THE BODY'S
RECOLLECTION
OF BEING

THE BODY'S RECOLLECTION OF BEING

PHENOMENOLOGICAL PSYCHOLOGY AND THE DECONSTRUCTION OF NIHILISM

DAVID MICHAEL LEVIN
Northwestern University, Illinois

Routledge & Kegan Paul
London, Boston, Melbourne and Henley

First published in 1985
by Routledge & Kegan Paul plc

14 Leicester Square, London WC2H 7PH, England

9 Park Street, Boston, Mass. 02108, USA

464 St Kilda Road, Melbourne,
Victoria 3004, Australia and

Broadway House, Newtown Road,
Henley-on-Thames, Oxon RG9 1EN, England

Set in 10/11pt Linotron Palatino
by Input Typesetting Ltd, London
and printed in Great Britain

Library of Congress Cataloging in Publication Data

Levin, David Michael, 1939–

The body's recollection of being.
Bibliography: p.
Includes index.
1. Phenomenological psychology. 2. Nihilism
(Philosophy). 3. Self-realization. 4. Body,
Human—Social aspects. I. Title.
BF204.5.L4 1985   128   84–17925
British Library CIP data also available

ISBN 0–7102–0149–4 (c)
ISBN 0–7102–0478–7 (pb)

To my brother
Roger Levin

Contents

CONTENTS

Acknowledgments

It is beyond my capacity to acknowledge in any adequate way the truth of my beholdenness. I cannot possibly name all the people, both living and dead, who have contributed in one way or another to the conception and production of this book. Nor can I possibly give adequate expression to the depth of my gratitude for their help and encouragement. With many, many friends in mind, I would like, at the very least, to name the ones who have contributed most directly and most consequentially. First of all, I want to thank my parents, who not only provided a true home for me during the time I needed to write, and gave me the benefit of a critical listening and response, but who also shared willingly in the trials of my commitment. Next, I want to thank my brother, Roger Levin, and my good friend at the University of Chicago, Eugene Gendlin, for the incalculable value of their deep questioning, and for suggestions which greatly helped me to clarify and extend my thought, particularly in relation to psychology and psychotherapy. I shall never forget the wonderful conversations we have had. Without them, it is possible that this book might never have been written. In any event, I am certain that, without them, it would not be the book which it is. The influence of their thinking is deep and pervasive. I would also like to express a very special gratitude to David Wood, who renounced the pleasures of a Christmastime interlude to read my manuscript in its entirety and give thought to its claims. If I cannot repay his kindness, I can at least keep it alive in the gathering of memory. Finally, I would like to thank Audrey Thiel for the excellence of her typing and for her superhuman patience in deciphering the labyrinthine palimpsest, at times virtually unreadable, which I gave her to work with.

Northwestern University (Evanston, Illinois) has been exceedingly generous in granting me the sabbaticals I requested and supporting the various costs I have faced in preparing this manuscript for publication. I am very grateful for this extensive support.

Part II of my 'Introduction' is a revised, expanded version of my essay, 'Heidegger's History of Philosophy: Recollection as Therapeia,' which originally appeared in *Reflections: Essays in Phenomenology*, vol. 2, no. 1, Winter 1981. Parts of this essay are reprinted by permission of *Reflections*, Ontario Institute for Studies in Education, Toronto, Canada.

Parts of Chapter 1 first appeared in my essay, 'Hermeneutics as Gesture,' published in *Tulane Studies in Philosophy*, vol. 32, 1984. I am grateful to *Tulane Studies*, Tulane University, for permission to reprint parts of this essay.

Chapter 2 is an expanded version of my essay, 'The Living Body of Tradition,' first published in *Religious Traditions*, vol. 5, nos 1–2 (1983). Parts of this essay are reprinted by permission of *Religious Traditions*, La Trobe University, Australia.

Chapter 3 is a revised version of my essay, 'Moral Education: The Body's Felt Sense of Value,' originally published in *Teachers College Record*, vol. 84, no. 2, Winter 1982. It is reprinted by permission of *Teachers College Record*, Columbia University.

Chapters 5, 6, and 7 are an expanded version of my essay, 'On Heidegger: The Gathering Dance of Mortals,' initially published in *Research in Phenomenology*, vol. 10, 1980. Parts of this essay are reprinted by permission of Humanities Press, Atlantic Highlands, NJ 07716.

An earlier version of the final part of Chapter 7 first appeared in my essay, 'Sanity and Myth in Affective Space: A Discussion of Merleau-Ponty,' *The Philosophical Forum*, vol. 14, no. 2, Winter 1982–3. It is reprinted by permission of *The Philosophical Forum*, Boston University.

I am grateful to Alfred A. Knopf, Inc. for permission to reprint lines from the Wallace Stevens poem, 'The Pure Good of Theory,' published by Knopf in *The Collected Works of Wallace Stevens*, New York, 1954. I am also grateful to Alfred A. Knopf, Inc. for permission to reprint a line from the Stevens poem, 'Things of August,' published in *The Palm at the End of the Mind*, New York, 1971. The quotation by W. S. Merwin in Chapter 1 is extracted from 'The Songs of the Icebergs' in *The Miner's Pale Children*, copyright © 1969, 1970 by W. S. Merwin. Used with permission of Atheneum Publishers. For British Commonwealth rights, the permission of Harold Ober Associates is hereby acknowledged.

ACKNOWLEDGMENTS

Excerpts from 'The Dry Salvages' and 'East Coker' in *Four Quartets* by T. S. Eliot are reprinted by permission of Harcourt Brace Jovanovich, Inc., copyright 1943 by T. S. Eliot, renewed 1971 by Esme Valerie Eliot. The excerpts are reprinted outside the United States, its dependencies, and the Philippine Islands by permission of Faber & Faber, Ltd.

Excerpts from *Sonnets to Orpheus* by Rainer Maria Rilke, translated by M. D. Herter Norton: First Part, Sonnet 16, first four lines, and Second Part, Sonnet 13, lines 9–11, are reprinted with world rights by permission of W. W. Norton & Company, Inc. Copyright 1942 by W. W. Norton & Company, Inc. Copyright renewed 1970 by M. D. Herter Norton.

Excerpts from *Duino Elegies* by Rainer Maria Rilke, translated by J. B. Leishman and Stephen Spender: The Second Elegy, lines 66–9, are reprinted in the United States and its dependencies by permission of W. W. Norton & Company, Inc. Copyright 1939 by W. W. Norton & Company, Inc. Copyright renewed 1967 by Stephen Spender and J. B. Leishman. Reprinted outside the United States and its dependencies by permission of St John's College, Oxford and the Hogarth Press.

The following are reprinted with world rights by permission of Harper & Row Publishers, Inc.: Nietzsche: Vol. I: *The Will to Power as Art*, translated by David Farrell Krell, copyright © 1979; Nietzsche Vol. IV: *Nihilism*, translated by Frank A. Capuzzi, copyright © 1982; *What is Called Thinking?* translated by Fred Wieck and J. Glenn Gray, English translation copyright © 1968; *The Question Concerning Technology and Other Essays*, translated by William Lovitt, English translation copyright © 1977; *Poetry, Language, Thought*, translated by Albert Hofstadter, copyright © 1971 by Martin Heidegger; *The End of Philosophy*, translated by Joan Stambaugh, English translation copyright © 1973 (British Commonwealth rights, Souvenir Press, London); *Being and Time*, translated by John Macquarrie and Edward Robinson, copyright © 1962 by SCM Press (British Commonwealth rights, SCM Press, London).

Preface

Section 1 Eros or Thanatos?

Nihilism, cancer of the spirit, is the challenge of the modern epoch. Nihilism is a 'sickness unto death' – a sickness in comparison with which even death itself may seem like a blessing. The danger of nihilism, and the deeper questions of essence which its historical actuality compels us to consider, constitute the principal background of concern against which the distinctive focus of this book, the figures of an emerging body of understanding, will be articulated.

At the very end of *Civilization and Its Discontents*, Freud asks us to contemplate the possibility of diagnosing the 'sanity' of an historical epoch, a civilization, or 'possibly even the whole of humanity.' Could we determine that the pattern of an entire civilization, or at least the pattern of a specific historical epoch, is the symptomatic manifestation of a collective neurosis? Would this kind of judgment make sense? Could it ever be justified? How could its truth be sustained? Freud is aware of the problems. Explicitly, he refuses to attempt such a diagnosis; but the fact of the matter is that the very formulation of these questions is sufficient to set the diagnosis in motion. And, in the final analysis, there can be very little doubt as to its disposition. In any event, Freud certainly did not hesitate to assert that,

> The fateful question of the human species seems to me to be whether and to what extent the cultural process developed in it will succeed in mastering the derangements of communal life caused by the human instinct of aggression and self-destruction. In this connection, perhaps the phase through which we are at this moment passing deserves special interest. Men have brought their powers of

1

subduing the forces of nature to such a pitch that
by using them they could now very easily
exterminate one another to the last man. They know
this – hence arises a great part of their current
unrest, their dejection, their mood of apprehension.
And now it may be expected that the other of the
two 'heavenly forces,' eternal Eros, will put forth
his strength so as to maintain himself alongside of
his equally immortal adversary.[1].

Since Freud, like Heidegger, was a reader of Nietzsche, I
think we may assume that the 'fateful question' which Freud
had in mind, when he called attention to symptoms of self-
destructiveness at work in our civilization, is the deeper question of nihilism: the very same question that Heidegger felt
a need to put at the center of his own later thinking. Heidegger, of course, took the standpoint of a philosopher; so
what mainly concerned him was not nihilism in its actual
historical manifestation, but rather nihilism in its essence,
about which he declared:

> With regard to the *essence* of nihilism, there is no
> prospect of, and no meaningful claim to, a cure.[2]

Just what he meant by this is, however, obscure, particularly
in light of the fact that he refrained as little as Freud from
the making of observations that can only be construed as
attempts at a diagnosis of our civilization. Be this as it may,
I do not claim to have any answer for the question with
which Freud's essay leaves us. But I would like to articulate
a worthy response, drawing, for the moment, on Freud's
expression of hope at the conclusion of the quoted text.
  In the study which follows, I would like to 'lend a hand'
to the still hidden, still unrealized power of *Eros*. For *Eros* is,
in truth, an immortal aspect of *Physis*: the sheer energy and
ecstasy of Being. It is also, however, a symbolic manifestation
of the primordial *Logos*, for it is the gathering of *Logos* as an
all-encompassing embrace. So the study I offer here has been
inspired by *Eros*; and this means that it is committed to
preparing for, and making use of, the historical opportunities
favored by *Eros*. Inspired by *Eros*, we shall challenge the
rule of *Thanatos* and contest the will to power which, in our
historical epoch, has finally brought forth the most terrifying
forces from the depths of its nihilism.

2

More specifically, as we shall see, this study will attempt to educe, by appropriately hermeneutical strategies, the hidden presence of *Eros* in *an emerging body of understanding*. It is a deep conviction of mine that our symbolic evocation of *Eros*, here, is an auspicious beginning, and that it may contribute in some small and unpredictable way to the opening of new historical possibilities – possibilities for a planetary existence of which our civilization has long been dreaming, but which it has never in the past been privileged to enjoy.

Although we shall be venturing a diagnosis of our affliction as a culture, and even risking the formulation of a salutary response, I would like to believe that we can do so with an appropriate sense of humility – and with a clear recognition that nihilism as an historical actuality is separated from the concealed 'essence' of nihilism by an abyss beyond our measure.

Section 2   The Crisis in Tradition

There is a deepening crisis in our Western tradition. On the one hand, it seems clear that we must break free of a dominant tradition which is taking us ever closer to the time of our annihilation through nihilism. On the other hand, it also seems clear that we cannot hope to escape the danger of nihilism without drawing strength from resources of spiritual wisdom which also belong to our tradition, but which the prevailing 'world picture' continues to conceal and suppress and exclude. Thus, if we cling to the dominant tradition, we are lost; but if we break away, we are in danger of losing touch with ancient traditions whose wisdom, long suppressed, might nevertheless now – even now – help to save us. A tradition can certainly be oppressive; it can stand in the way of growth, of life. But a retrieval of the 'origins' of that tradition (Nietzsche's 'genealogy of morals,' for example) can be emancipatory, a source of strength. How, then, can we take over the deeper, more concealed truth of our tradition? How can its ancient resources still be handed down in a meaningful and fruitful way?

In 'Metaphysics as History of Being,' Heidegger contends that,

> The tradition of the truth about beings which goes under the title of 'meta' develops into a pile of distortions, no longer recognizing itself, covering

3

up the primordial essence of Being. Herein lies the necessity of the 'destruction' of this distortion, when a thinking of the truth of Being has become necessary. But this destruction, like 'phenomenology' and all hermeneutical-transcendental questions, has not yet been thought in terms of the history of Being.[3]

Thus, at the same time that Heidegger argues for the 'destruction' of that which presently rules in our Western tradition, he can also insist on a *return* to tradition, and on a retrieval of its concealed wisdom. In keeping with this understanding, Heidegger therefore cautions us against a reactionary enslavement within the prevailing life of the tradition:

> The flight into tradition, out of a combination of humility and presumption, can bring about nothing in itself other than self-deception and blindness in relation to the historical moment.[4]

It is Heidegger's conviction that,

> [We] will only be able to wrest a destiny from it [our understanding of the present historical situation] if *within itself* it creates a resonance, a possibility of resonance for this vocation, and takes a creative view of its tradition.[5]

What Heidegger calls 'new spiritual energies' could indeed emerge from our tradition, but only, it seems, if *at the same time* that we repudiate that which presently dominates, we also prepare ourselves to receive, or to 'resonate' with, that in the tradition which has been deeply concealed, suppressed, or excluded.

In this regard, I would like to observe that the objective of this study is to retrieve for future history a *body of understanding* which our dominant tradition has kept in concealment. The retrieval is two-fold, since, first of all, this tradition has vigorously fought to suppress the life and truth of the body, and, secondly, the mainstream of our tradition has steadfastly excluded ancient spiritual teachings – traditions of ancient universal wisdom – which speak in archetypal and mythopoetic language of the body's deep ontological

4

understanding of Being and of the ways to bring it forth. Because this archetypal body of understanding belongs to the excluded traditions, its retrieval in and through this present work is simultaneously a radical break with the dominant tradition and yet also a renewal, which makes contact with, and continues, that which has always inhabited the most concealed interiority of the prevailing form of the tradition. Thus we may call the present work of retrieval a 'deconstruction' of the tradition, making it very clear by our choice of word that what is at stake is not a destruction, but rather, on the contrary, the potential for a genuine renewal.

Our attention to the emerging body of understanding, the body of gesture and motility *as* an emerging body of understanding, is accordingly conceived as a response to the crisis of tradition. For the body has served, from time immemorial, as the carrier, the place-holder, and the metaphor, of our tradition, passing on its culture, its history, its life. And yet, this same tradition has systematically distorted, suppressed, and concealed the body's essential being. The human body, as a body of deep ontological understanding, has suffered centuries of systematic misrepresentation – and not only in the reflections of our metaphysics. The body's suffering – for example, its dismemberment and reification in the history of metaphysics – is a worthy focus for our attempt, in the name of *Eros*, to articulate a critique of nihilism. Given this history, such a focus is already a contribution to the eventual deconstruction of metaphysics, and of the nihilism implicit in our Western tradition.

Inasmuch as nihilism is the negation (loss, absence, concealment) of Being, our attempt to deconstruct and renew the tradition must concern itself with the being of the body in its historical relation to Being as such. Focusing, therefore, on our embodiment as we experience it at this historical juncture in relationship to Being, we begin at once to free ourselves from the nihilism that is at work in our metaphysical tradition. In adopting this strategy for our study, we are only following in Nietzsche's footsteps. For the human body plays a decisive role, not only in Nietzsche's critique of metaphysics, but also in his diagnosis of the life-denying character of nihilism. The body is not only a metaphor for the crisis in tradition; it is also a metaphor for an historical moment in which the suffering of the crisis could at long last be significantly overcome.

PREFACE

I take his words very seriously. It is important that we really hear them well; it is important that they make a difference in our thinking. Now that I myself have worked in phenomenology for many years, I appreciate the great wisdom in his understanding. I am also aware, however, that, precisely because I have followed in Heidegger's footsteps on a path of thought, the phenomenological method he handed down, and with which I wholeheartedly consented to work, has unavoidably made itself, in a certain sense, obsolete. Heidegger's words thus apply to the work in this present study no less than to his own phenomenological reflections.

For me, what is ultimately most questionable in Heidegger's practice of phenomenology is perhaps its excessive formalism and intellectualism: after Heidegger's efforts, we need a phenomenology which is able to work much more comfortably and effectively with the dynamic character of our experiential processes; and we need a phenomenology which is capable of working with the body of understanding that is implicitly operative in our sensibility – in our feelings, our perceptions, our gestural comportments. Heidegger's phenomenology is *now* needed to translate the exceedingly formal ontology of the 'analytic of *Dasein*' into ontological articulations of the body of experience, whose emerging understanding is an explicitation and further unfolding of the body's own being as pre-reflective, pre-conceptual and pre-ordained relatedness-to-Being.

It may come as no surprise that I have taken the work of Merleau-Ponty as the basis for this translation. The present study undertakes to 'flesh out' the sense and significance of Heidegger's ontological interpretation of the *Dasein* by articulating the body of experience whose primordial attunement-to-Being (felt sense-of-being-in-the-world) constitutes an implicit, pre-conceptual pre-understanding (or a pre-ontological understanding) of the *Dasein*'s relatedness-to-Being (*Dasein*'s *Befindlichkeit*) and therefore also *an emerging body* of ontological self-understanding. Furthermore, as we specify the translation of Heidegger's formal ontology in terms of a hermeneutical phenomenology of gesture and motility, we make it possible to spell out the *stages* in a process of development. Thus we can in fact *initiate therapeutic transformations* in the *Dasein*'s way of being. For, the more clearly we can articulate the ontological dimension of our gestures and movements, and the more explicitly we can present the pre-ontological understanding implicitly carried by our embodiment,

the more we can prepare for an unfolding of this understanding in our lives which will be experienced as fulfilling
the development of our capacities for gesture and movement.
Merleau-Ponty's body of perception is therefore as central to
our project as Heidegger's thought of Being.

Section 6   Psychologism, Anthropologism, and Humanism

In his *Erinnerung an Martin Heidegger*, Medard Boss reports
that,

> He [Heidegger] confided that he had hoped that
> through me – a physician and psychotherapist –
> his thinking would escape the confines of the
> philosopher's study and become of benefit to
> wider circles, in particular to a larger number of
> suffering human beings.[31]

If we take this hope to heart – if, that is, we share it and
make it our own – then it seems to me that we need to give
thought to the *psychology* which characterizes the *Dasein* (i.e.,
the *logos* which speaks through, and as, the *Dasein's psyche*),
that we need to articulate this psychology as clearly as we
can in phenomenological terms, and finally, that we need to
understand the *psychotherapeutic* dynamics which are set in
motion by the ontological work of hermeneutical
phenomenology.

As is suggested by our extensive reliance on Freudian
psychoanalysis and Jungian archetypal psychology, as well
as by our use of material from clinical, developmental, interpersonal and transpersonal psychology, *our ontological interpretation of gestures and motility is informed by the recognition
that its hermeneutical phenomenology bears within itself the capacity
to bring forth significant revolutionary transformations: deep transformations in our awareness, our self-understanding, our comportment, and our social and cultural worlds.* And, *a fortiori*, our
interpretation is also informed by the *hope* that these changes
might be able to alleviate some of our deepest suffering,
or at the very least enlighten us concerning the underlying
ontological nature of our present affliction. The discourse
which is soon to follow this Preface is very much aware
of the immeasurable *therapeutic potential* in the ontological
disclosures of hermeneutical phenomenology; very much

17

aware of the fact that the process of developing ontological self-understanding is a process whose experiential dynamics are deeply healing.

In his history of metaphysics, for example, Heidegger attempts to 'deconstruct' the dualism of subject and object. But the overcoming of this dualism is not something that can be accomplished solely in the field of metaphysics. We must also understand, and be in a position to work with, *the immediately experienced dynamics* of this subject/object polarization. I am convinced that Freudian psychoanalysis can significantly deepen our understanding of the *ego-logical* processes: their formation, their structures, their modes of defense against openness and their corresponding strategies of objectification, their inherent strengths and weaknesses, and ways to heal their (ontologically related) distress. Likewise, I believe that the work of Carl Jung and Erich Neumann can supplement in essentially required ways Heidegger's formal analytic of the *Dasein*'s potential for becoming an authentic Self. Since the pre-conceptual, pre-reflective experience of our primordial relatedness-to-Being-as-a-whole would seem to be articulated first, and perhaps also most satisfactorily, in terms of the archetypal symbols of our body's 'collective unconscious,' a Jungian interpretation of cultural symbols, myths, and rituals of self-transformation can significantly clarify Heidegger's discourse concerning our deepest self-understanding and our existential possibilities-for-becoming. Furthermore, Jungian psychology can specify and enrich Heidegger's formulation of the three dimensions of human existence – the pre-ontological attunement, the ontical reduction in characteristic everydayness, and the expanded, authentic life of the ontological Self. For it draws on the resources of many different cultural traditions, to map the psyche's symbolic journey in great experiential detail: in the beginning, the time of the infant, we experience a wholeness and integration which are largely unconscious; in the middle, the time of our adulthood, we experience the affliction of a decentered ego lost in the material world; in the end, the years of our maturity and wisdom, there is the possibility of a wholeness and integration that would constitute the deepest fulfillment of our ontological self-awareness. *Heidegger's formal analytic of the three dimensions in the Dasein's unfolding self-understanding is very much in need of a corresponding developmental psychology of the Self – a psychology such as Jung's, with the appropriate depth and orientation.* Thus, despite the danger of psychologism, despite the possibility that the use of psychology in this study is vulnerable to misunderstanding, we shall make extensive use of psychological material – especially developmental material taken from the work of Freud, Jung, Carl Rogers, Jean Piaget, Erik Erikson, and Eugene Gendlin.

We shall also rely on texts that will be located in the discourses of cultural anthropology, despite the danger of anthropologism. I am certainly attentive to the possibility that our use of anthropological knowledge will encounter some suspicion and opposition, either because it is believed that there could be no universal wisdom from other cultures and other epochs that could speak to our present, historically unique situation, or else because it is thought that anthropology must be a positive science whose center of focus – human beings in their different cultures – necessarily excludes any deeper concern for the ontological dimension of human being. The first of these beliefs will be contested throughout the book, as we shall find again and again that the ancient wisdom of other cultural traditions and other cultural epochs can be enormously instructive. The second belief raises some difficult questions. It requires a more specific reply, and we shall soon give it our attention.

Anthropological knowledge provides 'eidetic variations' ('possible world' variations) on *our own* culture of experience. It consequently helps to free us from our cultural limitations and enables us to develop a new sense of the openness and richness of Being. For all we know this new and deeper understanding of Being in its diverse cultural manifestations may be able to generate an appreciation of new historical possibilities: opportunities that might be, in relation to our present historical situation, decisively emancipatory. But above all, perhaps, we need to bear in mind that the dimension of our being which is characterized by a primordial, pre-conceptual, pre-ontological relatedness to Being as a whole first comes to articulation in the form of archetypal symbols, mythopoetic narratives, and archaic rituals, and that cultural anthropology has given us access to the symbolic register in which this pre-ontological understanding first speaks and recalls us to ourselves. (Consider Heidegger's discussion of myth in *What Is Called Thinking?*)[32]

According to Heidegger,

> Anthropology is that interpretation of man that already knows fundamentally what man is and

19

hence can never ask who he may be. For, with this
question it would have to confess itself shaken and
overcome. But how can this be expected of
anthropology when the latter has expressly to
achieve nothing less than the securing consequent
upon the self-secureness of the *subiectum*?[33]

Because this present study makes intensive use of anthropological material, I feel a need to point out why this use does
not betray the ontological commitment of our project – why,
in other words, it does not reduce our thinking to anthropologism. I have called attention to this passage from Heidegger's essay on 'The Age of the World Picture' because it
helps to clarify the difference between, on the one hand, an
anthropological interpretation of human being in which this
being is *reduced or restricted* to the conceptual framework of
the interpretation and the question of our relatedness-to-
Being as such is systematically *excluded* from awareness, and,
on the other hand, a use of anthropological material which
avoids the formulation of an anthropocentric interpretation
of human being, and serves rather *to question and open up* our
culturally prevailing understanding of what it is, or what it
means, to be human. Considered by itself, our anthropological knowledge of other cultures neither limits nor betrays
the possibility of an authentic ontological interpretation. It is
my conviction that the way we shall be using such knowledge
in the course of this study is opening and not reductive,
liberating and not dogmatic.

Now, a similar kind of concern might perhaps be felt with
regard to our reliance on systems of knowledge in humanistic
psychology. Insofar as this similarity obtains, it will suffice to
say that my response would follow the form of the argument
articulated above. Unfortunately, however, there are also
other issues, and we need most urgently to consider them.

It might be thought that, according to Heidegger, it would
be impossible for us to rely on the traditional spirit of
humanism – and, *a fortiori*, on systems of psychology
committed to the vitality of this spirit – without betraying
the revolutionary ontological orientation of our project. But
I would like to show in what sense this understanding of
Heidegger's thought is seriously mistaken, despite the
courage and daring of its rupture with tradition.

Heidegger argues that,

> [*Dasein* is] drawn into the history of Being, but
> always only with regard to *the manner in which he*
> *takes his essence from the relation of Being to himself*
> and, in accordance with this relation, loses his
> essence, neglects it, gives it up, grounds it, or
> squanders it.[34]

And it might be concluded from this passage that the use of
humanistic psychology would necessarily *turn us away* from
an awareness and understanding of ourselves which needs
to take its measure by reference to our relatedness-to-Being.
But I do not see how this conclusion could ever be deduced
from what Heidegger's text has to say. In this study, we have
used systems of psychology (e.g., psychoanalysis, archetypal
psychology, clinical, developmental, and transpersonal) to
facilitate our ontological self-examination, our commitment to
taking stock, our process of contacting and articulating the
character of our deepest experience-of-existing, so that we
might more fully realize where we are, and how we stand,
in relation to Being. Whatever ontological reductions these
systems may insist on, or may effect in terms of their own
disciplines, it is possible for us to use them in a way that
deepens our self-awareness, enriches our self-understanding, engages our sensibility, and gives focus to our
perception: they can be used, not in a way that conceals the
ontological dimension, but rather in a way that enables us to
attend to it much more carefully and thoughtfully. Unless we
are informed by a *specific* understanding, an understanding
formulated in terms that make phenomenological reference
to what we are able to experience directly here and now,
there is not much value or meaning, not much hermeneutical
force, in the words of the text. Heidegger refers to the human
being who 'loses his essence, neglects it, gives it up, grounds
it, or squanders it.' Just what do these words mean? What
is their *purchase* on our experience of ourselves?
  Heidegger writes:

> the essence of man can never be *adequately*
> determined in its origin through the *prevailing* –
> that is, the *metaphysical* – interpretation of
> man. . . .[35]

It is his contention that,

21

the essence of man is determined by Being itself
from the essence of the truth of Being.[36]

Thus he wants us to read *Being and Time* both as 'an attempt
. . . to determine the essence of man solely in terms of his
relationship to Being' and as the failure of this attempt.[37] But
it would be an error to conclude from these bold statements
that the knowledge of psychology cannot help us to understand the character of this essence, or that the use of such
knowledge necessarily commits us to the notion that the
essence of man is determined by something *other* than our
relatedness-to-Being.

The later texts of Heidegger are sometimes read in such a
way that they seem to suggest an 'ontological difference'
which Heidegger surely could not have meant. It is an under-
standable ontical misunderstanding of the ontological difference between beings and Being to believe that we are necessarily *turned away from* the open dimension of Being insofar
as we are *attentive to* finite things in the everyday world. This
misunderstanding stems from the fact that Being is still being
thought dualistically – as if it were an object, one being
among other beings. I want to suggest that the consumm-
ation of the 'ontological attitude' consists precisely in our
capacity to maintain an open guardian awareness of the ontological (i.e., of Being as a whole) *while being engaged with
beings in our everyday life.* Being is not a being of another kind.
That difference is not the *ontological* difference. Being is rather
(we might say) a dimension, a field, a clearing-for: different
in *this* way.

In his 'Introduction' to *The Basic Problems of Phenomenology*,
Heidegger explains 'ontology' in terms which clearly articulate this understanding:

> Being is given only if the understanding of being,
> hence the *Dasein*, exists. This being accordingly
> lays claim to a distinctive priority in ontological
> inquiry. . . . Ontology [i.e., the philosophical
> meditation on Being] has for its fundamental
> discipline the analytic of *Dasein*. This implies at the
> same time that ontology cannot be established in a
> purely ontological manner. Its possibility is
> [necessarily to be] referred back to a being, that is,
> something ontical – the *Dasein*. Ontology has an
> ontical foundation, a fact which is manifest over

22

and over again in the history of philosophy down
to the present.[38]

Ontology does not happen by itself. Ontology is a work of
thought, and therefore it must be referred back to (or correlated with) the being who is thinking. As an undertaking of
human beings, ontology manifests the character of the
human being who is always already in relatedness-to-Being.
But ontology is not only the *articulation* of that relationship;
it is itself a dimension, or moment, within the very relatedness it is in process of disclosing and bringing forth.
Consequently, it cannot lay claim to a disclosure of the truth
of Being while suppressing the fact of its own *participation* in
modulating the relatedness-to-Being which is brought forth,
or comes to pass, by virtue of its own responsiveness.
Ontology must obey the phenomenological principle of
intentionality. What this means is that it must give adequate
consideration to that being, namely the *Dasein*, *for whom* a
relatedness-to-Being can matter, is questionable and worthy
of thought, and can become the concern of ontology.

What *kind* of consideration must we, or should we give to
this being called *Dasein*? 'Ontology has an ontical
foundation. . . .' Does this not suggest, even if it does not
strictly imply, that humanistic psychology, as a thoughtful,
high-level articulation of our experience-of-being-human and
a systematic contribution to our self-understanding, is to be
considered propaedeutic, or preparatory, with regard to the
laying of this foundation? However misguided it may be,
e.g., in placing its faith solely in the human will to power,
humanistic psychology is at the very least an honorable
attempt to listen to the *logos* of the psyche and give it an
articulate voice.

The crucial thing, it seems to me, is the distinction between
a psychology which *opens up* our human being to Being as a
whole and a psychology which functions, in effect, to *foreclose*
our potential-for-being in order to protect its own framework.
According to Heidegger, 'Dasein' is to be understood (translated) as 'openness-to-Being.' And this phrase is to be 'understood,' he says, 'in the sense of the ecstatic realm of the
revealing and concealing of Being.'[39] It is in keeping with this
understanding that he describes the task in *Being and Time*
as 'an analytic of human being which keeps itself ecstatically
open to Being.'[40] I think we may conclude from these statements that the systems of humanistic psychology which have

23

emerged in our culture are to be welcomed, and not ignored: they can be of great use, not only as therapies for mortals in need, but also in the laying of a 'foundation' for ontology, to the degree that their ways of articulating and working with our experience-of-being-human are felt, after due reflection, to be opening and deepening. This, in the final analysis, is the only test we have of the truth of our thinking, the only measure of our adherence to the project of ontology. Our thinking will always be genuinely ontological, Heidegger tells us, 'if it opens our human existence to [Being].'[41]

I am reminded, at this point, of Nietzsche's question, in Book Two of The Will to Power. 'How,' he asks, 'is truth proved?' And he answers: 'By the feeling of enhanced power.'[42] Earlier in the same book division, he observed that, 'One seeks a picture of the world in that philosophy in which we feel freest.'[43] This criterion (it is also Spinoza's) makes very good phenomenological sense. Thus, for example, we will find that the same criterion appears in The Interpersonal Theory of Psychiatry, where Harry Stack Sullivan calls our attention to 'the child's pleasure in manifesting any ability that he has achieved.'[44] It was, in fact, precisely this criterion which I had in mind when I spoke, earlier, of the experience of 'fulfillment' in regard to the deepening of our relatedness-to-Being. References to such fulfillment are not necessarily egocentric or psychologistic reductions of ontological experience. On the contrary, they may function to articulate how ontology is actually experienced. We need to understand this. If we do not, ontology is likely to remain a merely formal scholastic discipline, entirely cut off from its living existential truth.

Let us not overlook the fact that, in a discussion of the difference between truth and mere correctness, a discussion which we may well apply to the question of the value of psychology for ontological thinking, Heidegger himself defines the truth in relation to freedom: 'Only the true,' he says, 'brings us into a free relationship with that which concerns us. . . .'[45] But he at once concedes that, nevertheless, 'we must seek the true by way of the correct.' Thus, even if we consider that the various systems of humanistic psychology are at best merely 'correct', we must refrain from condemning the use of psychology – the use, for example, to be found in the present study – before we have carefully evaluated how it functions. I would like to claim that our use of psychology is opening and emancipatory, and that the measure *for this claim is determined solely by reference to Being.* What Heidegger says in regard to his questioning of technology may be translated with equal sense and power into a measure of the ontological significance of our own strategy of questioning, which makes use of psychological knowledge *in order to focus attention on our capacity for a deeper relatedness-to-Being.* Heidegger writes:

> We shall be questioning concerning technology, and
> in doing so we should like to prepare a free
> relationship to it. The relationship will be free if it
> opens our human existence to the essence of
> technology.[46]

For some time, now, Heidegger's so-called 'reversal' (*Kehre*) has been the subject of much speculation. It has also generated a good deal of confusion among the scholars. Some scholars boldly deny the turn, while others affirm it. Among the latter, however, there is no consensus regarding its timing. Different scholars place the reversal at different points in Heidegger's work. Even more scholars dispute the sense and significance of the turn. In *Being and Time*, Heidegger's major work *prior* to the turn, the 'Question of Being' is taken up for thought in terms of an 'analytic of *Dasein*.' *After* the turn, this strategy is explicitly repudiated and abandoned. But why? And what does it signify? Heidegger's own explanation has brought forth many very different interpretations.

In 'Nihilism and the History of Being,' a text presumably written from the standpoint of his reversal, Heidegger proclaims that the 'essence of man' is 'nothing human.' Rather, he says, 'It is the abode of the advent of Being. . . .'[47] A strange turn of thought! But it would seem that most scholars have been so anxious not to miss the turn and lose sight of their guide that they have forgotten to keep in mind the query which immediately precedes this most disturbing and thought-provoking statement. The question Heidegger addresses to us is this:

> Who, if he thinks, could escape being affected by
> the most extreme withdrawal of Being, sensing
> that in the withdrawal there is an exaction of Being
> – Being itself as such exaction – which applies to
> man in his essence?

25

If we forget or ignore this question, we will be misled into thinking, dualistically, that the reversal must consist in a turn away from human being: a turn away, therefore, from our experience-of-being and, of course, from the psychologies which are concerned with this experience and its historical unfolding. This, however, is a very dangerous and tragic misunderstanding. Nothing of this sort is meant, or could possibly be meant, by Heidegger's radical reversal.

The reversal does *not* consist in any dualistic turning away from beings (and least of all, from the beings who are human) in order to meditate, finally and more properly, on Being all by itself and as such – as if Being were just another being – a being to which we attend, or could attend, only by denying our attention to all other beings. On the contrary, the reversal constitutes a deeper, more radical, and much more powerful questioning of our *experience* as human beings. In any event, however, we cannot properly give thought to Being, Being in its truth, by blocking from awareness the reality of our relatedness, our ineliminable presence. Moreover, keeping our own being in mind, in terms of this relatedness, is not being self-centered; it is just the opposite, in fact, in the sense that the relatedness is decentering. Heidegger's question, in which he refers to our being 'affected' by the withdrawal of Being and our 'sensing' of its historical significance, should make this point very clear. What Heidegger's reversal reverses is, rather, the 'focus,' or the 'source,' of the ontological measure. The turning point in Heidegger's thinking is the affirmation of a new center, a new focus, a new origin. *Dasein* is said to be 'ek-static': the ecstasy of its primordial openness is at last proclaimed, and the self-enclosed Cartesian Self is exploded – an historical myth. Henceforth, the being of the *Dasein* is thrown off-center. Prior to the turn, Heidegger's analytic was fully centered on the being of the *Dasein*, as if this being were the ultimate source, or origin, of Being. Moreover, his use of hermeneutical phenomenology concerned itself *exclusively* with an articulation of the existentially most primordial and most universal structures of human being, as if Being could be *reduced* to the existential, but still subjective structure of the *Dasein*, and the 'Question of Being' could be *grounded* in the traditional way that is characteristic of Western metaphysics, i.e., by a regression to the specific being of a transcendental subjectivity.

After the turn, however, the project of interpretation becomes hermeneutically decentered; centered, instead, in the *Dasein's relatedness-to-Being*. Thus, the turn involves a revolutionary awareness, and an explicitly hermeneutical acknowledgment, that it is in relativity, in a relatedness Heidegger calls openness-to-Being, that a deeper truth of Being will make its appearance in the history of Western civilization. Openness-to-Being, the depth of our capacity for opening and the character of our receptivity to the presence or givenness (*Es gibt*) of Being, is to be our new historical measure of the truth which an ontological interpretation may claim. Ontological truth is not, as he once believed, a question of the *correspondence* between an interpretation of human being and the confirming presence of the existential structure described by that interpretation. Ontological truth is a question of *existentially dialectical process*: it is a function of the power of an interpretation to make a fundamental existential disclosure, a disclosure that opens us to changes in our existence, our dwelling. The truth of an interpretation can only be measured by reference to the depth, and the character, of the opening-to-Being experienced by those human beings who have deeply and thoughtfully encountered the interpretation in question. The truth does not consist in an event (*Ereignis*) which somehow comes to pass in absolute non-relatedness to the being of human existence. To interpret Heidegger's turn in *this* sense is to turn it into nonsense.

The difference between Heidegger's earlier and later understandings of the ontological task for modernity is not to be found in the starting points of his thinking; nor is it to be found in a turning-away from the original direction of his project. In both cases, both before and after the turn, we are directed toward Being; and in both cases, the starting point is human being – that which is closest to our understanding, and yet also farthest. Rather, the difference lies in the attitude, the character, of our *approach* to Being. Prior to the turning, our approach was totally determined by the analytic of being human (*Dasein*), i.e., human being was willed to be the sole measure, that which should define the approach. After the turn, however, what determined our approach was not human being, but Being itself. Thus, instead of perpetuating the limitations into which we as human beings have settled, Heidegger began to let Being itself illuminate our approach, our way to it. This is why we find, in Heidegger's later thinking, a different style of concepts: concepts, for example, which emphasize our capacity for openness, responsiveness, attunement, waiting, and letting-be. After the decisive turn, the starting point of ontology is still human being, and the direction of thought is still cast from human being into the truth of Being as such, but the approach, the *Weg*, is now determined by our attunement, our responsiveness, our capacity to wait, our willingness to let be.

Of course, if it be the very essence of 'humanism' to affirm the 'deification of mankind' – if, that is, it should be the essence of humanism to insist on putting mankind in the place traditionally occupied by God – then Heidegger's reversal *must* call for a turning away from the long tradition of humanism. But I believe that the implicit spirit of humanism is much deeper than the sum of its historical instantiations. As I have come to understand it, the spirit of humanism is not necessarily committed to making our human being the sole measure of all beings, and of Being itself as the whole. What it is certainly committed to, I believe, is the *well-being* of humanity. But I submit that, when this well-being is properly understood, it becomes clear that *it essentially requires us to develop, or deepen, our pre-given capacity for openness-to-Being*. And I therefore can see no reason why a new humanism cannot embrace this decentering in the very same spirit that called, in earlier historical times, for an origin whose centering absolutized the place of mankind.

Now, I have spoken of self-development and self-realization. In no sense do these concepts refer to self-aggrandizement; nor do they represent the old confidence, once identified with the spirit of humanism, in mankind's capacity to reach self-perfection. As we shall be using these concepts in the study which follows, they refer specifically to our capacity for deepening our openness-to-Being, and to the processes through which we develop or unfold this capacity. Thus, in the context of this study, 'ontology' is to be understood as the conception of a task which can never be finished, and in which we are committed only to calling attention, wherever and whenever possible, to possibilities for a deeper, more aware, and more self-fulfilling dimensionality of our historical existence as gesturing and self-moving beings. Ontological thinking is really nothing other than this rigorously sustained attending to openings – and by that I mean that, both as individuals and as an historical community, we need to realize not only our pre-given, pre-understood *potential* for a continuous deepening of our experience and understanding

28

of Being, but also the *opportunities* which come to pass for a richer, more meaningful *integration* of this ontological understanding into the very warp and woof of everyday life. It is the continuing opening and deepening which is genuinely ontological, not the articulation of an 'absolute certitude,' a 'true origin,' a 'first cause,' or an 'ultimate ground.' It is our commitment to ceaseless self-questioning, and to the building of a society in which such questioning is encouraged, which will make our living genuinely ontological, and not the answers and orthodoxies where we stop to rest along the way.

Because I keep to this understanding of ontology, I believe that there is, ultimately, only one point of reference for taking the measure of the communication which is sent on its way through this book. Like Heidegger, whose words I shall now repeat, I would like to see this present work 'measured by what we take ourselves to be, what we trust we are capable of, and what we dare as perhaps the extreme challenge, one we may just barely withstand.'[48] This is how, after the turn, we can 'wait' upon Being. This is how, after the turn, we can 'prepare' for the coming-to-pass of a new epoch in the history of Being.

Introduction

Part I
The Gift of Embodiment

the hint half guessed, the gift half understood, is
Incarnation.   T. S. Eliot, 'The Dry Salvages'

Man can embody the truth, but he cannot know it.
                                        W. B. Yeats[1]

if the body had been easier to understand, nobody would
have thought that we had a mind.
            Richard Rorty, *Philosophy and the Mirror of Nature*[2]

But the exile of the body in outward history has its
parallel in the exile of the soul in its migrations from
embodiment to embodiment. . . .
Gershom Scholem, *On the Kabbalah and its Symbolism*[3]

Come now, with all your powers discern how each thing
manifests itself, trusting no more to sight than to
hearing, and no more to the echoing ear than to the
tongue's taste; rejecting none of the body's parts that
might be a means to knowledge, but attending to each
particular manifestation.
                                        Empedocles[4]

Section 1   Giving Thought to the Body

In his *Economic and Philosophical Manuscripts* of 1844, Marx
argues that,

   the *senses* of social man are different from those of

non-social man. It is only through the objectively
deployed wealth of the human being that the wealth
of subjective *human* sensibility (a musical ear, an
eye which is sensitive to the beauty of form, in
short, senses which are capable of human
satisfaction and which confirm themselves as
human faculties) is cultivated or created. For it is
not only the five senses, but also the so-called
spiritual senses, the practical senses (desiring,
loving, etc.), in brief, human sensibility and the
human character of the senses, which can only
come into being through the existence of *its* object,
i.e., through humanized nature.[5]

This analysis, as it stands, is, I think, of the utmost importance. But Marx goes on to deepen it by his reference to
cultural history:

The cultivation of the five senses is the work of all
previous history.[6]

Since history is not only the past, but is also always in the
making, our sensibility is an unfinished social task, a current
social responsibility:

Sense which is subservient to crude needs has only
a restricted meaning. . . . Thus, the objective
realization of the human essence, both theoretically
and practically, is necessary in order to *humanize*
man's senses, and also to *create* the *human senses*
corresponding to all the wealth of human and
natural being.[7]

I would like to think of the present study, a work devoted
to the human body, as contributing to a collective task: the
humanization of our sensibility and the *culture* of our capacities
for perception.
   The urge I feel – to communicate, to share, to invite others
to participate in the transformative process I myself have
undergone – is very closely tied, for me, to the conviction
that, as Marx puts it so well, it is

the fully constituted society [which] produces man
in all the plenitude of his being, the wealthy man

endowed with all the senses as an enduring reality.
It is only in a social context that subjectivism and
objectivism, spiritualism and materialism, activity
and passivity, cease to be antinomies and thus
cease to exist as such antinomies.[8]

In words that may remind us of Thoreau's *Walden* essay,
'Economy,' Marx says:

The resolution of the *theoretical* contradictions is
possible *only* through *practical* means, only through
the practical energy of man. Their resolution is not
by any means, therefore, only a problem of
knowledge, but is a real problem of life which
philosophy was unable to solve precisely because
it saw there a purely theoretical problem.[9]

I do not regard what might be called 'the problem of
embodiment' as a purely theoretical problem. Indeed, since
understanding ourselves is a process of bringing forth new
possibilities for living, I will not treat the *understanding* of
embodiment as a purely theoretical problem. Hence the
thinking in this book has been rendered, from the very
outset, as an invitation that is constitutive of a practical social
task. This means that I must take the phenomenological articulation of our embodiment-as-it-is-experienced to be, in
part, a problem in communicative praxis. From that standpoint, the aim of the communication is to gather like-minded
people into an ancient collective dream, whose task, since
time immemorial, has been a new 'incarnation' here on earth,
together with the founding of a new, and more essentially
human community of self-fulfilled individuals. The full realization of our humanity in its *bodily* being, i.e., in its potential
for the relationships constitutive of sentient and sensuous
existence, is certainly not possible, and not in the end
conceivable, without the full support of a social and political
context. This study may prepare in some small way for that
kind of support; it is, in any event, an open invitation to take
part in the cross-cultural conversation.
   Whereas Heidegger, in *Being and Time*, undertakes to
involve us, as essentially social beings, in the collective task
of living 'an ontologically adequate conception of death –
that is to say, an *existential* conception of it,'[10] I would like to
involve us in the cooperative project of living an ontologically

adequate conception of our bodily nature, our embodiment as human beings. Here is where my project is indebted to Merleau-Ponty. Thanks to a thinking which significantly deepened in the course of an increasingly intense dialogue with Heidegger, Merleau-Ponty gives us another way of formulating the project which will engage us in this book. In 'The Intertwining – The Chiasm,' Merleau-Ponty proposes that we construe his work as a contribution to 'the architectonics of the human body, its ontological framework.'[11]

Bearing in mind that the body, as Marx points out, is the work of history, I would like to sketch now, as briefly as I can, the 'modern' history of this framework. We will break into the architectonic history at the point where Nietzsche enters. With Nietzsche's words, this history takes a radical turn; with his voice, the modern conversation finally begins. Nietzsche is really the first philosopher since the beginning of the Judaeo-Christian influence to espouse the human body in its truth, its beauty, and its goodness. He is the first philosopher belonging to the Judaeo-Christian world to repudiate the teachings of that patriarchal world and formulate – and in the most radical terms – what we are calling, here, 'the problem of embodiment.'

Section 2 Nietzsche

Nietzsche's 'retrieval' of the human body will not be entirely comprehensible, however, unless we consider it in the larger context of his 'return' to the spirit of classical Greece. (We might ponder, here, the message of Hölderlin's 'Home-coming,' a poem infused with the poet's enthusiasm for 'bringing back' the spirit of Greece.) A statement in *The Will to Power* will make this point very clear:

> German philosophy as a whole – Leibniz, Kant, Hegel, Schopenhauer, to name the greatest – is the most fundamental form of *romanticism* and homesickness there has ever been: the longing for the best that ever existed. One is no longer at home anywhere; at last one longs back for that place in which alone one can be at home, because it is the only place in which one would want to be at home: the *Greek* world! But it is in precisely that direction that all bridges are broken – except the rainbow-bridges of concepts! And these lead everywhere,

> acquire, because one continually sacrifices it
> again. . . .[22]

Sacrifices of the body, our countless crucifixions and mortifications of the sensuous flesh, will *continue* to test and try our developing consciousness. So Nietzsche considers that it could be useful for us to refer back to the ancient Greek experience, which seems to provide us, despite the passage of time and the difference of culture, with a clear paradigm or standard:

> When the Greek body and the Greek soul
> 'bloomed,' and not in conditions of morbid exaltation
> and madness, there arose that mysterious symbol
> of the highest . . . transformation of existence that
> has yet been attained on earth. Here we have a
> standard by which everything that has grown up
> since is found too short, too poor, too narrow.[23]

(Of course, even in ancient Greece, we find that there was also an incipient tendency, an 'unwholesome' tendency, to regard body and soul as irreconcilable polarities and to deny the body an understanding of its wholeness. In the *Charmides*, for example, Plato's protagonist asserts that it is 'the great error of our day in the treatment of the human body, that physicians separate the soul from the body.' The physician, he argues, must 'try to treat and heal the whole and part together.')[24]

So Nietzsche advises that 'We should study our organism in all its immortality.'[25] The body, he thinks, is even 'more mysterious' and 'more astonishing' than what is called the 'soul.' (He even goes so far as to suggest, for example, that we consider the human stomach as a 'divine' operation.)[26] Asking us to ponder the significance of the fact that 'The most spiritual men feel the stimulus and charm of sensuous things. . . ,'[27] he ventures to suggest that,

> Put briefly, perhaps the entire evolution of the spirit
> is a question of the body; it is the history of the
> development of a higher body that emerges into our
> sensibility. The organic is rising to yet higher
> levels.[28]

The notion of 'spirit,' then, is nothing more, at bottom, than 'a means through which the body desires to perfect itself.'[29] Or, in other words, it functions as our 'regulative idea' of the body's true perfection. Therefore,

> We want to hold fast to our senses and our faith in them – and think their consequences through to the end![30]

As we begin to do this, as we begin to *let* ourselves do this, what happens? Looking ahead, through eyes of faith, Nietzsche says:

> the spirit is then as much at home in the senses as the senses are at home in the spirit; and whatever takes place in the spirit must enkindle a subtle, extraordinary happiness and play in the senses. And also the other way around.[31]

Rather than an abasement of the spirit, is it possible that this reversal of our traditional attitude might enable us to (as he puts it) 'experience a kind of deification of the body'?[32] Might we not begin to experience a real *sublimation* of the flesh?

There is a Note, Note 820, published in Book III of *The Will to Power*, in which Nietzsche might be said to sum up the wisdom of his entire project:

> I desire for myself and for all who live, are permitted to live, without being tormented by a puritanical conscience, an ever-greater spiritualization and multiplication of the senses; indeed we should be grateful to the senses for their subtlety, plenitude, and power, and offer them in return the best we have in the way of spirit.[33]

But a Note in *Joyful Wisdom* communicates this vision in the more pointed form of a question and a task:

> How far is the truth susceptible of embodiment? – that is the question, that is the experiment.[34]

Since Nietzsche powerfully influenced Heidegger's thinking, I think it would be reasonable for us to turn, at this point, to Heidegger, to determine how he takes over this question, and the experiment it proposes. There is a very long and

complicated story here, but our efforts to unravel its more
puzzling knots will, I believe, be rewarded.

Section 3   Heidegger

What happens to the body in the history of thought at the
point where Heidegger takes up this question and makes of
it his own historical task? When we take an untutored look
at Heidegger's work, we come across many pages of text
concerned with our embodiment. Thus, for example, we find
a discussion of spatiality in *Being and Time*, where Heidegger
is observing that,

> *Dasein's* spatialization in its 'bodily nature' is . . .
> marked out in accordance with these directions [of
> right and left, up and down, front and back, and
> here and there].[35]

But then he adds, framing his words by parentheses:

> This 'bodily nature' hides a whole problematic of its
> own, though we shall not treat it here.

Oddly enough, however, this definition of his task does not
at all deflect him from a detailed phenomenological account
of human spatiality in relation to the body.[36] The conclusion
to which his account eventually leads us is a disclosure of
the fundamental ontological difference between the spatiality
of the human being and the spatiality of all other kinds of
being:

> because *Dasein* is 'spiritual,' and only because of
> this, it can be spatial in a way which remains
> essentially impossible for any extended corporeal
> thing.[37]

Even if we believe that Heidegger's attention to spatiality
is only for the sake of this ontological disclosure, we certainly
cannot dismiss obvious phenomenological analyses such as
this when we reflect on Heidegger's methodological deci-
sions, stated explicitly and often enough, to defer, or leave
aside, the 'whole problematic' of embodiment. Does he defer
it? If we hold that he does, we must at some point ask
ourselves: Why does he defer? – defer not just once or twice,

but again and again? Is it because the body is not important? Or is it because the problem is too difficult? But why would the body be a problematic too difficult for him to think through? And anyway, why does he *think* he is deferring it when, if we follow customary notions, we may be certain that, in point of fact, he is not putting it aside at all? Heidegger's methodological stance poses many unsettling questions for us. The human body is a very precious gift. We, as Heidegger's heirs, cannot in any case justifiably avoid the call to give it, in return, the gift of our thought.

Let us, for the moment, restrict ourselves to *Being and Time*, Heidegger's early, and still primary work. I would like to point out that, despite Heidegger's parenthetical remark, a careful reading of this work would in fact bring to light a surprising treasure of phenomenological material pertaining not only to the *spatial character* of our human way of being-embodied, but also, for example, to the traditional questions concerning the 'nature' and 'limits' of our perceptual and gestural capacities. Reading this book carefully, we will find lengthy discussions of bodily activities, such as hammering, in relation to *Vorhandensein* and *Zuhandensein*; the experience of hardness and resistance (1,3,B,20, p. 130); the ontological possibility of being 'touched' by something (1,5,A,29, p. 177); the character of hearing, its different modalities, and its potential as a capacity which we can develop; references to the sensuous character of our speech (*Rede*), e.g., intonation, modulation, pace, and style, or 'the way of speaking' (1,5,33, p. 205); the sensible and (dare we say it?) the ethical character of vision and its various modalities (for example, 'fixed staring,' pure theoretical 'beholding,' a vision 'diminished' under the rule of technology, a looking which opens with wonderment, a looking with lust and greed, and even the seeing of colors. Introduction, II,7,B).

If we continue our search by reading his other works, the same enigma appears. In 'What Are Poets For?' we find Heidegger has given thought to 'the still covetous vision of things.'[38] In that essay, and also in his studies of Herakleitos, we find Heidegger giving thought to our breathing. In 'Building Dwelling Thinking,' we find Heidegger entering the field worked by Merleau–Ponty, and deftly refuting the concept of an 'encapsulated body.'[39] In 'Science and Reflection,' we find Heidegger examining the origins of scientific theory in a specific 'way' of looking and seeing. In his essays on the pre-Socratics, but also in his works on language, we find that

Heidegger is attentive to the effort required of our hearing. Finally, in *What Is Called Thinking?* we find Heidegger carefully attending to our steps, paths, and leaps, as well as to the human propensity for stumbling, falling, and straying. (I would deny that these can be understood as 'mere metaphors'. But, even if I am wrong about this, their experiential impact is both incontestable and in need of further understanding.)

In what sense, then, does Heidegger defer attention to the problematic of our 'bodily nature'? Since he claims in no uncertain terms that he must postpone it, while to us it seems that he does not, we need to consider the possibility that two divergent conceptions are at stake here. I submit that this is indeed the case, and that the distinction with which we need to work differentiates (i) reflections on *the essence of our bodily nature* from (ii) reflections focused on *our various perceptual and gestural capacities* as human beings who are always already in relation to Being as such. Inasmuch as his reflections on *our bodily nature* never seem to get very far, and never seem to open up the matter for deeper thought, whereas, by contrast, his reflections on *our capacities*, as bodily beings, for maintaining an ontological relationship with Being invariably unfold our understanding of these capacities in deeply motivating and fruitful ways, it is not surprising that, in the end, Heidegger should divert his thought from the first to the second. He works where his thinking can bear fruit. Anyway, much of our puzzlement is abolished once we realize that Heidegger did not explicitly thematize the differentiation that we have finally had to make here.

Moreover, I believe that the making of this differentiation will help us to understand why the problematic of the body should appear, within the context of Heidegger's way of thinking, to be so unfruitful, so very difficult to work on. In large part, the explanation is to be found, I suggest, in the methodology of our tradition of metaphysics and epistemology, which assumes that such thinking must be the positing of an objective body for the contemplation of an abstract, disembodied, and purely theoretical mode of thought, and which accordingly authorizes the formulation of a 'problematic' whose amplitude of experiential sense is taken to be securely de-posited in the univocal propositional sequences of rational metaphysical discourse.

If thinking *is* our gift, uniquely our gift, then it should be *given* to the body *as* a gift, a gift *acknowledging and reciprocating* the gifts which the body, receptive to the sensuous presencing of Being, has passed on to it in the mode called 'givenness.' Indeed, thinking should give *itself* as a gift to the body. But in fully giving itself, it would not *insist* that the body's way of being must *conform* to its own set categories, would not *object* to the body's ownmost way of being and giving itself. On the contrary, thinking would *open* to the body, would listen, would shift into a more receptive attitude, an accepting attitude, an attitude whose spelling of graciousness the body would feel and find fulfilling.

We will note that, whenever Heidegger formulates the problematic in the *first* way, i.e., as a question of thinking the essential nature of the human body (or the bodily nature of the essentially human way-of-being), he is compelled to repeat the difficulty and repeat the deferment. But when, instead, he goes *directly* into the hermeneutical phenomenology of our perceptive and gestural being-in-the-world, then we find that he has *much* to say: about our hearing, our vision, our breathing, our gestures, our postures and bearing, our mooded ways of dwelling on, and experiencing, the earth. What *gives* him so much to say? And *from where* does his thinking draw its inspiration? In the passages where Heidegger's thinking about our bodily being is fruitful, his method, or strategy, is very different from the passages where it is not. It is *not* fruitful where he follows the tradition and continues to formulate a problematic for thinking in the 'objective' mode of essentialism. It is very fruitful where, instead, we find him thinking in an authentically *existential* way about the 'unfolding' of experiential capacities and processes. To be specific, we find him (i) *diagnosing* the afflictions we suffer and endure as perceptive and passionate beings, (ii) articulating the *opportunities* for an ontological development of our capacities, and (iii) himself taking some steps to prepare for this kind of development. Here, the method takes Heidegger *into* the body of lived experience, but into it more deeply than science and 'common sense.' Here, the method takes him in a questioning way into the *ontological potential for development* that is latent in our capacities as bodily beings.

There is great intuitive wisdom, then, in Heidegger's repeated postponement of what I am calling his 'first' method, or strategy. But Heidegger himself is not in a historically favorable position to appreciate this wisdom. Nor can he see clearly enough that, when he 'instinctively' turns to what I am defining as his 'second' method, he *is* able to think that 'same' problematic in a very fruitful way. What explains Heidegger's blindness? What explains the fact that he gives us very powerful evocations of our bodyhood while asserting at the same time, and with almost the same breath, that he is *not* able to tarry with the problem in a fruitful way? I would like to suggest that he cannot see what *we* can see – that is to say, cannot see his analyses of perceptual and gestural capacities *as* contributions to an ontological understanding of embodiment – because he is still too much enthralled by the traditional mode of metaphysical thinking which calls for the theoretical positing of objects-for-thought within the space of a subject-object structure.

Be that as it may, we find Heidegger reiterating, in his 'Letter on Humanism,' that 'the human body is something essentially other than an animal organism.'[40] And he argues, filling out his assertion, that metaphysics *does* think of the human being as *animalitas*, but *cannot* (as least, not with equanimity) experience 'our appalling and scarcely conceivable kinship with the beast.' But it must be acknowledged that Heidegger does little more, in this text, than call our attention to the problem. We will also find him touching upon – and still not settling – this most intractable of problems in *What Is Called Thinking*? Human being, he writes,

> is the as yet undetermined animal; the rational
> animal has not yet been brought into its full
> nature.[41]

Could it be that this future of fulfillment involves the emergence and cultivation of an entirely new attitude toward our physicality, our animal and fleshly nature? Heidegger's discussion of Nietzsche seems, I think, to suggest this. According to Heidegger, what we find when we scan the history of metaphysics with an eye to its representation of the human body, is that

> the two domains of being, animality and rationality,
> separate and clash. This rupture prevents man
> from possessing unity of nature and then being free
> for what we normally call the real.[42]

In this regard, it is worth noting what Heidegger argues in his Nietzsche work:

the essence of man can never be *adequately*
determined in its origin through *the prevailing*, that
is, the *metaphysical*, interpretation of man as *animal
rationale*, whether one prefers to give priority to
rationalitas (rationality, consciousness, and
spirituality) or to *animalitas* (animality and
corporeality), or whether one merely seeks an
acceptable compromise between these two.[43]

Now if a radically new strategy of thought is required, we
might well draw the conclusion that this strategy would need
to abandon not only the 'prevailing metaphysical interpretation of man,' but also the old question of the 'essence of
man' – or that, at the very least, it would be necessary to
avoid normal reliance on this notion of 'essence' as a way of
beginning the new path of thought. Thus, for example, it
might be a more promising strategy to begin as far from the
shadow of metaphysical thought as possible, consulting 'very
directly' our lived experience of being embodied.

Of course, there is no way that we can entirely avoid
metaphysics; but, in any event, it is crucial that we keep in
mind the precious lessons of our metaphysical past. Nevertheless, at this moment in history, every one of us understands, without much coaching, a 'direct' reference to exper-
ience-as-lived. So I should like to refer directly to the bodily
felt experience of (say) taking a stand, walking with humility,
and losing one's foothold; or, equally, to the bodily felt experience of the difference between staring and gazing; or,
equally, to the bodily felt experience of the difference
between grasping something with greed and holding it in a
way that lets go of the attachment. My faith in the value of
direct reference to experience is not at all moved by the old
conviction that experience is somehow innocent or pure.
Rather, it is moved by the conviction that we break out
of metaphysics with greater ease and greater completeness
insofar as we can bracket its categories while we get in touch
with our existential experience of embodied being and stay
close in an open way to its concreteness and specificity and
immediacy. At bottom, the problem with metaphysics lies in
the tendency to *reify* experience and exclude fresh encounter.
(It is in much the same spirit, I believe, that Foucault argues
for a radically new Marxism, based not on abstract and universal analyses but on 'specific knowledges'.)

But, for Heidegger, we must abandon our anthropocentric

interpretation (and his own, in *Being and Time*) of the project which announces itself in the history of philosophy as the attempt to 'determine the essence of man solely in terms of his relationship to Being.'[44] And it seems not to have occurred to him that in avoiding the route of metaphysics, he does not have to navigate forever a course of avoidance. Between the Scylla of a persistent anthropocentrism and the Charybdis of a paralyzing fatalism which awaits the external grace of salvation, there is the route of an experiential phenomenology focused on perceptual and gestural capacities. Out of this method, I believe that some new understanding of human being, as a mode of bodily being-in-the-world, might begin, hermeneutically, to show itself. This study is an attempt to justify such faith.

It is, I think, because Heidegger cannot clearly see this experiential route, a route which in fact he is already taking, that he must again and again raise the problem of embodiment, only to exile it at once to the margins of his text. And yet, despite this frustration, it is not possible for him entirely to avoid placing the matter in the very center of his textual focus. Indeed, it almost seems as if the body, moved by a life of its own, can insist on this placement, even when Heidegger would much rather contemplate other problems. Consider, for example, this passage from his fourth volume of *Nietzsche*:

> When we speak here about 'concepts' and
> 'grasping' and 'thinking' it is certainly not a
> question of a propositional delimitation of what is
> represented when we name these major rubrics.
> To grasp here means consciously to experience what
> has been named in its essence and so to recognize
> in what moment of the hidden history of the West
> we 'stand'; to recognize whether we do *stand* in it,
> or are falling, or already lie prostrate in it, or
> whether we neither surmise the one nor are
> touched by the other two. . . . Thoughtful knowing,
> as a supposedly 'abstract doctrine,' does not
> simply have some practical behaviour as its
> consequence. Thoughtful knowing is in itself
> *comportment*, which is sustained in being not by
> some particular being, but by Being. To think
> 'nihilism' thus does not mean to produce 'mere
> thoughts' about it in one's head, and as a mere

44

INTRODUCTION

spectator to retreat from reality. Rather, to think
'nihilism' means to stand in that wherein every act
and every reality of this era in Western history
receives its time and space, its ground and
background, its means and ends, its order and its
justification, its certainty and its insecurity – in a
word, its 'truth.'[45]

Now, I submit that this passage, to which we shall return
later on (cf. 'The Ground and Its Poetizing'), could not have
been written without a highly reflective awareness making
and maintaining its contact with the figure of the human
body, and itself taking a stand that depended on the experienced gift of this body. 'Concepts' (*Begriffe*) motivates his
reference to 'grasping' (*greifen*). The reference to 'standing'
is repeated and developed in a way that contests the possibility that Heidegger's words are meant only to sustain a
metaphorical conceit. Next, 'thoughtful knowing' is explicitly
characterized as comportment, practical behavior. And, in
order to reinforce this point, Heidegger denies that thinking
is the production of 'mere thoughts' in one's head. He may
even be understood to suggest that 'thinking' (in particular,
thinking in *his* sense, which makes it 'meditation-in-action')
does not 'take place' only up in the head, or in the brain.
Thinking is the *poiein, technē*; and to say that it 'takes place'
only in the head, or as a cerebral activity, is to perpetuate
the old metaphysical split between human being and world.
If *Dasein* is being-in-the-world, then 'thinking' can no longer
be conceptualized according to our traditional dualisms.

Finally, in the very last sentence we have quoted,
Heidegger speaks of space and time, further confirming the
initial sense that his earlier references to postures and
gestures are not to be construed as mere figures of speech.
Be that as it may, I should like to insist, at the very least, that
this passage lends itself to an interpretation which requires (i)
that we relate it to our way of being embodied, and (ii) that
we appropriately call into question the character of this bodily
being.

Let us continue our survey of texts, focusing on passages
in which Heidegger's attention is drawn to the human body.
In 'What Are Poets For?' Heidegger takes up for thought the
vexed problem of freedom, and again he cannot avoid placing
it in terms of the question of 'animality' and 'rationality':

45

> Plant and beast, 'In the venture of their dim delight,'
> are held carefree in the Open. Their bodily nature
> does not perplex them.[46]

As for the angel, whose being is 'higher' than ours,
Heidegger comments that,

> In keeping with this bodiless nature, possible
> confusion by what is sensibly visible has been
> transmuted into the invisible.[47]

Neither beast nor angel need confront the physical nature of
its being. The nature of our corporeality is an existential
question for us, and for us alone.

Heidegger's thinking, here, seems to be as strongly
influenced by Nietzsche as by Rilke. By this I mean to say,
not only that, after he began his period of intensive work on
Nietzsche's thought, it would seem to be Nietzsche, the
thinker with a dream of the spiritually transformed body,
who set out for him the very terms of the problem, but
further, that it would seem to be Nietzsche, too, who first
enabled him to get his bearing. After Nietzsche, he can begin
to escape from the terrible labyrinth of mortification in which
the tradition of metaphysics has successfully ensnared and
confused all thinking about the body. Let us consider the
dialogue which takes place between Heidegger and Fink in
the course of the twelfth session of their joint seminar on
Herakleitos (1966–7). Fink is recorded as saying that

> a human is not only a cleared being: he is also a
> natural being, and as such he is implanted in a
> dark manner in nature.[48]

And he elaborates:

> He [man] has the double character: on the one
> hand, he is the one who places himself in the
> clearing, and on the other, he is the one who is tied
> to the underground of all clearing.[49]

To which Heidegger replies:

> This would become intelligible first of all through
> the phenomenon of the body. . . .

And Fink then adds this:

> as, for example, in the understanding of Eros.

But, stresses Heidegger,

> Body is not meant ontically here. . . .

'[A]nd also not,' says Fink, 'in the Husserlian sense. . . .'
Whereupon Heidegger completes this thought by saying:

> but rather as Nietzsche thought the body, even
> though it is obscure what he actually meant by it.

Fink is then reminded of an especially important passage in
the text of Nietzsche's *Thus Spake Zarathustra*:

> In the section 'Of the Despisers of the Body,'
> Zarathustra says, 'Body am I entirely, and nothing
> else; . . .'

And he is prompted to comment that,

> Through the body and the senses, a human is nigh
> to the earth.

What he means is that the human being is one who 'belongs
bodily to the earth and to the flowing of life. . . .' But this
provokes Heidegger to formulate a major question:

> Can one isolate the dark understanding which the
> bodily belonging to the earth determines, from
> being placed in the clearing?

Does this mean (I wonder) that, in going *beyond* metaphysics,
our new and more radical thinking must *pass through* the trial
posed by the human body? Perhaps so, since we clearly need
to retrieve a new and more radical *experience* of Being as that
which is our 'ground.'[50] Whatever our answer, it is surely
striking that, somewhat later in the session, Heidegger
concedes that 'The body phenomenon is the most difficult
problem.'[51] That his confession really does bespeak his experience of the body as a 'matter for thought' may be read into
his final remark on the subject, which once again formulates
the problem without appearing to offer much more than a
hint as to the 'way out':

> The bodily in the human is not something
> animalistic. The manner of understanding that

accompanies it is something that metaphysics up till now has not touched on.[52]

Could it be that our patriarchal metaphysics has not been able to 'touch upon' the manner of understanding which accompanies our corporeal being because it has not allowed itself to be *touched* by the truth of the body, and because the only way it knows of getting in touch with the body's true nature is a way that does it an unforgivable violence? Let us conclude our initial examination of Heidegger's relationship to 'the problem of embodiment' by considering, very briefly, the matters to which he gives thought in the first volume of his work on Nietzsche, *The Will to Power as Art*. In 'Nietzsche's Overturning of Platonism,' Heidegger quotes Nietzsche's Note 820 (the one we cited at the close of our discussion of Nietzsche), and offers the following comment:

> What is needed is neither abolition of the sensuous nor abolition of the nonsensuous. On the contrary. What must be cast aside is the misinterpretation, the deprecation, of the sensuous, as well as the extravagant elevation of the supersensuous. A path must be cleared for a new interpretation of the sensuous on the basis of a new hierarchy of the sensuous and nonsensuous. The new hierarchy does not simply wish to reverse matters within the old structural order, now reverencing the sensuous and scorning the nonsensuous. It does not wish to put what was at the very bottom on the very top. A new hierarchy and new valuation mean that the ordering *structure* must be changed. To that extent, overturning Platonism must become a twisting free of it.[53]

One of the most promising 'twists' that Heidegger takes to free himself from our metaphysical tradition is to be found in his attention, for example in this work on Nietzsche, to the truth-disclosive potential in feeling. The body, as he notes, is 'internalized' in feeling.[54] What he is calling (still somewhat caught up in metaphysics) the 'internal experience' of the body is crucial, first of all, for our liberation from a frame of mind which hypostatizes the living body (the body as we live it). According to Heidegger, 'feeling' is

INTRODUCTION

that basic mode of *Dasein* by force of which and in accordance with which we are always already lifted beyond ourselves into being as a whole.[55]

What gives feeling its truth-disclosive nature, then, is that it is inherently directed toward an experience which is global and holistic. Our 'felt body' therefore *contests and counter-balances* the objective 'natural' body which we come to know only much later, and only through the influences of analytical science.

> Most of what we know from the natural sciences about the body and the way it embodies are specifications based on the established misinterpretation of the body as a mere natural body.[56]

Feeling and sensibility contest the reduction of the body to an isolated objective being. 'Where is the physiological,' he asks, 'or what pertains to bodily states?'[57] The body of feeling as we experience it, as we live it, *integrates* what objective thought would divide:

> Ultimately we dare not split up the matter in such a way, as though there were a bodily state housed in the basement with feelings dwelling upstairs. Feeling, as feeling oneself to be, is precisely the way we are bodily. Bodily being does not mean that the soul is burdened by a hulk we call the body. . . . We do not 'have' a body; rather, we 'are' bodily.[58]

Furthermore, as Heidegger observes in the fourth *Nietzsche* volume, the one which reflects on 'Nihilism',

> The essence of thinking, experienced . . . on the basis of Being, is not defined by being set off against willing and feeling. Therefore it should not be proclaimed purely theoretical as opposed to practical activity and thus restricted in its essential importance for the essence of man.[59]

Thus we may say that bodily feeling, sensibility, which is a mode of knowledge anterior to science, but not for that

49

reason (as Descartes insisted) necessarily inferior or 'confused', is fundamentally a contributory phase of thinking, in the sense that it *holds open for us* an access to a more 'universal' dimension of bodily being. According to Heidegger,

> Every feeling is an embodiment attuned in this or
> that way, a mood that embodies in this or that
> way.[60]

There is awaiting us, then, if we are prepared to go down into it, a preontological (or proto-ontological) attunement, an 'attunement woven into embodiment': an attunement, in fact, to Being as a whole.[61] (Incidentally, let me insist that my words 'go down into' are to be understood as a truth of experience, and therefore not a mere ornament of speech. The same must be said about the phrases 'raising' and 'lifting up,' which accurately articulate the actually lived experience of the second phase of phenomenological reflection. Thus, e.g., Heidegger speaks of phenomenology as attempting 'to raise the phenomenal content of the disclosing into concepts.')[62] Ontologically considered, our awareness of this feeling attunement – our retrieval of this perceptive, felt attunement as a 'guardian awareness' – is of the utmost significance, since it is that openness-to-Being which first acquaints us with the potential dimensionality of our being in a mortal embodiment. As we question the body of mood, going (down) into it ever more deeply, it seems that we move closer to that field of our being in which the ontological gift ('Es gibt') presents itself, i.e., is felt to present itself, in its deepest truth. 'Rapture' (*Rausch*) is the 'aesthetic' experience of this ek-static inherence in Being.[63]

Medard Boss, working very closely with Heidegger for many years, has this to say about 'attunement':

> Every attunement *as* attunement is a particular
> mode of the perceptive openness of our existence.
> The prevailing attunement is at any given time the
> condition of our openness for perceiving and
> dealing with what we encounter; the pitch at which
> our existence, as a set of relationships to objects,
> ourselves and other people, is vibrating. What we
> call moods, feelings, affects, emotions, and states
> are the concrete modes in which the possibilities for

being open are fulfilled. They are at the same time
the modes in which this perceptive openness can
be narrowed, distorted, or closed off.[64]

And he continues this step of thought with a remark whose
specific meaning we shall attempt to spell out in the course
of this study on gesture and movement:

Whatever its momentary attunement, the openness
that is our existence always determines as well the
particular breadth or narrowness, brightness or
obscurity of that existence.

Section 4   The Body in Question

Put briefly, perhaps the entire evolution of the spirit is a
question of the body; it is the history of the development
of a higher body that emerges into our sensibility. The
organic is rising to yet higher levels.

Nietzsche, *The Will to Power*[65]

The difference between the life of the spirit and that of
the flesh is itself a spiritual difference. . . .

George Santayana, *Platonism and the Spiritual Life*[66]

It is possible to make use of 'The Question of Being' to stake
out a *dimensionality* for the perceptive capacities of the human
body which will facilitate a process of ontological development. Inasmuch as Being is 'The Open,' the Question of
Being situates the human body in the spacious clearing of
the ontological difference. The ontological difference articulates for our perceptivity and sensibility a depth-of-field, an
open clearing, a dimensionality of meaningfulness which
draws us out of our ontically narrowed and impoverished
world and elicits from the inborn capacities of our bodily
nature their *intrinsic enthusiasm* for deepening and expanding
and enhancing the mortal experience of the openness of
Being. Understood as a *question* for our sensibility, our recep-
tive-perceptive capacities, the Question of Being lays out for
us the essential *difference* between the *affliction* of our *ontic*
existence and the *fulfillment* that is possible for us in our
ontological existence as beings perceptively open to the
presencing of Being and receptive by nature to the gifts of
the 'Es gibt.'

Instead of beginning, as Heidegger thinks he must, with the 'problematic' of 'the body' and its enigmatic duality of animality and spirituality, we may shift our methodological paradigm (as Nietzsche suggests) and focus on specific perceptual and gestural capacities. We may let our thinking, guided by The Question of Being, call our capacities for perceptive awareness and sensibility into the opening, questioning space of the ontological difference. Consider some specific modality of perceptual experience – our vision, for example. Vision, like the other modalities of perception, is a way of being-in-the-world. It is also, more specifically, a *capacity*. For those among us born with eyes that can see, seeing comes naturally. But, as the great painter knows, it is also, as a capacity, a skill. Vision invites development, invites cultivation. At birth, we are given a gift of nature and sent on our way. What we do with that gift, how we experience the potential-for-being inherent in that skill, is the question which defines our individual being (*Jemeinigkeit*). Since the skill *is* a gift, and in truth a 'dispensation' of Being, the most appropriate way of realizing it will be through a responsiveness that deeply and fully *inhabits* our visionary being and transforms every act of looking and seeing into a self-fulfilling gesture of rejoicing and thanksgiving.

The development or cultivation of our capacity for skillful vision needs, of course, a measure. The painter takes his standard from the tradition of painting. The critic takes his standard from the tradition of critical discourse. In a similar way, the surveyor, the pilot, the physician and the forest ranger each will develop a skill in vision according to the standards set by the nature of the work. But all of these measures are merely ontical. Once we begin to think of ourselves as visionary *beings*, however, a radically different measure confronts us. Of what are we really capable, by virtue of this gift, our *being* visionary? What fulfillment of our being *as* visionary can we, at the limit, envision? (We do not have to understand this 'fulfillment' in an egocentric or anthropocentric way. If vision is a gift of Being, the measure of fulfillment must come from Being. But that does not signify our occlusion from an *experiential sense* of this measure, as it governs our visionary being.) In asking these questions, we are articulating the ontological difference as a method for *calling into question* our everyday way of visionary being in its experienced *ontical* dimensionality. This 'calling into question' essentially consists in a 'diagnosis' of ontical 'pathology,' ontical 'affliction,' and it is effected by means of a phenomenology, guided by hermeneutics, that specifies the layout of opportunities for deepening, enhancing, and expanding our perceptual life *as* an experience of Being. The goal of the diagnosis is to recognize and make explicit the various disorders and afflictions of everyday life to which our visionary being is subject, so long as it remains inveterately restricted to the ontically limited dimension of the field of visibility.

Now, this diagnosis is an *Erinnerung*: it requires that we go very deeply into our experienced body of perception; that we go very deeply into our 'bodily felt sense' of the visionary experience; that we go very deeply, and with trust, into the unsatisfactory feeling and attunement characteristic of this experience; that we encounter the truth of this dissatisfaction in an open, enquiring manner; that we contact our need, and the great depth of our need, in that unfamiliar 'inwardness'; and that we respond, appropriately, to the 'felt sense' of what claims our attention, what we are needing, what lacking, what looking for. (I owe the concept of 'bodily felt sense' to Eugene Gendlin.) Diagnosis also requires a second phase, a *Wiederholung*, in the sense that we will feel a need to retrieve, from the very depth of our pain, our affliction, our ontical dissatisfactions, an experience of Being in its more hospitable, more wholesome dimensionality.

Recollection is much more than a process of contacting and retrieving. It is also a process of *developing* our bodily awareness and *cultivating* its capacities. Since the affliction is essentially a characteristic tendency of the ontical (and I would also add, here, the 'ego-logical') dimensionality of our visionary being, the therapeutic response must consist in going down *still more deeply* into the bodily felt sense of our visionary being, so that we make contact with its more open dimension. This 'more open' dimensionality of our visionary being is *always already* ours, so that, in the recollection, we are progressively realizing what we were *given* to understand all along. The open dimension is the primordial gift of vision that was given to us, at birth, *as* a gift of nature, a gift to our bodily nature as human being. But we naturally received this gift *without* awareness and understanding. The gift is our *pre-ontological* mode of vision, an open dimension of visionary belongingness, primordial attunement, spontaneous participation in the spectacle of light; it is *our original openness to Being as a whole experienced in its panoramic wholeness*. The gift is a bodily felt panoramic awareness, a felt sense of being well-integrated into the field of visibility as a whole.

In our visionary being, our capacity, there is a *pre-understanding* of our relationship with Being, an attunement darkly preserved in the primordial *body of feeling* which initially bears the 'destiny' of our visionary skill: a pre-conceptual understanding of our capacity, our inborn potential, for an authentically ontological experience with vision, and of the *openness* which is the true dimensionality of the Being of the field of visibility. We enjoy a rudimentary understanding, operative in the very first and simplest movement of our eyes, which *holds us open* to Being and continually recalls us to ourselves through our capacity for a feeling response to that which it is given to us to see. Thanks to this gift of a primordial understanding, it will never be possible for us totally to ignore our *need* for an explicit, understanding retrieval. And, inasmuch as the process of recollection returns us to the *truth* of our visionary being, the feeling which attends the illumination of this understanding is a deepening sense of individual fulfillment.

In order to avert a serious misunderstanding, I should like to reiterate, at this point, that my suggestion that we focus on individual fulfillment signifies neither egocentrism nor anthropocentrism. What makes this focus decisive is the fact that it is our only *test* of how we are faring, how well we are dwelling. Without such a test, how can we intelligibly speak of authenticity and fallenness, a history of the oblivion of Being, and the ontological difference? Without such a test, how could these differences matter? Heidegger's turning point (his *Kehre*) cannot possibly signify that we must turn our backs to the (ontical) world. We can, and can only, turn to face what Being gives while standing in the midst of our life-world. What the 'turning point' makes clear is the ontological *difference* between facing *only* ourselves, in order to understand Being, and facing ourselves by way of *questioning our capacity* to understand and receive the presencing of Being. In the latter event, there is an *Ereignis*, in the sense that this questioning is our only way of preparing ourselves to receive, *from Being*, the openness which is its measure.

To be sure, the question of the development of our capacities will at first appear like a merely ontical, or anyway egocentric and anthropocentric matter. But it is crucial to understand that, in asking the question and calling into question our actual realization ('performance,' in the vocabularies of linguistics and the behavioral sciences), we are *preparing* for a *radically new relationship* to Being by reference to the experienced character of our *present* relationship: we are *preparing* for the kind of relationship which Heidegger characterizes by speaking of receiving the determination of our capacities from Being itself,[67] because our self-questioning inaugurates a process of opening and deepening, a process by which we make contact with, and begin to retrieve, the primordial 'guardian awareness' (*Wahrnehmung*) of the ontological relationship that has been vouchsafed to us only by way of our embodiment – our capacity, for example, to experience, at least for a moment, a vision whose measure is determined not by itself (i.e., our 'normal' selves), but by Being itself.

The *anamnēsis* by which we go down into the pre-ontological (or proto-ontological) body of felt sense, deepening our contact with its panoramic attunement and holistic awareness, *lifts up* this dark pre-understanding into the clearer light of thought. (Thinking begins, fundamentally, in the feet. Its roots are there. But the level, or phase, or pre-understanding we mostly tend to contact and work with first is always significantly connected with the experiencing taking place in the region of the navel.) By virtue of this corporeal *anamnēsis*, our visionary being may progressively realize what it has been *given* to understand all along. Bodying forth this gift of understanding kept within the body (making it manifest, explicit, and articulate), we are *opening* into the clearing field of Being.

Section 5   The Rage of History

The history of philosophy is a secret raging against the pre-conditions of life, against the value feelings of life. . . .

Nietzsche, *The Will to Power*[68]

But the exile of the body in outward history has its parallel in the exile of the soul in its migrations from embodiment to embodiment. . . .
Gershom Scholem, *On the Kabbalah and Its Symbolism*[69]

What *is* the human body in the history of our relationship to Being? In his long work on *Heraklit*, Heidegger wrote of 'an unchained rage of history.'[70] I think this would be an accurate way of characterizing the historical experience of incarnation in the Judaeo-Christian tradition. Just as Heidegger must tell the history of metaphysics as a history of the oblivion of Being, so must we tell the history of the human body as a history of its ontological affliction. In metaphysics as in life, the truth of the body, or the body in its truth, is kept in exile. We *know* it only in its *epochē*, its errancy, its objectification and automation, its crucifixion, its rituals of mortification. The oblivion of Being denies the human body an assuaging awareness of the primordial experience of its openness, its enriching depth-of-field, its inherence in the wholeness of Being. The history of the being of the human body is a crucial part of the history of Being.

'Overcoming' metaphysics means overcoming the metaphysical misunderstanding of the being of the human body. It means overcoming our historically deep-seated guilt and shame, flaming into a terrible *hatred* of the body. The history of mind/dualism and the history of the subject/object dualism are two symptomatic manifestations of a violent, nihilistic rage in the very heart of our metaphysics. But to overcome metaphysics, we must do more than formulate a conceptual critique. We must *retrieve* the ontological body. We must actually *let go* of our dualistic, propositional way of 'thinking.' Metaphysical thinking takes place only in the theoretical 'mind,' and is always an 'I think (=represent to myself) that. . . .' Ontological thinking is radically different: it engages us in the opening *wholeness* of our being, and 'takes place' as much in the life of our feet and hands and eyes as it does in our head, our brains, or our 'mind.' Our thinking will not find its way back to a more primordial presencing of Being without first 'losing itself' as a metaphysical 'thinking' and going very deeply *into* the body of experience (*Wahrnehmung*).

Nietzsche realizes, though, that a methodic resurrection of the body's truth must sooner or later confront the cultural history of the body, which is a history of patriarchal humiliation and mortification. (In the Western discourse of cultural symbols, the body has always been associated with the feminine, and especially the matriarchal principle, while the mind (reason, law, intelligence, brainpower) has been traditionally tied to the masculine and the patriarchal. And Western metaphysics reflects this cultural and political division.) Nietzsche speaks, in a passage reverberating with strong emotion, of

My struggle against the feeling of guilt and the
projection of the concept of punishment [and self-
hate] into the physical and metaphysical
world. . . .[71]

And he speaks, therefore, of the need for a 'psychology of
metaphysics'[72] – a need for which, many years later, in his
'Working Notes,' Merleau–Ponty too is to speak. How else,
really, can we work through what Nietzsche describes as 'the
treacherous and blind hostility of philosophers towards the
senses,'[73] in order to experience the human body in a truth
that is finally *free* of our tradition of metaphysical re-
presentations?

It is *not* the senses that deceive. Our nose, of which,
so far as I know, no philosopher has ever spoken
with due respect, is as yet the most delicate scientific
[*physikalisch*] instrument in existence: it is capable
of registering vibrations where even the
spectroscope fails.[74]

Does the life of the spirit require the body's repression? Is
dualism the only way for the spirit to insist on its difference
from the flesh? Taking up the critique which Nietzsche
began, Max Scheler forcefully argues, in his diagnosis of
'Ressentiment in the Building of Morals,' that,

The ascetic ideal of life may be founded on an
estrangement from one's body which can actually
turn into hatred. I already indicated that this
attitude is frequently the consequence of repressed
impulses of hatred and revenge. This state of mind
is often expressed in reflections such as 'the body
is the prison of the soul,' and it can lead to diverse
forms of bodily self-torture. Here again, the
primary motive is not *love* of one's *spiritual* self and
the wish to perfect and consecrate it by disciplining
the body. What is primary is *hatred of the body*, and
the concern for 'salvation of the soul' is a pretense
which is often needed only later.[75]

Carl Jung also takes up the Nietzschean struggle to overcome
the metaphysical tradition and the destiny with which it has
burdened – and we might even say 'afflicted' – the mortal

body. In 'The Spiritual Problems of Modern Man,' for example, Jung declares that the 'recognition of the body cannot tolerate a philosophy that denies it in the name of the spirit.'[76] And he acclaims the time of a 'turning,' which begins 'a new self-appraisal, a reassessment of our fundamental human nature.'[77] For Jung,

> We can hardly be surprised if this leads to a rediscovery of the body after its long subjection to the spirit – we are even tempted to say that the flesh is getting its own back.[78]

We must think *beyond* 'the old idea of an antithesis between mind and matter,' in which, Jung believes, 'we are still caught.'[79] For Jung, this indicates that we must, as he says,

> reconcile ourselves to the mysterious truth that the spirit is the life of the body seen from within, and the body the outward manifestation of the life of the spirit – the two being really one. . . .[80]

I would like to point out, here, that Erich Neumann, perhaps Jung's most brilliant student, has translated this analysis of the body into the symbolism of the masculine and feminine principles, and attempted to correlate the history of our experience of embodiment (incarnation) with the historical transition from matriarchal to patriarchal rule.[81] (He needs of course to postulate, not implausibly, that the patriarchy emphasizes the supreme value of the intellect, which it locates in a head that is virtually detached from the rest of the body, while the matriarchy, devoted to the care of infants and children, is especially tied to the value of the body.) Since I am convinced that this interpretation makes sense, I consider that the 'mysterious truth' – the *difficult* truth – to which we must reconcile ourselves ultimately necessitates our involvement in a struggle to overcome the one-sided experience of the body which holds us in its thrall during the rule of the patriarchy. The human body will not, I think, be redeemed until the truth of the masculine principle is *brought into balance* – balance and harmony – with the corresponding truth of the feminine principle. This study of gesture and motility is intended to bring out the meaning of such a conjecture and will attempt, insofar as possible, to establish its claim to truth. Despite his offensive misogyny,

Nietzsche must be counted among the courageous few, mostly women, who have been responsible for the liberation of the human body – a liberation still, of course, underway – from the patriarchal repression of the body, an asceticism which denies the body its natural health, and its inborn 'will to power.'

Section 6   Thinking Underway

We should study our organism in all its immortality.
Nietzsche, *The Will to Power*[82]

We want to hold fast to our senses and our faith in them – and think their consequences through to the end!
Nietzsche, *The Will to Power*[83]

I think it is significant that Medard Boss, whose work enjoyed Heidegger's support, very fruitfully follows what I will call The Middle Way of Experiential Questioning. By virtue of this strategy, he avoids the *dilemma* which confronts all thinking that allows itself to be dominated by the traditional metaphysical formulation. For thinking thus dominated, it may well seem that, insofar as we must inevitably think our break with the tradition *within* that very tradition, we are constrained to begin our critical endeavor with the (theoretical) question, 'What is the essential being of the human body?' After all, it does at first seem reasonable to believe that this question *shifts* our attention to a 'deeper' level of understanding, a level *underlying* the polarities of both science and common sense. Yet this tempting strategy of understanding must be strongly resisted, because it formulates our question within the dualism of the tradition in a way that generates an unacceptable, unworkable dilemma and precludes the possibility of a radically new, and genuinely ontological answer. The difficulty with this formulation is that it concedes to the tradition precisely that which needs most to be questioned with vigor, namely, the representation of the perceptual and gestural 'situation' or 'event' (that-which-presences-primordially-in-our-experience-of-being) in terms of 'the body,' i.e., in terms of that which is not primordial at all, but is derivative, rather, from the spatio-temporal structure of the subject-object relationship.

It is not a fruitful strategy to give thought to 'the essential being of the body.' We are presumably questioning the entire

tradition of metaphysics. Therefore we must try to frame our
questions in a way that avoids the total domination of its
categories. The very fact that we find ourselves deeply
conflicted, *both* in our experience of 'the body' and in our
attempt to understand it in a way that appears to be 'ontological,' suggests that we must somehow find a more radical
alternative to the question Heidegger is often tempted to
ask. For him, it seems that 'thinking' is confronted by an
unresolvable dilemma: *either* we surrender to the traditional
objectification of the body that takes place both in science
and in common sense (and, equally so, in the other debates
of thought, i.e., empiricism and idealism, spiritualism and
materialism, physicalism and transcendentalism), *or* we ask
the 'ontological' question about the 'essence' of 'the human
body.' But, if we succumb to the temptation and formulate
the 'matter for thought' in these latter terms, we fall at once
into a self-defeating *resistance* to the domination of a dogmatically ontical thinking. If the first horn is clearly unacceptable
for 'ontological' thinking, the second, though *prima facie* more
acceptable, turns out to be no less problematic, no less
unfruitful, since its grammar of essentialism still carries *too
much* of the weight of our tradition.

Boss, learning well from Heidegger, undertakes a thinking
which is methodologically more fruitful, because the question
he implicitly asks is very different. *The question we need to ask
is: What is it to develop our perceptual capacity for responsiveness
and receptivity?* This *directly refers us* to our experiencing of
perception (and of gesture, motility, and bearing) as a
capacity for deepening our way of being-in-the-world. We
are avoiding a questioning of the 'body'; but we do so *in
order to respect that which presences primordially*, and whose
presencing is not adequately or properly understood through
the category of 'bodyhood,' regardless of how much we may
insist on getting to the 'essence' of the matter. Though Boss
never says so, the fact is that the question he asks is all the
more appropriately 'ontological' precisely because it *eschews*
the question about 'essence' in favor of a question directed
simply to our existential experience. Boss is able to put metaphysical 'thinking' very much out of action.

The problem is this: when 'thinking' frames the question
of 'essence,' it tends to *stand opposite* the body, secretly
detaching itself from 'the body' in a move that only perpetuates the conflict already inherent in dualism. 'Thinking,'
spellbound by the authority it wields during the rule of meta-

physics, is itself part of the problem. We must let go, finally, of our metaphysical conception of 'thinking.' We must simply *give* our thought *to* the body. We must take our thinking 'down' into the body. We must learn to think *through* the body. We must learn to think *with* the body. Thinking is not a question of 'bracketing' the body (Husserl's *epochē*), but a question of integrating awareness, living well-focused 'in the body.' For once, we should *listen in silence* to our bodily felt experience. Thinking needs to learn by feeling, by just *being with* our bodily being. Are we ready to let this body of experience tell us how to think its 'essence'? Are we, as thinkers, ready to quiet the conceptualizing mind in order to *listen* to the body's own speech, its own *logos*? To be sure, our 'thinking' will sound, and be, radically different. That, however, is precisely my point. I can see no other way for 'thinking' to break out of the history of Western metaphysics.

Boss asks, very simply, about *our capacities*. He *refers us directly* to our own bodily felt experiencing, so that we *become aware* of its character, aware of its satisfactions and afflictions, and begin to realize its inborn, gifted potential for development. *He draws us into a relationship with Being as such by focusing our attention on the immediately accessible opportunities we can find for developing and cultivating a greater openness, a more thoughtful responsiveness, a deeper receptiveness, a less conflicted contact.* This direct experiential reference to an immeasurable potential for development is the way he formulates the onto-logical question. This 'experiential questioning' is 'the middle way' by which he escapes between both the ontic and the insufficiently ontological horns of the dilemma. And the 'body' in question, here, is the body of Merleau–Ponty's depth phenomenology: neither the ontical body of 'common sense' nor the ontical body of science (which only reflects and encourages the errancy of our 'natural attitude'), but rather the body of deepening experience always already inherent in Being as a whole.

Since this ontological understanding of our bodily being remains more or less implicit, more or less undeveloped, in Heidegger's own account, I will attempt to expound this emerging body of understanding, aiming for a phenomenol-ogical concreteness of detail that may further bring out the ontological nature, the ontological bearing and destination, of the mortal human body. It is unquestionably fitting that Heidegger, following the path of Nietzsche's critique and adumbrating the problematic nature of the human body as

it is represented by our metaphysical tradition, should deliberately set aside, or anyway postpone, the ultimately necessary task of *thinking* the mortal body in the light of Being.
We, however, as the work of Medard Boss makes clear, need
not continue to exile in the margins the body which calls
forth this fundamental task.

Section 7   Merleau–Ponty

Thinking of Being needs an appropriate vessel: a body of
perception whose *Befindlichkeit*, a primordial, bodily felt
sense-of-being-in-the-world, grants us the potential in an
implicit pre-understanding of Being. In order to go beyond
Heidegger's difficulty, we must turn for help to the work of
Merleau–Ponty, whose philosophical vocation ended, as it
began, with an intensive phenomenological meditation – the
most fruitful we have so far – on the body of experience as
it is lived in a deepening awareness.

In his recent book, *Merleau–Ponty's Philosophy*, Samuel
Mallin asserts – and I would like to express my wholehearted
agreement with him – that Merleau–Ponty's most fundamental, most radical working principle, what he calls his
'thesis of the primacy of perception,'

> holds, first, that perception gives us the clearest
> case of our relationship to Being; secondly, that all
> other types of objects have a natural nucleus in, or
> must be based on, this perceptual relationship; and
> thirdly, that all the regions of a unified Existence
> necessarily interact in such a way that they
> 'borrow' or 'imitate' the logic of the most primordial
> region, [which is] perception.[84]

Now, in Merleau–Ponty's *first* large work on the problem of
embodiment, a book entitled *The Structure of Behavior*, every
one of the historically major theoretical understandings of
the human body is subject to a rigorous conceptual and
methodological critique. This book laid the foundation for his
next large work, the *Phenomenology of Perception*, in which his
earlier hints, promising an alternative, and more adequate
understanding of the body, are taken up as points of departure for a detailed phenomenological explicitation. The basic
standpoint from which he speaks is nicely formulated in a
passage from this second major work:

As far as the body is concerned, even the body of
another, we must learn to distinguish it from the
objective body as set forth in works on physiology.
This is not the body which is capable of being
inhabited by a consciousness. . . . It is simply a
question of recognizing that the body, as a
chemical structure or an agglomeration of tissues,
is formed, *by a process of impoverishment*, from a
primordial phenomenon of the body-for-us, the body
of human experience or the perceived body. . . .[85]

To be sure,

when science tries to include my body among the
relationships obtaining in the objective world, it is
because it is trying, in its way, to translate the
suturation of my phenomenal body on to the
primordial world.[86]

But the point Merleau–Ponty wishes to make is that this
translation is doomed eventually to failure, since it is possible
only on the basis of an anterior understanding of the body, an
understanding which essentially owes nothing to the science
which constitutes an 'objective body' in the observable
spatio-temporal world. This is not to say, however, that the
only truth which it remains for us to espouse is a body of
purely subjective experience:

At the same time as the body withdraws from the
objective world, and forms *between* the pure subject
[as espoused by idealism and intellectualism] and
the object [pursued by our physical sciences] a
third genus of being, the subject loses its purity and
its transparency.[87]

So his *Phenomenology of Perception* attempts to flesh out for us
this 'third genus' of corporeal being, bringing it to articulation
in a discourse that facilitates a reflectively deepening *experience* of our own embodiment.

But the *Phenomenology of Perception* is a work whose promise
of radicality is not (yet) fulfilled. For one thing, it is, as the
author himself later acknowledged, still too Cartesian, too
steeped in the heady brews of idealism: in the end, it perpetuates the very same philosophies of 'consciousness' which

conspired in the suppression of the body's own truth. But there is also a second shortcoming, viz., that it fails to penetrate the primordial dimensionality of our embodiment, and it consequently misses a truly radical understanding of our *pre-ontological* bodily attunement, as well as – of course – our *ontological* 'destination' as a body fulfilling the calling of Being. In fine, then, it must be said that, in his *Phenomenology of Perception*, it is the mundane body of everyday life, the body enjoyed by a mature *egological* consciousness, which is brought into the light of reflection. For a more radical explicitation of the body, for a boldly hermeneutical phenomenology strongly influenced by his renewed contact with the work of Heidegger (and especially with Heidegger's 'later' work), we must concentrate, rather, on 'The Intertwining – The Chiasm,' and also on his 'Working Notes' for the book he never got a chance to write. It is in these continually astonishing manuscripts from his later period of thinking, manuscripts published posthumously under the title *The Visible and the Invisible*, that we will find, but in the most painfully truncated form, Merleau–Ponty's still tentative gesturings toward what he wanted to call 'the architectonics of the human body, its ontological framework.'[88]

I would like, therefore, to turn now to these extremely difficult, daring, and more radical manuscripts, where we will be able to see, as if the fateful moment were not yet entirely past, the absolutely *shattering* effect of the collision between the author who conceived the *Phenomenology of Perception* and the later works of Heidegger, to which – I think we may presume this – the first returned for a re-reading that manifestly opened up his thinking in the most explosive manner. 'The Intertwining – The Chiasm,' together with his 'Working Notes,' tell the story, if we read between the lines, of this decisive event, decisive, in fact, not merely for Merleau–Ponty's own thinking, but also for the future of the entire phenomenological movement.

After the collision with Heidegger, Merleau–Ponty starts over. His new beginning is not, however, entirely disconnected from his earlier work. A careful reading of *Phenomenology of Perception* will in fact discover a number of passages which already adumbrate the perspective unfolded in his later writings. One of the passages in question is this:

I am not, therefore, in Hegel's phrase, a 'hole in

Being,' but a hollow, a fold, which has been made
and can be unmade.[89]

There is sublime vision here. But the transpersonal and
cosmological dimensions of personal existence to which this
passage alludes were not very clearly brought to light, of
course, until its author began to work out the crucial notions
of 'The Intertwining – The Chiasm.' Eventually, and inevitably, we find him wrestling with the subject-object relationship of classical metaphysics: wrestling with it and finally
breaking out of its powerful and familiar hold. The relationship, he says, is a 'doubling,' a 'mirroring'; subject and object
belong together like the two sides of a leaf.[90] (He also speaks,
in that same text, of hinge and pivot, trying in many different
ways to undo the metaphysical knot.)

But the deconstruction of this rigid subject-object polarity
ultimately must take place, as he patiently shows us, in the
context of a radicalized phenomenology of embodiment. And
it is at this point – the point, I mean, where he fully realizes
what this means – that he makes his most consequent break
with the entire history of metaphysics. The crucial notion in
this deconstruction – the notion which, in no uncertain
terms, proclaims his irrevocable breaking away from the fate
of this long history – is the notion of 'flesh.' This one notion
alone deconstructs, in just one devastating sweep, not only
the dualism of subject and object, but also the egology and
objectivity of the body – and indeed, the entire complex of
metaphysical representations within which the human body
had been held captive. 'The flesh (of the world or my own),'
he writes, 'is . . . a texture that returns to itself and conforms
to itself.'[91] It is 'the formative medium of the object and the
subject. . . .'[92] Due to the inherent nature of the flesh, 'a sort
of dehiscence opens my body in two,'[93] and the human body
therefore 'remains incomplete, gaping open.'[94] The notion of
flesh makes possible a radically deeper understanding of the
human body as a phenomenon of a *field* of Being: an opening
and a clearing, '[M]y body sees,' he notes, 'only because it
is a part of the visible in which it opens forth.'[95] But even
this formulation is inadequate, for it is still likely to conjure
up a representation of the body as located rather like a 'thing'
in its field. A more radical formulation of its field-character
would, for example, be this:

My flesh and that of the world therefore involve

clear zones, clearings, about which pivot their
opaque zones, and the primary visibility, that of the
quale and of the things, does not come without a
second visibility, that of the lines of force and
dimensions, the massive flesh without a rarefied
flesh, the momentary body without a glorified
body.[96]

In the *flesh* of the personal, egologically constituted body,
we must recognize a *pre-personal* past – the integrated but
'unconscious' body of the infant and the child in us – as well
as the possibility of a *transpersonal* future: an existence whose
flesh is medium for a selfless commitment of energy. It is,
we might say, this notion of an elemental flesh which serves
to *liberate* the metaphysically delimited body; for it enables
us for the first time to think 'carnal being' as 'a being of
depths . . . a being in latency.'[97] It is a notion which *releases*
the body from restrictive representations and reifications and
opens it out, a 'primordial' body unfolding like the bud of a
flower in the morning sun, opening out into the expansive
field of worldly being. It is a notion which retrieves, for a
thought committed to radicality, what Walter Pater's Marius
wanted to call 'the deep original materialism or earthliness
of human nature itself, bound so intensely to the sensuous
world. . . .'[98] Merleau–Ponty declares:

> [M]y body is made of the same flesh as the world
> . . . and moreover . . . this flesh of my body is
> shared by the world. . . .[99]

But we must be cautious and wary, because, although the
notion of flesh is a novelty, and may therefore escape at
first the full weight of our metaphysical tradition, it can be
captured all too easily and itself reduced to a non-threatening, and eventually familiar term within the tradition of
our metaphysical discourse.

> We must not think the flesh starting from
> substances, from body and spirit . . . but we must
> think it . . . as an element, as the concrete emblem
> of a general manner of being.[100]

And, at another point in the text, he says this:

> The flesh is not matter, is not mind, is not
> substance. To designate it, we should need the old
> term 'element,' in the sense it was used to speak of
> water, air, earth, and fire, that is, in the sense of
> a *general thing*. . . . The flesh is in this sense an
> 'element of Being.'[101]

'Flesh' is a notion which finally makes it possible for us to articulate the human body with respect to its ontological dimensionality: its inherence in the field of Being as a whole, and the destiny, or ideality, for which this inherence claims us. Merleau–Ponty's retrieval of the flesh is an event of the greatest significance. Thus, for example, if space had permitted, I would have liked to include a chapter on the 'body politic,' because I believe that this flesh, an 'intercorporeality' defined by 'intertwining' and 'reversibility,' schematizes and models at the most primordial level an ideal body politic whose wild nature implicitly contests the polarizations, reifications and alienations that have prevailed throughout our history.[102] The notion of 'flesh' introduces an ontological dimension to our embodiment which precedes and underlies the socialized and politicized body (the body, for instance, of capital investment in an age of technology): it is a field of 'wild being' whose elemental intertwinings and reversibilities constitute the intercorporeality of an 'initial community' which could provide a radical grounding for political theory and critique. Merleau–Ponty's notion articulates a corporeal schema which roots the human body, as a local opening and clearing, in the multi-dimensional field of Being; and it accomplishes this in a way that discloses a new historical project for the ontological truth of our incarnation as human beings. 'Flesh' is a notion that clarifies the existential structure which, in purely formal terms, Heidegger calls 'openness-to-Being,' for it articulates the embodiment-character of our responsiveness and elicits its potential for development on the basis of our initial *Befindlichkeit*, our most primordial sense-of-being-in-the-world. After our passage through Merleau–Ponty, it is my hope that, against the background of Heidegger's texts, we may begin to read into our metaphysical tradition the *emerging* body of understanding.

Can we break out of a framework which has allowed us to experience the gift of embodiment only in terms which betray it? Is there a new historical prospect? Or are we constrained to suffer a future of dismemberment, torn between a mechanistic *physics* of the body and a no less injurious *metaphysics*? Nietzsche, Heidegger and Merleau–Ponty seem to be struggling, all three of them, toward the new historical opportunities in a phenomenological hermeneutics of the body. But with Merleau–Ponty's retrieval of the elemental flesh in its primordial ecstasy, we can at last begin a truly ontological discourse concerning the body, for this is the first time in Western philosophy that we can work with a notion of embodiment which recognizes its true topology and specifies its ek-static openness as the basis for our organs of perception, gesture, and movement.

Furthermore, there is an ideal which is implicit in the body of radically reflective experience: an ideal I would describe in terms of its 'spirituality.' Merleau–Ponty's notion of 'flesh' moves us very much *closer* to an understanding of the body's 'participation' in this spiritual dimension of existence. Thus, we might say that, ultimately, the gift of embodiment, the gift which is still so little understood, is the favoring of a local apotheosis in the vast field of Being. Embodiment is not a curse, not an affliction, but the only opportunity we shall be given to learn the poetry of mortal dwelling. If we are attentive to this poetry, I think we have reason to believe that, with the emerging of a new body of understanding, a new historical epoch could dawn on our horizon.

Part II
Recollection in the Epoch of Nihilism

And the ear of our thinking, does it still not hear the cry?[103]

Section 1   The Epoch of Nihilism

In his *Introduction to Metaphysics*, Heidegger observes that,

> The spiritual decline of the earth is so far advanced
> that the nations are in danger of losing the last bit
> of spiritual energy that makes it possible to see the
> decline (taken in relation to the history of 'Being'),
> and to appraise it as such.[104]

Seeing our epoch in this light, Heidegger undertakes a task

which he calls 'recollection.' His hope is that, through the recollection of our cultural history, we may be enabled to contact and retrieve 'new spiritual energies.'[105]

Further specifying his diagnosis of our epochal affliction, Heidegger writes (in words that could equally well be those of Jung):

> the world is darkening. The essential episodes of this darkening are: the flight of the gods, the destruction of the earth, the standardization of man, the pre-eminence of the mediocre.[106]

And he adds:

> Darkening of the world means emasculation of the spirit, the disintegration, wasting away, repression, and misinterpretation of the spirit.[107]

I am sure that, if we relate Heidegger's words ('darkening,' for example) to our body of experience, we can, all of us, make contact with a felt sense of the cultural phenomenon to which Heidegger is pointing. But Heidegger wants to focus our attention, for the most part, on the history of philosophical discourse. Thus he writes, for example in 'Metaphysics as History of Being,' that,

> The tradition of the truth about beings which goes under the title of 'meta' develops into a pile of distortions, no longer recognizing itself, covering up the primordial essence of Being. Herein lies the necessity of the 'destruction' of this distortion, when a thinking of the truth of being has become necessary. . . . But this destruction, like all 'phenomenological' and hermeneutical-transcendental questions, has not yet been thought in terms of the history of Being.[108]

It is Heidegger's conviction that the history of metaphysics, in which this history of Being is reflected, is the historical unfolding of the tendency for the Being of our thought to undergo a progressive, and increasingly alarming, 'concealment.' 'Concealment,' however, is only *one* of the ways by which Heidegger attempts to bring this history to words. In *other* words, the history is a process of human 'forgetfulness'

(*Seinsvergessenheit*), corresponding to the 'oblivion' of Being; a progressive narrowing and restricting of the *field* in which (and as which) Being presences, to which there correspond, in the realm of human experience, an ever-deepening despair and complaints of dread. (*Angst*, 'anxiety,' stems from a Latin root which recognizes very clearly the symptomology.) Still another word of diagnosis appears in 'The Age of the World Picture,' where Heidegger speaks of his growing sense that there is, in our age, a terrifying 'loss of Being'.[109] (Inasmuch as the experience of depression, which psychiatry understands as a response to inconsolable loss, has today become an epidemiologically significant pattern of affliction, it would be worth considering how we should interpret the *ontological* dimension, which the historically outstanding symptomology and prevailing diagnostic categories inevitably conceal.)

In his 'Letter on Humanism,' Heidegger speculates about the ontological interpretation of our cultural affliction:

> Perhaps what is distinctive about this world-epoch consists in the closure of the dimension of the hale. Perhaps that is the sole malignancy [*Unheil*].[110]

This perception of 'closure' assumes special significance, in the context of Heidegger's understanding of human being (*Dasein*). For the very word by which we are called, in German, articulates the character of our most fundamental existential project:

> The *Da* is the clearing and openness of what is, as which a human being stands out.[111]

What makes us 'outstanding' individuals is our capacity for responding in individuating ways to the ontological calling; and it is the gift (*Gunst*) of the capacity which defines our historical responsibility. Thus Heidegger relates the task of thinking to the clearing: the openness of which we are capable and into which we are cast by the existential character of our mode of being:

> Thinking conducts historical ek-sistence . . . into the realm of the upsurgence of the healing.[112]

But what is the basis for Heidegger's faith in thinking? This is an important question, but we must keep in mind

Heidegger's insistence on a thinking which is rooted in an understanding of our cultural history. According to Heidegger, the thinking which bears the work of healing must be a process of recollection, since, as he argues in his *Introduction to Metaphysics*,

> The basic fallacy . . . consists in the belief that
> history begins with the primitive and backward,
> the weak and the helpless. The opposite is true.
> The beginning is the strongest and mightiest. What
> comes afterward is not development but the
> flattening that results from mere spreading out; it
> is the inability to retain the beginning; the beginning
> is emasculated and exaggerated into a caricature
> of greatness taken as purely numerical and
> quantitative. . . .[113]

Recollection is therefore called upon to retrieve a rich and full beginning which preceded the 'loss of Being' and the history of 'decline.'[114] As Kierkegaard points out, with a gently healing expression of irony,

> Recollection has the great advantage that it begins
> with the loss, and so it is secure, for it has nothing
> to lose.[115]

But Heidegger's understanding of cultural history, his philosophy of history, was more strongly influenced by Nietzsche – perhaps more than we might have supposed. In any event, I would like to call attention to a passage which I consider to be of great importance for the thinking at stake in this book. The passage is taken from *The Will to Power*:

> I set down here a list of psychological states as signs
> of a full and flourishing life that one is accustomed
> today to condemn as morbid. . . . My claim in this
> matter is that what is today called 'healthy'
> represents a lower level than that which under
> favorable circumstances *would be* healthy – that we
> are relatively sick – [116]

For Nietzsche, 'what would be healthy' was anticipated by the Greeks of antiquity, at the glorious dawning of Western civilization. Thus, he believes, as does Heidegger, that, in

71

the course of history, a destructive tendency has predominated, and that nihilism, the 'malignancy' characteristic of our technological civilization, is growing and spreading beyond our power to resist the madness of its final destruction.

The diagnosis of our collective pathology is crucial. I, however, am ultimately *more* concerned to articulate, at an ontological level, our possibilities for well-being. Thus, although I shall not endeavor to catalogue, as Nietzsche does, the 'states' of health and illness, the thinking which develops in the course of this study is certainly committed to a vigorously *experiential* focus – a hermeneutical phenomenology that is able to elicit, from *within* the pathology itself, the encouraging existential opportunities for a radical turn in our historical destiny.

In this regard, I would like to call attention to the text of 'Nietzsche's Overturning of Platonism,' in which Heidegger proclaims the power of recollection to initiate *revolutionary* transformations in our historical existence:

> The more clearly and simply a decisive inquiry
> traces the history of Western thought back to its
> few essential stages, the more that history's power
> to reach forward, seize, and commit grows. This
> is especially the case where it is a matter of
> overcoming such history. . . . The greater a
> revolution is to be, the more profoundly must it
> plunge into its history.[117]

Section 2   Recollection and The Body of Understanding

According to Heidegger, recollection is the 'repetition of a possibility of existence that has come down to us.'[118] It is a retracing of steps in order to retrieve an understanding which will prepare us for new steps forward. Recollection is not at all a *passive* form of enquiry; nor, for that matter, is its emerging body of understanding required to be docile, submissive, and fatalistic. On the contrary, we need to realize, first of all, that recollection, as a process of self-understanding, cannot possibly make contact with our history (what Nietzsche called our *Entstehung*) without interacting with present reality and changing its future course (its *Herkunft*). Consequently, the existential decision to begin the arduous work of recollection is *itself* a commitment to the truth of revolutionary action. The fact that Heidegger speaks of 'preparing' and 'awaiting' must not conceal the character of this underlying commitment. The words Heidegger uses – words like 'prepare,' 'await,' and 'receive' – must be understood in a sense which contests, and is therefore already beyond, the metaphysical dualism of action and passion, activity and passivity, doing and not doing. The 'retrieval' we undertake in a Heideggerian 'recollection' is thus partly a discovering, partly an inventing: it is *neither* purely and solely, because the articulation (explicitation) of experience is a hermeneutical process that touches and transforms the experience which has been brought out in this way.

It is in this same spirit that I would like, here, to initiate a further development in the process of recollection by calling attention to the methodological possibility of (i) focusing this process on our experiencing of gesture and movement, and especially on their distinctive character in the present historical epoch, and (ii) making explicit, as a symptom of modern nihilism, our technological way of understanding this body of experience in relation to the primordial claim of The Question of Being. What I need to do in this section, therefore, is outline *the emerging body of understanding* as it figures in the work of recollection that has generated the subject of this book.

The present study is motivated by the strong conviction that, to the degree that metaphysics is powerfully determined by the nihilism of which it is both a reflection and a symptom, we need to respond to the threat of nihilism by retrieving an experience attuned to the presencing of Being-as-a-whole which is, so far as possible, outside the domination of our metaphysical tradition and its one-dimensional technological rationality. While I acknowledge that no *complete* freedom from metaphysics is possible, nor even desirable, I believe that we can enter an 'experiential space' of *relatively* much greater freedom than we have been accustomed to assume for ourselves.

I submit that our *embodiment* is the gift through whose receptivity and responsiveness we may begin to retrieve that redeeming experience of Being. Precisely because, since the very beginning of metaphysics, the gift has been rejected and the body sent into exile, the historical return of the body, a return of the long repressed, is uniquely qualified to bear at this time the thoughtful response to nihilism and the corresponding renewal of our cultural tradition.

The study offered here is, then, a work of recollection in two interdependent senses: (i) it is committed to the retrieval of the glorious body of experience exiled by our predominant cultural history and therefore, also, to the emergence of a radically *new* body of understanding; and (ii) it is committed to the retrieval of an experience of Being to which only the historical retrieval of the body in its lived wholeness can contribute. It should be evident, from what I have just claimed, that the first retrieval, i.e, the retrieval of the exiled body, is at least as much dependent on the retrieval of a deeper experience of Being as the latter is on the former: the lived body, the true 'corps phénomenal' (in the language of Merleau–Ponty's *Phenomenology of Perception*), can only be redeemed to the extent that we are able to prepare for an historically new experience of the presencing of Being.

In any event, though, it seems clear to me that at this time, we are needing to make contact, and stay in touch, with that dimensionality of our being which *resists* the destructiveness of nihilism most intensely, most immediately, and most instinctively. At the limit, it is the body of experience which understands affliction, and the brutality of enslavement, alienation, repression, and humiliation. At the limit, it is the body of experience which understands the historical *need* for resistance. But I want to insist that, however much it may be brutalized, it is also the body of experience which bears the most uncompromised implicit understanding of the revolutionary opportunities that could favor us at the present historical moment with an opening up of the 'healing dimension.'

In developing a radical response to nihilism, our work of recollection must accordingly divide its focus in two. (i) In order to understand how and why our way of being has contributed in its own way to the historical danger of nihilism, serving the technology of its destructiveness with an ignorance and confusion that metaphysics has not dispelled but encouraged, we need to understand, very specifically, the inveterate tendency of our experiencing to close and narrow and welcome restriction. We need to understand the tendency to conform, to normalize, to secure and control. We need to understand the avoidance of impermanence and the 'constancy' which regulates perception. We need to understand fixation and the dread of creative change. We need to disclose the *specific essence* of nihilism *by way of* our experience of embodiment: getting in touch with the *existential meaning* of nihilism as it lays claim to our bodies, dimming and diminishing our vision, twisting and using our gestures, deafening our ears, seizing the very alignment of our posture.

(ii) But our response to nihilism remains very much in danger until we also begin to understand how our gift of being bears within itself an inherent potential for changes: how, by grace of what Heidegger calls 'our inherence in Being,' we always enjoy an inherent capacity for opening to the presencing of Being and deepening our experience of its dimensionality. Thus, it is clear that we need to articulate how the presencing of Being has already laid out the 'topology' of an historical journey out of the wasteland – how it is always clearing a way for our planetary well-being. However, this too calls for a process of recollection which gradually retrieves the lost body of ontological experience.

What the trajectory of our thinking is, I hope, beginning to make explicit is the 'therapeutic' character of the work of recollection. This interpretation is unquestionably supported by the textual passages we have been considering, though it is certainly true that Heidegger leaves this matter largely unthought. As soon as we make it explicit, however, I think we will be struck by the deep kinship between Heidegger's process of recollection and the process of *anamnēsis* which is described in the *Symposium*, and which Sokrates induces in working with Meno, the slave-boy. Heidegger, of course, only makes use of recollection as a procedure for working out the unrealized possibilities concealed in the beginnings of the history of philosophy. Rather like Husserl's *Sinnesgenesis*, his use of recollection is strictly formal, or logical: it is exclusively focused on the historical unfolding of metaphysical *concepts*. For Sokrates, however, *anamnēsis* is conceived, more broadly, as a procedure for educing in the individual an unrealized *a priori* knowledge. And what recommends it, in his eyes, is the fact that it is the most compassionate, most respectful way of facilitating the soul's recollection of its *a priori* wisdom. *Anamnēsis* is not only *paideia*; it is also a process of *therapeia*. But Heidegger believes that the recollection he initiates *also* retrieves a 'spiritual' wisdom: not only a *concept* of Being, but ultimately, an *experience* of Being that has somehow been concealed (lost and forgotten) in the course of Western history. Thus, even though the explicit matter for thought is a progression of concepts in our cultural history, Heidegger's recollection is also, like *anamnēsis*, a way of retrieving a lost experiential wisdom for authentically *individual* initiatives. But Heidegger's recollection is historical: the individual's retrieval of his ownmost possibilities-for-being is *mediated* by a meditative gathering up of the historical sense of Western metaphysics. It thus *differs* from the Platonic *anamnēsis*. Summarizing the preceding argument, then, I am making three distinct claims. (i) Both Sokratic *anamnēsis* and Heideggerian recollection are *individual* initiatives in response to a sense of loss and need. (ii) Both undertake the retrieval for the sake of a deep 'spiritual' wisdom, the knowledge enjoyed by a soul (*psyche*) 'prior to' its entanglement in the 'worldly' world. (iii) Finally, both attempt to retrieve, or 'bring forth' a wisdom present in concealed form from the very beginning of worldly life.

I now want to take my argument another step. The fourth claim I wish to make, bringing Heidegger together with Merleau–Ponty, is (a) that we can translate Heidegger's recollection into the process of radical reflection that Merleau–Ponty sets in motion in his *Phenomenology of Perception*; or, conversely, (b) that we can interpret the process of radical reflection in such a way that its most radical phenomenological disclosures constitute the beginning phase, and experiential grounding, of the recollection which takes place, in Heidegger's ontological thinking, with a focus on the history of metaphysical concepts.

If we believe that our *concepts* are rooted in *experience*, and if we understand experience to be *embodied* in our being-in-the-world, then we are constrained to acknowledge (a) that the intellectual recollection of a history of concepts (e.g., the concept of 'Being as such') must be *existentially* radicalized, so that it works as a process rooted in the body of experience; and, conversely, (b) that the *ontically focused* process of radical reflection ultimately calls for an *ontologically* radicalized interpretation which commits it to articulating its understanding of perception and motility by focusing on the primordial openness and responsiveness to Being which is given to us for our development in the gift of embodiment. When recollection and radical reflection are working together, as they shall in the following study, they initiate a *doubly* radical movement of thought, focused on the emergence, or retrieval, of a radically new *body* of understanding.

Heidegger's recollection of the history of metaphysics is a

thinking which attempts to *approximate* the experience of Being at the beginning of this history. Our recollection, though, as he knows, is bound to our time, our culture. We cannot possibly bring back, as it was, the life-world of Greek antiquity. The ancient's experience of Being and ours could never be entirely the same. Nor should we even *hanker* after an experience which, in any event, we cannot hope to replicate, since it is luminously apparent to us, at this moment of history, that what disclosed itself in their world also concealed from them the history of unconcealment as the history of Being, and therefore concealed from them that *necessity of concealment* whose history and significance we alone, and not they, have been privileged to experience and challenged to understand. In the very moment when we are compelled to recognize our *loss* of Being, our broken understanding is *favored* with the truth of unconcealment as the revolutionary history of Being. The objective of recollection is not, therefore, to bring back the actual experience of the beginning, but to experience the reaching out, and *stretch* ourselves in such a way that our pre-understanding of Being is opened up, and we are enabled to retrieve a relatively more opening, more primordial experience from within ourselves.

Now, as I have already noted, this recollection of Being is a process which has two distinct phases: (i) going down 'into' oneself, into the 'innermost,' or most individual depths of oneself (*Er-innerung*) and (ii) re-claiming, or bringing forth, the potential to be developed (*Wiederholung*). The passage through these phases is crucial, inasmuch as the authentic recollection is *not* a 'repetition' in the sense that it attempts to replicate the experience of the past with a slavish submission to its historical precedence, but is rather a 'repetition' in the sense that, in its own appropriate way, and in keen awareness of its own time, it prepares us to undergo an *original* experience of Being – an experience whose disclosiveness is somehow emancipatory. (What we share with the ancient Greeks, by virtue of our 'recollection,' is not *their same experience* exactly as they lived it, but rather participation in a moment of disclosure, a moment which is possible precisely because, between them and us, *there is an ineliminable difference, there is an unabridgeable distance*.)

What I want specifically to argue, though, in the fourth of my claims, is that these two phases need to be interpreted – need, I mean, especially as a response to the technological alienations of our present historical situation – *not only* in the way Heidegger's own thinking demonstrates, but also in the way my reference to Merleau–Ponty was meant to adumbrate, namely: as a process by virtue of which we go into the innermost body of felt experience in order to *develop* an inborn potential for opening to the presencing of Being as such, and *redeem* thereby the primordial claim on our existence that our inherence in Being has already laid out.

The full measure of my argument for the incarnation of Heideggerian recollection will not become apparent until we have worked through the material in the study that follows this Introduction. What I will attempt here is only a very brief, introductory mapping of the being of the human body – the body which presents itself to the hermeneutical process of recollection as an auspicious 'instance' of the topology of Being.

According to Heidegger, we human beings are 'always already' gifted with a pre-ontological understanding (or, in other words, an ontologically attuned pre-understanding) of the presencing of Being as such. By grace of our 'ecstatic inherence,' our *Befindlichkeit* in (the field of) Being as a whole, we are always, in a way, attuned to this presencing as such, and always find ourselves already implicitly 'called,' already implicitly claimed, by the potential for development that it lays down and opens up for us. Now, Heidegger interprets this pre-ontological understanding as a 'primordial' attunement by (and to) the presencing of Being as a whole (and as such): an attunement of such a primordial nature that our most basic, most universal existential possibilities for a deeper, richer, and more understanding relationship with Being i.e., an authentically *ontological* relationship, are always already implicitly laid down for us 'from the very beginning.' Thus, the existential possibility of an ontological understanding is to be retrieved by acknowledging, and appropriately receiving, the gift of our primordial, pre-ontological understanding (our ontologically attuned pre-understanding). The pre-ontological (or proto-ontological) already *is* ontological, except for the fact that it lacks a developed awareness which would integrate its understanding into the substance of our daily life.

I submit that, if this account is an accurate rendering of Heidegger's analytic interpretation of *Dasein*, then it implicitly authorizes the interpretation of recollection with which we shall be working. Our account has introduced three concepts fundamental to Heidegger's interpretation: the

INTRODUCTION

concept of 'attunement,' the concept of 'primordiality,' and
the concept of 'pre-understanding.' Each one of these implicitly refers, I suggest, to a body of deeply felt (but not yet
existentially articulated) experience. Furthermore, our case is
greatly strengthened when we consider some of the texts
I have already quoted, which show beyond question that
Heidegger understands, and in fact has explicitly acknowledged, that it is through our *sensibility* (Heidegger's word is
'Gemüt') that we first become acquainted with a *wholeness* of
presence which radically differs from technologically constituted totalities – a wholeness which differs so radically, I
believe, that the recollection which gets in touch with it is
empowered to contest such totalization. So I think we may
conclude that, implicit in Heidegger's thinking, there *is* a
deep body of feeling, an incarnation of deeply felt awareness,
that we now need to retrieve in a hermeneutical leap of
thought. When I refer, in this study, to an emerging body
of understanding, what I have in mind is a radically new
body: a body brought forth through a hermeneutical reading
of texts that we have coordinated with a self-reflective discourse focused phenomenologically on our gestures and
movements as we actually experience them, and opening up
for further explicitation a new understanding of our historical
existence.

But we need, at this point, to give more consideration to
Merleau–Ponty's method of radical reflection, which we are
going to radicalize by taking it down more deeply than he,
down into the most elemental roots of our being, our bodily
ek-sistence. From our reading of his *Phenomenology of Perception*, we know that Merleau–Ponty effectuates a reflection
which discloses, beneath the structure of subject and object,
a 'stratum' of experience that he characterizes as 'more
primordial': a dimension of our incarnation that is (in his
words) 'anonymous,' 'prepersonal,' and 'pre-ontological.'
And according to him, this elemental dimension – which he
called, near the end of his life, by the word 'flesh' – is an
exhilarating experience of felt integration and wholeness: our
bodily felt sense-of-being-in-the-world.

Now, it requires only a little more work to radicalize the
process of recollection and take it still deeper. When we go
more deeply into this dimension of our incarnation, I submit
that we make contact with, and can appropriately retrieve,
our corporeal, bodily felt inherence in the field of Being as a
whole. But it is precisely the retrieval of the ontological pre-

understanding (or the pre-ontological attunement) *in this primordial, mooded inherence* which constitutes the ultimate objective of our work of recollection, interpreted as a task of radical reflection.

For me, however, the work of recollection cannot be only an isolated individual's undertaking. As an historical task, it is always also social, and the communication of the process is a gathering of the body politic around a matter that urgently calls for our thought.

Section 3   The Recognition of Our Affliction

Needful is the articulation [*legein*], as well as the mindfulness [*noein*] of this: that Being is.

Parmenides[119]

And if the kingdom of darkness erupts after all in full force, then let us throw our pens under the table and go in God's name where the need is greatest and our presence the most useful.

Friedrich Hölderlin (1799 letter to his brother)

In the first chapter of his *Reflections on the Causes of Human Misery and upon Certain Proposals to Eliminate Them*, Barrington Moore, Jr points out that it has never been possible to reach widespread agreement, even among the population of one and the same culture, regarding the true nature of happiness, whereas, in his words,

> Matters stand otherwise with misery and suffering. . . . If human beings find it difficult to agree upon the meaning and causes of happiness, they find it much easier to know when they are miserable. . . . In straightforward factual terms, it is also possible to recognize certain widely recurring causes of human suffering. . . .

Thus he concludes that,

> [a] conception of the unitary nature of human suffering, unitary at least in comparison with human happiness, is helpful in resolving some of the vexing issues of the proper role that subjective

80

evaluations and moral judgments may or ought to play in social analysis.[120]

These reflections, which come from a scholar eminent in political science, have encouraged me to develop the direction of thought which we shall examine in this section. I strongly agree with the perception Moore communicates, and I should like to say something quite similar as an explanation for, and as a justification of, the kind of focus to which the thinking articulated in this study is methodologically committed.

As the communicativeness of all great literature attests, in its spanning of historical epochs and cultural worlds, it is the open and sincere sharing of that which has been directly experienced in a thoughtful way which transcends most completely, or anyway most satisfactorily, the inevitable discontinuities that can so easily separate different people, different historical epochs, and different cultures.

Although it is true that we are, in an important sense, deeply rooted in our own historical situation, and therefore continually find ourselves bound by its inherent limitations, it is also true that we are favored by its opportunities. Under these conditions, it is not surprising that we often turn to the *universal* wisdom handed down in the great texts of earlier historical epochs and other cultural traditions. For the greatest texts of other times and other cultures never cease to *share* with us the universal wisdom they have gathered, so that, despite the incontestable reality of our situatedness and theirs, it *is* nevertheless possible for us to derive from the transmission of their wisdom a greater *specific* understanding of both our historical limitations and our historical opportunities.

Although we are, in an important sense, the slaves of a technological 'rationality' that has, in our time, suddenly begun to make manifest its essential truth as an historical unfolding mostly beyond our domination, it is possible – and I believe always will be possible – for us to *resist* in specific ways the effects of 'enframing' (what Heidegger calls 'das Ge-stell') where they immediately hurt us, where we feel them. At the very least, we can *speak* from out of that place in our experience where the enframing most deeply touches us with pain. We can speak . . . or we can cry out. And we can always somehow share, in communications that make a direct experiential contact, the power of our resistance.

Resistance is not ever enough; but it *can* be the beginning of a creative historical response. And the communicativeness which shares both the experience of affliction and the experience of resistance multiplies in the most wonderful ways our emancipatory possibilities.

The individual's most personal and most deeply felt *response* to the specific afflictions that are characteristic of his own historical epoch must always be, I think, the first and foremost *source* of a critical and creative historical (i.e., social) response. This is perhaps especially true in a time such as ours, when we are importuned by a mad succession of abstract theoretical models, and abstract theoretical frameworks, which are communicated not only without any significant impact, but even without any concern over the failure of their communicative *praxis*. Furthermore, the body of experience will often be *superior* to the formulation of abstract 'philosophical' propositions, since the abstractions are more easily destroyed by the skeptical questions to which they themselves gave rise.[121] Precisely because of this problem – the difficulty, I mean, in undertaking an ontological reflection starting out, not from experience, but from a theoretical model or paradigm – *our* distinctive focus, which attempts to retrieve the intrinsic openness in the body of felt experience as an historically effective way into the authentically ontological understanding of human existence, would seem to promise an auspicious beginning.

In this particular study, our concern will be focused on the articulation of an *individual* response to the crisis of our time. Our focus on individuality ('Jemeinigkeit,' in the language of *Being and Time*), like our receptivity to the 'universal wisdom' of other cultures and other times, is itself an attempt to transcend the crisis. Those among us who would deny us any access to a 'universal wisdom,' or who would equate the process of individuation articulated in this study with the rage of narcissistic indulgences that mock it, only play into the hands of an ever-deepening nihilism. Our focus on an *individual* appropriation of traditions of universal wisdom and on an *individual* response to nihilism denies neither the historicity nor the sociality of such a concern. The question of understanding the nihilism in our technological 'world-view' and finding 'within ourselves' an appropriate response *cannot* be reduced to a question of alleviating exclusively individual sufferings through processes of 'self-development' and 'self-realization' that involve the individual apart from

INTRODUCTION

the social and cultural world. In fact neither the 'causes' of
individual suffering and misery, nor the opportunities for
individual initiatives on behalf of revolutionary possibilities,
can be isolated from the limiting and enabling conditions of
their larger historical context. And, as a universal wisdom
reminds us, even this larger context is itself dependent upon
a 'dispensation' to which we can, in the end, only allude,
calling it (for example) the 'Es gibt' of Being.

In a time when ideologies are suspect, when absolute and
transcendental foundations are impossible, when the very
attempt to *grasp* the rational meaning of our historical existence can only intensify the grip of nihilism, when onto-
theologies cannot be taken seriously and revelations and
epiphanies can only be called psychotic, *where* can there be
any 'resistance' to nihilism, where any standpoint for
critique, where any hope, if not in those places where the
authentic individuals stand out, those places near the abyss,
I mean, where the individuals who are deeply thoughtful
and deeply feeling *attempt* to respond, to question, and to
share with one another whatever can be shared? Where can
a *fresh response* to technological nihilism, and a *creative appropriation* of its hidden gift of possibilities, come into being, if
not, ultimately, in those individuals who are most deeply in
touch with their pain, who understand the nature of their
suffering, and feel a need to diminish the misery of their
epoch?

In the Herakleitos Seminar he gave with Fink (1966–7),
Heidegger remarks:

> For Hegel's thinking . . . need consisted in the
> fulfillment of what is thought, whereby fulfillment
> is to be understood literally as the reconciliation of
> the immediate with the mediated.

And then he suddenly asks,

> But how about us? Do we also have a need?[122]

What can we 'do' with this question? There are many things
we can do, but I think we need to sit quietly with it, so that
we can listen to our body of deeply felt wisdom. Of course,
our need is immeasurable, is at times so utterly over-
whelming that it cannot speak; and the reversal of destiny
which would *meet* our need – that, too, is a strain on our

powers of thought and utterance. But, in *Human, All Too Human*, Nietzsche observes:

> How strong the metaphysical need is, and how
> difficult nature makes our departure from it, may be
> seen in this, that even in the free spirit who has
> cast metaphysics aside, the highest workings of art
> can easily sound a tone from some string which has
> long been mute – even if it has been torn
> out. . . .[123]

Nietzsche's reference to a 'metaphysical need' is insightful. As an interpretation of our cultural history in relation to nihilism and the Being of metaphysics, it foreshadows Heidegger's attempt to deconstruct metaphysics by working out an ontological reinterpretation of Nietzsche's understanding. In *Being and Time*, for example, Heidegger offers the following diagnosis of our affliction:

> In everydayness, *Dasein* undergoes a dull
> 'suffering,' can sink away in the dullness of it, and
> evade it by seeking new ways in which its
> dispersion in its affairs may be further dispersed.
> In the moment of vision, indeed, and often just 'for
> the moment,' existence can even gain mastery over
> the 'everyday' [i.e., over its inherent suffering], but
> it can never extinguish it.[124]

In a later text, 'Nihilism as Determined by the History of Being,' Heidegger amplifies this diagnosis. After a long and, so to speak, formal analysis of 'the essence of nihilism' in 'the history of Being,' Heidegger breaks off. Is he (he muses) 'escaping from true reality?' This query he answers as follows:

> What does the *essence* of nihilism . . . signify as
> opposed to the reality – which alone is effective –
> of *actual* nihilism, which sows confusion and strife
> everywhere, which instigates crime and drives us to
> despair? What is the nothing of Being, which we
> have considered, in the face of the actual an-nihil-
> ation of all beings, whose violence, encroaching
> from all sides, makes almost every act of resistance
> futile?[125]

Now Heidegger wants to say that,

> We hardly need to illustrate in detail the spreading
> violence of actual nihilism, which we all personally
> experience to a sufficient degree, even without an
> ivory-tower definition of its essence.

I appreciate his point, but I cannot entirely agree. Different
ways of experiencing, of perceiving, are possible; and it could
be the case that there is a sense, or a way, in which we have
not yet 'actually' *experienced* the destructiveness. Could it be
that we are still needing to *experience* it in its actuality, and
that it is only by way of this deeper, more deeply *felt* experience that we may enjoy a superior understanding of the
essence? Let us keep this matter in mind as we continue our
reading:

> Furthermore, Nietzsche's experience, in spite of the
> one-sidedness of his interpretations, deals with
> 'actual' nihilism so forcefully that, by comparison,
> our attempt at determining the essence of nihilism
> appears insubstantial, not to say utterly useless.
> When every divine, human, material, and natural
> thing is threatened in its existence, who would want
> to trouble himself about something like the
> omission of the default of Being itself, even granting
> that such a thing takes place and is not merely the
> subterfuge of a desperate abstraction?

This is certainly an appropriate question. But the question I
want to ask here is: What are our alternatives? Are we
compelled to choose between the Scylla of a merely factual
(ontical) account of 'actual nihilism' and the Charybdis of an
'utterly useless' abstraction about the 'essence of nihilism'?
Would it be feasible, for example, to 'work' hermeneutically
with our actually felt experience of nihilism – at whatever
level of depth that actuality may place us – in order to make
contact with a more authentically ontological body of experience and retrieve its more primordial awareness for our
understanding? Heidegger's reflections continue:

> If only a connection between actual nihilism, or
> even the nihilism experienced by Nietzsche, and

the essence of nihilism as thought here were at least perceptible.

Indeed. But I would like to point out that Heidegger's frustration here could in part be a consequence of his own failure to break out of a metaphysical tradition which persists in conceptualizing our experience in dualistic ways. Perhaps, if Heidegger had been able to work in a more direct phenomenological way with the emerging body of felt experience, he would not have despaired so profoundly.

Be that as it may, let us continue our reading. Jumping ahead a few pages, we will find an important reference to the experience of *need*:

> As the veiled and extreme need of Being, however, needlessness reigns precisely in the age of the darkening of beings, our age of confusion, of violence, and despair in human culture, of disruption and impotence of willing. Both openly and tacitly, boundless suffering and measureless sorrow proclaim the condition of our world a needful one.[126]

And yet, it is Heidegger's perception that our neediness continues to grow, since our awareness of this need, and our ontological understanding of it, are becoming more concealed from us. Where, then, does Heidegger leave us? On my reading of the text, he leaves us with the conviction that we need to make a more deeply thoughtful contact with our present experience of 'needlessness'.[127] This is helpful, but we need to find a more satisfactory *way* of making this contact, and I submit that we can make his point the basis for further steps of thought.

But Heidegger, for his part, remains convinced that,

> Even the immense suffering which surrounds the earth is unable to waken a transformation [*Wandel*], because it is only experienced as suffering, as passive, and thus as the opposite state of action, and thus experienced together with action in the same realm of being of the will to will.[128]

'It almost seems,' Heidegger says, 'as if the being of pain were cut off from man under the dominance of the will;

similarly the being of joy.'[129] (John Stuart Mill once observed that, 'One of the effects of civilization – not to say one of the ingredients in it – is, that the spectacle, and even the very idea of pain, is more and more kept out of the sight of those classes who enjoy in their fullness the benefits of civilization.')[130] So he ponders a crucial question:

> Can the extreme measure of suffering still bring a transformation here?[131]

The paradoxical depth of our affliction is, as Kierkegaard argued in *Sickness Unto Death*, that we are not authentically in touch with the gift of healing in the very center of our affliction. Heidegger states it this way:

> the fracture of his fragmentation does not yet reach down to man in his essence, despite all the unspeakable suffering, all the distress that all too many men endure. The pain that arises from the rift of that which is, does not yet reach man in his essence. What did we say at the end of the first lecture? 'We feel no pain. . . .'[132]

So Heidegger begins to focus our awareness on the *specific character* of the experience of pain that is distinctive of our historical epoch. His interpretation tends to remain, however, disembodied:

> A sign of this [veiling of the ontological difference] is the metaphysico-technological reaction to pain, which at the same time predetermines the interpretation [*Auslegung*] of the essence of pain.[133]

Heidegger does, though, have this to say, in his essay on 'Language':

> we should not re-present pain anthropologically as a sensation.[134]

Sensationalism is an *epochē* (reduction) symptomatic of our technological epoch: a way of *avoiding* the true depth of our body of felt experience. Sensationalism turns us away from the disclosive *presence* of the pain, and therefore from its primordial *truth*. What it offers is a mere *re-presentation* of

87

pain; and its image of the fragmented body is determined by the classical paradigm of Newtonian physics. For me, therefore, the paradigm-shift Heidegger's words suggest is a shift from *re-presenting* the pain to *being with it* in the wholeness of an experience that lets it simply be present. What Heidegger does not seem to appreciate is that, by staying so faithfully within his own cultural tradition, he was not able to benefit from the continued existence, outside the Judaeo-Christian world, of ancient traditions of wisdom which understand this 'presence,' and which can still hand down their teachings about how to 'work' with pain and need in that dimension of experience. In part, then, his frustration and pessimism are due to the fact that he is not familiar with these living traditions of wisdom. Anyway, to the degree that we can simply be *present* with our pain, we are engaged in a process that *opens* to a new dimension of its truth, and we therefore make ourselves available for a new disclosure of its deeper historical meaning.

What Heidegger recognizes very clearly is that, in his words,

> The pain which must first be experienced and borne
> out to the end is the insight and the knowledge
> that lack of need [*Notlosigkeit*] is the highest and
> most hidden need which first necessitates [*nötigt*] in
> virtue of the most distant distance. Lack of need
> consists in believing that one has reality and what
> is real in one's grip and knows what truth is,
> without needing to know in what truth *presences*
> [*worin die Wahrheit west*].[135]

Thus, it would seem to be Heidegger's belief that, in our present historical situation, we must *begin* the process of breaking away from our metaphysical tradition by *accepting* our participation in the history of Being,

> only in the form of an essential need which
> soundlessly and without consequences shakes
> everything true and real to the roots.[136]

I am sensitive to the experience which lies behind Heidegger's contention. But I would argue, nonetheless, that we are somewhat more fortunate than he supposes. First of all, Heidegger himself has shared with us experiences of thought in which he communicates, from out of his own affliction and need, a participation in the history of Being which is filled with the rejoicing of a different truth. Secondly, as I have already suggested, I believe that, thanks to Heidegger's trail-blazing, we may now be enabled to go more deeply into the phenomenology of our suffering need, to retrieve from the body of feeling something of its depth of integration and wholeness, its primordial grounding, and its gestation of a body of understanding whose gestures and movements are already attuned by a different moment in the history of Being. The goal of recollection is not to capture the past for a slavish repetition, which in any case it is not possible to accomplish, but rather to find/create new historical opportunities for ourselves. The truth in the work of recollection is therefore to be judged not by an accurate *correspondence* to the objective reality of a past epoch and another culture, but rather in terms of the character of the *transformation* by which a deeper understanding of the past significantly *alters* the course of the future. I think we may know, better than Heidegger, how to bring forth such an understanding from out of the body's *Befindlichkeit*, its primordial felt sense-of-being-in-the-world.

CHAPTER 1

The Bearing of Thought

Introduction

The title of this chapter is a phrase I have lifted out from one of Heidegger's essays on language.[1] In the context of that essay, the focus is on thinking. The body, that to which his word 'bearing' (*das Gebärde*) alludes, remains, however, unthought. And yet 'thinking,' for Heidegger, is no longer to be understood as a coherent succession of disembodied *cogitationes*. In the wake of Heidegger's deconstruction, are we not compelled to ackowledge that, so long as the bearing of the body, the body as that which bears thought, has not been raised up into explicit awareness, the tradition of Cartesian metaphysics will continue to hold us in its power? In the framework of that tradition, as Merleau–Ponty has argued, 'thinking' is intellectualized, while our embodiment is re-presented as a physical substance and reduced to the ontology of a mechanism determined solely by physiological laws.

Our title shifts the focus. What now calls for thought is the bearing of the body, which is . . . bearing the life of our thinking. Thinking is thus embodied; at the same time, the metaphorical truth of the body, what the tradition has suppressed over a long history, is finally retrieved, finally resurrected. Even in Heidegger's thinking, thinking is denied its gift of embodiment: the truth of the metaphor, the truth of the 'bearing,' makes its appearance in the text, but only in the shade of meaning. The body's presence is still concealed by a reticence which is familiar, and undoubtedly cultural. Our focus will attempt to let the metaphor bear out its historical truth in a discourse oriented by Being. What *is* a body 'well-fitted' (as Spinoza might have said) to the bearing of thought? What *is* the bearing of our body, when it bears our 'thought of Being'?

The etymology of 'bearing' focuses our attention on the manifold nature of the body of thought. (i) 'To bear' means 'to give birth,' 'to gestate.' It indicates, therefore, a gesture or movement which is essentially and intrinsically creative. As we shall see, the one whose bearing understandingly realizes and fulfills this creative gift is one who 'dwells' on the earth in a 'poetizing' way. (ii) 'To bear' means 'to give,' 'to bring forth,' 'to make appear.' Thus, the bearing of thought must be understood in relation to our skillfulness (*technē*), and our capacity for practical activity in general (*phrōnesis*), but also, and more deeply, in relation to the primary experience of truth as an event of disclosing (*alētheia*). (iii) Finally, 'to bear' means 'to carry,' 'to convey,' 'to transmit,' and 'to support.' The bearing of thought must accordingly be understood as a keeping and protecting and sharing – and not only of the *matter* which calls for thought, but also of the call to thinking itself. As we focus on our bearing, taking the word in the sense of conduct or comportment, we shall attempt to unfold these three dimensions of its meaning.

In the bearing of thought, what is the character (*ethos*) of our comportment? Here we give to the formalism of Heidegger's theoretical question a decidedly 'practical' orientation. Since *Dasein* is an openness for Being in the midst of the world, it is appropriate for us to consider how the 'thought of Being' is to be *borne* in the world through our *bodily* comportment. Thinking, for Heidegger, can no longer be considered as a purely theoretical activity carried out by a transcendental ego; it manifests, rather, a possibility of our being-in-the-world. But Heidegger's account of this being-in-the-world needs further explicitation, above all with regard to our comportment. In the context of our present study, the character of this comportment is to be understood in terms of our gesturing and our motility.

Reflecting, in *Walden*, on the 'Economy' of the human condition, Thoreau is moved to observe that 'man's capacities have never been measured; nor are we to judge of what he

THE BODY'S RECOLLECTION OF BEING

can do by any precedents, so little has been tried.' But then he remembers the time when he was preparing the ground for a crop of beans, and he suddenly becomes aware of a cosmological dimension, a cosmological *measure* for his comportment:

> We might try our lives by a thousand simple tests;
> as, for instance, that the same sun which ripens
> my beans illumines at once a system of earths like
> ours. If I had remembered this it would have
> prevented some mistakes. This was not the light in
> which I hoed them. The stars are the apexes of
> what wonderful triangles.[2]

What *difference* does this kind of remembering make? We might want to say that this remembering is the receiving of a gift, the *hint*, perhaps, of something which could, in time, give us a certain *access* to the dimensionality of the ontological difference. We might also say that the remembering gives to the hoeing body a new experience of wholeness; for the body is in fact re-membered, placed in the wholeness of a deeper and more nurturing dimensionality of Being.

Just as we are beings who need to give thought to Being in the realm of language, both saying and thinking that Being is, so are we beings who need to give thought to Being in the thoughtfulness of our posture, our stance, our gait and comportment, and in the thoughtful gestures of our hands. In *every* enactment of our embodied being, our relationship to the Being of beings is in question. In every disposition of our embodiment, the existential possibilities in this relationship lay claim to our guardian awareness, and appeal to our capacity for a manifest (hermeneutical) responsiveness. Every gesture and every movement takes place within the dimensionality of the ontological difference, measured by the depth we open up. Moving within this space, moved by its indifferent grace, we are charged at all times with questions of motivation. Regardless of our level of awareness, regardless even of the degree of our caring, our bearing continually bears witness to the enabling presence of a field of Being. How might we bear this charge with grace and dignity? And what difference would we like our bearing to make in the world of our brief passage?

92

Part I

The Genesis and Unfolding of Human Motility

The subject of our immediate concern, here, is human motility: not only our motility as we *actually* experience it, but also our motility as we *could* experience it in the richness of its unfolding. Our motility is a wonderful capacity: it is the capacity we enjoy, as human beings who exist (ek-sist) embodied, for self-initiated movement. We will reflect on motility first, before taking up, in the second part of this chapter, the question of our gestures, because our first concern is for the being of the human body *as a whole*. Motility is of special significance for the path of self-realization, for it involves the body *in its wholeness*. To be sure, our gesturing also mobilizes the body as a whole; but in gesturing, the body as a whole is backgrounded, while the processes of signifying and communicating are gathered into a powerful focus through the movement of our most articulate organs (our limbs and face).

'Movement' and 'motility' refer to the body's meaningfully organized behavior, and, except when these terms are explicitly distinguished from 'gesture,' they will be understood to *include* a reference to our gestures, which always involve some sense of movement. When, however, 'movement' and 'motility' are distinguished from 'gesture,' then they will refer only to behavior for which the body in its entirety, and as a physiognomic whole, is mobilized, as in, for example, walking and running. 'Gesture' is also a word for meaning-bearing behavior, but it must be distinguished from 'movement' and 'motility' in virtue of the fact that it refers to behavior which (1) is concentrated in, and primarily mobilizes, the upper limbs of the body, the expressiveness of the face, and our organs of speech, and which (2) explicitly expresses, or is intended to communicate, specific figures of meaning. Sometimes, what have just been called 'movements' may also be described – and perhaps more appropriately – as gestures, insofar as they explicitly express, or are intended to communicate, specific figures of meaning. Thus, for example, when Samuel Johnson kicked a lamppost to refute the Bishop of Cloyne, his kick is more accurately described as a gesture than as a movement. In comparison with our 'mere' movements, our 'gestures' bring forth more differentiated articulations of meaning. In our present study,

93

we shall also be thinking, however, about the postures, positions, dispositions and attitudes of the body, and about two
in particular, viz., standing and sitting. These are meaning-
bearing comportments, but it is clear, of course, that they are
not movements, even though they are *like* movements in one
respect, for their meaningfulness characteristically gathers up
the body in its physiognomic wholeness. It is equally clear
that, according to the first criterion formulated above, they
are *not* like gestures. And yet, because they are always
charged with meaningfulness, not only to articulate explicit
figures of sense (for example, when one turns away from a
stranger or stands up to show respect), but also to bring
about and bear some vital understandings of Being, they may
well be considered, and sometimes will actually be referred
to, as 'gestures.'

We will by no means ignore the *interpersonal* dimension of
motility: our motility in, and as, our being-with-others. Most
of our attention, however, will be concentrated on the
unfolding of the ontological dimensionality. This exclusive
concentration is unfortunate, but also unavoidable. The interpretation of motility in the dialogues of our interpersonal
world constitutes a task which remains: an urgent task for
our future work.

Now, we will note that our motility takes place in a *field*
of many dimensions. Our existence, as beings gifted with
the capacity we call 'motility,' is *dependent* upon this field.
Our being is *grounded* in the *openness* of this field. Thus
grounded, our being is in a sense co-extensive with, or to-
be-identified-with, the *open being* of the motility-field *as a
whole*. The field of our motility is the *layout* of a field of Being:
it is how Being manifests, how Being presences, in relation
to our motility. Consequently, in the light of the Question
of Being, even our motility (our capacity for self-initiated
movement) is fundamentally at stake. The Question becomes
a question *for* our being insofar as we understand that *we*
are beings for whom there is ('Es gibt') this capacity called
'motility'. (We are beings for whom our own being is always
in question.) Specifically, then, I think we need to ask
ourselves: of what are we capable? This question focuses
attention on our capacity to *develop* the character of our
primordial relationship to Being as a whole *by virtue of* our
motility. What is at stake? Among other things, we may say:
Our groundedness, our rootedness, our autochthony, our
balance and upright stature, our bearing and carriage, our

steadiness of gait, our path, and the goals on this path: in sum, every aspect of our motility *in relation to Being as such.* Our ever-deepening guardian awareness of this ontological dimension is what I mean, in brief, by 'the genesis and unfolding of motility.'

In the phenomenological disclosure of the primordial *Logos,* a *Logos* which articulates itself in the depth of the phenomenon of motility, our ontological interpretation will attempt to describe – or, in effect, to diagnose – an inveterate human tendency to lose touch and forget, err and stray, lose our footing, stumble and fall. This interpretive description, however, cannot avoid prescribing, in that very same process, the trajectory of a radically different kind of movement: a movement strong and graceful, shaped by its deeper awareness, poised in its unpretentious care-taking; a movement headed in the direction of a life outstanding for the authenticity of its individuation and for the exemplary character of its passage in the midst of so many needful sentient beings.

In the first part of this chapter, we are going to respond to the Question of Being in an historically new way, viz., by formulating the task of fundamental ontology as an articulation of our most fundamental *topology.* What should make this formulation especially significant, I think, is the fact that it enables us to think this Question in terms of a process of incarnation whose experience of motility has been called into question – and correspondingly motivated to move towards a more thoughtful life of 'authenticity.' It will be recalled that 'authenticity,' the process of *becoming* oneself, requires being *true* to oneself. But this *Jemeinigkeit* requires, in turn, a commitment to developing the *deepest* truth of one's Selfhood, namely: an *individual* realization of the universal relatedness-to-Being which defines every one of us in a primordial way from the very beginning of our worldly existence.

Our formulation recognizes the unavoidable *connection* between, on the one hand, the project of fundamental ontology, which articulates our being in its relatedness-to-Being, and, on the other, the analysis of our potential for authentic Selfhood, which discloses how the Self emerges through its relatedness-to-Being. Our formulation recognizes the *need* for an explicitation of fundamental ontology which overcomes its history of theoretical formalism and translates it into a language which can speak more directly, and with deeper therapeutic effect, to the emerging *psyche*: a language which will speak, that is, in *direct reference* to the *body* of lived experience. In case it be objected that the language of this translation is 'psychological,' I would like to observe that the articulation of fundamental ontology which Heidegger works out in his 'analytic of the *Dasein*' is *already* an inherently therapeutic process. Our translation, which interprets fundamental ontology as a fundamental *topology*, places our motility in the deepest, most radically open matrix of experience; and it *opens* our experience of motility to the transformative potential that abides at the very deepest levels of our well-being.

Let us clarify this argument by reflecting, for a moment, on the *interpersonal* dimension of our motility. According to Heidegger, being-with-others (an interpersonal *Mitsein*) characterizes an essential dimension of our openness-to-Being (our *Dasein*). This suggests that *authentic* existence calls for the development of our capacity for 'solicitude,' the fulfillment of the 'Care' whose structure Heidegger's analytic brings to light. What comes to light, then, when we focus, through the lens of this analysis, on the deepest accessible structures of our motility? Can we contact these structures in process of formation? Can we follow their emergence? I submit that we will eventually contact a sensuous-emotional field of motivating energies, a primordial field of tensions, pulses, and waves of attractions and aversions, whose intertwining intensities manifest a very strong inveterate tendency to constitute bodily centers of ego-logical (subjectively- and objectively-polarized) comportments, centers, that is, of purposive, ego-serving behavior, while providing, at the very same time, the layout of an opportunity for the development of a *Self* whose centeredness is achieved, rather, through the *openness* of its solicitude. (We should at least note, in passing, the succession of phases, our words for which all stem from the same root: intensities of energy, tensions, intentionalities, and tendencies.) Although the primordial field of our motility is so constituted that its intertwining tensions manifest a very strong inveterate tendency to condense into ego-centric bodies that are moved by polarizing motivations (subjective intentionalities), the deeper *truth* of the matter is that the intertwining of tensions (intense, primordial intentionalities) is *already* a rudimentary form of interpersonal solicitude. The encompassing field of our motility is therefore *always and already* a transpersonal compass of compassion – if we are

96

ready to get our bearings from its layout and can move as its importunings would move us.

The conclusion which I would like to draw from this account is that, as we let go of the ego-logical, ego-centric structure which typically characterizes our present experience of motility in its personal-interpersonal field, going (as it were) *beneath* it in an attempt to make contact with our more primordial attunement by Being as a whole, what we encounter, along the way, is a *prepersonal* and, in fact, a *transpersonal* dimension; and our contact with the motivating energies at work in this dimension of our experiential motility-field can have profoundly therapeutic effects, radically transforming our experience, for example, of the very *ground* of interpersonal solicitude.

Heidegger's fundamental ontology calls attention to the ek-static 'Care-structure'. This structure obviously assumes great significance, for Heidegger, in the unfolding of our ontological calling. The account we have been working on here attempts to spell out some unrecognized factors in this significance. In particular, our account suggests that the transformative process reverberates through many dimensions. As we deepen our awareness in the dimension of our relatedness-to-Being-as-a-whole, it seems that we become intensely motivated to develop our capacity for solicitude in fulfillment of the original ecstasy (*ek-stasis*) of the Care-structure. But I submit that the converse is also true: as we develop our capacity for solicitude, it seems that our capacity for a deeper ontological relatedness, a richer attunement by, and to, Being-as-a-whole, will begin correspondingly to unfold.

It is definitive of our human way of being (the being of a *Dasein*) that we are finite openings-for-Being localized as bodies within the field of Being as a whole. The ek-static openness of the primordial Care-structure (our interpersonal *Mitsein*), which is fulfilled in the development of our capacity for solicitude, is a *fundamental* dimension of this more general openness-for-Being. In opening ourselves to others, and especially to others in need, we *are* opening to Being; in developing the one, we develop the other. Compassion, or solicitude, essentially involves an awareness of universality and wholeness: we are not alone; and we are not whole, without caring for others. Thus, to the extent that we are deeply *moved* by a deep compassion and can *feel* this compassion in the form of a strongly *grounded* motivation to move

97

through the world for the sake of others, we are in fact also unfolding our more fundamental capacity to move in the motility-field of Being, moved not by the subjective springs of our own volition, but rather by grace of the 'energy' of Being as such.

To move with compassion is to move *in response to* the calling – the sufferings and needs – of other sentient beings. But when deep compassion is the motivation, to move and to *be* moved are one and the same. (In its encounter with this openness, the tradition of metaphysical dualism, which regards moving and being-moved as absolute opposites, must concede that it is shattered.) Being moved, then, by such compassion, we are on the way (*unterwegs*) to developing a deeper understanding of that more fundamental movement which consists in moving in a responsiveness to the field that discloses its openness as such. Being moved by such compassion, we are allowing *a new body of understanding* to emerge: a body whose movement consists (for we can also put it this way) in being moved *by grace of* Being as a whole. Compassion is a *calling* which *lays claim* to our motility from the very beginning; and it makes this claim because the openness it lays out for our movement originates in the motility-field of Being as a whole: compassion is the way Being, which 'needs' us, calls us out of ourselves and into its enriching openness; it is through movements taking place in the openness of compassion that Being first touches us and moves us to sense its still deeper, and much more mysterious, claims on our guardian awareness.

The authentic human being, whose ontologically experienced motility we have schematized, is one who understandingly appropriates the topological configuration of corporeal capacities as a local disclosedness, a local field of highly motivated energy, 'originating in' and 'emerging from' a still more primordial clearing of Being. According to this interpretation, our motility claims our attention at this level as the 'animation' or 'activation' of an elemental *flesh* inseparable from its situational field and functioning as an immediately meaningful disclosure, both in and of Being. This utterly open field of Being, and its expansive space of disclosure and horizon, constitute a dimension of motility whose primordial topological presence is a truth concealed not only by our 'normal,' consensually validated mode of motility, a motility characteristic of everyone and anyone, but concealed also by its projection in the present-to-hand ontology of our tradition of theoretical reflection.

From 'the very beginning,' i.e., always and already, the field of motility is *an elemental syntax* of motivations, an array or layout of possible routings, orchestrating and choreographing our bodily postures, gestures, attitudes and comportments. ('Layout' is one of the ways I am translating the word *legein*, which appears in Herakleitos, Fragment B50. *Legein* will be considered more fully in the second part of this chapter, where we take up the ontological destination of our gestures. The words 'orchestrate' and 'choreograph' both derive from ancient Greek words for the movements of dance. These concepts will be the subject of our reflections in the final chapter.) Our ontological interpretation is meant to call attention to, and consequently *open up* the basic overall layout of the motility-field for human existence; our goal is a reflective *disclosing* of the depth and dimensionality of this field – its most fundamental openness-to-Being. Our interpretation is an attempt, moreover, at clarifying the way that this layout, *as* place (*topos*) for the primordial 'working' of the *Logos* (i.e., Being), *lays claim* to our motility by orchestrating and choreographing our field of existential possibilities.

Bringing together Heidegger's ontology and Merleau–Ponty's phenomenology of motility, this interpretation continues the work of both and initiates further steps on the path of our experience of Being. We are giving formal ontology a moving embodiment; at the same time, we are setting Merleau–Ponty's phenomenology of the body in a much deeper, and more primordial dimension, so that the motility he describes is introduced to existential claims and opportunities which originate in the primordial dimension of openness cleared by Being and which only come to awareness when our experience of motility is articulated in relation to our capacity for deeper ontological attunement. Briefly stated, our interpretive approach consists in pushing the hermeneutical power of Merleau–Ponty's phenomenology to its most radical limits, so that we can begin to see how the prepersonal, pre-ego-logical dimension of motility, the dimension of orchestration which the *Phenomenology of Perception* calls 'primordial' and which, in his much later work, the philosopher calls the elemental 'intertwining,' suddenly *opens out* into an even more primordial dimension – that, namely, which Heidegger calls our 'attunement' by Being-as-a-whole.

As awareness of this more open dimension grows, our (experience of) motility at the other levels (prepersonal, personal, interpersonal and transpersonal) invariably undergoes corresponding transformations. It is for this reason that, as our philosophical reflections unfold, we must try to maintain an unprejudiced dialogue with psychotherapy, developmental psychology, and traditions of spiritual awareness.

The human being 'begins' life endowed with a body genetically pre-coded, genetically pre-programmed, for movement. This infantile body of movement is, however, an *ancient* body, a body which, from the very beginning, belongs as much to the culture of our ancestors as it does to nature. It is the body of our 'collective unconscious,' and it therefore cannot be adequately understood in terms of 'proper' concepts: it is a body whose motility calls for interpretation through archetypal *symbols* – symbols such as Merleau–Ponty's 'intertwining.' Even prior to the emergence of culturally generated patterns of meaning, the infant's body is, and finds itself, always and already *invested* with meaningful orchestrations of movement; orchestrations which originate in the field of motility as a whole. (Consider the pre-given configurations of meaning with which our egological motility-body finds itself always already invested: consider, e.g. the pre-cultural meaningfulness in our turning-to-face, our turning-away-from, our rotating body, our holding-back, our taking-a-stand, our fallenness, our uprightness, our flexibility, our unconscious favoring of right or left, our attitudes towards up and down, the above and the below, and our bodily felt differentiation between what is in front of us and what is behind.)

The infantile stage of development is a phase in our human life during which the motility is *without* an ego-logical subject or agent; that is to say that the infant's motility-body and the enabling field of clearing are still relatively undifferentiated. Since the motility-body has not yet been personally 'owned,' it still *belongs*, experientially, to the primordial field, Being as a whole, which presences 'for' it in the worldly form of the taken-for-granted: a reliable ground and a field of clearing. The infant's body, and *a fortiori* the 'sublimated' body of the child which we still carry around with us in the course of our normal adulthood, belong to, and are charged by, their primordial attunement to, the worldhood of the motility-field as a whole. By grace of this topological belonging and attunement (*Zugehörigkeit*), the body of motility exists in the world with a *pre-ontological understanding* of its ownmost way of being.

The child's body of motility becomes, of course, progressively more socialized, more 'humanized.' The child's body is shaped, according to the image of its culture, into the well-tempered body of everyone-and-anyone: the primordial orchestrations of motility opened up for him pre-ontologically gradually fall into line, constituting a life-world already regulated by social conventions, cultural styles, ethnic identifications, role-introjections, and especially significant interpersonal associations. The original routings are routinized; a free motility finds itself increasingly organized, sedimented into habitualities; the archetypes, functioning primordially as corporeal schemata, are increasingly *fixed* into typical patterns of movement, consensually validated styles of gesturing and posturing, a familiar signature. However, the motility characteristic of 'das Man,' of 'Jedermann,' manifests our 'inveterate tendency' to become absorbed in an unnecessarily narrow, needlessly restricted world-field of purposive, dualistically polarized, and mostly ego-centered action. There is no felt awareness of the larger field, the open horizon, the background, and the ground underlying; no sense of a more pervasive and more universal field-continuum as the more original source of our motility, and as having already laid out for us a certain elemental configuration, a certain life-world, the very *possibility* of *possible* movements, *possible* courses and routings. There is no body of understanding with an existential awareness of our deeper inherence, our intertwining, in the vast topology of Being.

But we are not necessarily 'stuck' in this restricted field, not necessarily immobilized by the boundaries which are imposed on us by virtue of our initiation into a social world and our education into the ways and traditions of our culture. There can be no doubt that each generation of mortals has needed, and continues to feel a need for, this corporate initiation and education. The ego-logical motility characteristic of everyone-and-anyone is a *necessary* acquisition for our natural, normal, and spiritually most fulfilling development. But there is *no need* for us to restrict ourselves to such standard and typical forms of motility, once we have reached the stage of our ego-logical adulthood; *no need* for us to con-form, to limit our motility-experience, in obedience to a state of conforming. In truth, our deepest well-being *depends* upon the 'resoluteness,' the 'moral character,' of our transgression, our eventual *release* from these standards of a 'fallen' experiencing of the human capacities for motility. Our *deepest* well-being *calls*, in truth, for a 'resolute' *movement* of 'authenticity' (*Jemeinigkeit*): a motility which takes place, both as experience and in understanding, as a dynamic center of energy-awareness within a radically deepened vector-field of disclosure, a vastly expanded field, and presencing, of Being. I submit that the personally felt *truth* of this radical calling, permeating and motivating us even in the cells of our musculature and jointure, *calls into question* the adult ego's standard of normality, and together with this, the ontology which reflects it; and I suggest that this calling of thought arises precisely from the personally *experienced* topology of our primordial, elemental, pre-ontological openness-to-Being.

Being, according to Heidegger, claims us. Being 'claims' us by calling each mortal into the deepest recollection of that which has been most deeply excluded from a 'normal' everyday existence. 'Being claims human being for grounding its truth in beings.'[3] The question that most calls for thought, then, is this:

> how [each human being] is claimed by Being for
> history and cor-responds to this claim. . . .[4]

Although the *character* of the human response is endlessly various, differing from epoch to epoch, from generation to generation, from culture to culture, and from person to person, it is nevertheless 'inevitable' that, when we stop to reflect, we find ourselves, as human beings, both already *claimed* by the attunement, and already *living* in a response. Thus, Heidegger says that,

> our nature is *already open* to the claim of Being. Yet
> even this openness to Being, *which thinking can*
> *prepare*, is of itself helpless to save man. A real
> openness in his relatedness is a necessary though
> not sufficient condition for saving him.[5]

Now, it would be a mistake to suppose that this ontological claim, which we have also characterized, following Heidegger, as a 'calling,' is nothing but a cognitive event in the 'mind.' Such could not possibly be Heidegger's understanding. And yet, he has very little to say about how the claim is experienced, how it actually calls us. I submit that our motility constitutes a body of genuine understanding, and that this motility-body enables us to *feel* our inherence in the field of Being as a whole. I submit that the claim calls to us *through* our motility, and that motility *opens* us to *feeling* the initial claim and *being moved* by our sense of its significance. Because motility necessitates a certain level of awareness with regard to our attunement by the field *as a whole*, every movement we make automatically opens us to the claim in this attunement, so that it may reverberate through the body and move us with its call. The body of motility, the body of pre-ontological understanding, *belongs* to Being by grace of its pre-ordained attunement (*Zugehörigkeit*) to the field as a whole. Thus, as we move through this field, as we move in its clearing, we are ineluctably opened to feeling, initially in a bodily way, the gift ('Es gibt') of its bearing. And we are enabled to move with the enlightenment of its grace.

As we begin to feel the call in our body of pre-understanding, as we begin to *sense* the significance of our attunement, the ontical fact of our belongingess-to-the-field becomes an ontological *question* that cannot be avoided; and our very existence becomes the answer. Our decision *is* how we live: how we are moved to comport ourselves, how we bear witness to that which has moved us, the kind of stand we take, and the various postures and positions by which we continually manifest what we have understood of the attunement.

The calling, a bodily felt sense of the true nature of our motility as a dynamic mode of being-in-the-world, calls us into the region of existential struggle and decision; that standpoint, namely, from which we begin to understand that neither the worldly, practical motility of everyone-and-anyone, nor the present-to-hand ontology to which it gives rise, can constitute the ultimate ground of truth, the ultimate source of meaningfulness. Thus we find ourselves faced with a need for authentic 'decision.' Either/or. Either we seek, or we avoid, an ontologically appropriate motivation and an ontologically attuned configuration of movement. Either we seek, or we avoid, a deeper, more thoughtful grounding. Either we seek, or we avoid, a motility more deeply in touch with its elemental field of sense and purpose. As those beings who are gifted with *distinctive capacities* for 'motility,' either we seek, or we avoid, an existence moved by the truth of Being, committed to the continuation of its unfolding as a topology for our dwelling. Either we will find ourselves deeply *moved* by the ontological calling which comes to us pre-ontologically (i.e., by way of our embodiment) from the primordial *topos* of Beings as a whole, and we will resolutely *move ourselves* with an appropriate beholdenness; or else, I believe, we will find ourselves *driven* by an ontological anxiety, taking flight in the face of a threat to the structural rigidity, and perhaps the very survival, of our ego.

The traditionally contemplative mode of thinking, the mode exemplified by Heidegger himself, can certainly constitute an authentic response to the orchestration (calling) whose *Logos* is a primordial topology for our motility. But, as soon as we recognize the presencing of Being in the gift ('Es gibt') of this topology and are prepared to acknowledge that the calling can lay claim to our guardian awareness through the pre-ontological orchestration (attunement) by grace of which the human body is moved, then I question whether we can continue to be satisfied with the purely contemplative mode of response. What I think we need, instead, is a mode of thinking which is genuinely comfortable working hermeneutically by direct phenomenological reference to our experience of an emerging body of understanding. For what we need is a thinking which actually deepens our contact with the choreography of the motility-field as a whole: a thinking which can actually take us into the depths of our topological attunement and help us to articulate our *felt sense* (our implicit, pre-ontological understanding) of the claim laid down for us in this primordial attunement. What we need, to put my argument in other words, is a thinking which can help us to reclaim our felt sense of being-open-to-Being as a way of being open, in our motility, to the grace of the field through whose clearing we move and pass.

Now, the typical adult motility is ruled over by an egological subject that has completely lost touch with the primordial choreography of Being, and with the field of clearing it prepares for our movements. Nevertheless, this self-destructive rule *can* be overthrown, since the motility it governs is called into question not only by the philosopher's radical deconstruction of traditional metaphysical responses to the Question of Being, but also, and much more immediately, much more powerfully, by the occasionally undeniable *unsatisfactoriness* of our typical, ontologically forgetful experience. (Consider, for example, how most people today experience walking, and how the linear system of concrete sidewalks we build reflects our attitude and our experience.) But it is at precisely this moment that the philosopher's words *could be* most helpful in motivating an existential movement in the direction of an ontological awareness. First of all, the philosopher can call attention to the fundamental errancy in the conception of motility that prevails in our traditional ontology. (Consider, for example, the problematic nature of the metaphysical distinction between activity and passivity.) Secondly, as Heidegger himself demonstrates, the philosopher is in a position to articulate the matter for thought in a way that calls attention to this unsatisfactoriness. Thus, for example, philosophical thinking can make the pathology, the actual pattern of symptoms, more explicit – more explicit, I mean, precisely *as* a pathology, *as* a pattern of affliction. Thirdly, the philosopher can shed light on the *connection* between this ontical pattern and the deeper condition of pathology which underlies it, viz., our forgetfulness of Being and the fallenness it brings to pass. Fourthly, the philosopher can actually help us to make better contact with the pathology itself, so that our neediness – or at least our need for existential change – might be more deeply and more lucidly *felt*. And, finally, the philosopher can resume the movement of reflection begun by Merleau–Ponty, following its trajectory into the dimensions of our pre-ontological orchestration, and retrieving, by way of our bodily felt *sense* of ego-logical motility, a guardian awareness, already available, of the most primordial choreography and the utterly open field which it prepares for us. By articulating this dimension in a way that makes it accessible to us in our very embodiment, philosophical thinking can help us to open up our motivational field to the seemingly limitless energies of Being as such.

Insofar as that phase of the process of personal development which we have been calling the phase of an 'authentically individuated Self' may be said to begin with the emergence of a certain guardian awareness of Being and a certain existential understanding of our inherence in the openness of Being as a whole, I would like to argue that, once our (experience of) motility has been grounded in ever-deepening understanding of the topological presencing of Being, our motility as such may become the principal medium and metaphor for the journeying of an authentically individuated Self. The Self's motility is not any longer the motility of an ego-logical agent; nor is it the routinized, standardized, consensually validated motility of everyone-and-anyone (*das Man*); rather, it is the poetizing motility of someone gracefully

105

following his own path, and passing through the world in a way that somehow enriches all the beings of earthly dwelling. In the final chapter, we shall complete our hermeneutics of gesture and movement with an interpretation of the Self's motility which reads in its orchestration the 'gathering dance' of Being.

It will be noted, of course, that this project of interpretation continues the historical task of the tradition, which concerns itself first and foremost with the question of Being. I assume that it will be noted, furthermore, that, because we are focusing on our experience of motility, we have needed to take very seriously the *grounding* of this experience. But it might therefore be thought that our project is inevitably committed to the ultimately nihilistic foundationalism that has determined the character of all thinking taking place under the spell of our metaphysical tradition. Such a conclusion, however, would be totally wrong-headed. The truth, I believe, is just the opposite. I believe that, for a careful reading, it will be clear that our project *deeply undermines* the dogmatic, absolute grounding which all the different systems of traditional foundationalism invariably insist on proving. I believe, in fact, that the grounding whose presence for our motility we shall be attempting, hermeneutically, to disclose, contests in the most radical way the reified grounding affirmed by tradition.

There are at least three factors which account for the critical difference, namely: (i) the fact that, in our project, the question of grounding is understood as calling for direct phenomenological reference to our lived experience, so that we can avoid the dogmatism that invariably threatens all modes of thinking which work with concepts not actually *rooted* in our experience; (ii) the fact that, in our project, the grounding in question is derived, not from the exigencies of a 'pure reason' or the 'logical necessity' of some 'system' of thought, but rather from *an emerging body of understanding*, so that the arrogant, lofty standpoint of traditional metaphysics is immediately denied its 'unquestionable' authority; and (iii) the fact that, in our project, grounding is explicitly understood as a hermeneutical process of continually unfolding our experience of Being, so that at no point is a final moment of completeness allowed to determine the work of thinking. Furthermore, these three factors make it extremely difficult for our project of grounding to remain under the spell of the atomism required by the mechanistic thinking that dominates our modern technological epoch, for atomism necessarily presupposes, i.e., requires, a finite, completed, free-standing totality, whereas the grounding which we shall be attempting to explicitate involves an unfolding relationship that essentially *depends* on the elemental Earth, the utterly untotalizable and ever-elusive presencing of darkness.

The very nature of the motility-body is inimical to a rigidly placed, context-free standpoint; it is an ever-shifting configuration of energy which *resists* the arrogant isolation, as well as the immobility and paralysis, which that willful stance-and-posture entails. Thus, we can call into question all totalizing ontologies which claim an absolute standpoint, a fixed point of origin, and a complete understanding of the ultimate foundation by staying close to the experiential motility-body and its field: getting in touch, in a reflective way, with our experienced *sense* of motility: being well-grounded, being moved, being motivated to move, being at rest, being at a standstill, being stuck in a standpoint, being uplifted, being upset, and being well-balanced – to name only a few of the more primary modulations that register the character of our being in this field. It is my conviction, therefore, that the being of our motility-body constitutes a field of great promise for any attempt at overcoming the ontological reifications of our metaphysical tradition. Our radicalized reflection is certainly committed to the disclosure of universal and invariant characteristics of motility; it certainly does undertake to articulate the most fundamental structures of our motility as a hermeneutical phenomenon of Being. But the radicality of our project demands that we *deny* the possibility that we can enjoy some absolute standpoint from which to assert a final or total conceptualization of the primordial dimension. From our radicalized standpoint of understanding, the possibility of a deeper and more primordial dimension, a field of expanded, and indeed expanding horizons, is always acknowledged, always accepted, always allowed for.

From *our* standpoint, the 'present-at-hand' ontology of subject-object and cause-effect correspondences, the ontology which lies behind all the abstract re-presentations of agency and motility proposed again and again by disinterested theoretical reflection, appears as just one of many possible ways to interpret the being of our motility. We need to appreciate that the traditional re-presentations owe their metaphysical possibility to a much more primordial experience of motility. In particular, we need to realize that the rational grounding for motility which gets asserted in traditional metaphysics is the product of a reflection depriving itself of feeling and moodedness, a reflection that has lost touch with *the bodily felt truth* of its field of Being.

Our project breaks with the history of Western metaphysics, for it does *not* claim to lay bare the ultimate and absolute foundation of motility – the most primordial grounding that we can conceive as at all possible. Rather, it claims only *to call attention*, at each step along the way, to a more open field of significance, and *to articulate* a process of opening, deepening, widening, and self-enriching understanding, while staying closely in touch with our practical field of embodied worldly living.

The narrowing, restraining, and self-limiting experience of motility that is characteristic of the ego-logical adult in our modern technological world has indeed a genesis – and a cultural history – that we can clearly trace. But our ultimate goal in this study is not so much the recollection of our primordial choreography as it is, rather, the attempt to read, in the gift of this choreography, a story for our future. If we could be moved by a different attunement, could we not enjoy some *release* from the pattern of affliction that is characteristic of our motility in the present historical epoch? Is there no possibility of relief from the obsessive, compulsive, disjointed patterns of motility, which seem to drive us – all of us – ever more rapidly and ever more blindly on the way to our madness and collective annihilation?

Since the symbolism of the primordial is appropriate in telling the story of our genealogy, our psychogenesis as ontological beings, I would like to suggest that the body of motility is rather like a text that is very much in *need* of existential, ontological interpretation. Since the topology of Being is a *Logos* which, in laying down the vectors of the motility-field, *pre-inscribes* this layout into the elemental flesh of our being, the topology is a *topography*. The *Logos* is a writing, a *grammar* of motility, a topology pre-inscribed like an esoteric text upon the primordial flesh; and it gathers this flesh into the shape of a motility-body at the center of a spatial field. The body of motility is like a *palimpsest* of endlessly interpretable fields of sense: a multi-layered text of mortal experience woven from the intertwining codes of Being. We are therefore proposing a reading or interpretation of the most primordial text accessible at this time: a text that we find very deeply inscribed into our elemental flesh. The text inscribed is a text that *alludes* to the most primordial context, the field of motility as a whole, which pre-scribes our possibilities-of-being, and to which we can always return in order to sense in a feeling way.

Our reading of this text is neither more nor less than an interpretation, limited and vulnerable, as all interpretations are. Nevertheless, I would like to claim that it *opens up* the being of our motility to a dimensionality of Being that is more open, more meaningful, more universal, more integrated, and more holistic. Our collaborative reading of this hidden, or anyway obscure, text returns us to a deeply fundamental stratum of embodiment, articulating a phenomenon which presents itself as the potential groundwork for a gathering dance of mortals in the open clearing of Being.

In closing this abbreviated existential-ontological interpretation of the being of the body of motility, I would like to cite a Tibetan (Buddhist) rDzogs-chen text from the eighteenth century: the text, written by the scholar 'Jigs-med gling-pa, is called, in its English translation by Dr Herbert V. Guenther, 'The Tantra of the Reality of Transcendent Awareness [symbolically referred to as] Kun-tu bzang-po, the Quintessence of Fulfillment and Completion.'[6]

In the First Chapter, 'Explaining the Ground and the Gates to Samsara and Nirvana,' the Being of the 'ground' is described, in a language which contests the distinction between psychology and cosmology, as being 'a pervasive medium in which the intentionality of a mind does not yet operate.' Out of its dynamic, however, a certain configuration of 'motility (*rlung*), present in the analytic and synthetic functions of a mind and activated by the traces of positive and negative actions and of the emotively toned patterns of attraction, antipathy, and indifference . . . begins to stir.'

According to the text,

> In this way the activity of the six senses awakening
> to their objects marks the emergence of the
> subjective mind operating in the subject-object
> dichotomy (*yid*). In favoring the emotively toned
> and constituted aspect of mind . . . which is the
> egocentricness of conscious life, it occasions the
> five basic emotively toned action- and reaction-
> patterns, the twenty subsidiary ones, the fifty
> mental events, and the eighty-four thousand
> interpretations and judgements, so that everything

without exception is set for the origination of
Samsara [i.e., the world of human existence as a
realm of suffering, misery, and all forms of
destructiveness].

Here we are reading an interpretation of the body of motility
as the body of a living being, a being whose flesh is deeply
inscribed by its experiencings of pain and suffering and
sorrow. We are reading an existential-ontological interpretation of the motility-life of everyone-and-anyone, the normal
adult who is living in the everyday world at an ego-logical
stage (level, stratum) of development. This interpretation
hermeneutically traces the genesis of the human way of being
as a psycho-physical process of ancient provenance,
emerging from an elemental field of motility and developing
or unfolding itself into the spatiality of an ego-logical structure, an ego-logical configuration of disclosive spatiality
already implicit as an 'inveterate tendency' within the primordial layout (*Logos*) of the field-as-a-whole. The text is thus a
'recollection' of the history of Being as an errant, wayward,
and fallen modality of human motility. As Guenther remarks,
'The underlying assumption is the psychologically verifiable
fact that man is capable of ascending to the highest levels of
spiritual awareness and also of falling into the deepest abyss
of misery and suffering.' It is an interpretation which *situates*
the human motility-body, *as* a psycho-physical process of
existential-ontological development, within a cosmological
dimension of Being. (Experientially speaking, we must ask,
for example: what happens to our motility, and to our understanding of its (felt) sense, when our individually and
culturally characteristic gestures, gestures typical of everyone-and-anyone, and the gestures which correspond to our
technological epoch, are explicitly *situated* in a cosmological
field of meaningfulness? Do we feel a shift, a new reach? Is
there a sudden shift in the intensity-level, the experienced
energy, of our motility?)
    The text also articulates the *truth* of this process in terms
of a motility so *related* to its field of Being as a whole that it
finds itself in the *fulfillment* of its various capacities. Thus we
read:

Although the transcending awareness which knows
reality as it is in reality, is, in view of its continuity,
not a different substance from the pervasive

THE BEARING OF THOUGHT

medium of the all-ground, it is said to be a change
in its modality. It is like awakening from deep sleep.
But although here the senses wake up to their
objects, they are not affected by the appearance of
these objects. . . .

And the motility-body which *incarnates* this transcending
awareness is accordingly said to be, at the level of its greatest
spiritual self-fulfillment and self-realization, 'a free unim-
peded movement.' 'Samsara,' says Guenther, 'is basically a
descriptive term for the observable fact that man, in ignorance of his real being, is driven by his actions and emotions,
while Nirvana refers to the experienceable passage beyond
suffering.' The Chapter concludes with the observation that,

inasmuch as this capacity cannot be thwarted by
reification into external objects and by avidity and
listlessness, everything is set for the origination of
Nirvana [i.e., the world of human existence as a
realm of well-being, a realm in which human
motility understands itself as, and is, a clearing for
the truth of Being in the depth of its beauty and
goodness].

The Second Chapter, 'Explaining the Split into Samsara
and Nirvana,' emphasizes that we need very much to 'know
what the ground is,' since its presencing 'comprises both a
path of freedom and one of errancy.'
As Guenther points out, 'there is a danger that . . . we
may center all our attention on the developmental phase [of
ego-logical adulthood] and lose sight of the "all-ground," or
even identify the "all-ground" with the ground underlying
one particular direction of the development.' As such, of
course, the field of motility is not 'sullied by karmic actions
and emotively toned action- and reaction-patterns.' Whence,
and why, do such patterns of errancy arise, constituting the
world of Samsara, the world we know most familiarly, the
everyday world of everyone-and-anyone? The Third Chapter
answers as follows:

When the noetic capacity by its inherent dynamic
has stirred from the all-ground and is about to
meet its object, the all-ground cognitiveness (*kun-
gzhi'i rnam-par shes-pa*) has risen; it is as if the

111

(indeterminate) psychological make-up (or the pervasive medium which makes a 'mind,' in the strict sense of the word, possible) has been roused from its deep sleep. The concrete objects of the five senses are not yet really present; but a very subtle cognitive capacity which tends to grasp its objects *has* risen and makes itself ready in every respect to receive the impressions of the objects of the discursive mind, like a mirror. This receptivity is confronted with [a field of] objects [organized] by the five senses operating according to their structure (*rtsa*) and their specific motor activity (*rlung*). . . . Then, through emotionality and mentation it arranges the action- and reaction-patterns of attraction, antipathy, and indifference, and so sets up the cause-and-effect [world] of Samsara in a total manner. . . .

By contrast, a motility that is *thoughtfully in touch* with its encompassing and underlying field, a motility free of emotively toned dualities, enjoys a life-world whose 'ground' is a great initial gift, 'the path a great self-authentication, and the goal a great self-freedom.' According to the text, 'Nirvana' may be said to 'begin' when our motility is *deeply in touch* with the five senses and their respective fields and zones (vision, hearing, tactility, taste, and smell); for, at the level of synaesthesia, the stratum of 'intertwining,' there arises a 'great transcending awareness,' and our motility-body is *moved* by a vision which the author of this text, inspired by Kun-tu bzang-po, describes – for our benefit – in a Chapter entitled 'The Path of the Magnificent Appearance of the Ground.' His description, at once phenomenological and symbolic (hermeneutical), reaches us in these terms:

Out of its realm the radiant light of the magnificent appearance of the ground, representing a pattern of communication in the highest perfection, comes as a self-arising appearance where the light shed by the lamp of self-arisen analytical awareness marks the beginning, that of the lamp of distant vision marks the gates through which the ground appears, that of the lamp of pure value reveals the beauty of the ground that has appeared, and that

112

of the lamp of glittering colors illumines the
distinct features of the ground that has appeared.

When motility, ontologically speaking 'an ultimate continuity,' is (i) thoroughly integrated with the four lamps of
vision (i.e., when our motility is in touch with, and arises
from, the stratum of a synaesthetic intertwining), then '(ii)
the felt knowledge of reality becomes more and more intense,
(iii) cognition attains its fullest measure, and (iv) reality reigns
alone.' The existential 'goal,' which is 'self-freedom,' is then
'perfectly present in the light of the path,' a path which it
would be appropriate to call a path of 'self-authentication.'
   According to the tradition, such an existence lays claim to
a motility whose essence is to be found in its 'communicativeness.' And the *heart* of this 'communicativeness' is a motility-
body moved by, and in the service of, the greatest and most
far-reaching compassion.
   Summarizing the significance of the text as a teaching of
unsurpassable wisdom, Guenther writes that

> two basic paths are open. Man may give himself
> over to the world and its ultimately futile aims, or
> he may see the fleeting character of the world and
> give himself over to his [ownmost] existential
> possibilities in the face of transcendence. In this
> connection, the tradition that derives from
> Vimalamitra expressly speaks of a path upward to,
> and being, a path of freedom, and a path going
> downward and getting lost in a maze of
> bewilderment, in the flickering appearances
> distorted by subjective aims and biases. It here so
> happens that man strays away from 'existence'
> (*sku*) into mere 'organismic being' (*lus*). . . .

When, however, we are resolved to appropriate our human
way of being in relation to Being-as-a-whole, then, as
Guenther puts it, 'there reigns the freedom of the spirit
moving in a realm of values which alone can give [fulfilling]
meaning to human life.' I propose to take these words as
an existential-ontological interpretation of that motility-body
whose distinctive potential-for-being we have always and
already experienced, even here and even now, experienced,
therefore, even in our most errant and most ungraceful
moments.

TABLE 1.1
The genesis and unfolding of motility

Stages of Life Development	Stages of Existential Development	Dimensions of Personality	Relatedness to Being	Predominant Characteristics of Motility
Maturity	Selfhood: *Jemeinigkeit*	Transpersonal	Ontologically ontic (aware openness-for-Being)	Grounded, poised, balanced, graceful, flowing, relaxed, open, dance-like, free, serene, agile, manifesting equanimity, ready to let go, tender, gentle, caring, mindful, lively, firm, fitting
Conventional adulthood: *das Man, Jedermann*	Egohood	Personal-interpersonal	Ontically ontological (closed and forgetful of Being)	Unstable, rigid, stumbling, off-balance, awkward, errant, falling, disjointed, tight, violent, careless, unyielding, indifferent, driven, obsessive, compulsive, defensive, closed, holding back, grasping, clinging, restless
Infancy	Pre-ego-logical	Prepersonal	Pre-ontologically ontic (primordial openness-for-Being)	Pre-ontological attunement (primordial orchestration and choreography)
Collective unconscious, biophysical ecology-body				

Explanation of Table 1.1

(1) The earlier stages are transcended, but still preserved in a certain latency. In Hegelian terminology, the earlier stages are sublated (*aufgehoben*). Thus, for example, Selfhood is not a fixed or final state. Nor is the continuation of its 'achievement' ever permanently assured. At any moment, and possibly even *just* for a moment, an individual Self may lose his footing, slip and fall back into a more comfortable pattern of egohood. The same may be said of the establishment of the ego's rule. The ego is a construct whose structuring of experience in terms of subject and object is continually emerging from, and subsiding back into, a pre-ego-logical dimension of awareness (e.g., when sleepy, exhausted or very relaxed). Likewise, the adult always carries within him the daydreams and memories of the child he once was; the adult never entirely loses, or at least never wants to lose, the child's capacity for enchantment. And the person's entrance into the transpersonal field does not *normally* involve taking leave of the consensually validated personal and interpersonal fields. In cases where the person does leave these fields behind and merges with the transpersonal intertwinings, a form of psychosis has taken place and Selfhood is not to be enjoyed. We must also point out that *submergence* in the ontological is sheer madness. Openness-for-Being must take place *in* the everyday world of ontical relationships. Moreover, no matter how far we move on the path of ontological thought, it is always possible for us to stumble and fall, or to go astray. But, whereas we are typically and for the most part forgetful, we certainly can become, for the most part, more thoughtful, more vigilant in recollecting the clearing of Being.

(2) The second stage in each of the axes is the stage of existential possibility. It is only at this stage that we are susceptible to the call of conscience, the reminders of our guardian awareness. It is at this stage that one initiates an existential movement of decision and commitment. Most of us live either all the time or most of the time in the zone of the second stage. It may be unsatisfactory, even painful; but at least it is familiar. Authentic experiential processes *begin* when we realize the possibilities for

115

further self-development and commit ourselves to learning from the joys and sorrows of the adventure.

(3) The possibility of self-development requires a *hermeneutical* return to retrieve for further unfolding the as yet undeveloped potentialities always already implicit in the earlier stage. The ego moves on to Selfhood by retrieving the lost gifts of infancy: for example, the openness of his prepersonal field, or the experience of primordial attunement. The personal journey into the transpersonal dimension likewise requires a hermeneutical process, a return to the field of prepersonal awareness, for there is a sense in which the essential *difference* between the prepersonal and the transpersonal is simply a question of awareness and understanding. The same may be said, *mutatis mutandis*, for the difference between the ontological and the pre-ontological, and for the processes through which our ontical existence becomes more fully an ontological openness-for-Being. In regard, specifically, to our motility, the ontological achievements of groundedness, balance and grace depend upon a bodily experienced hermeneutical recollection of our *pre-ontological* orchestration and choreography. It is crucial to recognize, however, that our self-development as an emerging body of understanding *requires* that the hermeneutical retrieval take place in, and as, a *bodily sensed, bodily felt* process. It is not sufficient to work through a hermeneutical recollection of the 'history of Being' solely as an intellectual, or contemplative exercize. *That* history needs to be *connected* to *our own developmental history* as beings embodied.

(4) The column under the words 'Characteristics of Motility' includes some of the more noteworthy characteristics belonging to our *gestures* as well as our motility in general.

Part II

Hermeneutical Gestures

Introduction

In his *Existential Foundations of Medicine and Psychology*, Medard Boss reminds us that,

To exist as *Dasein* means to sustain and maintain
the clearness of a world-spanning realm of
perception, to hold open this realm into which
whatever can be may shine forth and be perceived
in its meaning and its place.[7]

This passage sets in motion a tension of readings. For us,
the words 'sustain' and 'maintain' invite an interpretation in
terms of the body of understanding slowly emerging from
our study. The latter even makes visible, right on its face,
the fact that its concept originated in a gesture of the hands.
'World-spanning' and 'holding open' are words which immediately suggest gestures of our embodiment, although they
may certainly be read in a sense that refuses their truth
and turns the reference to such gestures into nothing but
embellishments of metaphor. For us, however, the body is
always to be understood as metaphorical; but we shall adhere
to the conviction that the more enriching truth for our present
historical situation calls for a reading which gives these words
their power, as metaphors, to *open* us to specific gestural
experiences.

In this part of the chapter, we shall focus our thinking on
'hermeneutical gestures.' The grammatical ambiguity in this
title already announces the double focus of our study. We
shall be reflecting, here, on *the disclosive capacity* of our
gestures. But we shall also reflect on the fact that the work
of articulating this capacity is *itself* a disclosive, hermeneutical
gesture. Thus, we shall not be concerned only with the
gesture *as* hermeneutical; we shall also be concerned with an
interpretation of hermeneutics *as* gesture. Our emerging
body of understanding requires *both* a hermeneutics of
embodiment and an embodiment of hermeneutics, for it
turns out that each of these tasks calls upon the other in a
circle of hermeneutical interdependency.

Section 1   Heidegger's Essay on Herakleitos,
Fragment B50

Fragment B50 may be understood as saying: 'When you have
been listening not to me, the mortal speaker, but to the *Logos*,
it is wise to agree [*homologein sophon estin*] that the One unifies
all things.'[8] *Legein* and *logos* are the words of Herakleitos:
mere fragments, though, of his thought. They are words that
refer, let us say, to articulation – gestures of articulation.

According to Heidegger, these ancient words will be most fruitfully opened up at this time in history when they are understood, hermeneutically, to mean a *gathering* and *laying-down*. This is an 'ontological' understanding, because it retrieves, and opens up, a primordial experience of Being.

Now, Heidegger's thinking has a two-fold focus: first and foremost, an understanding of the *Legein* of the *Logos*, that toward which Herakleitos directs our listening; and secondarily, the *legein* of our own mortal *logos*. According to Heidegger, *homologein* describes the essential character of our own *logos*, our own articulatory capacity, insofar as it is, or could become, more ontologically appropriate, more responsive, to the claim primordially laid down for us by the *Legein* of the *Logos*. But Heidegger is mainly concerned to bring out the more 'formal' ontological character of the mortal *homologein*. He does not recognize the need to specify it as an ontological question (a *Seinsfrage*) referring us directly, i.e., phenomenologically, to *our own experience* as gesturing beings, beings born with a unique grace in motility. What he has not thought through defines our present task. For we do need to ask ourselves: What *is* mortal *legein*, what is its character, understood as articulatory gesture, when thinking places it, by virtue of the relationship called *homologein*, in the ontological dimension of the *Legein* of the primordial *Logos*?

In response to our historical need as I perceive it, I shall therefore propose a hermeneutical reading of Heidegger's interpretation. That is to say, we shall undertake a further opening up of the Fragment by applying Heidegger's method to his own interpretation. What I am proposing is (i) that we take *logos* and *legein* to refer, not only to the articulatory gesture he calls 'speech,' but also to articulatory gestures in general, and (ii) that we take 'gathering' and 'laying-down,' Heidegger's translations for the Greek *legein*, to refer specifically to the *embodied characteristics* of this *legein*. In our attempt at working out such an interpretation, Merleau–Ponty's phenomenology assumes a role of decisive importance.

In accordance with our new reading of both Heidegger and Herakleitos, the 'Question of Being' will call our gesturing, and our motility in general, into question. It will motivate, perhaps, a shift in our focus, our awareness; at the very least, it will certainly question our motivation. It could also touch us in our innermost being, and move us to take the measure of our gestural being, recollecting the dimensionality of the ontological difference as the difference between our gesturing in its inveterate ontical everydayness (i.e., as forgetfulness of Being) and a gesturing opened up by its intrinsic aware-ness to the field of Being as a whole. As we shall see, this question (*Seinsfrage*) summons us to consider the *character* of the ontologically hermeneutical gesture. What, then, is ontological hermeneutics, when it takes the embodied form of a human gesture?

For our purposes, the principal claims which Heidegger makes are as follows. (i) '*Legein* properly means the laying-down and laying-before which gathers itself and others.' (60) (ii) 'To gathering belongs a collecting which brings under shelter.' (61) (iii) This sheltering means a sheltering and securing 'in unconcealment.' (63) (iv) This gathering is a 'preservation' and a 'safekeeping.' (61) (v) 'Every gathering is already a laying. Every laying is of itself a gathering.' (62) (vi) '*Logos* occurs essentially as the pure [primordial] Laying which gathers and assembles.' (66) (vii) 'The original *Legein*, laying, unfolds itself early and in a manner ruling everything unconcealed as saying and talking. *Legein* as laying lets itself be overpowered by the predominant [ontical] sense, but only in order to deposit [i.e., lay down] the essence of saying and talking at the onset under the governance of laying proper.' (63) (viii) '*Legein* is a laying wherein saying and talking articu-late their essence . . .' (63) (ix) 'Hearing is actually [i.e., in truth] this gathering of oneself which composes itself on hearing the pronouncement [of the *Logos*] and its claim. Hearing is primarily gathered hearkening.' (65) (x) 'We have heard when we *belong to* the matter addressed.' (66) (xi) 'If there is to be proper hearing, mortals must have already heard the *Logos* with an attention which implies nothing less than their [respectful] belonging to the *Logos*.' (67) (xii) 'Proper hearing occurs essentially in *Legein* as *homologein*.' (66) (xiii) 'As such, the proper hearing of mortals is in a certain way the Same as [the *legein* of] the *Logos*.' (67) (xiv) But we must think this Sameness with great care, because, 'precisely as *homologein*, it is not the Same at all. It is not the same as the *Logos* itself.' (67) (xv) Rather, proper hearing, as *homologein*, 'rests in the Laying that gathers, i.e., in the *Logos*.' (67) (xvi) 'Mortal *legein* lies secured in the *Logos*.' (74) (xvii) 'The Laying that gathers assembles in itself all destiny by bringing things and letting them lie before us, keeping each absent and present being in its place and on its way. . . .'

(72) (xviii) 'When proper hearing, as *homologein*, is, then the fateful comes to pass, and mortal *legein* is dispatched to the *Logos*. It becomes concerned with the [primordial] Laying that gathers.' (68) (xix) The primordial *Legein* of the *Logos* is not 'the overcoming of mortal *legein*, nor can [our] *legein* be a simple copying of the definitive [i.e., measure-giving] *Logos*.' (75) (xx) The *Legein* of the *Logos* 'can be nothing other than the essence of unification, which assembles everything in the totality of simple presencing.' (70) (xxi) 'The Laying that gathers has, as *Logos*, laid down everything present in uncon- cealment. To lay is to secure.' (70) (xxii) 'The *Logos* by itself brings that which appears . . . to appearance. . . .' (64) (xxiii) '*Logos* is in itself *and at the same time* a revealing and a concea- ling. It is *Alētheia*.' (71) (xxiv) '. . . disclosure is *Alētheia*. This and the *Logos* are the Same.' (70)

Our contribution to the hermeneutical process will now begin. A new body of understanding begins to emerge, I believe, as soon as we see that, if *legein* and *logos* are words which may be understood very broadly as 'articulation,' then the essence which Heidegger's thinking hermeneutically discloses, namely the gathering and laying-down, may in turn be understood as the essence of what I should like to call an 'articulatory gesture.' In this chapter, therefore, I wish to focus our attention on the essential character of *our own* articulatory gestures insofar as they are, or could become, more 'appropriate' to the claim primordially laid down for them by the *Legein* of the *Logos*. Our question, therefore, is this: what is the essential character of our articulatory gestures insofar as the experience to which they bear witness could be called *homologein*? This question throws before us, however, a long trajectory of thought. We will need to venture many new steps before we can reach for the answer.

Section 2   Thinking With Our Hands

I exercize occult and subtle power,
Carrying water, shouldering firewood.
              Zen Master Koji[9]

When the 'mental' is regarded as a self-contained separate realm, a counterpart fate befalls bodily activity and movements. They are regarded at best as mere external annexes of mind. They may be necessary for the satisfaction of bodily needs and the attainment of

external decency and comfort, but they do not occupy
a necessary place in mind nor enact an indispensable role
in the completion of thought.

John Dewey, *Democracy and Education*[10]

According to our tradition of metaphysics, the human body
is not capable of thinking. Thinking takes places only in the
'mind' and this 'mind' is contingently located in the region
of the head – which, for that reason, is often not counted as
part of the human 'body'. Our tradition is not easily liberated
from this dualism, because it has been very deeply
committed, for many centuries, to the Judaeo-Christian ideal
of asceticism and its path of renunciation. When we read
Descartes, for instance, it becomes evident that his epistemo-
logical and ontological dualism of mind and body is not only
the projection of a new historical dream, a mechanistic vision
of humanity which inaugurates the modern technological
world; it is also, in the final analysis, a reflective manifestation of the dualism inherent in our religious experience of
good and evil. We certainly have tended to see an incurable
split in our moral nature, a split which is repeated in every
dimension of our being. The body, it seems, is inherently
evil; it is a perpetual source of sin, moral weakness and
limitation, cognitive error, perceptual illusion. When meth-
odically separated from the body, the mind is essentially
unpolluted and free of evil propensities. Nothing so noble,
so lofty, as the power of thought could ever take place in the
lower body.

Unfortunately, however, this understanding only perpetuates the moral and spiritual affliction. If we are ever to break
out of the suffering reflected in this tradition, we must first
of all acknowledge that we can think, for example, with the
capacity right in our hands. Until we acknowledge this, it
will not be possible for us to retrieve for the future that *more
primordial* experience of the presencing of Being which our
technological sensibility tends to conceal behind its projection
of a reified ontology forgetful of Being. Yet this retrieval will
probably be crucial for our capacity to realize new historical
possibilities. What accordingly differentiates Heidegger's
sense of 'thinking' from the more familiar sense still dominant in our tradition is precisely the fact that 'thinking' in his
sense is most certainly not a Cartesian *res cogitans*. Although
Heidegger's 'thinking' is not yet sufficiently incarnate, it can
help us, nevertheless, to retrieve the more primordial experi-

ence from its concealment in our history. This is a point to which we shall soon return.

In *Phenomenology of Perception*, Merleau–Ponty argues that,

> To know how to type is not, then, to know the place of each letter among the keys, nor even to have acquired a conditioned reflex for each one, which is set in motion by the letter as it comes before our eye. If habit is neither a form of knowledge nor an involuntary action, what is it then? It is knowledge in the hands, which is forthcoming only when bodily effort is made, and cannot be formulated in detachment from that effort.[11]

Our unwillingness to acknowledge this wonderful intelligence inwrought in the hands themselves makes us profoundly *indifferent* to the ontological difference, and to the potential-for-being of which we are capable by virtue of the gift of our hands.

In a lecture published in *What Is Called Thinking?* Heidegger recognizes this need and undertakes a sustained meditation on the hands and their craft:

> 'Craft' literally means the strength and skill in our hands. The hand is a peculiar thing. In the common view, the hand is [merely] part of our bodily organism. But the hand's *essence* can never be determined, or explained, by its being [just] an organ which can grasp. Apes, too, have organs that can grasp, but they do not have hands. The hand is infinitely different from all grasping organs – paws, claws, or fangs – different by an abyss of essence. Only a being who can speak, that is, *think*, can be handy in achieving works of handicraft.
>
> But the craft of the hand is richer than we commonly imagine. The hand does not only grasp and catch, or push and pull. The hand reaches and extends, receives and welcomes – and not just things: the hand extends itself, and receives its own welcome in the hands of others. The hand holds. The hand carries. The hand designs and signs. . . . Two hands fold into one, a gesture meant to carry

man into the great oneness. The hand is all this, and this is the true handicraft.[12]

And Heidegger then points out the *need* for giving the maintenance of thought to our hands:

> Every motion of the hand in every one of its works carries itself through the element of thinking; every bearing of the hand bears itself in that element. All the work of the hand is rooted in thinking.[13]

When we genuinely struggle to understand this rootedness, we will discover, I believe, that the *reverse* of what Heidegger says is also a truth: there is a thinking of Being, a maintaining of thought, which is rooted in the work of the hands. To be sure: 'Thinking,' as Heidegger says, 'guides and sustains every gesture of the hand.'[14] But we must not overlook Heidegger's observation that, 'We have called thinking the most excellent handicraft.'[15] Once we have repudiated Cartesianism, we can begin to explore the suggestion that our handicraft reaches its highest fulfillment when it becomes an embodiment of thinking. By the same token, once our thinking is no longer compelled by its Cartesian past, we can begin to appreciate how the 'thinking which guides and sustains every gesture' – the 'thinking' at stake in Heidegger's deconstruction of Western philosophy – is not an intellectual, contemplative act taking place in the mind and governing from above the movements of the lowly gesture. Heidegger's intention was to articulate a 'thinking' radically different from the cognitive processes of our tradition. The thinking of concern to Heidegger will be understood much better, I believe, as the *character* of the gesture. Thinking, then, *is* the thoughtful gesture. The thinking and the gesture are one and the same. Our reversal, giving thought to a body, continues the overturning of the history of metaphysics to which Heidegger contributed, but which he in no sense completed. I am arguing that one of Heidegger's most striking failures to break out of the traditional framework of thinking can only be redeemed when we have let the body of understanding emerge from its historical exile.

THE BODY'S RECOLLECTION OF BEING

Section 3   Being in the Grip of Technology

> In holding fast, or grasping, the whole universe vanishes.
> In letting go, or releasing, the individual world appears,
> in which everyone asserts his true existence.
>
> Katsuki Sekida, *Two Zen Classics:*
> *Mumonkan and Hekiganroku*[16]

In *Psalm* 115, there is a brief but powerful reference to the gesturing of our hands. The text reads as follows:

> Their idols are of silver and gold,
> The work of human hands.
> . . . . They have hands but cannot feel,
> legs that cannot walk.

The conventional interpretation assumes that these lines refer only to idols, and that they mean only to warn us against idolatry. But another meaning, deeper and more hidden, also suggests itself, namely: as far as the idols are from manifesting our characteristically human capacity for gesturing with feeling, just so far are we from realizing our God-given *capacity* for gesturing with the grace of holiness. The lines are not only meant as a warning against idolatry; they are also meant to warn us against the temptation to forget the spiritual calling which informs our humanity and distinguishes our hands from the hands of the idols and the grasping organs of the other sentient beings. In other words, the lines are meant to call us back to ourselves; in particular, they call into question the caring and compassion by which our hands are moved. The Psalm does not want us to take for granted the ontological difference between our own hands, the hands of human beings, and the hands of idols. Only ours are challenged to be moved by feeling.

Our gestures bespeak *capacities*: not only capacities for doing, but also capacities for being.[17] These capacities are deeply motivated by their inborn skillfulness (*Geschicklichkeit*): the gift (*Geschenk*) we are given at birth. At birth, we are given a gift of nature and sent (*geschickt*) on our way. Whatsoever we do with that gift, how we experience the potential inherent in our skillfulness, decides our story (*Geschichte*), our individual fate, our mortal destiny (*Geschicklichkeit, Schicksal*). Some of us will, in the course of time, realize the gift in this skill. Some will not. But in any case, it is appropriate (*schick-*

lich) that we realize the true measure of our articulatory capacities, in that we have appropriately experienced our indebtedness and belongingness (*Zugehörigkeit*), appropriated our capacity to develop, and responded in the most appropriate way to the original, unchosen appropriation of our articulatory being (our mortal *legein*).

Etymology tells us that 'to gesture' means 'to bear,' 'to bring forth,' 'to give birth,' and 'to make appear.' This gesturing of our hands is a *legein* – what for the moment we shall simply define as an articulation which brings forth a *logos*. (In this sense, every gesture is a *phenomenological* event.) Our gesturing is, moreover, a *technē*, a skill, an articulatory *capacity*: something, then, that we can measure by considering both the character of our effort and the nature of that which this effort makes appear. For, to speak of capacity, of skill, is to acknowledge the significance of development and to assume some responsibility for that process. But I suggest that, if the capacity in question is recognized as a *gift* (as our 'giftedness'), then the most appropriate *reception* of the gift would be a bearing of this responsibility which transformed every gesture into a movement of rejoicing and thanksgiving. But what, typically, motivates our gestures? What do our gestures typically bring forth? To what do they actually give birth? What kinds of beings do they make appear in the world of their restless activity? How do our gestures contribute to the appearing of beings in the truth (i.e., the unfolding dimension) of their Being? What *reception* of this giftedness, what *character* of response to its calling, actually appears in the field spanned by our gestures? Can we assert that the gestures we make are really *open* to whatever beings the sensory-motor field happens to bring forth? The way our hands *are* does not touch, does not reach to, the way they *could* be: the way they *would* be, were we to realize their ingrained destiny of character and maintain their inherent gifts of skill. Our skillful hands are a most precious gift. We readily pay lip-service to this matter of fact; but, even when we develop a skill of the hands, we take the fact of the *gift* for granted. We neglect to reciprocate. Do we feel any *need* to reciprocate by giving our hands the gift of our thought, our guardian awareness?

Now, according to Heidegger, we are called upon to maintain the 'element of Being' in which our gestures take place. In the terms of our present study, we need to translate the 'element' of Being' into articulations of the sensory-motor field as a whole. But, for the moment, we are not going to consider gestures in their relatedness to the field of Being as such. Rather, we shall extend our meditation by focusing on the bodily felt sense – the bodily felt character – of our gestures in their relatedness to various touchable, manipulable things, things which are tangibly in Being: things like the wood which a cabinetmaker works. There is a tactful way of handling things, a way of manipulating, which is mindful of their dimensionality, the span of their presence, and which holds beings, keeps beings, and maintains beings in the immeasurable richness of their Being. The hands therefore can *give* to Being our gift of thought *whenever* they handle things with appropriate skill, and with *care* for their being. Thus, Heidegger wants to call our attention to the true cabinetmaker who, true to himself and to the enchantment in things, 'makes himself answer and respond above all to the different kinds of wood and to the shapes slumbering within the wood.'[18] By virtue of patience, delicacy of touch, and gentle, careful motions, the cabinetmaker's craft becomes an event (*Ereignis*) of disclosing, a moment when the field of the gesture's encounter gives birth to, or makes appear, a 'new thing,' and the emotional depth of the field's reserve of enchantment is somehow itself made sensible for our emerging body of emotional understanding. Whenever this kind of skillfulness is at work, and wherever this kind of sensibility, this kind of reverence, is still handed down, as the gift of ancient tradition, there I think we will find a *living* response to the nihilism of our technological epoch.

The child's first concepts (*Begriffe*) are really corporeal schemata of com-prehension formed in the process of grasping (*greifen*) and manipulation. Consequently, the adult's encounter with tangible, re-movable beings, and the adult's comprehension of Being as such, will tend to be determined in ways that *correspond* (i.e., co-respond) to the initial character of the enquiring, learning gesture. The circumstances of early life, and the kinds of gestures they elicit – gestures of violent emotion, for example, in response to gestures of rejection, abuse, and indifference – set the predominant character of the original concept. If we are concerned about pathologies in the character of our comprehension, we should look to afflictions in the character of our prehensions. We need to attend to the ways we 'use' our hands and experience their 'activity'. We need to sense in a bodily way the tone (*Stimmung*) of our gestures, and become more aware of how that tone is related to our technological modes of production. Since the origin of technology refers us back to the *technē* of our hands, a more developed awareness of the productive character of our gestures would contribute to a radical critique of technology and would help us to recognize otherwise concealed opportunities for a new response to the nihilism in our technological machine. The truth of the matter is that new historical initiatives have *already* been placed in our hands. Can we retrieve new concepts for our technology from the ontological awareness always implicit in the very grasp of our hands?

Giving thought to the use of his hands, Heidegger wants to tell us that,

> 'Using' does not mean the utilizing, using up, exploiting. Utilization is only the degenerate and debauched form of use. When we handle a thing, for example, our hand must fit itself to the thing. Use implies fitting response. Proper use does not debase what is being used – on the contrary, use is determined and defined by leaving the used thing in its essential nature. But leaving it that way does not mean carelessness, much less neglect. On the contrary: only proper use brings the thing to its essential nature and keeps it there. So understood, use itself is the summons which determines that a thing be admitted to its own essence and nature, and that the use keep to it. To use something is to let it enter into its essential nature, to keep it safe in its essence.[19]

In other words, we are appropriately caring in our use when we relate 'to the thing in hand according to its nature, thus letting that nature become manifest in the handling.'[20]

Heidegger turns this matter of use into an ontological problem. He thus deepens in a very radical way the significance of the industrial nihilism first articulated by Marx. According to Heidegger,

> Where anything that is has become the object of representing, it first incurs, in a certain manner, a loss of Being.[21]

Whatever else we might want to say about this loss, we are

127

certainly justified in observing that such objectification always entails an experience of affliction. David Krell is therefore speaking very accurately when he uses a word from psychopathology to describe the metaphysical *grasp* of 'truth' that prevails in our epoch of technological objectification:

> 'the true,' 'truth' in the traditional metaphysical sense, is a *fixation* of an apparition; it clings to a perspective that is essential to life but in a way that is ultimately destructive to life.[22]

Heidegger details the connection between truth and use. We need to continue Heidegger's astute examination of this connection. The experience of truth which predominates in our world is a reflection of the prevailing use of our hands and the ways we characteristically handle and use things. According to Heidegger, the prevailing truth is the fixation of a willful grasping and clinging. But the same can be said about our typical, consensually validated ways of handling things and using things. Thus, just as the modern experience of truth (truth restricted to correctness) is cut off from the richness of a more primordial experience of truth, so our handling and using of things is cut off from the actuality of a more enriching encounter with the depth of their thingly presence. This more primordial presence is an openness, or depth, which eludes metaphysical re-presentation; but it also eludes that objectifying grasp of technology. This grasp is a gesture whose essential character we might describe by using Heidegger's word, *Ge-stell*: the word suggests a gesture which is moved by the need to secure, or tie down, for its permanent possession.

The grasping gestures characteristic of our technological world are powerful, but they cannot reach into the essential nature of things. In this regard, such gestures are tactless transgressions. The careful touch, which is open to *feeling* what it touches and uses, gets in touch with a thing's essential nature more deeply and closely than the hand which willfully grasps and clings, moved by strong desires (i.e., by attractions and aversions), or than the hand which is indifferent to the beauty of the thing in the wholeness of its truth. This is why I have argued that the rooting of gesture in thinking requires attention to the body of felt experience.

A bodily felt guardian awareness, being the mode of our original tactile understanding, our global pre-comprehension of things in a primordial mood of tactile openness, is our most *tactful* way into the opening depth of things. Touching with equanimity, handling with tact, we leave things whole and intact. Touching with a restraint that is not deformed by renunciation, we let things yield the richness of their more intangible nature, their deeper and otherwise inaccessible nature. Handling things without greediness, our hands will be filled with a palpable wealth. Maintaining things in accordance with the dictates of our guardian awareness, the *objects* of technology can perhaps be transmuted into the *things* they originally were and essentially are. Even when we *use* things, we can be moved to *keep* them in a way that also lets them be *free* of our use. The hammer, the piston, the knot and pulley are certainly useful; but they are also manifestly beautiful – and not only when they are left to stand in their own intactness, but even when they are actually being used, if handled by hands receptive to the moving beauty of their presence.

What *is* our capacity to be touched, and moved, by that which we are given for our touching? What is the *character* of our touch? By what are we touched, by what moved? Touching *presupposes* our capacity to be correspondingly touched, and this primordial reciprocity calls into question our inveterate tendency to polarize the tactile field into a subject and its object and lose touch with Being as a whole. Are we capable of touching things, capable of handling and manipulating things, with a sensibility that I should like to call *Gelassenheit*? (*Gelassenheit* means equanimity, the capacity to let go and let be.) The 'properly human' gesture, in touch with the intrinsic 'value' of Being, will skillfully practice a movement free of ego-logical attachments. Touching a deep, and deeply hidden truth, the thoughtful maker of cabinets touches the wood he is using with fingers sensitive to the precise needs of the wood. He lets his fingers, and the work of his hands, be *attuned by* the wood. The wood *speaks* through its grain, and the hand is *moved* in response. He takes pride in his tools, and handles them with a timeless care. As he planes the wood, he caresses the grain. In the flow of his movements we will observe poise and grace; and in his gentle touching and holding we may sense a visible tact. Even the gesture by which he returns the plane to its hook takes place with the slowness and the intensity of a deeply felt meditation. For a moment, the sensori-motor field is opened up, and there is (*es gibt*) a space of enchantment.

This example is helpful in clarifying the character of the enlightened touch, the gesture whose equilibrium, or neutrality, embodies *Gelassenheit*. But it is also helpful in formulating our fundamental *political* problem. For the modern factory, the modern office, and the modern store, and most of the other workplaces of our world, are not in any sense 'spaces of enchantment.' Does our example merely serve, then, to call attention to an untruth? Or does it at least suggest the futility in our ontological account? The example poses a challenging question, an existential Either/Or. Should we repudiate the ontological account on the ground that, as the example seems to demonstrate, it defines an ideal too far-removed from the situations of modern living? Or should we acknowledge the ideality of the account and regard its ontological difference from actuality as defining for us a difficult, but worthy political task? Formulated in the simplest possible terms, an important part of the task would be to bring about institutional organizational changes in the places where people work, so that gestures more nearly embodying the ontological attunement whose fulfillment we have described might have an opportunity to develop. It certainly seems to me that the possibility of facilitating such changes in the field of political action offers itself as a subject eminently worthy of thought. It is my conviction, moreover, that, if political action progressively cleared a space for the taking-place of thoughtful gestures, thinking itself might reach a deeper, much clearer understanding of the historical essence of technology and how to relate more appropriately to the nihilism in its ontology. If Being is now in the grip of technology, then an intelligent political response to the danger it holds would seem to consist in efforts to build a new society, a new community, in which conditions favorable to a deeper understanding of technology, together with conditions hospitable to the gestures most responsive to a radically different ontology, could be continually tried, tested, measured against the ontological difference they would make.

Let us now consider our technological ontology in more detail. The various beings of our world are present for us in many modalities of presencing. Even one and the same thing can present itself in numerous different ways: as present, as near and close, as past, as distant, as absent, as a perception, as a memory, as an image, as a fragrance, as a sound. Beings presence, presencing in different modalities. For our immediate purposes, though, what is of particular concern are the two modalities which Heidegger differentiates at a more comprehensive level of interpretation, viz., being-ready-to-hand (*Zuhandensein*) and sheer extantness (*Vorhandensein*), and which he then subjects to a very radical critique from the standpoint of a more fundamental dimension of Being. Now, according to Heidegger, the (ontical) presencing of all (worldly) beings, regardless of their modalities, is always dependent upon the primordial presencing of Being as such. For this more primordial presencing consists in an event of receding, or clearing (*Lichtung*), which opens up the field of experience as a whole in a way that allows all beings whatsoever to give, or present themselves in keeping with the conditions of their nature. But Heidegger's 'history of Being' demonstrates that the reified, atomistic ontology which serves our technology of nihilism conceals and denies the primordial openness, or clearing, as which Being in its wholeness presences. To be sure, it is this very receding, withdrawing, or self-concealing of Being which makes it possible for all beings to presence, just as it is the receding, withdrawing, or self-concealing of a visual background which makes it possible for a succession of figures to arise, emerge, and stand out in a light of relief. But in what sense is it necessary that we continue to deny the primordial event of Being? Heidegger's 'history' is an attempt to remind us that the ontology holding sway in our epoch is an indication of our forgetfulness-of-Being; that it is a symptom of our being out of touch with a more primordial experience of Being; and that Being as such, the fields of Being in all their depth, openness, and intactness, can now only appear in the grip of a nihilistic technology.

Relative to the presencing of the fields and their clearings, the presencing of beings in the two modalities of readiness-to-hand and sheer extantness must be considered to be derivative and secondary. Whenever the openness of Being *as such* is encountered in a way that reduces it to these modalities, or whenever beings are encountered in a way that excludes awareness of the more primordial dimension of their presencing, the symptoms of an affliction peculiar to our epoch are manifest. Insofar, however, as thinking succeeds in effecting a radical recollection of Being, there is an acknowledgment of the primordial openness and clearing, and the presencing of beings in the modalities of readiness-to-hand and sheer extantness will be maintained intact in the deeper fields on which they depend.

Readiness-to-hand is the modality of possibilities in which beings variously presence when they are encountered within the field of instrumental relationships. The various possibilities which can unfold in this modality of Being are manifest in many different kinds of situations, for example: when a tool breaks, or breaks down, and becomes unusable, or when we confront some kind of interference with our use of the tool (e.g., when the tool is lost or misplaced). *Sheer extantness* is the modality in which beings presence when they are encountered as containing possibilities of their own, possibilities seemingly independent of our projects, our concerns, and our needs. Although the sheer extantness of Being is the condition which *lets there be* beings variously presencing in the modality of a readiness-to-hand, it is beings variously presencing in the *latter* modality which *first make it possible for us* to shift our awareness (perhaps in deep ontological anxiety) to the level or dimension of sheer extantness (where the nothingness of beings may quite suddenly present itself as a real possibility). Readiness-to-hand is a presencing of beings in response to (or in correspondence with) practical, and more specifically instrumental comportments. Relative to such presencing, the sheer extantness of beings is brought forth in response to more theoretical, more contemplative, or more disengaged comportments – comportments which often are called forth only in situations where something useful, something ready-to-hand, is no longer useful, no longer ready-to-hand for the realization of our worldly projects.

Heidegger's words for the two derivative modalities of presencing, viz., *Zuhandenheit* and *Vorhandenheit*, implicitly remind us that, although it is Being itself, presencing in and as a primordial field of openness, which lets beings presence in their readiness-to-hand and sheer extantness, the historical domination of these secondary modalities, and their fateful concealing of the more primordial presencing of Being, must be ascribed in due measures to the work of our hands. To be sure, a long history mediates the connection between our gestures and the domination of these modalities in our modern technological economy. Nevertheless, the connection was originally, and I believe still is, even today, a matter of decisive significance. Specifically, what I want to argue is that the domination of the two modalities, a domination without which the nihilism of our technological epoch is really not conceivable, is a function of the ontologically forgetful character of our gestures. It is first and foremost through the medium of our gestures – the ways we typically touch, grasp, hold and handle things – that we have participated in the event (*Ereignis*) of Being which is the bringing-forth of beings in their readiness-to-hand and sheer extantness.

I am not suggesting that these modalities are intrinsically nihilistic. My claim is rather that the danger of nihilism comes from the *concealment* of the more primordial dimension of Being; and what is dangerous, therefore, is our *loss of contact* with this dimension of our gesturing. As the history of our civilization has unfolded, this loss of contact continues to extend the depth of the concealment. Thus, we are needing, at this time, to regain our gestural contact with the intactness of Being and retrieve from our guardian awareness of that contact a radically different way of grasping the presencing, the gift and givenness, of Being.

The gesturing of our hands is determined, for the most part, by ego-logical motivations. Our hands typically belong, that is, to an ego-shaped body. And they are moved in an attunement-to-Being that is regulated and modulated by the particular historical situation which that ego-body is fated to inhabit. In our present epoch, gestures of grasping, seizing and clinging, gestures of rage and violence, and gestures of mechanical indifference seem increasingly to prevail. If our experience of beings, and of the Being of all beings, is indeed powerfully determined by our technological world-epoch, and if this technological world-epoch can in turn be traced back to a life-world shaped by the activity of our hands, then it would seem reasonable to suppose that, should we find within ourselves the capacity to cultivate an awareness which modifies our way of relating to the things we touch and handle, we could indeed begin, albeit with small and insignificant gestures, to *break out* of the reductive nihilism of our present historical epoch, and begin, with a different experience of truth, to hold open for human existence a new historical possibility. This new historical possibility is to be found, I submit, right in our hands.

In the epoch of modern technology, the presencing of Being as such, and likewise the presencing of the Being of all the beings we encounter, are subject to a powerful reduction. Everything in our world must be made for permanent availability and total control. Our technologically conditioned ontology is a reflection of hands that are motivated by the will to power: the need to dominate and control, the need to hoard and secure. The gesturing of our hands is not only the first, but also the foremost manifestation of *das Ge-stell* – the setting down or placing which makes something permanently present and always available for our use.

Can we renounce the gestures of such willfulness? Can we learn to let go? Can we balance our grasping and hoarding and clinging with gestures that let go and let be? Can we learn to enjoy being empty-handed? Can we cultivate gestures of tenderness and caring, so that some of the rage and some of the violence in our world might be transmuted into energies, of better purpose? The overcoming of nihilism and the coming-to-pass of a new way of being with all that which presences requires, I believe, that we learn how to *root* our gestures in the tact and contact of their proper field – that field of Being which has already made a clearing for their movement and already given them an initial *sense* of the deepest meaning of openness. If we can begin to reverse the inveterate tendencies which presently govern our gestures, then a radically different ontology, and a radically different basis for our technology, might eventually come within reach and fill our emptied hands with the gifts we have learned how to receive and maintain. In 'The Turning,' Heidegger says:

> If enframing [*das Gestell*] is a destiny of the coming
> to presence of Being itself, then we may venture
> to suppose that enframing, as one among Being's
> modes of coming-to-presence, changes.[23]

We know very little, and can be sure of less. But, as Heidegger observes, it would be wise for us to comport ourselves with dignity, for the lesson of our history is that 'another destining, yet veiled, is waiting.'[24]

Section 4   The Cosmological Extension

For if our body is the matter upon which our
consciousness applies itself, it is coextensive with our
consciousness. It includes everything that we perceive; it
extends unto the stars.
    Henri Bergson, *The Two Sources of Morality and Religion*[25]

134

our hands spread out in prayer as the eagles of the
sky. . . .

Talmud Pesahim (118a)

Michelangelo painted for the Sistine Chapel an archetypal
gesture – a gesture of reciprocity in the drama of its cosmological extension. In his depiction of 'The Creation of Man,' we
see the hand of God reaching down from the heavens and
the hand of Adam as it reaches up from the Earth. Their arms
are stretched to the limit, their fingers touch. The meeting of
hands, that 'point' where they meet, initiating a binding
contact, is an event of awesome dimensions. It can move us
with the might of a thunderbolt. It can shake us with the
strength of an earthquake. The gesture extends the mystery
of their communication across all generations of mortals and
across the infinity of space which separates us from the
Creator. The painting re-presents an experience of primordial
presence as it is bodied forth in its archetypal gesture.

Translating Heidegger into the language of an ontological
embodiment, Medard Boss writes that,

> The human being exists as a spanning, hearing, and
> holding-open of a realm of perception that is
> responsive to the presence of whatever phenomena
> reveal themselves in it.[26]

The painting shows us this existence in the clarity of a
gesture; but the gesture it shows invites us to experience a
reaching-out that places the human existence in the time and
space of a religious cosmology. It schematizes for us the
mythic history of an archetypal gesture; it hands down Old
Testament cosmology as a 'corporeal schema' for our emerging
body of understanding.

Heidegger's discussion of Fragment 26 in Eugen Fink's
Heraclitus Seminar of 1966–7 bears directly on the matter at
hand.[27] The crucial words, he tells us, are haptesthai, which
means 'to be brought together,' haptomai, which indicates a
'reciprocal touching,' and anchibasiē, which means 'coming
into nearness'. While Eugen Fink focuses on the phenomenon of touching as an immediate contact, Heidegger wants
to call our attention to the expansiveness of the enabling field
and to the character of the touching as a gesture which reaches
across the distance and spans it. Heidegger emphasizes, first
of all, that the Greek words imply that the touching is already

135

taking place at a distance, because 'coming into nearness' necessarily *presupposes* a sense of the touching. In other words, we can touch, and we can be touched, even at a very great distance. And the sense in which this is true is not, as some might want to argue, 'merely metaphorical,' in contrast with the sense in which two sentient beings are said to make *immediate contact* in their touching. The truth is, rather, that the touching which takes place at a distance, the touching which is a coming-into-nearness, is the more *primordial* sense, the more primordial *experience*: it is that which *lets* the touching, in the sense of an immediate contact, take place. Secondly, Heidegger emphasizes that neither the expanse of the distance nor the touching as such can be adequately understood in the language of objective thought. The expanse of the field in which *this* touching takes place cannot be measured: in view of God's presence, we must accept that it is immeasurable. Nor can the *presence* of the movement, the lived trajectory of the gesture, be adequately re-presented through our metaphysical re-presentation of movement. We need to understand these matters before we can begin to realize the possibility which Michelangelo's painting holds open for us: the possibility, that is, for a cosmological extension of our gestures – and of our capacity for being touched, even at an immeasurable distance.

In his *Existential Foundations of Medicine and Psychology,* Medard Boss begins to articulate the unfolding of this cosmological extension, starting out from the most familiar kind of situation and gesturing, in three phases, into the expansiveness of the world-field. It is worth paying attention to the succession of manoeuvers by means of which he points our awareness into the cosmological dimension of being-in-touch. I have introduced numbers into the text in order to clarify the phases of his extension:

> When I direct someone toward a windowsill with a
> gesture of my right hand, my bodily existence as
> a human being does not end [1] at the tip of my
> index finger. While perceiving the windowsill . . .
> [2] I extend myself bodily far beyond this fingertip
> to that windowsill. In fact, bodily [3] I reach out
> even further than this to touch all the phenomena
> of my world, present or merely visualized re-
> presented ones. . . .[28]

136

(This formulation parallels the one Heidegger makes in 'Building Dwelling Thinking,'[29] where he repudiates the view that we are nothing but 'encapsulated bodies' standing and moving in a space to be defined by Euclidean geometry and Newtonian physics.)

How far do we try to reach? What is the extent of our capacity to be touched? By what compass are we moved? Does the beauty of the stars reach into the heart? Is a deeper sense of the immeasurable vastness in which we move able to *enrich* our gestures? Would our gestures, enriched by this sense, finally begin to bring forth, then, a new astrology, a new astronomy, a new physics, a new geometry, a new mathematics, a new cosmology? And might we not also reach a better understanding of how we mortals could dwell more harmoniously with one another? Extending our gestures into the sky above, into the cosmological field that opens up beyond that and into the dimension of greatest enchantment, rejoicing with uplifted arms like the magicians of ancient Palestine, we hold ourselves open for the wisdom so powerful that it can touch us only from afar. And who can say how, in our time, the gestures of mortals might build a future world, a new social order, if, at long last, they were deeply rooted in the cosmological field and could receive some wisdom from the mystery of its laws?

Section 5   Lending a Hand to Being

if one is not firm and brave within oneself, one has nothing to bestow and cannot stretch out one's hand to protect and support.

Friedrich Nietzsche, *The Will to Power*[30]

Wherever he touches, it becomes a work of art; whatsoever he says becomes poetry. His very movement is aesthetic. If you can see a Buddha walking, [you will notice that] even his walking is creativity; even through his walking he is creating a rhythm, even through his walking he is creating a milieu, an atmosphere around him. If a Buddha raises his hand he changes the climate around him immediately.

Bhagwan Shree Rajneesh,
*Only One Sky: On the Tantric Way
of Tilopa's Song of Mahamudra*[31]

It is one's own spiritual nature in enlightenment

that responds to the 'external' world, comes into contact with objects, raises the eyebrows, winks the eyelids, and moves the hands and legs.

Suzuki Daisetz, *Essays in Zen Buddhism*[32]

In 'The Turning,' Heidegger asserts that,

thinking is genuine activity, genuine taking a hand, if to take a hand means to lend a hand to . . . the coming to presence of Being.[33]

I would like to focus our reflection, here, on the gesture named by this text. Perhaps our efforts will be rewarded with the gradual emergence of a new body of understanding. What I would like to consider, first of all, is the way that lending a hand, as a gesture in which we are both active and passive, simultaneously giving and receiving, utterly defies re-presentation within the dualistic framework of metaphysics. When we genuinely lend a hand, we transcend the skin of our ego. The ego-logical structure of subject and object can be abolished as it has been initiated – by a gesture of the hand.

In his chapter on 'The Body as Expression, and Speech,' Merleau–Ponty argues that 'speech puts up a new sense, if it is authentic speech, just as gesture endows the object for the first time with human significance, if it is an initiating gesture.'[34] But when is a gesture *most fully actualizing* its truth as 'initiating'? I would like to suggest that 'lending a hand to Being' is a helpful answer to this question.

'Lending a hand' is also an answer to the 'Question of Being': an answer, I believe, which serves a need of our time. The 'Question of Being' motivates a shift in our focus, and from the point of its dislocation, it calls our gesturing into question. It questions our motivation; it touches us in our innermost being and deeply moves us; it moves us to recollect the true dimensionality of our gestural being. The Question is hermeneutical; it formulates the 'ontological difference' as a difference between our gesturing in the forgetfulness of our ontical everydayness and an ontologically deepened gesturing which is mindful of the tangible givenness of Being. It formulates, therefore, a task, which challenges us to take the measure of our gesturing by situating our motility within the immeasurable dimensionality of the sensori-motor field of Being as a whole. It invites us to extend our awareness of the fact that every gesture we make takes place within the clearing of this field. It invites us to meditate on what this placement means to us. But the thinking it invites is no longer the intellectualizing which typifies our metaphysical tradition; rather, it is an effort to remain in contact with the presencing of Being as a whole by virtue of a thoughtfulness continually bodied forth through our posture, stance, gait, stride, and gesturing.

Our gestural capacities bear within their motility an ingrained destiny: a bodily sensed potential we are called upon to make our own. And we appropriately own up to 'destiny' as we begin to realize the extent of our commitment to the maintenance of Being. The thoughtful maintenance of beings, moving out of respect for their ownmost, and even their most intangible ways of being, never fails to lend a hand to the coming-to-presence of Being. There are many ways to lend a hand to Being. What is, perhaps, essential is only that our gesturing toward beings – for example, our touching, handling, pointing, and writing – *hold beings open* to the field of their being: that we relate to the various beings of our world in a way that *maintains* their contact, and our own, with the primordial clearing of space that let them, and us, first meet in the enchantment of presence.

Now, we have already observed that lending a hand to Being initiates a process in the gestural field which can only be understood, according to the indispensable categories of our tradition, as a movement that is simultaneously active and passive. The 'passive' character of the process consists in the fact that this is a gesture which is moved by its sense of belonging (*Zugehörigkeit*), moved by its attunement (*Stimmung*) to the sensori-motor field as a whole. The gesture is a movement which holds itself open to the felt orchestrations of the field. It is a gesture which is receptive to the solicitations of the field and moves in response to this guidance. Such a gesture is no longer initiated by the metaphysical ego; it is a manifestation or articulation of Being itself, and emerges from the gestural field as a whole. Such a gesture lends a hand to Being by maintaining a tact which lets the field as such determine its movement, its purpose, its goal, its trajectory.

But lending a hand must also be described in terms of its 'active' character. Considered in these terms, the gesture is one which is committed to a hermeneutical disclosure of the gestural field *as* a dimension of Being. Such a gesture lends a hand to Being by moving in a way that maintains for the community of mortals a moving recollection of the sensori-motor field *as* that gift of Being by grace of which our gestures first become possible. In its 'active' role, then, our lending a hand to Being is a question of gesturing in a way that continually lets the field as such be present – present, I mean, as that clearing by grace of whose attunements and orchestrations the gesturing is enabled, or empowered, to be. In this sense, therefore, we lend a hand to Being to the extent that our gestures are able to make explicit the ontological truth that is generally concealed by our consensually validated reality: the truth, namely, that what fulfills our hands is an awareness that they belong (*gehört*), in the end, not to 'us,' but to the intactness of Being. Lending a hand with every single gesture we make is our only way of rejoicing and giving thanks for this grace. Lending a hand may be writing to communicate the grace of Being in the gestural field.

Section 6   The Implicit *Legein* of Our Motility

I want to argue, here, that Heidegger's interpretation of the Heraklitean *legein* is confirmed by our motility – that if we cultivate a phenomenologically vigilant awareness in our motility, we will eventually encounter the *implicit* (ontical) *legein* which has always and already defined the (ontical) character of our gestures and movements. Merleau–Ponty will be extremely helpful in establishing the phenomenological evidence for this hermeneutical demonstration. My strategy for using his work to this purpose consists of two steps: first we will push his method of radical reflection (which is, as I have already argued, a stage of 'recollection') into the dimension of our experience where we can encounter the primordial layout, the matrix and *logos* of our motility; then, second, we will explore this layout until we can find the entrance into the ontological *depths* of this field: depths where, as we shall argue, the layout which Merleau–Ponty has articulated may be finally identified with the primordial *Logos* – that which Heidegger calls Being as such.

According to Merleau–Ponty, the human being enjoys 'a global bodily knowledge which systematically embraces all its parts.'[35] I take this to mean that we enjoy a body-knowledge which functions as an integrating, unifying 'gathering' – in other words, as a *legein*. Furthermore, we are obliged to acknowledge that our embodiment is also organized around a *second* 'gathering.' For this innate 'gesture' of physiognomic integration, a spontaneous functioning of the body which is *concealed* in the ontical understandings of both common sense and our various objective sciences, even touches and embraces *the motility-field as a whole*, and is, in fact, a 'gathering' of the *field*, since it is clear, for example, that 'we can, in recollection, touch an object with parts of our body which have never actually been in contact with it.'[36] In his critique of empiricism and intellectualism, Merleau–Ponty observes that the gesturing of my hand 'is not [intelligible as] a collection of points.'[37] What this means is that a series of points along a linear trajectory cannot accurately graph the topology of even my simplest gesture. The truth of the matter is that, as he says, 'Each instant of the movement embraces its whole span. . . .'[38] It is the concept of gathering, then, and not the concept of points, which graphs the human gesture. (In passing, let us note Merleau–Ponty's use of the word 'embrace.' This word, which appears twice, is a hermetic trace of the presence of immortal Eros.) As he reflects on the observations which record the fate of Schneider, a patient suffering from serious motor disorder as a result of lesions damaging the brain, Merleau–Ponty begins to *see* what Schneider's gestures lack and what 'normal' gestures enjoy, namely, a certain style of movement, a certain deeply implicit 'melody.'[39] And he calls this 'melody' an 'intentional arc': 'It is this intentional arc which brings about the unity of the senses, of intelligence, of sensibility and motility.'[40]

Now the point I wish to make is that this 'melody,' this 'intentional arc', is to be disclosed in its deeper truth as a *gathering* and *laying-down*. Concealed within every gesture and movement we make, there is an implicit ontical *legein* which is always and already engaged in (i) laying down an encompassing field of motility, (ii) gathering up the compass of the field into a focal, purposive trajectory, and (iii) gathering the gesture itself into a unified, intelligible whole. This *legein* of the gesture (the *logos*) is not normally experienced with much awareness. For this reason, Merleau–Ponty wants to characterize the deeper experiencing of the melody as taking place, *during the gesture*, in a prepersonal or anonymous level of awareness. But his phenomenological work unquestionably demonstrates that it is possible for reflection to elicit this concealed *sense* of the body's motility and retrieve the truth (*alētheia*) of this awareness. (I would like to remind the reader that the etymology of our word, 'awareness,' connects it with the German words *Wahr*, *Wahrnis*, and *gewahren*.)

Of course, our *use* of 'radical reflection' in order to recollect (i.e., re-collect and gather up) the inherent *legein* of our motility is a step of decisive importance. Nevertheless, both Heidegger's Question of Being and Merleau–Ponty's method of radical reflection pressure us to go *still more deeply* into the truth of our motility. For the Question of Being reminds us that we need to bring to light the essential *relationship* between the character of the mortal *Legein* and the primordial *Legein* of the *Logos*. It reminds us that we need to understand the *relationship* between the gathering and laying-down that are characteristic of the gestures of *mortals* and the gathering and laying-down of the *Logos* itself. And it reminds us of this relationship *in order to challenge us* to continue deepening the reach and range of our experience of motility *as* an awareness of Being. By the same token, Merleau–Ponty's method of radical reflection will not come happily to rest in the hermeneutical disclosing of the melodic arc of intentionality. By virtue of its persistent 'radicality,' a 'reflection altogether more radical than objective thought,' it too challenges us to go more deeply into the experienced nature, or being, of human motility.[41] It thus becomes feasible to continue our ontological path of thinking with the help of Merleau–Ponty's method of radical reflection.

Section 7   Motility and the More Primordial *Legein*

Going still more deeply into the felt experience of gesturing and moving, we find ourselves 'returning' to a still more primordial 'stratum' of corporeal intentionalities that, even without our awareness, are always already functioning. Going beyond Merleau–Ponty's account, but still using his method of radical reflection, we eventually encounter a dimension of our motility-experience in which it is possible for us to realize the thorough-going, on-going 'interaction' – one might even say the 'interpenetration' or 'interweaving' – of the immeasurable *Legein* of the primordial *Logos* and the measured *legein* of our own mortal motility. Putting this in other words, I will argue that there is a dimension of our motility-being where, if we are sufficiently open to experiencing it, we can reach an implicit awareness of the truly primordial *Legein* as it touches our flesh, takes hold of our embodiment, outlines for us its measure, and lays claim to our motivation. Merleau–Ponty argues that, 'We must return to the *cogito* in search of a more fundamental *Logos* than that of objective thought.'[42] We can, and must, make the attempt to trace 'objective being' to its rootedness, its inherence, in a 'pre-objective' being: a 'pre-logical' dimension of our experienced embodiment that is to be found and retrieved by a reflection that parts company with the subjectivity of the *ego cogito* and its co-emergent object in order to recollect, 'beneath the subject,' a more primordial, anonymous structuration, a more original dynamism, a 'prepersonal tradition.'[43] This radicalized reflection is necessary because both common sense and its reflection in the objective sciences tend to lose touch with the more open experience that always underlies them. Thus, when I 'think,' I *reduce* the field of my being, whereas, 'when I perceive, I belong, through my point of view, to the world as a whole.'[44] Recollecting this belongingness, this 'gathering' inherence in the world as a whole, we regain for our gestures a lost dimension of significance.

According to Merleau–Ponty,

> My personal existence must be the resumption of a prepersonal tradition. There is, therefore, another subject beneath me, for whom a world exists before I am here, and who *marks out my place* in it. This captive or natural spirit is my body, not that momentary body which is the instrument of my personal choices and which fastens upon this or that world, but the system of anonymous 'functions' which *draw every particular focus into a general project.*[45]

Thus we discover that there is 'a communication with the world more ancient than thought,'[46] a *legein* which has always and already 'marked out' for us, as a general project, the place and the field of our motility. The fact is that the prepersonal body-subject is itself already functioning as a *legein*, anonymously gathering the motility-field into a pre-ego-logical center. And yet, from the standpoint of our personal life, our life as it is ruled over by the ego, the prepersonal existence that precedes it is a condition of dispersal lacking a true center. The ego's story, therefore, is that no true gathering and centering can take place until the emergence of an ego-body with a personal life. There is an important sense, we must admit, in which this story is true. In any case, what Merleau–Ponty says is this:

> This anonymous life is merely the extreme form of that temporal *dispersal* which constantly threatens the historical present. In order to have some inkling of the nature of that amorphous existence which preceded my own history, and which will bring it to a close, I have only to look within me at that time which pursues its own independent course, and which my personal life utilizes but does not entirely *overlay*. Because I am borne into personal existence by a time which I do not constitute, all my perceptions stand out against a background of nature. While I perceive, and even without having any knowledge of the organic conditions of my perception, I am aware of *drawing together* somewhat absent-minded and dispersed 'consciousnesses': sight, hearing and touch, with their fields, which are anterior, and remain alien, to my personal life.[47]

I want to say that all the 'gatherings' of which we are capable – those that take place at the prepersonal level and those taking place at the personal level – essentially depend on the even more primordial layout and gathering of the *Logos* itself. The *Legein* of the *Logos* enters into a primordial communication with us through the *legein* of our prepersonally organized motility. Its primordial gathering of our 'temporally dispersed consciousness' takes place in the darkness of anonymity. And it always underlies the gatherings which take place in the prepersonal field and in the ego-logical consciousness of our personal life. But the gatherings of our personal life are ruled over by the ego, which overlays the primordial contact between the *Legein* of the *Logos* and the *legein* of the prepersonal field: overlays it, that is, in a way which both conceals it and restricts it. It is possible, however, to penetrate this ego-logical masking and make contact, in a more fulfilling sense, with the underlying *Legein*.

Presencing in our world as the gathering layout, by grace of which we may enjoy a space of freedom in which to move, the *Logos* serves, as Merleau–Ponty says of space, 'to embrace every being that one can imagine.'[48] (It is in this sense, i.e., as gathering and embracing, that the primordial *Logos* may be identified with the archetypal symbols of the immortal Eros.) The *Legein* of the *Logos* is a 'universal setting,' granting our motility a basic (con)text and syntax. It lays down an organized field of co-ordinates and trajectories; it orients our movements to the possibilities of our world; it anchors and aligns the body; finally, it offers itself as a sort of 'corporeal schema' to orchestrate and choreograph the *sense* of our motility:

> The word 'here' applied to my body does not refer to a determinate position in relation to other positions or to external co-ordinates, but the laying-down of the first co-ordinates, the anchoring of the active body in an object, the situation of the body in the face of its tasks.[49]

For Merleau–Ponty,

> To have senses, sight for example, is to possess that general setting, that framework of potential, visual-type relations with the help of which we are able to take up any visual grouping. To have a body is to possess a universal setting, a schema of all types of perceptual unfolding and of all those inter-sensory correspondences which lie beyond the segment of the world which we are actually perceiving.[50]

The *Legein* of the *Logos* is accordingly to be called the 'origin' of our world-space: it is that ek-static topology, that elemental inscription of a 'primordial field,'[51] by grace of which it first becomes feasible for us to find our bearings and move about in the spaciousness of our world.

> Everything throws us back onto the organic relations between subject and space, to that gearing of the subject to his world which is the origin of space.[52]

In our bearing, therefore, insofar as it is a bearing of thought, we carry with us, and translate into appropriate action, the gathering of the primordial *Logos*.

This, in sum, is how the gathering-and-laying-down of the

Logos presences – and works – within the motility-field of our experience.

Section 8   Transpersonal Gatherings

Opening Conversation

(1)   My personal existence must be the resumption of *a prepersonal tradition*. There is, therefore, another subject beneath me, for whom a world exists before I am here, and who marks out my place in it. This captive or natural spirit is my body. . . . Space and perception generally represent, at the core of the subject . . . a *communication with the world more ancient than thought*.

Merleau–Ponty, *Phenomenology of Perception*[53]

(2)   We are a movement of a hand within millions of seasons. . . .

Hyemeyohsts Storm, *Seven Arrows*[54]

(3)   You don't make much money if you work with your hands. You can't make the turnover. But I have no regrets working so slowly. I began in a world without time.

Horry Rose, Saddler[55]

(4)   the hours I could pass in Rome watching a rope-maker who in his craft repeated one of the oldest gestures in the world . . . exactly like that potter in a little Nile village, to stand beside whose wheel was, in a most mysterious sense, indescribably fruitful for me.

Rainer Maria Rilke[56]

(5)   I have a lot of my grandfather's features, although I'm not as tall as he was. I have his hands. Hands last a long time, you know. A village sees the same hands century after century.

Gregory Gladwell, Blacksmith[57]

(6)   My wife went round, keeping her eye open for bolts, latches, handles, grates; drawing them and finding out their dates, and I made more of them as exactly as you're not likely to tell the difference. Mind you, it took time. It took hours. But it was a fine thing for me to have something lying on the

bench before me made by one of the old men,
and my hands doing again what his had done.
Gregory Gladwell[58]

(7) I have a very clear, keen memory of myself the day
after I was married: I was sweeping the floor.
Probably the floor did not really need to be swept;
probably I simply did not know what else to do
with myself. But as I swept that floor I thought:
'Now I am a woman. This is an age-old action,
this is what women have always done.' I felt I was
bending to some ancient form, too ancient to
question. *This is what women have always done.*
Adrienne Rich, *Of Woman Born*[59]

(8) You, my friend, are lonely, because. . . .
We with words and finger-pointings,
gradually make the world our own, perhaps its
weakest, most precarious part.
Rainer Maria Rilke, *Sonnets to Orpheus*[60]

(9) On Attic steles, did not the circumspection
of human gesture amaze you? Were not love and
farewell
so lightly laid upon the shoulders, they seemed to
be made
of other stuff than with us?
Rilke, *Duino Elegies*[61]

(10) their hands extended in gestures out of the dreams
of men.
W. S. Merwin, 'The Songs of the Icebergs'[62]

In *Beyond the Pleasure Principle*, Freud speaks to us of 'Eros,
the preserver of all things.'[63] According to Freud, 'the Eros
of the poets and philosophers [is that] which holds all living
things together.'[64] Thus, where Eros is at work, we will
encounter a movement to 'combine organic substances into
ever larger unities.'[65] Now, I have already noted the symbolic
identity of the *Logos*: since the gathering of the *Logos* is, in
essence, the gesture of embrace, the gesture which brings
together, receives, and welcomes, the *Logos* to which the
thinker attunes his listening is the *same* as the hermetic Eros
of which the poet forever sings. This identification suggests
that we have been right all along in focusing our attention
on the body of feeling, or more specifically, on our *felt sense*

147

of gesture and motility, as a way of articulating the emergence of a new body of ontological understanding.

In 'The Question Concerning Technology,' Heidegger
himself, in fact, connects his sense of the 'gathering' with
the question of our sensibility, our 'moodedness' and 'attunement.' As is his wont, he makes the contact through etymology, a science which is itself concerned with gathering: the
gathering of all word-stems which derive from the same root-
word near the origin. What Heidegger actually says is that,

> The original gathering from which unfold the ways
> in which we have feelings of one kind or another
> we name 'Gemüt.'[66]

The original word, *ge*, seems to bear the sense of 'gathering.'
From the standpoint of our embodiment, I translate this to
mean that the 'original gathering' is the gesture of the *Logos*
in which our body of feeling, the body of our ontological
pre-understanding (i.e., our pre-ontological understanding),
is always already rooted. But, if this be so, then the evolution
of our humanity consists in a rooting of the gestures of our
body of feeling (i.e., the gestures 'made' by this body) in the
gesture of the original gathering. What Heidegger says is
that, 'To be human means to take gathering upon oneself.'[67]
But, as we have seen, this gathering is the gesture by which
we must recognize the presence of immortal Eros. Therefore,
it is appropriate for us to continue the passage which
Heidegger begins by considering the claim that to be human
means to take upon oneself the careful work of Eros.

On a less symbolic level, what I suggest this means is that
the fulfillment of our capacity for becoming more fully human
depends upon, and calls for, *a body of feeling whose gestures
are gestures of love* – of caring, of solicitude, of compassion,
of loving kindness. To be human is to take upon oneself the
challenge and commitment of a new body of understanding:
one which is *rooted* at long last in an open and attuned
sensibility (our pre-conceptual pre-understanding of Being)
and in whose gestures this understanding is *brought together*
with the careful work of Eros. Our essential humanity
consists in gestures of gathering, gestures of loving embrace:
gestures which unfold their contact with all beings from out
of their contactful attunement to the original gathering, the
gesture of our encompassment by which the primordial *Logos*

manifests (in the symbolic language of theology) the presence of its 'universal love.'

But Eros works in many different dimensions: (i) the gathering and laying-down of *a primordial field* (where, of course, it is identified with the *Legein* of the *Logos*); (ii) the *prepersonal* gathering, where it is at work in the darkness of anonymity and unconsciousness; (iii) the *personal-interpersonal* gathering, where its work is centered in an ego-logically structured world; and (iv) the gathering of a *transpersonal* field where it develops the preceding gathering (the personal one) beyond its inveterately limited reach by retrieving the *more extensive* gathering which has always taken place already in the *prepersonal* field of our sensibility, our moodedness (our *Gemüt*, our *Stimmung*). The gathering which takes place in the prepersonal field is determined by our moodedness, our belonging attunement-to-the-whole; its contact is pervasive, its extension vast. For, it is in the essential character of our sensibility to desire intactness and wholeness and universality . . . and also tactful community. However, it must be conceded that the gatherings in this field are without (a body of) awareness and understanding. Thus we must conclude that our entrance into the transpersonal dimension of Being takes place when our gathering begins to embody the character of our *prepersonal* sensibility, and of course the pre-ontological understanding it bears, in a gesture whose vast extension is related to the emergence of a deeper awareness and understanding. For the moment, we shall concentrate on the gestural gatherings which take place in a transpersonal field.

The textual passages which open this section of our meditations on gesture are highly instructive. The saddler makes contact with a timeless world; because he works out of his centeredness in love, his hands work in a world without time. His hands gather in the timeless. The blacksmith also works with love, and his hands become one with the hands of many generations of his village's smithies. His hands gather into themselves the hands of ancient craft. So perhaps the loneliness of Rilke's friend is related in some way to the difficulty of belonging to the transpersonal field. Rilke's *Elegy* emphasizes, certainly, the discontinuities, the moments of isolation and segregation, which make such belonging a difficulty. But he also speaks of gestures of tactful embrace, gestures that gather in love and farewell. And he speaks as one enchanted by the living presence of these gestures carved in stone. Thus, we come to Merwin, another poet, who sings of the dream, reminds us to dream. He gathers us into the song of his understanding, reminding us that the material of the transpersonal matrix is the same as the stuff of our dreams. All the opening texts, then, evoke a gesture of gathering, a gesture in the hands of Eros, an extension of our humanity taking place in a transpersonal field of existence.

Now, what defines this field? Let us consider, as a beginning, two lines from *Proverbs* 31:

> She stretches out her hand to the poor;
> She reaches out her arms to the needy.

These lines call attention to traditional gestures of the women in our culture. They are focused on the *gestures* which model virtues of character, gestures strong in the virtue of solicitude – gestures moved by the needs of others and moving freely for the sake of others. Although the lines are specifically intended to formulate an ideal schematization, a standard, for the gestural being of the woman, I would like the words to provide a basis for some more general consideration of how all mortals, we in the time of our dwelling, could touch more enrichingly upon the lives of others. In the reading I would like to propose, the lines would say that every mortal who continues these gestures continues the influence of a transpersonal field on the moral life of a culture; they would say that every mortal who maintains these gestures, moved in tactful regard for the preserve of all beings who may appear in the world, takes a hand in a gathering of the transpersonal field.

But why does our reading of these lines make them situate these gestures in a transpersonal dimension? Are we denying that the gestures are personal? Certainly not. It is *always* as a deeply felt *personal* gesture that one participates in the transpersonal field. Would it not be sufficient, however, to say that what is in question are *personal* gestures taking place in an *interpersonal*, or *social* world? I think not. After all, we must recognize that the discourse in which these gestures are evoked takes part in the theodicy of *The Old Testament*. In a theological text, our gestures must surely be considered from the standpoint of eternity. The social world of interpersonal relationships is essentially constituted by gestures that are more limited in their reach and range.

In the lines from *Proverbs*, the hand is stretched out to the poor of all times and all places: not only to the living, but even to the poor who are dead and the poor not yet born. The hand in question is stretched out in a *repetition* of an archetypal gesture, a gesture whose original belongs to the body of the collective unconscious, guardian of the realm of the spirit – which means that it is also stretched out *beyond the present*, to serve as an example for all the generations of mortals who will be coming into this world poor in the wisdom of love and compassion. Likewise, the arm which reaches out to the needy through the words of this text reaches out beyond the measure of our consensually validated reality. In fact, there are many ways in which the reach of this gesture goes beyond the horizons of our social world. It reaches out, for example, in a responsiveness to historical needs so deeply repressed, or so deeply misunderstood, that they are not even recognized as needs until the gesture has reached them and brought them out with its kindness. And it reaches out to communicate with all the beings of the ocean and all the beings of the sky, taking care of *their* needs, too. And inasmuch as even the plants are present in their ecological need, the reach of this gesture naturally extends itself to the needs that are manifest in the realm of vegetation.

The most crucial fact for our discernment of the transpersonal field is, I think, that genuine participation in this field begins by virtue of a personal commitment to developing the body of awareness and understanding whose potential is already implicit in our belonging to a *prepersonal* field of existence. Here I must point out that Merleau–Ponty lucidly articulates the nature of the prepersonal field, but he neglects the dialectical spirit in his own methodology, and fails to realize that, when the nature of our existence in this field is taken up into reflective consciousness, we inevitably undergo a certain transformation, a certain modulation, in our awareness. (Self-reflection always changes the person engaged in that kind of a process.) He therefore also fails to realize that the character of our prepersonal existence holds within it a potentiality-for-being which holds us open to a richer, more extensive world, and that our entrance into this dimension is a question of our commitment to developing that potential.

What defines the spirit of gestures in the transpersonal field of awareness is the fact that there is a commitment to maintaining a body of contact with the modes of responsiveness, openness and attunement that function much more spontaneously in the dimension of the prepersonal field than in the field normally constituted by our merely personal life.

151

Whereas our personal life is normally restricted by the identifications to which the ego is attached, our prepersonal life is not yet restricted by an ego's conditions. Gestures taking place in the transpersonal field have contacted the more open sensibility of the prepersonal field and let go of the ego's barriers. (By way of the prepersonal field, 'I am already,' says Merleau–Ponty, 'in communication with others.')[68] Touched by the pervasive communicativeness of the field, by its spontaneously reciprocal acknowledgments of kinship, these gestures have retrieved its synergies for the needs of daily living, and continue the 'participation mystique' by letting themselves be moved by its finer attunements.

What further defines the spirit of gestures in the transpersonal field is the felt sense of a deep continuum, and of a pervasive orchestration of harmonies, through which such gestures are tuned and moved. Just as the *prepersonal* field is a field of sensibility organized by the flowing and intertwining of emotionally toned energies, so the *transpersonal* field, where these energies need to be fulfilled, is a field of responsibility in which interdependencies are freely acknowledged, and pervasive responsiveness and reciprocity prevail; a field whose gestures are governed by a deeply felt sense of the interpenetrating currents of communicativeness which underlie our collective being, always circulating among us in the field of our most fundamental moodedness and already gathering us together into the dream of a universal community.

Our entrance into the transpersonal field is therefore of the greatest *ontological* significance. The awareness and understanding which define the character of gestures in this field are necessary *preparations* for the emergence of gestures even more openly attuned, even more responsive, to the tactful clearing of our way that is the original gift of Being. The hermeneutical openness of the ontological gesture requires a long and arduous preparation. I submit that some of this preparation needs to take place in the transpersonal field, where our gestures have learned to communicate, through the field, with the gestures of other times and places, learned to be touched from afar, learned to overcome the ontological anxiety which keeps us in a solipsism of the ego, learned to move in a more open responsiveness and attunement to the presencing of beings, learned the ecstasy in a continuous extension of that fundamental *ek-stasis* which

Heidegger calls *Dasein*'s 'Care' and Freud, our immortal 'Eros'.

We have already considered, in our section on technology, how our more careful gestures get in touch more deeply, and more fulfillingly, with the being, or presence, of the things we handle. The things we handle will always *reciprocate* the treatment they receive in our hands. Thus, when our gestures become very caring, they *receive back* from the things we have handled with care a much deeper disclosure of their ontological truth. The same may be said of our gestural involvements with other people. We are surely familiar, all of us, with the fact that our gestures of love and kindness invariably constitute an interpersonal space in which people spontaneously *open up*, freely *reciprocating* those gestures by sharing more deeply of themselves. I take this to be evidence that the gestures inhabited by Eros gather more deeply, more extensively, from the immeasurable reserve of beings. Gestures of love and kindness bring us closer to other sentient beings; thus, through gestures of this character, we come closer to experiencing the beautiful truth of their spiritual being.

This phenomenon explains the significance of the transpersonal field for the emergence of a radically new body: our body of ontological understanding. But I would like, nonetheless, to reformulate my argument in another way. When our awareness and understanding have reached a place in their unfolding where we can begin to experience ourselves as participating in the continuum of a transpersonal field, a field of synchronicities, interdependencies, and intertwining, interpenetrating existences, it seems to me that our capacity for loving and caring undergoes a very radical shift in its openness-to-beings. What this means, of course, is that our gestures will be correspondingly *moved* by their sense of belonging to such a field. But, as the gestures are centered in a deeper, more thoughtful caring and moved by a deeper, more expansive love, the gathering of beings brought forth in response will take place in a reciprocity deep enough to open up a vast new field, full of mystery, for our maintenance of the Being of beings.

I am hopeful that the account we have just completed succeeds in clarifying this question of maintenance without reducing our sense of the mystery. It is very sad that, in our present epoch, the power of technology continues to expand,

while the field of spiritual wisdom is being increasingly
closed off.

Section 9 Gesturing Recollection

There is a need for those who will sanctify all activities,
not only eating and drinking – and not merely in
remembrance of them and to become one with them, but
this world must be transfigured ever anew and in new
ways.

Friedrich Nietzsche, *The Will to Power*[69]

Our being-in-time cannot be understood without giving
thought to the body. Our sciences assert that memory is
stored in the body. Whatever the validity in their claims, we
do know from our own (phenomenological) experience that
traces of memory are borne by our body's unconsciousness,
and that these traces can speak to us of our past through our
retrieval and clarification (articulation, explicition) of our
body of feeling and sensibility. Thus, we understand at once
the communication which Jean Cocteau wrote into his diary.
In this communication, Cocteau writes of the time when he
returned to the village where he spent his childhood and
found that he was able, trailing his finger along a wall familiar
to him as a young boy, to retrieve that past so dear to his
heart, to feel it once again, and be touched by its most
sensuous element:

> Just as the needle picks up the melody of the record,
> I obtained the melody of the past with my hand.
> I found everything: my cape, the leather of my
> satchel, the names of my friends and my teachers,
> certain expressions I had used, the sound of my
> grandfather's voice, the smell of his beard, the
> smell of my sister's dresses, and my mother's
> gown.[70]

In this example, it is the poet's finger, and not the brain or
the mind, which retrieves the memory. The finger retrieves
the trace of his memory by retracing its original gesture, its
original articulation, in a touching of the wall. Now memory,
understood as recollection, is *always* (i.e., essentially) a gathering and collecting.[71] For Cocteau, an entire childhood past
is gathered, intact, into the centeredness of a living present;

and it is gathered in the deeply felt contact of a gesture of gathering. There is love in the repeating gesture, and the gathering in this love extends itself to embrace the gathering and recollecting of the trace. Thanks to the gesture of his finger, gathering a deeply felt experience, he is able to remain in touch with his distant past.

I have begun the reflections in this section with the poet's report, because I want to take such memory for granted as the basis for the next steps in our interpretation of gesture as a hermeneutical movement. Even when Cocteau's experience is recognized, however, the next step requires a leap of thought. We need to understand, therefore, that only the passage through personal experience can make the step compelling.

The difficult step consists in recognizing that Heidegger's recollection of the history of Being *can* be undertaken – and, in fact, if our old metaphysics is to be deconstructed successfully, then it certainly *needs* to be undertaken – as a recollection which questions the body's experience of Being and retrieves the moments of that history from the stages of development through which our body of pre-ontological understanding has been destined to pass in the time of its dwelling.

The point I want to make with the help of Cocteau's experience of recollection is that, since the body always carries for us a pre-ontological experience of Being (i.e., an ontological pre-understanding of Being), the process of undoing our forgetfulness-of-Being (our *Seinsvergessenheit*) *needs* to involve, and *can* very fruitfully involve, a retrieval of this body of primordial experience, *as well as* the strictly intellectual recollection of the history of Being which, as we know, engaged Heidegger. I am arguing not only for a possibility, but also for a need. Just as thinking calls for a recollection of *concepts* of Being to overcome a history of Being that is reflected in the history of our metaphysics, so it must eventually call for *embodiments* of recollection that will reverse our inveterate tendency to *fall in line* with the ontological commands of our technologized world and *lose touch* with the primordial *Legein* of Being, whose elemental choreography is always already orchestrating our motility within the space first opened up by its clearing.

If philosophical *concepts* of Being are rooted in our *experience*-of-Being, and our experience-of-Being resides in a body whose perceptivity, sensibility, and motoric capacities are primordially attuned by Being, then the philosophical deconstruction of metaphysics needs to be, and just as surely can be, accompanied by a corresponding process, taking place in the fields of our embodiment.

Merleau–Ponty's method of reflection exactly fits our needs. Practised in its radicality, this method is a genuine *anamnēsis*, a genuine recollection of Being, in the sense that (i) it is concerned with our returning to an *a priori* 'knowledge,' namely, that which, *from the very first*, we have *always and already* been given to understand (i.e., a pre-conceptual, pre-ontological understanding of our mortal being in its relatedness-to-Being-as-a-whole), and (ii) it is concerned with our capacity to recollect *the presencing of Being*, i.e., the experience which Plato wanted to call a 'vision' of the forms. Heidegger's recollection takes the form of a reading of the history of Being. But his recollection does not involve the body. To that extent, it perpetuates the very metaphysics it sets out to deconstruct. (Even Plato, after all, acknowledged the need to inaugurate the recollective process by working with the body's appreciation of beauty.)

The method of radical reflection makes it possible for *our motility itself* to become the *route* of our recollection of Being. But it must be understood that the key to the workability of this method as a process of recollection is to be found in our body of feeling and sensibility. This is the body which reverberates to the 'claim of Being.' This is the body which is kept in attunement by a primordial orchestration of that claim. This is the body to whose guardian awareness (*Wahrnehmung*) Being lays claim by laying out a primordial field for its moodedness.

Heidegger contends that recollection is:

> the listening response which belongs to the claim
> of Being, as determination attuned by the voice of
> that claim. . . . Recollection of the history of Being
> returns to the claim of the soundless voice of Being
> and to the manner of its attuning.[72]

I submit that the claim of Being claims us first, and claims us foremost, in the dimension of our capacity for feeling, i.e., in the dimension of our body's primordial attunement. Since we are always *touched* by the claim through our body of feeling, the process of recollection must at some stage be channeled through our bodily felt *sense* of the meaning inherent in the claim. By consenting to work through our felt sense of the gesturing in virtue of which the character of our existence is bodied forth, the process of recollection can make contact with a primordial wisdom, a guardian awareness of Being that is preserved in the body of our collective unconscious. Recollecting this wisdom, gathering it up for the caring of our everyday life, we bring back for the joy of our days the experience of being gathered into the centeredness of Being's compass. Thus, with *every* gesture we make, and not only with the gesture of our most memorable moments, we can experience the gathering of a recollection like Cocteau's. And, with every gesture we make, we could experience a gathering even deeper, and more far-reaching in its historical significance, than the gathering that responded to the poet's need and healed his painful loss.

Section 10   The *Homologein*

Isan kicked over the pitcher. So wonderful is his Zen that every movement of his foot and hand is shining with the truth.
      Shibayama Zenkei, *Zen Comments on the Mumonkan*[73]

Legein is rooted in *apophainesthai*, to bring forward into appearance. . . .
      Heidegger, 'The Question Concerning Technology'[74]

The *gift* (the 'Es gibt') of the *Logos* is: the laying out of a clearing and the gathering of a continuous field. And the *receiving* of this gift takes place in the anonymous, prepersonal dimension where our motility first makes contact with the topology of the *Logos*. But the giving of this gift *lays claim* to our motility – a claim we may well feel a need to redeem by recognition and guardian awareness. We can, as it were, redeem our beholdenness (our *Schuldigkeit*) insofar as we disclosively re-collect the original *Legein*, now overlaid by the paths of our forgetfulness, gathering up into the time of our own re-membering that by the grace of which our motility was first enable to become, itself, a laying-down of co-ordinates and a coherent gathering of motivating energy. Through the grace in the re-membering, a turbulent and fragmented body is gathered up into its felt wholeness.
      The primordial laying-down-and-gathering-of-a-field, i.e., the effective presencing of the *Logos* in our world, sets mortal

beings in motion. But if our thinking is deeply moved by the Question of Being, then it responds by setting in motion a process of recollection. This process *opens* us to the claim on our motility that has *already* been implicitly acknowledged by our body's guardian awareness. The claim of the *Logos calls* for our articulation; it calls for a response from our own mortal *legein*. With the concept of the *homologein*, our re-membering responds to this claim, and it gathers our still undeveloped pre-ontological capacities for motility into the melodic wholeness of their most appropriate ontological fulfillment.

Our everyday forms of motility – the characteristically ontic forms of human motility – take place, in truth, in a field or clearing of Being with whose immeasurable dimensionality we naturally tend to lose touch, despite the reminders kept alive in our cultural myths. The Being of this field, in which we may always recognize the working of the primordial *Logos*, articulates through our bodily nature the very possibilities for movement which ground, and clear an open space for all actual passages of human motility. The Being of this field essentially outlines, and sets in motion, the schema of corporeal opportunities for deepening our natural capacity to 'bring forth.' Since reflection re-collects, in the *depth* of our motility, the primordial articulations of the *Logos*, the *deepening* of our capacity points to our skillfulness in bringing forth this primordial articulation – making it luminously manifest in the 'elegance' of our gestures and movements. ('Elegance' refers here, by way of etymology, to the *perfection* of our *legein*.)

In regard to human motility, a natural capacity *awaiting* its most appropriate alignment and fulfillment, the Question of Being *calls* attention to the primordial claim on our grounding, our alignment, and our gestural grace; it calls attention to a claim which the clearing and grounding *Logos* has *already*, i.e., pre-ontologically, set in motion. The Question *gathers* our customary motility into a thoughtful recollection of the openness of Being which is always already presencing *for us* as the *clearing* we need to move in and the *ground* we need to stand on – the ground we need, in fact, to stand being ourselves. When our ontical motility responds to this ontological claim, thoughtfully celebrating the inherence of the gift (the *'Es gibt'*) in the very movements themselves, the *homologein* is a wondrous epiphany in Being.

THE BEARING OF THOUGHT

In his essay on 'Alêtheia', Heidegger argues that, for Herakleitos,

> the revealing-concealing gathering is identified as
> being entrusted to mortals in such a way that their
> essence unfolds [and is fulfilled] in this: their
> correspondence or noncorrespondence to the
> *Logos*.[75]

Now, *homologein* is the word Herakleitos seems to use for this correspondence. The question of the *homologein*, therefore, is the question of *our* correspondence. We are responsible for responding to the gift with which we have been entrusted in a way that truly and most appropriately corresponds to it. When mortals are responsive in this way,

> they can, in *their* way, accomplish the lighting (bring
> it to the fullness of its essence) and thereby protect
> it.[76]

Heidegger speaks of us as mortals who are capable, as he puts it,

> [of] bringing the lighting with them in their own
> way, preserving it and handing it down in its
> endurance.[77]

But he does not flesh out these words by clarifying the (onto-logical) difference they could make in our gestural being. Without this fleshing out, his words invite a reading which reduces 'bringing the light' and 'handing it down' to mere ornaments of speech. Such a reading misses an opportunity to let these words schematize for us the possibility of a new body of understanding.

The *homologein*, binding mortal *legein* to the *Legein* of the *Logos*, is a relationship which takes place through the guar-dian awareness that lives in the very flesh of our motility. As the *Legein* of the *logos* is a setting-down-and-gathering which sets in motion the *ek-stasis* of our motility, the *homo-logein* that can shine forth in mortal *legein* will be a *corre-sponding* gesture, an articulation that *repeats* the primordial gesture in an appropriate way, that is to say – with her-meneutical elegance and grace. (When I speak of 'repeating,'

I mean, of course, an *original* repetition: a *Wiederholung*.)

We know that, for Heidegger, *Dasein* (human being) means: a being who stands out in the openness, a being-which-opens. To be human, therefore, is to instance this *ekstasis*. So our *homologein* consists in a motility moved by our understanding that *this* motility is the 'same' as the motility of the primordial *Logos*, in the sense that, like the *Logos*, *it itself* sets down, and *it itself* can gather and open. But we need to understand that the *homologein* is nevertheless *not* fully appropriate, *not* authentically finished, until the primordial *Legein* is, *as such*, articulately bodied forth in a human motility whose very gestures and movements, being the 'same,' *pay homage* to their source.

Our very motility (our *own* clearing of space, our *own* laying-out and setting-down, and our *own* ways of opening and embracing and gathering) is called upon to become the route of this *homologein*, this radical recollection: a 'truthing' (an *alētheia*), a disclosive event (*Er-eignis*) within, and also of, the primordial articulation of the *Logos*. The *homologein* takes place *only* when the hermeneutical character of our motility, *as* a form of mortal *legein*, *brings* the primordial *Legein* into presence *as* the primordial, and brings it forth in the *truth* of its *own* primordiality, i.e., as that event (*Er-eignis*) of gathering and setting-out by grace of which our own mortal *legein*, in gestures and movements, first becomes feasible.

Thus we may say that the *Logos* 'needs' our motility to disclose its presencing in the very *giving* of that (clearing, grounding, and gathering) by grace of which our own ontical *legein* is first set in motion, and on which our motility essentially depends. But there is a danger in saying this unless it is understood, first, that we mortals are the ones in need, needing to commemorate the ontological clearing, the laying-down, and the gathering of the *Logos*, without which our own ontical clearing, laying-down, and gathering would never have become feasible. Furthermore, it must also be understood that our own motility enjoys ontological fulfillment only insofar as it can appropriately repeat the original *Legein* in the celebration of a hermeneutical disclosure. Putting this second point in another way, we need to understand that, for our mortal *legein* to accomplish the correspondence of the *homologein*, it is *not sufficient* that our gestures, and our motility in general, *repeat* the gathering of the primordial *Logos*. Nor is it even sufficient that the repetition take place in an intellectual *awareness* of its correspondence. The *homologein* does not truly take place (*er-eignet*) until the gestural repetition (i) discloses itself *as* a repetition and (ii) recollects the *presence* of the primordial *Logos* in order to disclose it in its truth (or 'unconcealment') as the original *Legein* which brings forth the very *being* of our field of motility. What this means is that our own mortal *legein* must consist of gestures and movements *capable* of bringing forth the *Legein* in a celebration that lets it come into its own (*er-eignet*). The correspondence in the *homologein* is not, therefore, a matter of achieving certain 'correct' gestures and movements in conformity to some pre-established worldly conventions. Rather, it is a question of the 'truthing' of our *legein* in gestures and movements which spontaneously, and yet with skill, bring forth (*apophainesthai*) in an ontologically disclosive way (*alētheuein*): a question of gestures and movements, then, which gracefully *inhabit* the truth (*Wahrnis*) of Being, maintaining and protecting (*wahren, bewahren, gewähren*) the enchanted field of its clearing.

Section 11   The Gathering of the Circle

Since your mind has been since the very beginning a
  deity
its body is a mandala and its speech a mantra –
a reach and range of pristine cognitions
in which everything is spontaneously perfect.
Long-chen-pa, Sems-nyid ngal-gso[78]

If, in this final section of the chapter, we now gather together the results of our preceding analysis, it will be noted that we have described human gesture, human motility, at *six* distinct levels of being. (Our ordering, here, is not from the standpoint of their development and unfolding but from the standpoint of our reflective steps.) At each level, our gestural being is disclosed as a *legein*, a gathering-and-laying-out. But the deeper we go into the being of our gesturing, the closer we get to an experience of the deeper 'mystery': our inherence in, and our dependence upon, the primordial *Legein* of the *Logos*, the motility-field of Being as a whole. (1) First we find the ontic level of naive and unreflective everyday experience (the level of the 'natural attitude', the level of conformable behavior belonging to 'everyone-and-anyone'), where gestures of clearing, gathering, and laying-down are always already taking place, but *without* any guardian awareness and understanding. (2) Next, we achieve the deeper level of 'objective thought' (the level of Western science, Western metaphysics, and ontically limited, uncritical cultural understandings), where motility, ontically understood (and ontologically concealed) in terms of Euclidean geometry, Newtonian physics, classical neurophysiology, mechanistic psychology, and traditional metaphysics, is mapped out in linear time along a linear series of points simply added together in physical space. (3) and (4) Then we reach the two deeper levels encountered by radical reflection, where motility is encountered, first of all, in the experience of the 'intentional arc,' a melodic gathering and laying-down, and then, secondly, in the more primitive, pre-ontological experience of an anonymous, prepersonal, non-ego-logical clearing, laying-down and gathering which is not of my own 'doing,' and on which, in fact, my own motility necessarily depends for its feasibility. (5) But, reaching these levels, we encountered the possibility of centering our gestures and movement in the more extensive gathering of the transpersonal field. And finally, (6) we leaped to the level of ontological thinking, where the ontical motility of mortals is disclosively articulated as (i) having been already determined (*bestimmt*) by the *Legein* of the primordial *Logos*, and (ii) as continuing to call for a fulfillment which can only take place through the on-going cultivation, or deepening, of an individual appreciation of Being within the field of our motility.

Now I submit that the first two understandings are levels which assume, and work entirely within, the *traditional* theory of truth as correspondence – a correspondence between an articulatory gesture and the reality it signifies; whereas the second two levels are understandings which begin to recognize that the traditional theory of truth is essentially *derivative* from a more primordial experience of truth as unconcealment, hermeneutical disclosure. It is only in the even more radical ontological understanding of the fifth level, however, that the gesture is understood in the context of a hermeneutical theory and is accordingly disclosed as the taking-place of a hermeneutical event of Being. Thus, it is only when the fifth and deepest level of awareness is bodied forth that the articulation of the ontological difference begins to appear in all its beauty as the space-clearing 'gesture' of the *Logos* and its primordial gathering of all beings.

What I have called, above, the cultivation of an 'appreciation' of Being means that we *develop* our capacity to gesture and move – or, more specifically, that we develop our *natural* gestures, which are *already* clearing an open space, laying-down, and gathering – in such a way that, by the character of these gestures, we gather into our collective memory, re-collect and bring to living presence, the primordial clearing, laying-down, and gathering of Being itself, giving thanks in the very joy of this embodied recollection to the primordial 'gesture': thanks for the *field* it has laid down, and thanks for the *motility* its own gathering has made possible and set in motion.

Now that we have gained some clarity concerning the hermeneutical character of our gestures, and have supple-mented Heidegger's interpretation of the mortal *legein* by explicitating the sense in which gathering, *legein*, articulates the very *essence* of all human gesture, I would like to explore the connection between the traditional symbol for hermeneutics, which of course is the circle, and the move-ment of the gesture of gathering, which is manifestly obedient (*gehörig*) to the wisdom that is outlined by that ancient mythic symbol.

The gesture of gathering is certainly an archetypal gesture – a gesture, moreover, of particular symbolic significance. A gathering is inherent in the gestures of mothering, protecting, and harvesting. By virtue of their *actual* gathering, their exemplary caring and loving, welcoming and receiving, these gestures manifest and fulfill that gathering which is the very *essence* of gesture as such. The circle is a symbol for this essence – a symbol, in fact, which seems to transcend the enclosure of cultural boundaries and gather into its embrace the dreams of many peoples. The symbol is the idealized *schema* for the embodiment of these dreams.

As a symbol for the hermeneutical method, the circle demonstrates the fact that processes of reflection, and enquiry in general, can have no absolute beginning, no abso-lute end. It demonstrates, further, that every beginning is also an end, and every end is also a beginning. The circle reminds us therefore, that all our understandings are *preceded* by a field of pre-understandings whose origins will forever elude our grasp: the circle reminds us to consult our unclear *sense* of how things are for us; it reminds us to listen to our body of felt sense, as the surest route to a deeper, more articulate understanding. And the circle shows us that no matter how far we journey, we must always come back to ourselves. We may reach out, for example, to understand another culture, but we cannot, in the end, risk forgetting ourselves and the place of difference where we are standing. The circle shows us that the advancement of understanding must continually go back to the assumptions and conditions that represent its beginning standpoint in order to progress to a new clearing. The circle reminds us that hermeneutics is a circuit of recollection: there is always a leaving and a returning; but somehow, the returning is never a full returning, and the leaving is never a final leaving. And this is how it is with the forgetting and remembering, or the rejecting and accepting, of any tradition.

Let us now focus on the *character* of the gesture which is represented by the hermeneutical circle. The gesture which most sharply differs from it is the gesture which moves in a straight line toward its goal. More than any other, the hermeneutical gesture, always circuitous, is the gesture of *culture*, whereas the more direct gesture, the gesture of the straight line, is the gesture which comes from our untutored nature. This latter gesture is the gesture moved straightaway by desire, by strong ego-logical attractions and aversions, or moved by a kind of careless indifference. It is a gesture which tends to be impatient, possessive, grasping and greedy, always seeking the most immediate egocentric satisfaction. It is a gesture which inscribes a trajectory of opposition and conflict between its object and itself. Naturally, it tends to be aggressive, willful, manipulative. It is, in fact, a gesture of objectification befitting the will to power of our modern technological epoch, an epoch in which everything is required to be ready-to-hand, always available, permanently present within the reach of our gestures.

Depicted in its archetypal form, i.e., as a circle, the hermeneutical gesture manifests a very different character. It is, of course, a welcoming, gathering into a whole; but the whole it makes is open, not totalized. The arms inscribe an *open* circle: they embrace, yet what is enclosed within remains free of constraint. As a gathering which encircles, the hermeneutical gesture inevitably alludes to a center, something precious and worthy of protection. But the center is only *evoked* by the encircling: the gesture makes no move to point to it *directly*. The embrace 'lends a hand' to the presencing of such a center; it articulates a central point. But its mode of articulation is oblique, metaphorical. What, then, is this center? Speaking ontically, and therefore ego-logically, we would note that there is 'nothing' in this center – nothing at all. In the center of the hermeneutical circle, 'there is' only emptiness, the presencing of an absence, the absencing of a presence. No origin. No goal. And this is true even if, ontically and literally speaking, 'something' *is* there. For the encircling motion of the gesture clearly acknowledges that which *is* as its center. and yet it is equally clear, equally legible from its comportment, that nothing is there to be grasped, nothing to be posited, nothing to be possessed, nothing reached.

What makes this gesture the paradigmatic gesture of culture is precisely this continual self-restraint, this continual inhibition of natural desire, desire transmuted into a movement that flows with grace in its attunement to a deeper centeredness. We note that the circuit repeatedly *postpones* the possibility of ego-centric satisfaction: there is a sort of continuous bending or deflecting of desire, a sublime reshaping of its bodily metaphored character. Is the circuit a turning towards or a turning away? Without the normal polarizations of subject and object, we cannot say. The gesture, in any case, continually defers a full comprehension, a direct return to its central point of origin. By the same token, it endlessly defers the objective certainty of a direct access to the apparent goal, the absolutely central meaning. The gesture represented by the hermeneutical circle is a living exemplification of ontological tact, or reserve, of circumspection, of reverence. It is a gesture which belongs to the maintenance of Being, for its very *restraint* discloses the unreachable, the *space* of ontological difference as such.

The hermeneutical circle symbolizes gestures of gracious humility: gestures of selfless waiting, letting go, letting be. It symbolizes gestures which body forth the attitude which Heidegger has called *Gelassenheit*: gestures of equanimity in which the polarizing, objectifying tendency has been neutralized and the motivational energies are held in a dynamic balance. The circle can symbolize these gestures – can symbolize, in fact, the very essence of these gestures – because it is, after all, the material trace, the inscription that has been left, taking its shape from the very gesture it symbolizes. Handed down from generation to generation, it holds our attention as a re-presentation of the gesture's living presence. Inscribed by innumerable generations of hands, the calligraphy of the circle continues to gather the peoples of different cultures into the embrace of its encompassing wisdom.

Thus far, our account has concentrated on the hermeneutical circle in relation to our gesturing. But to complete this account, we must also consider the circle in relation to the motility of our body as a whole. Here our attention must be focused on circumambulation, a movement which the people of many cultures consider to be sacred, and which they have embodied in the gatherings of their ancient ceremonies. This is because circumambulation is a movement which actualizes in an exemplary way the very essence of the gathering. Like the gestures of gathering, it too can become ontologically hermeneutical: a *homologein* which *lays down* a welcoming space, an open and receptive clearing, for the elusive presencing (unconcealment) of Being. Symbolically, its very distancing, its aware deferral of a move to occupy and master the center, keeps and maintains the truth, or space, of the ontological difference. The circumambulatory movement serves to remind us that the ontological fulfillment of our motility, i.e., the realization of its pre-ontological potential, essentially consists in an attitude of caring – an attitude which can only be *true* when it is willing to be hermeneutical.

Before we have experienced our capacity for movement, the *Logos* has already outlined for us the whole of the field in which we are gathered. Circumambulation is forever nearing the origin of its centeredness, forever turning towards the point of its grounding. And yet, it preserves the distance and protects, symbolically, the hidden compass of its field. It is in this kind of movement, in movement bearing this character, that a guardian awareness of Being, a *Wahrnehmung*, a taking care of the truth, is most articulately bodied forth. Perhaps, then, it is in movements which understand the spirit of circumambulation that the presencing of the *Logos* would be most appropriately welcomed into the world of indifference where mortals must try to dwell.

According to the fourteenth-century scholar, kLong-chen rab-'byams-pa, one of Tibet's greatest teachers of Buddhism, 'mandala' (*dkyil-khor*) means: 'to surround any prominent facet of reality with beauty.'[79] It seems to me that, in the gestures and movements which body forth the hermeneutical essence of gathering, a *mandala* of great beauty is brought into Being. What would it be like for us to dwell in a world that welcomed the earth and the sky, all our gods and all mortals, into the vast circle of its recollection?

CHAPTER 2

The Living Body of Tradition

Introduction

Opening Conversation

(1) Only human beings have come to a point where they no longer know why they exist. They . . . have forgotten the secret knowledge of their bodies, their senses, their dreams.
Lame Deer, Sioux Medicine Man[1]

(2) Philosophy is not a particular body of knowledge; it is the vigilance which does not let us forget the source of all knowledge.
Merleau–Ponty, 'The Philosopher and Sociology'[2]

(3) [History must become] once again what it should be for the philosopher: the center of his reflections, not, as an object-nature . . . but on the contrary [as] the place of all our questions and wonders. . . . To choose history means to devote ourselves body and soul to the advent of a future humanity. . . .
Merleau–Ponty, 'The Indirect Language'[3]

(4) My personal existence must be the resumption of a prepersonal tradition. There is, therefore, another subject beneath me, for whom a world

167

exists before I am here, and who marks out my
place in it. This captive or natural spirit is my
body. . . .

> Merleau–Ponty, *Phenomenology of Perception*[4]

(5) the body is history.

> Merleau–Ponty, 'The Indirect Language'[5]

(6) Put briefly: perhaps the entire evolution of the
spirit is a question of the body; it is the history of
the development of a higher body that emerges
into our sensibility. The organic is rising to yet
higher levels. Our lust for knowledge of nature is
a means through which the body desires to perfect
itself. Or rather, hundreds of thousands of
experiments are made to change the nourishment,
the mode of living and of dwelling of the body;
consciousness and evaluations in the body, all
kinds of pleasure and displeasure, are signs of
these changes and experiments. In the long run, it
is not a question of man at all: he is to be
overcome.

> Friedrich Nietzsche, *The Will to Power*[6]

(7) As the vehicle of tradition, human consciousness
collectively takes over the role formerly played by
the biological factor. Organs are now no longer
inherited, but are transmitted.

> Erich Neumann, *The Origins and History of
> Consciousness*[7]

(8) the tradition of perception. . . .

> Merleau–Ponty, 'The Indirect Language'[8]

(9) It is characteristic of cultural gestures to awaken
in all others at least an echo, if not a consonance.

> Merleau–Ponty, 'The Indirect Language'[9]

(10) Just as our bodies still retain vestiges of obsolete
functions and conditions in many of their organs,
so our minds, which have apparently outgrown
those archaic impulses, still bear the marks of the
evolutionary stages we have traversed, and re-echo
the dim by-gone in dreams and fantasies.

> Carl G. Jung, 'Two Kinds of Thinking'[10]

(11) When I turn toward perception, [I] find at work in

my organs of perception a thought older than
myself, of which those organs are merely a trace.
Merleau–Ponty, *Phenomenology of Perception*[11]

(12) the body of history. . . .
Merleau–Ponty, 'The Indirect Language'[12]

(13) Just as the body has its evolutionary history and
shows clear traces of the various evolutionary
stages, so too does the psyche.
Carl G. Jung, 'Two Kinds of Thinking'[13]

(14) Millions of years of ancestral experience are stored
up in the instinctive reactions of organic matter,
and in the functions of the body there is
incorporated a living knowledge, almost universal
in scope, but not accompanied by any
consciousness. During the last few thousand years
the human mind has laboriously made itself
conscious . . . of some meager fragments of what
the cells, functional systems, and organisms
'knowingly' do in their adaptations and reactions.
By reason of this incorporated knowledge the
pleromatic phase of the uroboros is also intuited
as one of primordial wisdom. The Great Mother
has a wisdom infinitely superior to the ego,
because the instincts and archetypes that speak
through the collective unconscious represent the
'wisdom of the species' and its will.
Erich Neumann, *The Origins and History of
Consciousness*[14]

(15) The more primitive the psychic level, the more it
is identical with the bodily events which rule it.
Neumann, *The Origins and History of Consciousness*[15]

(16) In this 'deeper' stratum we also find the a
priori, inborn forms of 'intuition', namely, the
archetypes of perceptions and apprehension,
which are the necessary a priori determinants of
all psychic processes. Just as his instincts compel
man to a specifically human mode of existence, so
the archetypes force his ways of perception and
apprehension into specifically human patterns.
Carl G. Jung, 'Instinct and the Unconscious'[16]

(17) These we consider to be the older primary

processes, the residues of a phase of development in which they were the only kind of mental process.

Sigmund Freud, *Collected Papers*[17]

(18)   The body stands for wholeness and unity in general, and its total reaction represents a genuine and creative totality.

Neumann, *The Origins and History of Consciousness*[18]

(19)   the self is . . . felt to be identical with the body and with the world of the ancestors. . . . The [so-called] totem ancestor represents [for the primitive mind] the 'ancestral experience within us', which is incorporated in the body ['our ancestral body'] and is at the same time the basis of our individuality.

Neumann, *The Origins and History of Consciousness*[19]

(20)   The difference between the life of the spirit and that of the flesh is itself a spiritual difference. . . .

George Santayana, *Platonism and the Spiritual Life*[20]

(21)   We will therefore have to recognize an ideality that is not alien to the flesh, that gives it its axes, its depth, its dimensions.

Merleau–Ponty, *The Visible and the Invisible*[21]

(22)   so it is with our ideas and reasonings: they have a certain body, but it is a shapeless mass, without form or light, if faith and divine grace are not added to it.

Michel de Montaigne,
'Apology for Raymond Sebond'[22]

In this chapter, we shall reflect together on the living body of tradition. The conversation of remarks to which we have just attended is meant to provide the skeleton of our interpretation. It is hoped that by the time we have concluded the hermeneutical reflections of this chapter, the skeleton will be fleshed out in an intelligible and significant form, viz., as an ontological framework for the embodiment of spiritual life in keeping with a religious tradition.

How is the wisdom of a spiritual tradition kept alive? How is the liberating truth of a spiritual tradition passed on from the old to the new generation? These questions constitute the problematic of this chapter. Our focus, however, will be on the human body: the body as primary ritual bearer, and original metaphorical text, of such transmission. In an important sense, the body is, or is at, the very source of all our knowledge. But how well do we know, or understand, this body? Our 'very own' body is not really, or not fully, our own. It is the deposit, in fact, of a secret wisdom, secret not only because of our extensive ignorance, nor even because very little of its potential, its endowment, has yet been touched, but also because the wisdom itself has been given to us in secret, and necessarily inscrutable ways: concealed, first of all, within the impenetrable mystery of nature; but concealed, too, within the hermeneutical symbolism of religious traditions, which do not reveal their treasures of wisdom except to those who will *willingly surrender* their body of pre-conceptions in order to learn a spiritual life. We must remember that the body of wisdom is the bequest of more generations than we could ever count: as an ancestral body, an 'ancient' body of genetically encoded reproduction, for example, it is the biophysical element which binds our existence to that of our mortal ancestors, even the earliest; as a cultural body, it transcends the chains of nature, participates in the shaping of history, and serves, whether we will it or not – though our willingness makes a difference – as an impressionable medium for the transmission and sedimentation of cultural norms, values, and meanings.

We do not have to accept, and in this study will not in fact accept, the arguments of depth psychology in favor of the concepts of the individual and the collective unconscious. *A fortiori*, we will not make use of their conceptual distinction between consciousness in the mode of awareness and consciousness in the mode of the unconscious. *The distinction which these concepts are intended to draw can be made in other terms, namely, by way of the experienced body.* The 'unconscious' which, in Jung's depth psychology, is called 'collective' can in fact be articulated very well in terms of the body's primordial and archaic attunement; its automatic, and always already functioning intentionalities; its generous endowment of inherent dispositions and propensities; its latent, and sometimes involuntary perceptivities; its implicit structures of pre-understanding; and its always accessible felt sense, however inchoate and untutored, of what is basically good, basically true, and basically beautiful.

Working without the benefit of an appropriate phenomenological understanding of the body as we experience it, depth psychology was *forced* into a theoretical framework which could conceptualize 'depth' only in terms of an unconscious consciousness. For the depth psychology of Freud and Jung, and even for the innovative theory which Erich Neumann later formulated, where 'the body' refers to 'a psycho-physical organism,' there is a false understanding of the body: an understanding which fails to escape a Cartesian dualism and its consequent materialization and mechanization of the body. Thus, for example, when Neumann takes up, for reflection, our 'ancestral body,' he is still not able to avoid conceiving it exclusively in terms of its biophysical causality, its material efficacy; and, correlatively, he is unable to imagine the possibility of a therapeutic process whereby we might undertake to appropriate for ourselves – in a reflective, but nonetheless emotionally salutary procedure – the store of meaningfulness made available through that ancestral bond, the gift of that genetic code.

Neumann's contrast between inheritance and transmission, however, is useful. The 'ancestral body' is therefore two-fold: in the first instance, to be sure, it is claimed by, and belongs to, the ancestral chain, an undecoded code of organismic and environmental attunements; but in the second instance, it is claimed *by us*, and belongs to our ancestral origins only by virtue of a gift of thought, an act of dedication. The ancestral body is both the body we have inherited biologically from our ancestors, and also the body we have received from them through the processes of cultural transmission. By the same token, our body *already belongs* to culture and its history by the decree of nature; and yet, this historicity is different from, and must not be confused with, that other historicity – the one which only comes to pass, always most precariously, within the context of human culture, and which is, as Santayana points out, a culturally original moment: a cultural history which we have expressly chosen, and make over, in a perpetual vigil, into our own. The 'collective unconscious,' I want to say, is not other than that *gesturing* of the personality *through which* the dream of our community, the unrecognized dream most latent in the ancestral body, comes spontaneously to articulation, and enters the circle of cultural conversation.

In one of the passages at the very beginning of this chapter, Merleau–Ponty asserts that, 'to choose history means to devote ourselves *body and soul* to the advent of a future

humanity.' I share this concern. But I also want to understand this choice, as he does, in terms of our incarnation –
an adventure in what Nietzsche has called 'the body's self-
perfection.' As the medium which receives the shape of our
past and holds open our future, the human body is, in a
sense, the pivot, the hinge, on which this fateful adventure
in our humanity ultimately turns. The acculturated body is
the deposit, the sediment, of generations of tradition, but it
is also the metaphor of every historical transition. The body
is a living symbol of tradition, because it knows *instinctively*
that it must embrace creative metamorphosis in order to
survive.

This chapter is focused on *the embodiment of tradition*. That
is to say, we shall be reflecting on how a spiritual tradition
survives, how it renews itself, by way of, or in the medium
of, its embodiment. But this means that we must also reflect
on the fact that spiritual traditions are always *traditions of
embodiment*. I shall argue that spiritual traditions survive in
renewal only if they include teachings and practices that
constitute a tradition of *embodiment*: a tradition, in fact, of
perpetual incarnation – that 'sublimation' of the flesh, by
virtue of which the time-honored traditions of spiritual life
may be taken over again and again, and borne anew, again
and again, through the creative existence of generations of
mortals.

According to Heidegger, time, history, and tradition constitute fundamental dimensions of *Dasein*'s ecstatic nature as
Caring. *Dasein* always finds itself already thrown into the
ecstatic structurings of these dimensions: in its *Befindlichkeit*,
it finds itself always already bound, always already attuned
to these structurings; and it finds itself, therefore, always
already held in beholdenness (*Schuldigkeit*). Thus, the understanding of these dimensions realizes the very heart of
Heidegger's task for thinking, especially as he formulates it
in *Being and Time*. But Heidegger does not introduce the
question of embodiment into his formulation of the task,
even though, since *Dasein* is always embodied, and indeed
always finds itself *already* embodied, it would seem *necessary*
that we give the gift of our thought to the *Befindlichkeit* of
embodiment. More specifically, Heidegger attempts to think
the thrownness, the attunement, the binding, and the
beholdenness of *Dasein* in the dimensions of time, history,
and tradition; but he does so *without* taking up the question
of the body, even though – as I am wont to believe – it is by

virtue of the body, the body first and foremost, that *Dasein* is claimed and appropriated, bound and beholden, and decisively *thrown* into the ecstasy of an original attunement, in relation to time, history, and tradition. It is because *Dasein* is embodied that it finds itself ecstatically decentered in a threefold field of time, a repetition of history, and a living tradition. It is because *Dasein* is embodied that it finds itself inscribed into a time, a history, and a tradition to which it always and already belongs – belongs, I mean, *before* the possibility of decision, and in truth as the fundament which lays down the very possibility of this decision, in the resoluteness of an existence binding itself to the understanding of this claim, this belongingness.

The body is always already temporalized: it is born; it lingers and persists a while; it perishes. The body holds us, keeps us pledged, to the corruption and mortality by which our existence is ultimately called into question. But the body returns, through its death, to the cosmological time that defines the elemental. And time calls, time speaks to *Dasein* through the very pulse of its being: through the rhythmic measure of its heartbeat, through its cycles of rest and motion, its cycles of need and satisfaction, its pattern (*Logos*) of breathing, and the melody in its gait and stride.

The body is always already thrown into a history, as well. And, in truth, *Dasein*'s historicity, its ineluctable belonging-to-history, can be traced back, ultimately, to its incarnation. The genetic code, for example, is that gift of Being by grace of which we belong to the biological history of mortal generations. And it is into the circle of this history, which we are just beginning to decode in a science of codes, that we humans are gathered: gathered to be *claimed* in the responsibility of a story. Furthermore, as soon as we begin to move and gesture in response to the presence of the human Other, we are held by our culture in the corresponding beholdenness of our bodies. In every human voice, there are echoes of the mother's tongue, echoes of significant teachers, respected elders, close friends; and there are accents, too, which bind the voice to the history of a region, a culture, and generations of ancestors. The athlete of today repeats the race of the Olympic torch-bearers, bearing the history of centuries in the very span of his body. The carpenter of today repeats the gestures of skill which have always constituted his handicraft; and it is only by the grace of that ancient gesture that he belongs to the tradition of the craft as it has been handed down from generation to generation across thousands of years. Analogously, the mother nurses her child, repeating thereby one of the oldest of human gestures. In these ways, and in countless others, *Dasein* is held open to its history and tradition, and is granted the chance to find in this beholdenness the deepest dimensionality of its fulfillment as an historical and tradition-bound being.

The text which follows this introductory statement is concerned less with the body in time, and rather more with the body in history and tradition. More specifically, it undertakes a hermeneutical reflection which focuses our attention on the body of *Dasein* as it is claimed, bound, and appropriated by the symbolic practice of religion. Underlying this focus is my conviction that it is always the office of religion to hold open for *Dasein* the deepest, most opening and most liberating possibilities for understanding the nature of its belonging-to-history and realizing its appropriation by tradition.

Part I
Religion and the Ritual Binding of the Body

Opening Conversation

(1) Through faithful devotion, the organs of sense are fed.

Milarepa[23]

(2) The eternal wisdom is tasted in every tastable thing: it is delight in everything delightful.
Nicholas Cusanus, 'De Sapientia'[24]

(3) consecratory gestures. . . .
Merleau–Ponty, *Phenomenology of Perception*[25]

(4) the symbolic accentuation of the body, and the sanctification of everything pertaining to it. . . .
Erich Neumann, *The Origins and History of Consciousness*[26]

(5) Every man is the builder of a temple called his body. . . .
Henry David Thoreau, 'Higher Laws'[27]

(6)   the psychophysical unity reacting as a whole by
      means of meaningful acts which are not the
      outcome of individual experience but of ancestral
      experience, and which are performed without the
      participation of [thematizing] consciousness. This
      ancestral experience is rooted in the body and
      expresses itself organically through the body's
      reactions.
                        Erich Neumann, *The Origins and History of
                                      Consciousness*[28]

(7)   As the child of a tight-rope walker is from his
      earliest years made supple in his back and in every
      muscle, so that, after daily practice, he is sheer
      suppleness and can carry out every movement,
      absolutely every movement, in the most
      excruciating positions, yet always easily and
      smiling: so with prayer to the absolute majesty.
                        Søren Kierkegaard, *Journals 1853–1855*[29]

(8)   Pain and discomfort are among the earliest factors
      that build consciousness.
      Neumann, *The Origins and History of Consciousness*[30]

(9)   The development of ego consciousness is paralleled
      by a tendency to make itself independent of the
      body. This tendency finds its most obvious
      expression in masculine asceticism, world
      negation, mortification of the body . . . and is
      ritually practised in the initiation ceremonies of
      adolescents. The point of all such endurance tests
      is to strengthen the ego's stability, the will, and
      the higher masculinity, and to establish a conscious
      sense of superiority over the body. In rising above
      it and triumphing over its pains, fears, and lusts,
      the ego gains an elementary experience of its own
      manly spirituality. To these tribulations is added
      an illumination by the higher spiritual principle,
      whether this be vouchsafed by spiritual beings in
      individual or collective visions, or by the
      communication of secret doctrines.
      Neumann, *The Origins and History of Consciousness*[31]

(10) It is so truly the mystery of the kneeling, of the
      deeply kneeling man: his being greater, by his
      spiritual nature, than he who stands! . . . He who

kneels, who gives himself wholly to kneeling, loses
indeed the measure of his surroundings, even
looking up he would no longer be able to say what
is great and what is small. But although in his
bent posture he has scarcely the height of a child,
yet he, this kneeling man, is not to be called small.
With him the scale is shifted, for in following the
peculiar weight and strength in his knees and
assuming the position that corresponds to them,
he already belongs to that world in which height
is – depth – and if even height remains
unmeasurable to our gaze and our instruments:
who could measure the depth? . . .

Rilke (in a letter to his mother, 17 December 1920)[32]

(11)   The limbs of which thou hast formed us, the spirit
which thou hast breathed into us, the tongue thou
hast placed in our mouth: these sanctify and
acknowledge the sway of thy presence. Every
mouth shall adore thee, and every tongue shall
give thee voice; every knee shall bend in thought
of thee; every being shall bow down to show thee
humility; every heart shall open to receive and
thank thee, and even the invisible elements of our
bodies shall sing psalmodies unto thy name. As it
is written: All my bones shall say, 'O Eternal, who
is like unto thee?'

Hebrew Liturgy of Morning Worship[33]

(12)   Blessed art thou, the Eternal, our God, King of the
Universe, who has formed man in wisdom, and
created in him various apertures, tubes, veins and
arteries. Before thy glorious throne it is manifestly
known that, if but one of them be open [when it
should be closed] or closed [when it should be
open], it would be impossible to exist and endure
in thy presence. Blessed art thou, O Lord our
God, who healeth all flesh, and worketh many
wonders.

Talmud Berakhoth[34]

(13)   Incorporated knowledge and unconscious
purposivity must be regarded as essential marks of
every organism.

Neumann, *The Origins and History of Consciousness*[35]

(14)   Were our mouth filled with song as the sea is with
       water, and our tongue with ringing praise as the
       roaring waves; were our lips full of adoration as
       the wide expanse of heaven, and our eyes
       sparkling like the sun or the moon; were our hands
       spread out in prayer as the eagles of the sky, and
       our feet as swift as the deer – we should still be
       unable to thank thee and bless thy name, Lord
       our God, and God of our fathers, for the one
       thousandth of the countless millions of favors
       which thou hast conferred on our fathers and on
       us. . . . Therefore, the limbs which thou hast
       apportioned in us, and the soul which thou hast
       placed in our mouth, shall all thank and bless,
       praise and glorify, extol and revere, hallow and do
       homage to thy name.

Talmud Pesahim[36]

In his *Metaphysische Anfangsgründe der Logik im Ausgang vom Leibniz*, Heidegger asserts that, 'In the project of the for-the-sake-of-which as such, human being gives itself primordial binding.'[37] There are many dimensions of binding, and 'logic' is certainly one of them. But the dimension of our *existential* binding, the binding of our Being as a whole, and therefore, of our being in relation to the meaning of Being, is the overarching concern of the 'spiritual' traditions. It is the mortal human body, however, which bears the first aspirations, and the primary weight, of our spiritual life. And I can think of no tradition of spiritual life, no culture of the sacred dimension of human existence, which does not crucially depend on the thoughtful bearing of the mortal body. Insofar as the maintenance and the transmission of a tradition of spiritual life are entrusted to the practice of what we call 'religion,' the appropriate ritualization of the body, and a consequent sanctification of the mundane flesh, inevitably become matters of the most fundamental concern for 'religion.'

I would like to begin with a preliminary definition of 'spiritual awareness.' Like all definitions, mine will be of limited value; but this limitation does not mean that it cannot be useful, at the beginning, for the organization of our thinking. 'Spiritual awareness' is our richest, deepest, most open and most meaningful experience-of-Being; it is that attitude in which we hold ourselves most open, and most receptive to, the primordial presencing (i.e., primordial unconcealment) of Being. It concerns our experience-of-Being in the primordiality of its unconcealment, its truth. The function of a religion, then, is – or should be – to maintain a binding commitment to the development of this spiritual awareness in the life of a cultural community.

I would like two points to be clear, however, before we proceed to reflect on the question of ritual. (i) The primordiality of 'spiritual awareness' – its service in the preserving, protecting, and cherishing of our primordial sense-of-Being in all its depth and openness – signifies that *it underlies every socio-political order*, and indeed must bear the ultimate responsibility for a vigilance which keeps this order *open* to the primordial presencing of Being. (ii) But, conversely, the *socio-political order must assume responsibility* for creating and maintaining conditions that are really *congenial* to the development of 'spiritual awareness,' since it is *precisely those conditions* which ultimately *protect* the political economy against a technological organization of its power and the nihilism of a totalitarian regime.

Now, a careful reading of history seems to suggest that even the most anarchic, most subversive forms of 'spiritual experience' sooner or later need, for their survival, some kind of 'anchorage' in the institutional structures of our life-world. In other words, they need the *support* of 'routine' religious practices, ecclesiastical institutions, liturgical texts, and a variety of discourses and documents. At the center of every religion, therefore, we find the objects and practices of its ritual. Rituals are the 'materialization' of religion: its way of ensuring some continuity with everyday life, and with the original spirit of the past; its way of reminding, teaching, and transmitting; its way of touching our bodies, our flesh, and reaching into the very heart of our being. Rituals are the bearers of religious tradition. Thus, if we feel a need for some religious tradition, we tend to feel some corresponding need to participate in those rituals that make a place for it in our world. But a religious tradition needs to be continually renewed, or else it will die. If it is not open to change in response to the changing needs of different historical situations, it will not be able to transmit the spiritual awareness that would keep us radically open to Being in its primordiality, despite historical conditions which are constantly pressuring us to accept a much more restricted experience.

I am therefore concerned with a fundamental question:

179

how is it possible to appropriate the rituals of a religious tradition in a way that is *creative*, and yet also *in keeping* with the spirit, or the 'spiritual awareness,' of the sacred tradition? Unless we can answer the challenge in this question, it will be necessary to *reject* these rituals altogether, as nothing but *obstacles* to our spiritual growth, in order to find our way, once again, into an openness of experience which would grant us the presencing of Being in its primordial richness.

In this chapter, we shall examine the nature of spiritual life from a rather unusual standpoint: our experience of embodiment as it passes through the ritualization of a religious tradition. Because this examination will adhere to the phenomenological method, it is hoped that, in the course of this chapter, it will become clear that, just as the phenomenological *epochē* suspends the 'natural attitude' as doxic modality in the context of our existential beliefs and convictions, so the religious appropriation of the body through its tradition of rituals, which is itself a kind of *epochē*, suspends the natural attitudes of the human body – suspends, that is, its natural postures, bearing, gestures and movements – in order to facilitate the emergence of a deeper, and more spiritual, modality of awareness.

Ritualization is an *epochē* aimed at achieving a 'sublimation,' or an 'apotheosis', of the flesh. (The prayers which appear at the beginning of this section, as well as all the other prayers which appear in this chapter, should be experienced as *visualizations*, aides to the realization of this sublimation. They are included for this purpose.) Ritual is aimed at a metamorphosis in the very nature of our incarnation. In essence, this metamorphosis is a process of sanctification. The process begins – universally, it would seem – with rituals of purification, acknowledging the body's spiritual needs and cleansing it, symbolically, in preparation for its more difficult tasks. These rituals also undertake to *separate* it, somehow, as the destined bearer of a spiritual bearer of a spiritual life, from the profane demands of its mundane existence. The ritually consecrated body, sheltered within the precincts of a sacred space and devoted to performing the appropriate sacred gestures, or the appropriate sacred tasks (whatever modes of comportment may be spelled out by the tradition), thus becomes, in itself, a moving sanctuary for the preserving disclosing of that which is ever transcendent, opening, liberating.

Religion is a tradition of rituals which *bind and fasten* the body: it binds us to the performance of special tasks, special postures, gestures, and movements; it dedicates the body to the incarnation of a spiritual life, promising that the body's careful adherence to such strict regulation will not be experienced, in the end, as its restriction, but rather, on the contrary, as its dream of health, well-being, and liberation. Through ritual, then, through the ritual practices of its tradition, the living body is completely reshaped. We are touched and moved in every cell and fiber. Our limbs are gently bowed, bent and folded, and our posture and bearing regulated, so that we can begin to feel *in a bodily way* the meaning of devotion, and the value of service. And our various organs and sensoria, the 'gates' and 'pathways' of awareness, are deeply relaxed, or widely opened, so that we can begin to experience the healing presence of that which, since time immemorial, religious traditions have called, in one way or another, the 'holy,' the 'sacred,' and the 'divine.' The ritual *epochē* 'stops the world'; it begins, and intensifies, our bodily felt sense of the deeper reality.

Rilke, in a letter, brings to words what I think is the experiential essence of the process:

> It is certain that the divinest consolation is contained in humanity itself – we would not be able to do much with the consolation of a god; only that our eye would have to be a trace more seeing, our ear more receptive, the taste of a fruit would have to penetrate us more completely, we would have to endure more odor, and in touching and being touched be more aware and less forgetful – : in order promptly to absorb out of our immediate experience consolations that would be more convincing, more preponderant, more true than all the suffering that can ever shake us to our very depths.[38]

The poet speaks, here, of openness and receptivity. It is not, of course, a question of some causal sequence, as if we should *first* be opening and receiving, *then* rejoicing and giving thanks. For rejoicing and giving thanks are *themselves* ways of opening and receiving – and, in truth, the most appropriate. Furthermore, since *sensory* experience is *receptive* experience, the goal of the spiritual process is to make *sensing itself* a receiving-which-gives-thanks. Thus, for spiritual fulfillment, our sensory reception of the phenomenal gift of Being needs to exemplify this integral character.

Western philosophy and psychology have worked for a very long time, however, with distorted re-presentations of sensory receptivity. Merleau–Ponty is helpful, though, in breaking the spell of this picture:

> Sense experience, thus detached from the affective and motor functions, became the mere reception of a quality, and physiologists thought they could follow, from the point of reception to the nervous centres, the projection of the external world in the living body.[39]

Until we have given up our attachment to the traditional conception of sensory receptivity, it will not be evident that a much richer and more fulfilling experience is really possible.

The beauty of our spiritual life depends upon an incarnation which can bring it to fulfillment; it *needs and uses our senses* to complete its realization. This is the gift of our senses. That is why, in *Psalm* 19 (verses 10–11), we are told about the ordinances of God in language which appeals to our sense of taste:

> The ordinances of the Lord are true, they are righteous altogether. More to be desired are they than gold, yes than much fine gold; sweeter also than honey and the honeycomb.

If it is difficult to believe that the fulfillment of spiritual awareness requires a process which works through the senses, then we need to understand that this process *binds and thoroughly transfigures* the senses. Thus, Nicholas of Cusa, whom we quoted at the beginning of our reflections on ritualization, has boldly asseverated that our spiritual gifts 'cometh not to perfection without the senses.'[40] Yet he also argues that,

> he who seeks after [eternal] wisdom with intellectual motion is already inwardly touched by the foretaste of the sweetness, and its reception into the body renders the body almost incorporeal.[41]

It is customary to understand the spirit's final salvation,

its release from the sufferings and defilements of body, as the *separation* of soul from the element of the flesh. According to the traditional Western story, the soul, filled with repugnance and hate towards its body, which during our lifetime holds it as a captive, or hostage, longs for the moment of death, when it is finally free to leave the realm of mortality, the realm of suffering and the doing of evil, and may return to its abode of bliss. But there is a different and more subtle understanding of this release. The soul's liberation, its redemption, need not be taken to mean that it *detaches* itself from the body – a position which presupposes, in any case, a metaphysical dualism whose sense, whose very intelligibility, is by no means obvious, clear and distinct, let alone true. Rather, once we have understood the human body as an ongoing process of embodiment, as, in Merleau–Ponty's words, a 'perpetual incarnation,' then we may interpret the theological notion of the soul's release to be the dream of a complete *metamorphosis* of the flesh. Release is a question not of separation, but of the achievement, *in one's lifetime*, i.e., *prior* to the time of death, of a transfiguration of our embodiment: a transfiguration whereby the flesh of the body and the spirit of the soul have finally achieved a relationship of harmony, integration, and non-duality. The notion of salvation (redemption) as a *real* separation is coarse and vulgar; it is very much in need, now, of deconstruction. 'In need,' I stress, 'now': because the traditional conception, and the traditional story, are no longer credible. And there is a danger that, if the truth be identified too closely with this particular conceptualization, this particular story, truth itself will be repudiated. Our concern, here, is to renew or restore the liberating truth which informs the ritualized body of the religious traditions.

If we carefully examine even the most familiar religious texts of our own Judaeo-Christian tradition, and keep our eyes and ears especially attuned to the implicit meanings that are buried within their textures, we will then discover some amazingly coherent, lucidly articulate references to this crying need of the spirit, this dream of a complete transformation of the human body. Moreover, we will also discover extremely precise *regulative principles* regarding the nature of this transformation, carefully describing, for our benefit, how it is to be undertaken, how it affects us, how it is experienced, and how it would serve the spiritual life of the religious tradition.

Since we will soon take up the question of liturgical texts and their relationship to traditions of ritual incarnation, it might at this point be useful for us to examine the spiritual experience of writing. Since writing is a gestural process, our reflections will continue the thinking we began in the preceding chapter, where we explored, in experiential terms, the nature of the hands and the character of their gestures. I propose that we briefly focus, now, on the writing of sacred texts and on the gesture of writing as a religious, and consequently a ritualized, act of spiritual incarnation.

Due to the singular importance of our hands, many religions, and perhaps even most (even many of the so-called 'primitive' ones) have recognized the need to 'bind' the gestures of the hands, and commit them to spiritual practice, in accordance with rituals of a religious, or sacred, nature. Such ritualization helps us mortals to attend to the nurturing of bodily feelings and bodily awarenesses the meanings of which would normally go unnoticed or unattended, or which perhaps would otherwise not even exist. Rituals involving the body – the hands, for example – can awaken some very special corporeal latencies: motivations, intentionalities, skills and dispositions; dimensions of bodily being which our everyday activities in 'the natural attitude' do not require, and do not therefore encourage.

In cultures where writing replaced oral communication as the primary gesture of memory, bearing thus the weight of tradition, the spiritual life appropriated the process of writing and bound the gesture to a religious service. Writing was originally, it seems, a sacred gesture – a ritualized gesture of piety, celebrating the presence, or the efficacy, of a divinity visible both in the grace and elegance of the gesture itself and also in the darkness of the inscription which that gesture makes, and leaves behind. As such, writing became a skill of immeasurable dimensions. (In a poem called 'The Pure Good of Theory,' Wallace Stevens speaks of being 'Touched suddenly by the universal flare/For a moment, a moment in which we read and repeat/The eloquences of light's faculties.') But writing long ago *ceased* to embody any sacred, or even cosmological significance. And we of today give no thought at all to our writing, except to regard it as a basic instrumental skill needed to communicate a multitude of worldly concerns. Not even in our Western religions do we find any present attention to this matter.

And yet, writing is, and has to be, one of the most sacred

of all our ritualized gestures, since, without it, the sacred liturgy itself could not possibly exist. Moreover, the *handing down* of religious traditions – traditions of understanding as well as of ritual practice – depends on writing in a most decisive, most fateful way. For, in its character as a gesture, writing is perhaps one of the most direct, most immediate *incarnations* of a religious tradition. In the production of manuscripts, in the producing of liturgical texts whose spellings, the shapings of light and shadow, retrace for vision the inwrought scriptural process, the hand shows forth – the hand hands down – the felt presence of divinity, and the truth of the spiritual life impressing its experience into the very play, the very warp and woof, of its legible textures.

There is a point in the *Meno* when Socrates is prompted to say, 'I asked you to deliver virtue into my hands whole and unbroken. . . .' Socrates believes that this kind of delivery is possible only when the teacher teaches, not by precepts, but by example, being himself a virtuous man. So, too, in the matter of writing, as a gesture in the maintenance and transmission of the religious truth, the religious experience. *Unless the gesture of writing itself embodies its spiritual tradition in the most exemplary, most self-evident, and most illuminating manner, the tradition will be fatally corrupted in the very act by which it is inscribed and handed down.*

Writing is an act of submission: a gesture that voluntarily binds itself, first of all, to the visibility of a grammatical virtue; but it is also, in the context of an uncorrupted religious tradition, a ritualized discipline and practice, a gesture binding itself to the transcendent mission of its tradition and selflessly effacing itself, but in the most visible, most effectively traceable way, before the spiritual wisdom which it submits to the vision of a reader in the moment of enlightened transmission.

Where, then, can we find what Stevens calls 'A hand of light to turn the page. . . ?'[42] In the ritual of sacred writing, the work of the gesture must be understood hermeneutically, as the completion of a process of reading. The writing ultimately belongs, in its absolute obedience, to the graphology of light; to *Alētheia* as the logic of light and darkness, concealment and disclosure. Without light, there could be no writing. The hand which moves with the understanding – the hand which is *moved* by this understanding – answers to the poet's call. But the obedience (*Zugehörigkeit*) of the gesture needs to be clarified in relation to the historical traditions which flourished once both in Europe and in China, and in which the process of copying assumed a significance that remains quite enigmatic to the modern mind.

Walter Benjamin explains, however, that,

> the power of a text is different when it is [merely] read from when it is [also, and simultaneously] copied out. . . . Only the copied text then *commands* the soul of him who is occupied with it, whereas the mere reader never discovers the new aspects of his inner self that are opened by the text . . . because the reader follows the movement of his mind in the free flight of day-dreaming, whereas the [reading] copier *submits* to its command. The Chinese practice of copying books was thus an incomparable guarantee of literary culture, and the transcript a key to China's enigma.[43]

What will probably spring to mind first, though, is the spectre of an utterly immobilized society: a society not only paralyzed but dying, precisely because of this oppressive and very exclusive culture of reading, copying, and writing. And yet, there is also something attractive, something compelling, and even, I feel, deeply convincing, in the practice which Benjamin describes. Is there an inherent value in this practice? What is the *potential* of which we are being reminded?

What is copying? To start with, we might suggest this: copying is *binding* oneself to write (to follow with one's hand) what one reads (follows with the eyes). And reading? Reading is *binding* the eyes to gestures which follow what is written. (We tend to overlook the complex sorts of trainings involved in learning how to read. We forget, or ignore, the linearity, for example, and what other subtle values culture successfully incorporates along with its lessons in reading. In ordering the scanning of the eyes, culture also teaches a certain kind of rationality: staying in line, patience, perseverence, concentration, first things first.) But writing, too, is a form of binding. For we (learn to) write by binding the hand to imitate, and reproduce, what the eyes (are learning to) read. Since binding is always in question, what needs to be thought is, broadly speaking, the moral *character* of this process. To be specific: is it enslaving, or is it liberating? The binding also establishes our *belonging*. Once we have learned how to read and write, we belong in a new way to our culture; we are inscribed in the fullest sense into the Book of Life and Death. What, then, is the *character* of our belonging? And how is it being taught? How transmitted?

We always learn to write by *copying* what we are given to read; and what we are given to read is a text, a textue of 'significant' marks. In *What Is Literature?*, Sartre holds that the reader must first 'render himself passive' in order to respond, in the end, creatively. And he concludes from this that, 'the man who is reading has raised himself to the highest degree.'[44] Does this claim put reading in a different light for us? Does it suggest a defense of reading that might parallel Benjamin's vision of writing? But of course, this passivity and obedience need not be, and in fact could not be, exclusively, and not even primarily, a *slavish* passivity. Skillfulness in reading and writing has always signified opportunities for individual and political liberation. Be this as it may, however, the fact is that, in the reading and writing of ancient China, and likewise in the literary copying of mediaeval Europe, a completely different kind of 'passive binding' was at stake.

In the examples of these two cultural traditions, we encounter a truth that is at first very difficult to grasp: the most spiritual form of reading and writing is the process of copying. The copying that flourished at the height of those traditions demanded a gesture of the most intense, most self-restrained devotion, reproducing without the slightest mistake, reproducing with the most perfect accuracy, and by a writing which originated in a mythic gesture that was capable of gathering and disseminating the blessings of light, a manuscript of unquestionable authority. The act itself, the copying, requiring, as it did, the most intense meditative concentration, poise and steadiness of hand, as well as the virtues of patience, devotion and humility, reached its spiritual fulfillment not in the calligraphy as such, but rather as a gesture of compassion, reaching out towards other mortals, mortals in need of guidance, and handing down to them, in the most beautiful, most gracious way, the authoritative guidance by which they so desperately need to be touched.

Perhaps the best way to get at the nature of the process which both Benjamin and Sartre must have had in mind, when they proclaimed the great virtue in the passivity of copying and reading, would be to reflect very briefly on the *character* of the gestures which are, or which ideally might be, involved. Bringing the process of copying somewhat closer, or at least bringing it into our own culture, we might visualize a monk living in the Europe of the Middle Ages, concentrating in a meditative way on the copying, the exact replication, of a precious religious manuscript. What needs to be noted, first, is this: that to every signifying mark, every tracing of thought which appears on the surface of the original text, there corresponds a gesture – the gesture, namely, which produced it. Thus, for example, the shape of the mark, and its relationship to the other marks in its context, provide a tracing, a track, of the gesture which brought it forth. Variations in the width of the mark, and in its darkness, or opacity, correspond to variations in the pressure of the hand, and to the variations in timing and flow – the rhythm, the melody – of the movement. And they correspond to the eyes' sense of beauty, which is to say, in part, movements that are, and are felt to be, most 'natural.'

Now let us suppose, visualizing the object of our supposition as vividly and as intensely as we can, that, first of all, the gestures which produced the original text were the gestures of a monk whose piety, faith, and simple devotional life truly *exemplified* for his community the very highest values of the religious tradition; and second, that the gestures which brought forth the text visibly and tangibly *embody* the meditative quality and character of his mortal life. Then it seems to me that the character of that life would be woven into the character of the characters which appear on the surface of the text, constituting its texture, and a meaning intrinsically present; and that the copying or transcribing of that text could therefore be a process valuable in and of itself, quite *apart* from the purely cognitive meanings conveyed through the *words* of the text. For, after all, the surface of the text one faces is a texture which reflects, which reproduces, the very gestures which brought it forth. Consequently, the transcribing of the text, involving both a reading which engages the eyes in a replication of the manual gesture, and a writing, which of course engages the copyist's hand, would transmit in the most direct, most tangible way the virtues most cherished by the tradition.

The religiously motivated soul will feel, after all, the ancient pressure to transcribe its rhythms, the measure of its spirit, into the 'delirium' of a scriptural gesture. The reading and copying of the original sacred text inscribes into the flesh, the very musculature of the copier, the grace, the balance, the measure, which the original gesture, and the original text, so perfectly embody. The monk's submission to copying is therefore not at all slavish; rather, it is the humility and compliance of love which enables him to learn, and pass on, what it is that his tradition, reaching through the generations even from its most intangible depth, has within it to teach.

In the modern age of mechanical reproduction, when the endistancing of representation replaces, and postpones, the experience of felt presence, writing has not only been deprived of its vision of a divinity made tangible, but also has lost touch with its inwrought meaningfulness, and with the pressure of its virtue, as the incarnation of a holy life.[45] The loss of scriptural skill is indeed, then, a fateful loss. For the sake of the living body of religious tradition, the gesture of writing *needs* to be given the gift of our thought. Then, and only then, manifesting the non-dual, two-fold character of yielding, viz., as that which renders by virtue of its capacity to surrender, and which receives the most by giving and giving way – only then, I believe, will the gestures of our hands know how to hand down their own most precious gifts.

Once upon a time, when writing was a skill for the high priests, it was understood that writing not only hands down the illuminations of a tradition, but also teaches, at the same time, the nature of the discipline, the ritual required to hand it down. But more basic even than this is the teaching of writing as a gesture both personal and more than personal: a religious gesture of great compassion, a gesture signifying only itself, and handing on directly, apart, that is, from the externally signified meaning of the text, the most essential values of spiritual life to be maintained by that body of tradition.

But, of course, the time for calligraphy, the time for the copying of sacred texts, is gone. What, then, is the use in proclaiming the virtue in those arts? I would like to say that, even in our profane, technologized world, there is a guardian awareness which it is possible to retrieve from our gestures of reading and writing. Reading and writing are essentially ritualized gestures, even when they have lost their sense of any contact with the sacred and the holy of the old tradition. And they are still gestures which essentially belong to the communicative gatherings of culture. The very processes of reading and writing are processes which, in their own right, successfully teach many of the qualities of character highly esteemed by our culture. In reading and writing, in the very gestures themselves, we are *claimed* by those qualities, but claimed precisely in and through our freedom; and our character is ordered, is formed and in-formed, by way of a *mimesis* which incarnates its rationality, deeply inscribing it into our body of awareness. Thus, it remains as an exciting possibility that a *new sense* of existential meaning, a *new sense* of something worthy of our deepest devotion, could some day emerge from the ritual binding to which our culture invariably subjects us.

Part II

The Text of Flesh: Our Primordial Text

Opening Conversation

(1) You shall place these commandments of mine in your heart and in your soul, and you shall bind them for a sign on your hand.

Deuteronomy 11:18

(2) Why does it no longer happen that a god marks a man's forehead,
Prints, as before, the stamp on the stricken?

Hölderlin, 'Bread and Wine'[46]

(3) all our so-called consciousness is a more or less fantastic commentary upon an unknown text, one that is perhaps unknowable but still felt.

Nietzsche, *Dawn of Day*[47]

(4) The body is to be compared, not to a physical object, but rather to a work of art.

Merleau–Ponty, *Phenomenology of Perception*[48]

(5) woe to the flesh that does not preserve its purity. . . . May the tenderness [of thy touch] be moved toward all flesh; [and] thy glorious holy name shall be blessed by all flesh. [For] the instruction of thy law healeth all flesh.

Service for Yom Kippur[49]

(6) [The task of genealogy] . . . is to expose a body

190

totally imprinted by history and the process of
history's destruction of the body.

Michel Foucault, 'Nietzsche, Genealogy, History'[50]

(7) The flesh is not matter, is not mind, is not substance.
To designate it, we should need the old term
'element', in the sense it was used to speak of water,
air, earth and fire, that is, in the sense of a *general
thing*. . . . The flesh in this sense is an 'element' of
Being.

Merleau–Ponty[51]

(8) the body is solidified or generalized existence, and
existence a perpetual incarnation.

Merleau–Ponty, *Phenomenology of Perception*[52]

In 'Freud and the Scene of Writing,' Jacques Derrida muses
on the fact that,

From Plato and Aristotle on, scriptural images have
regularly been used to illustrate the relationship
between reason and experience, perception and
memory.[53]

This is so, except that, by writing this, he casts away in
shadow – as we shall presently see – the ancient scriptural
image of his own ancestors, the Jewish people. The tradition
is not only Greek; it is also Palestinian, Semitic. Anyway,
forgiving him this forgetfulness, we read on:

Psychical content will be represented by a text
whose essence is irreducibly graphic. The structure
of the psychical apparatus will be represented by a
writing machine [as in Freud's mystic writing pad,
for example].[54]

And he therefore asks what the psyche must be if it can be
represented by a text. Pursuing this question, we might ask:
What is the process of embodying a liturgical tradition, if it
be such that it can be represented by a text? As we shall see
very soon, the liturgical and scriptural texts *themselves* connect
the human body to the image of a text. But they also hide in
shadow the full significance of this connection. Our concern,
here, is therefore hermeneutical, as well as phenomenological: to shed some light on this connection between body and

191

text, so that we may see more clearly how the textual *image* helps us to understand the transmission of a religious tradition.

If we accept Julia Kristeva's definition of 'text', then the process of embodying a liturgical tradition is indeed a text-centered process; but the sense in which this is so turns out to be much deeper, much more complicated, than we might at first have thought. Here, then, as a point of departure, is Kristeva's definition, which she proposes in her essay on Mallarmé's *Up coup de dés*:

> Let us designate as a text any linguistic *practice* in which the operations of the genotext appear in laminar form in the phenotext, so that the phenotext serves as a projection of a genotext and invites the reader to reconstruct from it the entire signifying process.[55]

First, suppose that we construe 'the reader' to belong to the tradition of some devotional community, so that the invitation is understood as religiously binding. Second, suppose we take the 'phenotexts' to be the *visible* texts of the liturgy. Third, suppose that the 'genotext' is an *invisible* text – a text of Nature or Destiny (*Moira*): a text, we might say, which is inscribed by God's own hand. And finally, suppose that the text, as liturgical, belongs to a tradition of ritualized embodiment – that the text, in other words, is a *religious* text which concerns the performance of those rituals by virtue of which the religious tradition is embodied, and successfully transmitted from generation to generation. (A tradition of ritual embodiment ensures the *transmission* of that tradition, and consequently its *continuity*, in a perpetual reincarnation.) Then Kristeva's definition could be taken to imply that the visible texts of the liturgy bind those mortals who have thoughtfully encountered them to reconstruct, or interpret, their significance through a never-ending process of embodiment.

But how should we characterize this process? Is it simply a process of liturgical readings? Surely not, since it is *written into the liturgy* that we, in reading the visible liturgical phenotext, are invited to transform our embodiment, weaving, stamping, or, in effect, rewriting, the liturgical sense of the text into the very flesh of our body. Is it, then, a *simple* process of writing? Not quite, since it is written – in the liturgical texts – that what we 'write' into our flesh in the binding of ritual *always* turns out to have been 'written' *already*, 'written' invisibly, in the primordial, or divine, genotext. So, if the embodiment is a 'writing,' it is the 'writing' which makes a 'copy': by the 'copying' of liturgical phenotexts, which are *themselves* mere 'copies' (the visible dimension) of the genotext, the embodiment ultimately 'copies' the original, and of course *authoritative*, genotext. But the matter is further complicated by the fact that the originality of the genotext, and even its basic authority, are shrouded in impenetrable mystery. The genotext is invisible, as is its author. Is the liturgy just its projection, its trace, its copy? Or could it be that the genotext is in fact a *projection* of the liturgy – a myth, a fiction? We must now interpolate these obscure questions into the context of the embodiment process.

In 'The God's Script,' a short story by Borges, the author invites us to imagine the idea that, on the first day of Creation, God thought to write 'a magical sentence with the power to ward off . . . evils. He wrote it in such a way that it would reach the most distant generations and not be subject to chance.' And, he speculates, while searching for this formula, that awesome sentence with the secret of health: 'Throughout the earth there are ancient forms, forms incorruptible and eternal. . . . A mountain could be the speech of God, or a river. . . . Perhaps the magic would be written on my face; perhaps I myself was the end of my search.'[56]

Perhaps Borges' fiction is a poetic lie; that is to say: a hermeneutic truth. For the fact of the matter is that Borges simply recasts in modern print the shadow of an ancient truth: a truth which has been protected, despite everything, by the sacred texts of our religious tradition, which tell us, in partially veiled allusions, about the nature and origin of writing, and of inscription generally, and which claim to recognize, engraved upon the human flesh, the invisible handwriting of God, compassionately transmitting, for the benefit of all human beings, the secret of their – of our – embodiment. This secret, dispelling diseases, even madness, spells out the way to health, the way of ancient wisdom. As Gershom Scholem explains:

> Everybody carries the secret trace of the
> transmigration of his soul in the lineaments of his

forehead and his hands, and in the aura which
radiates from his body.[57]

Now, we certainly could construe this as nothing but metaphor. The hope of this study, however, is to demonstrate
that such an interpretation would miss a significant experiential truth.

In the *Book of Psalms* (139:16), it is stated that the secret
trace, the secret spell that brings mortals their health, is in
fact a text: 'in thy book, all my members were written.' But
the text is *identified* with the human body. Thus, for example,
in the text (a *piyyut*) for the second day of the service which
commemorates the Jewish new year (*Rosh Hashanah*), we find
a most powerful prayer. It reads:

O deign to hear the voice of those who glorify thee
with all their limbs, according to the number of
the two hundred and forty-eight affirmative
precepts. In this month, they blow thirty sounds
according to the thirty members of the soles of their
feet; the additional offerings of the day are ten,
according to the ten in their ankles; they approach
the altar twice, according to their two legs; five
men are called to the law, according to the five
joints in their knees; they observe the appointed
time to sound the cornet, on the first day of the
month, according to the one in their thigh; they
sound the horn thrice, according to the three in
their hips; lo, with the additional offering of the
New Moon, they are eleven, according to their
eleven ribs; they pour out the supplication with
nine blessings, according to the muscles in their
arms; they contain thirty verses, according to the
thirty in the palms of their hands; they daily repeat
the prayer of eighteen blessings, according to the
eighteen vertebrae in their spine; at the offering of
the continual sacrifice, they sound nine times,
according to the nine muscles in their head; in the
two orisons they blew eight times, according to
the eight vertebrae in their neck; their statutes and
law are contained in five books, according to the
five perforations; he hath ordained the six orders of
the *Mishnah*, according to the different
imaginations of the heart and inward parts; also the

kidneys, the loin, the imagination, thought, belly, bowels and their moods; the animal life [instinct], spirit, rational soul, perception, skin, flesh, veins and bones. . . . Shall all lift up the eye, and pierce the ear, and open the mouth, that with tongue and speech of the lips, and from the sole of their feet to the head [they] may show the particulars of their good acts.[58]

Gershom Scholem writes that,

Long before the Kabbalah the Talmudists played with the idea of a correspondence between the commandments of the Torah and the structure of man. . . . Thus, each member of man's body was made to fulfill one of the commandments.[59]

If this correspondence should seem, nowadays, to be nothing but the word-play of magic or myth, is that not because we, we moderns of the scientific epoch, have been denied the full teachings of our tradition? Where is the living tradition, now? Where is that tradition which once transmitted, from old to young, the *experiential* significance of this correspondence? The tradition which taught and preserved the healing of our embodiment, the healing of the flesh and our release from its suffering, through which alone the beauty of our spiritual life can blossom, is now gone. The continuity of the tradition has been all but completely forgotten – or (if we may translate Freud) deeply repressed. Still, as long as these texts, these prayers, are extant, the healing wisdom of this most ancient tradition is not, and will not be, entirely lost. Can we, in fact, restore it? Perhaps we can, if, even to some extent, we succeed in fleshing out, in the moving language of human experience, just what these texts concern, so that we rescue them from the perverse fate of mysticism.

It becomes crucial, here, to understand and appreciate the role of narrative imagination in the process of healing. Even if the correspondence be, in a sense, nothing but a wonderful waking dream, that is not to exclude the possibility that, precisely by such wakeful dreaming, or guided visualizations, our experiencing of ourselves, and above all, of our embodiment, may be profoundly changed. Wakeful dreaming is, as such, a form of therapy – perhaps, in fact, one of the most ancient, most powerful methods of healing. The liturgical texts could be said to describe, then, the dream of a cosmological correspondence. And they do this with a spell-binding poetry that *moves us to respond* in such a way that the de-scriptions *of* experience become prescriptions *for* experience. And, since these are techniques that do actually cure, the texts succeed in *making* themselves true (true descriptions, that is). Nor is this truth a mere isomorphism between text and flesh; for the possibility of the truth, here, is not different from the possibility of a cure. And this means that the texts are true because they have not forgotten the original text, inscribed upon our flesh, and of which they are merely the true and faithful translations.

We need, at this point, to consider the phenomenology of the visualization process. We need, that is, to understand how (the reading of) liturgical texts, texts gestated out of a religious tradition of ritual embodiment, can effect spiritually significant transformations – sublimations of the flesh. I would like to make use of Jung's depth psychology. But we must bear in mind, of course, that, in our account, what Jung calls 'the collective unconscious' refers to what Merleau–Ponty would recognize as the most archaic, most primordial dimension of our *embodiment*, and that, as John Welwood (a clinical psychologist) has accurately put it, the 'primordial archetypes,'

> instead of being seen as inborn psychic structures
> or contents of the collective unconscious, may be
> understood as universal patterns of body-in-the-
> world.[60]

Now, in 'The Structure of the Psyche,' Jung suggests that,

> the unconscious, as the totality of all archetypes, is
> the deposit of all human experience right back to
> its remotest beginnings. Not, indeed, a dead deposit
> . . . but a living system of reactions and aptitudes
> that determine the individual's life in invisible ways
> – all the more effective because invisible.[61]

Since the collective unconscious 'contains the whole spiritual heritage of mankind's evolution,'[62] Jung asserts, in another essay, 'The Relations Between the Ego and the Unconscious,' that,

> Access to the collective psyche means a renewal of
> life for the individual, no matter whether this
> renewal is felt as pleasant or unpleasant.[63]

By the same token, we may say that our returning to the
primordial dimension of our incarnation, the field of our
wholeness in relation to Being, means the *beginning* of a
process of recentering ourselves in an expanded bodily felt
awareness: the Ego's recognition, once it has reached a place
of personal stability and maturity, that it is feeling a healthy
need for a still deeper grounding, and a more meaningful
attunement, in the openness of Being. Erich Neumann
argues, therefore, that

> Ego consciousness evolves by passing through a
> series of 'eternal images,' and the ego, transformed
> in the passage, is constantly experiencing a new
> relationship to the archetypes.[64]

The Ego's metamorphosis involves it in an 'interior' journey;
and its access to the collective unconscious (the 'ancestral
body,' as Neumann calls it) is essentially a rite of passage – a
passage into self-recognition by way of the archetypal images
which the body holds in its latency, and which the ritual
patterns prescribed by ancient spiritual wisdom often have
the power to awaken. In an extremely important essay,
'Concerning Mandala Symbolism,' Jung writes:

> Knowledge of the common origin of these
> unconsciously preformed symbols has been
> [almost] totally lost to us [as a basis for the
> transmission and cultivation of our religious
> traditions]. . . . And when we penetrate a little
> more deeply below the surface of the psyche, we
> come upon historical layers which are not just dead
> dust, but alive and continuously active in everyone
> – maybe to a degree that we cannot imagine in the
> present state of our knowledge.[65]

Now, as Neumann points out,

> Archetypes take the form of images only where
> consciousness is present; in other words, the
> plastic self-portrayal of instincts is a psychic process

197

of a higher order. It presupposes an organ capable
of perceiving these primordial images. This organ
is consciousness. . . .[66]

Although Neumann unfortunately speaks, here, of
consciousness, I think we may understand him to be referring to the phases of a process in which archetypal images
of Being emerge from the primordial configurations of our
embodiment, are bodily sensed, i.e., registered in a pre-
conceptual body of understanding, and finally raised into the
articulate speech (*logos*) of self-understanding. In the gift of
embodiment, we will find the gift of what Neumann
describes[67] as a 'primitive body symbolism': ancient archetypal images that are responsive to appropriately attuned
inducements (e.g., the ritual prescription of particular
gestures, movements, or postures) and emerge spontaneously from the body's primordial participation in the wholeness of the field of Being,[68] bearing within them the symbolic
power to help us retrieve, from the depth of our own embodiment, the existential meaning of an authentic ontological
understanding. (The continued presence, in a culture, of its
traditional religious symbols, themselves the cultural projection of archetypal images originally carried within the primordial body, will protect the perpetual reincarnation which is
human existence, so long as they are transmitted from generation to generation in ways that directly correlate their
wisdom with the body's capacity to retrieve them from its
own *felt sense* of being.)

Let us now examine in more phenomenological detail the
religous appropriation of the visualization process as a liturgically guided, liturgically prescribed *ritualization* of the human
body: a process in virtue of which the essentially limited, and
naturally suffering, ego-logical body undergoes a spiritual
sublimation in the keeping of its religious tradition, and in
consequence of which the religious tradition itself is
embodied in a medium which can renew it, and will continue
the transmission of its wisdom. For this final phase of elucidation, however, we will require the help of Merleau–Ponty.
Although his *Phenomenology of Perception* does in fact take up,
albeit very briefly, the imaging of the body, our principal
source of insight must rather be his essay on 'The Child's
Relations with Others.' A most basic point, for our purposes,
is his claim, there, that,

> To the extent that I can elaborate and extend my
> corporeal scheme, to the extent that I acquire a
> better organized experience of my own body, to that
> very extent will my consciousness of my own body
> cease being a chaos in which I am submerged and
> lend itself to a transfer to others.[69]

This passage is extremely condensed. In order to spell it
out and develop, at the same time, my own account of this
process, which Merleau–Ponty is calling, here, the 'extension
of my corporeal scheme,' I would like to articulate its
elements in a sequence of steps that I hope will be congenial
to our sharing of thought. (1) Liturgical texts hand down,
from generation to generation, a tradition of symbolic images.
(2) These images include, as perhaps their most powerful
species, images of an archetypal nature. (3) Many of these
archetypal images are in fact corporeal images or schemata,
in the sense that they are representations of corporeal
patterns that originated in the primordial dimension of our
embodiment (the so-called 'collective unconscious' of our
'ancestral body'), whence they were retrieved and projected
in culturally preserved traces. (4) The corporeal images are
therapeutic, or healing, in that they put us in touch with the
well-spring of our need for a spiritually deepened conscious
life. That is to say, they appeal, they call, to our deepest
spiritual needs and longings *as they are carried* in the metaphors of our body's innermost sense. (5) The corporeal
images arise from the dimension of our body's pre-conceptual, pre-ontological attunement, and manifest our body's
felt pre-understanding of its participation in the wholeness
of Being. Because they arise from this dimension, they are
akin to the dream-images which constitute what Freud calls
'primary process thinking'. They are deeply satisfying, fulfilling our deepest dreams of being.

(6) Let me give an example of how images can serve to
elicit what, in *Phenomenology of Perception*, Merleau–Ponty has
called our 'implicit or sedimentary body of knowledge.'[70]
There is a text, written by a Tibetan scholar of Buddhism, in
which it is said that 'object and subject are like sandalwood
and its fragrance.'[71] Now, this is not an archetypal image.
But it is an image which bypasses rational, objective thought
in order to speak very directly to our 'implicit or sedimentary
body.' In fact, it speaks to that level of our understanding
precisely because *that* is the level where it will resonate with

a truth we unquestionably *sense* but have not been able to articulate with the clarity of a conceptual understanding. (7) Merleau–Ponty contends that 'the body can symbolize existence because it brings it into being and actualizes it.'[72] When they are genuinely archetypal, the corporeal images function as models, paradigmatic schemata of an ideal body. They schematize for our benefit the transcendence of our suffering incarnation and make present the possibility and desirability of a corresponding 'perfection' of our spiritual being.

(8) The schemata of spiritual accomplishment can be very effectively concretized and actualized through patternings of ritual that bind, discipline, and organize our experienced embodiment, making our bodily being humble and compliant, open and receptive, and filled with enthusiasm, kindly bending us toward the light of the inscribed teachings. Thus, the body in prayer is concentrated on shaping itself in conformity with its relationship to the ideality cherished by its spiritual tradition. The Christian, for example, makes himself small by kneeling in prayer to his God. This smallness is the body's way of schematizing the humility of a child of God. (I refer the reader to the letter which Rilke wrote to his mother, quoted earlier, at the beginning of Part I, in which he describes his experience of kneeling.) The Buddhist demonstrates a total submission of the will in which nothing is held back by prostrating himself flat on the ground. The Hebrew, however, prays mostly in the upright posture and, when filled with enthusiasm, his arms will be uplifted and his hands, as it is said in *Talmud Pesahim*, will be 'spread out in prayer as the eagles of the sky.' (The reader is referred, once again, to the passages quoted at the beginning of Part I.)

(9) The ritual schematizing of archetypal images can effect significant changes, shifts that we can feel, or sense, in the emerging of a new body of understanding. The shifts can take place, however, only in the hospitality of the open space that is constituted by the *difference* between the ideally schematized embodiment and the embodiment as which we have submitted to the schematizing process. (10) The transmission of spiritual wisdom by way of such schematizations involves what Henri Wallon first called a 'postural impregnation.' If we were to take over Husserlian terms, however, we might describe an 'intentional transgression,' involving a process of 'coupling' and the effecting of an 'associative sense transfer.'[73] (11) The liturgical texts produce corporeal shifts

by inducing a process which is at once active and passive, or rather, a process which it is altogether beyond the power of these metaphysical concepts to describe with fidelity to our experience. Despite this difficulty, we might want to speak, here, again drawing on Husserl, of active and passive syntheses of sense. (12) This ritual process is one of the most precious gifts of spiritual culture, for it binds us to the life of the 'ancestral body'. (13) The ancient and tradition-bearing provenance of the images that are synthesized therefore vouchsafe the continuity of the tradition in the new life of this ancestral body.

Many influences stamp, misshape and mutilate the body which emerges from the primordial field of Being. The routines of school and work contribute to the dismemberment of the body just as surely as the more violent interventions of political terror. Our cultural history has certainly not been kind to the human body. Even in education, where some greater enlightenment might be presumed to maintain the dignity of embodiment, our history tells a story of regimentation whose conclusion it is not difficult to foresee. But I do not believe that we are bereft of opportunities to reverse the course of history. Various spiritual traditions remain alive, even now; although they have not avoided degeneration, the challenge of responding to the crying need of our epoch may yet create conditions more favorable to their renewal as sources of revolutionary experience and liberation. I still have faith in the concealed wisdom of the ancestral body.

Michel Foucault, however, seems to perceive a more hopeless crisis, but I believe that he has restricted his perceptions to an ontical body whose history he himself has cut off from the history of Being. The history of Being may be a history of its oblivion; but even in its concealment, it keeps open a more promising destiny than a history which remains altogether silent about the body of ontological understanding. According to Foucault, it was Nietzsche's experience of suffering, and his conviction that the human body 'manifests the stigmata of past experience,' that moved him to assign to his genealogy (*Herkunft*) the task of exposing 'a body totally imprinted by history and the process of history's destruction of the body.'[74] But Foucault's emphasis on the body's mortality is in need of a counterbalance. In fact, Nietzsche's genealogy gazes prophetically into a future of redemption at least as much as it avows the ravages of the past. Nietzsche is quite certain that, out of the flesh upon which suffering has inscribed its message, a rejoicing life of the spirit could eventually emerge. For Nietzsche, it simply is not true that, in Foucault's sense, the body is 'totally imprinted by history.' For Nietzsche, the writing of a *Herkunft* is inseparable from the vision of an emergence (*Entstehung*).

Keeping this historical problematic in mind, let us continue to explore the wisdom still at work in extant traditions of ritual process. If we turn back to one of the prayers which we cited at the outset of this section, we may find ourselves asking questions such as these: *How* is God's 'tenderness . . . moved toward all flesh'? *How* is God's 'glorious holy name . . . blessed by all flesh'? And finally, *how is it possible* for the 'instruction' of divine law to 'heal all flesh'?[75] In order to focus our reflections on the question of the suffering and healing of the flesh, we must attempt to understand how the 'text' of divine law, and the liturgical texts which refer that law to the body, bear on these ways of the flesh. Perhaps the best material for thought, given the attention to pain on which both Nietzsche and Foucault insist, would be the reference to the body that we find in the prayer of Grace by which religiously thoughtful Jews conclude their meal. Before rising from table, they softly chant:

> We will give thanks unto thee, O Eternal, our God
> . . . for thy covenant, which thou hast sealed into
> our flesh.[76]

The orthodox interpretation understands this prayer as referring solely to the ancient rite of circumcision, the act by which the Jewish people as a whole repeatedly seal their historical de-cision to observe the sacred covenant. This interpretation, while certainly not false, is yet a tragically restricted understanding. For, in the first place, we must note that the word in the text does not denote only circumcision. Etymology discloses that the word also means 'sealed': it is, in short, a two-faced *hermeneutical* word, a word which indicates a hermeneutical, and in fact a scriptural, kind of phenomenon. 'Sealed' protects the truth of which circumcision would remind us, viz., that the ancestral body of the Jewish people was created by grace of a primordial incision or inscription: the writing and attesting of the divine signature, the grammatology of the original divine de-cision.[77] According to Irving Friedman, the covenant is related *both* to the word of the tongue *and* to the circumcision of the foreskin: the Hebrew term *milah* refers, it seems, both to word and to circumcision.[78] The two are really one and the same. By 'sealing' the tongue, Jews *bind* themselves to speaking words of truth, words of compassion and benevolence, words so filled with love and joy and worship that they move the air in a polyphonic song. Likewise, by the 'sealing' of the foreskin, Jews make a sacred offering of their ancestral body, an offering, in particular, of the encoded sexual organ. In the ritual of circumcision, the patriarchy sanctifies the male organ of sexual union and procreation; and it reminds the male, guardian of the ancestral body of tradition, to infuse into his experience of sexual embrace and union the joyful wisdom of godly love. In properly consecrated union, even a separation from God (in keeping with His fateful decision) can be erased and healed.

It must also be noted that, at *Deuteronomy* 10:16, we find the rite of circumcision related also to the binding of the heart:

> Circumcise, therefore, the foreskin of your heart,
> and be no more stiffnecked.

This context surely establishes, I think, not only that circumcision is symbolic of a process of *opening*, but further, that the very *essence* of circumcision – the heart of the matter, as it were – lies in the fact that the *incision opens*. Circumcision therefore corresponds to the breaking open of a path: the process which Freud, in his early years, called 'Bahnung.' It is, to be sure, a transgression against the flesh, a ritual act which *wounds*; but in wounding, it also opens. It is also an act of theft; yet it *gives* in exchange a gift for thought which is far more precious than what is taken.

In his 1895 *Project for a Scientific Psychology*, Freud wrote that 'pain leaves behind it particularly rich breaches [*Bahnungen*].'[79] Circumcision, as the ritualized infliction of pain, brings about much more than a traumatic neurophysiological memory-trace (in Freudian language, an *Erinnerungsspur*). Indeed, it initiates the ancestral body into a spiritual process which Jews call 'remembrance.'

Circumcision is a tremendous encounter with the Lawful Word, the commandments of God that are meant to seal the entrustment of virtue into man's memorial body. In sealing the covenant, God *pro-grammed* our bodies. (This insight persists, oddly enough, in our scientific thinking about the genetic 'code'.) But this pro-gramme is originally, as the word itself informs us, just a *potential*. In linguistic theory, it would probably be called our 'competence': a very special one, however, since the text is woven, invisibly, into the very texture of our flesh. It is, as it were, the secret, hidden scripture: that scroll of interior light by reference to which our life (or, as linguistic science would say, our 'performance') may always be properly guided. The pro-gramme is, therefore, a truly unshakable *standard* or *norm*, a secret code of behavior, inscribed for safe-keeping into the very flesh of our bodies. However, the circumcision only *breaks open* a passageway: what happens thereafter is up to us. The pro-gramme, after all, is not a 'real' seal; it is only the ideal *promise* of one. The 'real' seal, of course, can only be placed at the very end; for it is the sentence of one's death. Thus, to say that the religious body of tradition is inscribed with the Law of God is to concede that the truth of this body exists *only in deferment*, or delay. It is, in fact, precisely to *remind* Jews of this pro-grammed deferment, and to warn them against the possibility of 'erasure', that the seal of the covenant is put into visible writing, i.e., into the visibility and legibility of liturgical texts. But the inscription itself actually exists only in, or only by way of, this *difference*, which we have articulated here as the temporal delay – the temporal interlude, the separation and exile – between the mere potential of a capacity and the holy life in which that potential would be wholly realized and fulfilled.

Hence, we are compelled to acknowledge that there is, in fact, no 'original' text at all. The 'original', which is traditionally understood to be invisible, exists *only* as an *absent* text. (And its 'author,' of course, is likewise absent: absent in a hiddenness which foreshadows the 'death' of God in the Judaeo-Christian world.) In truth, the inscription takes place only after the fact, or, as Freud would say, *nur nachträglich*: only, that is, after the transformative encounter with the liturgical texts of the tradition. Considered in this light, circumcision is a *first* encounter, traumatic precisely because its significance cannot be known until many years later, when, thanks to an encounter with liturgical tradition, the human body begins, perhaps, to *embody* the visible scriptures and *make them visible* as a living body of tradition. *After the fact*, that is to say, only in the living body of tradition, do I realize, 'in my organs of perception,' as Merleau–Ponty puts it, 'a thought older than myself, of which those organs are merely a trace.' (See the text cited at the beginning of this chapter.) But this ancient thought, older than myself, and always already at work, is a weave of archetypal symbols, binding our perceptual body into the maternal textures of the world. Thus, it is precisely of this body of primordial inscription, this text of ancient thought, this body of instincts and genetically encoded wisdom, that Derrida's 'programme' holds true: 'We must speak,' he writes, 'of the indissoluble union of the signifier and the concept signified.'[80] There is 'indissoluble union' at the beginning, because, in the attunement of the infantile body, the painful encounter with the significant texts of a religious tradition has not yet taken place; and there is indissoluble union at the end, union in death, since the body is always *returned* to the primordial context of Being. The question, then, is whether in that span between birth and death, the living body has compliantly bound itself to the spiritual duties of liturgical tradition. The liturgical texts really belong to the *middle*, the interlude of life, which is also, perforce, the time of exile and alienation: the time, as Derrida would say, of maximum *dissemination*, which only the gathering of liturgical re-petition can bring to an end. The 'original text,' read as a body inscribed with the divine code, and belonging to the beginning and the end, is myth, is dream. And yet, the tradition of liturgical texts understands that, because it is a myth which serves us mortals as pre-text to spiritual exertion and devotion, it meets our most desperate need for encouragement.

However, we must somehow be taught how to *read* the liturgical texts, so that they illuminate for us the *ritual performance* by virtue of which the invisible text, the text of Law which is inscribed upon the scroll of our flesh, is to be *made visible* in its beauty, *legible* in its truth and goodness. And this requires that we bend every effort to understand the liturgical tradition by *translating its meaning* into the meaningful context of our daily life. Otherwise, the human potential for well-being granted us by virtue of these texts will remain unfulfilled, our lives the merest shadow of what, in the context of their truth, they might have chanced to become. Without the inherent wisdom in this primordial text of flesh, our mortal existence is bereft of its most profound meaning and value. And, in the fall of our mortality, we will not know the refreshing spring of joy in a life which is visibly *moved* by the inwrought text of spiritual wisdom.

In the print of the texts, we will read the shapes of thought's embodiments, cast in articulate shadows. Do these shadows foreshadow our translation of their wisdom into the sanity of our lives? Or will they, instead foreshadow a continuation of our period of mourning, exiled from the healing light of a new awareness? We must not forget that the divine inscription may also be read as the engraving of our fate: the seal, and shadow, of our death.

Part III
The Fleshing out of the Text

man cannot know
What passes in his members till periods of Space and
    Time
Reveal the secrets of Eternity; for more extensive
Than any other earthly things are Man's earthly
    lineaments.

William Blake, Milton[81]

In his discussion of how the Kogi (Indians living in the mountains near Santa Marta in Colombia) train their youth for the priesthood, Reichel-Dolmatoff observes that,

> Many of the songs and recitations are phrased in
> the ancient ceremonial language which is
> comprehensible only to an experienced mamá
> [priest], but which has to be learned by the novices
> by sheer memorization. During these early years,
> myths, songs and dances become closely linked
> into a rigid structure that alone – at least, at that
> time – guarantees the correct form of
> presentation.[82]

And he points out, further, that,

> One of the main institutionalized teaching concepts
> consists in iterative behavior. This is emphasized
> especially during the first half of the curriculum,
> when the novices are made to repeat the myths,
> songs, or spells until they have memorized not only

the text and the precise intonation, but also the
body movements and minor gestures that
accompany the performance. Rhythmic elements
are important and the learning of songs and recitals
is always combined with dancing or, at least, with
swaying motions of the body. This is not a mere
mechanistic approach to the learning process and
does not represent a neurally based stimulus-
response pattern, but the child is simultaneously
provided with a large number of interpretive details
that make him grasp the context and the meaning
of the texts.[83]

According to this author,

The novices have ample opportunity to watch their
master perform ritual actions, a process during
which a considerable body of knowledge is
transmitted to them. . . . Now that they
themselves begin to perform minor rituals, the
recurrent statements contained in the texts,
together with the identical behavioral sequences,
become linked into a body of highly patterned
experiential units.[84]

Through these ritual repetitions, the human body becomes
'a body of esoteric knowledge,' a body which the Kogi themselves call a 'loom of life': that gift of Being upon which the
Kogi elders, guardians of their spiritual tradition, painstak-
ingly weave into existence a sacred body of understanding.
The Kogi may seem primitive to technologized eyes. But they
are astute enough to realize that, if the body of understanding vouchsafed a religious tradition is to avoid reification,
and the fate of an eventual death, it must be kept alive as, and
kept alive in, a tradition of embodiment. And that involves a
tradition of consecratory rituals, teaching and sharing the
ancient wisdom of the tribal ancestors. Even for the Kogi,
these rituals are partly liturgical: rituals of reading, and actually performing, what amount to textual *prescriptions* for the
translation of textual meanings into a 'new' body of understanding. Furthermore, the Kogi are astute enough to realize
that their tradition of embodiment, their tradition of ritual,
is at the same time the embodiment of their tradition: that,

namely, by virtue of which the tradition stands its only chance of surviving.

What perhaps most captures my attention, in this anthropological report, is the question of pedagogical method. The Kogi apparently see great value in a teaching which works very directly with the process of embodiment; and they accordingly put great weight on the ritual education of the body as primary locus, primary ground, of 'conceptual' understanding. In the matter of education, the Kogi are anything but primitive, for their method of transmitting the ancestral tradition is a way that is meant to ensure the continuity of their collective spiritual life, but without suppressing the creative potential for spontaneous individual understandings. And this is something which still needs to be incorporated into our own theory and practice, even though, many years ago, John Dewey gave it a very forceful, very articulate formulation. Thus, in *Art as Experience*, for example, he argues that,

> sense, as meaning so directly embodied in
> experience as to be its own illuminated meaning,
> is the only signification that expresses the function
> of sense organs when they are carried to full
> realization.[85]

Dewey is convinced, in fact, that,

> There is no limit to the capacity of immediate
> sensuous experience to absorb into itself meanings
> and values that, in and of themselves . . . would be
> designated 'ideal' and 'spiritual.'[86]

If we were to turn back, at this point, to the beginning of this chapter, it would be evident that our reflections on the body in its bearing of thought have now brought us to the pedagogical process surrounding the reading of visible liturgical texts – texts which explicitly *lay claim* to the character, and the spirit, of our incarnation, and undertake the cultivation of that potential to which they lay claim by working with the ritualization of the body. However, before we can properly appreciate the crucial role of the body in the realization of that understanding which our spiritual tradition holds open for us, it might be useful to spell out the 'textual' interpretation of the flesh suggested in the preceding section, going over, once again, the function of the 'original' and 'secondary' texts in the context of ritual incarnation.

According to the liturgical texts we have been considering – the texts, namely that I have just called 'secondary' – we mortals receive, as our destined being, an elemental body of nature, an emblematic existence, upon whose flesh a secret and invisible text – the 'original text' – has always, and already, been engraved. According to some of the texts, of course, it is the hand of God which makes the fateful inscription. Anyway, the interpretation to which we will adhere in this chapter is that this 'original text' is the encoded prescription, and the normative pro-gramme, of our corporeal nature: our genetic inheritance, our neurophysiological system of functions, and indeed, the totality of our original corporeal endowments, capacities and dispositions. But this 'original text' is encoded; we do not know how to read it. Or, in other words: we do not initially know, and therefore need to learn, of what we are fully capable. Our *natural* body is the gift of an innate potential: an implicit meaning, or entrustment of meaning, whose full realization – the explicit fulfillment whose truth we call 'sanity' and 'health' – is the task, not of nature, but only, rather, of culture. The 'secondary texts' respond, therefore, to our need for instruction, our need for very specific guidance. And this responsiveness is especially needed, clearly, with regard for the explicitation and realization of our implicit capacity, our capacity precisely as bodily beings, for incarnating the well-being of a spiritual life. The liturgical texts, decoding the pre-scriptions for well-being that are invisibly in-scribed into our flesh, make possible the fulfillment which is first pro-mised in the prescription.

The decoding and guidance take the form, first of all, of a reading: the reading of the liturgical texts pre-scribed by the religious tradition. This reading is itself an act of devotion, a gesture by virtue of which we actively appropriate the tradition being handed over to us, and by virtue of which, moreover, we perform a sacred task. But the reading pre-scribes a second decoding, viz., the actual *performance* of pre-scribed postures, gestures and movements. This is the phase of ritualization, where textual meanings are read as providing precise *schematizations* of the spiritually developed, spiritually fulfilled human body, and are translated accordingly into the body's own idiom of understanding. As we perform the pre-scribed rituals with greater and greater skill and grace, we are progressively in-habited, correlatively, by a *living, breathing, muscular, and moving understanding* of the visible, legible texts, bearers of our tradition. At the same time, of course, our understanding of the 'original' text, i.e., our understanding of our 'supersensible destination' as mortal embodiments of the truth of Being, likewise becomes very much clearer, since it is an understanding which exists only by virtue of its being (increasingly) embodied.

Thus, with the passage of time, time continuously repeated in the performative reading, 'inner' and 'outer' texts will eventually begin to coincide. Were there no longer any difference between them, our understanding would be complete, that is to say: by virtue of the satisfactory performance of the rituals prescribed by the 'outer' texts, the hidden sense of the 'inner' would be fully translated. We would finally *become* the one true text. However, the ambiguity in the word 'sense' should serve to remind us that meaning, embodied in the sensuous element, is subject to endless translation, endless dissemination. So that our relation to the texts is *always in question* as a sentence of becoming. The infinite existential value and inexhaustible meaningfulness of the archetypal text thus continues to unfold – not only in our own life, but also in the lives of all the living beings whom we chance to encounter.

This process of ritual embodiment is what I want to call the 'fleshing out' of the liturgical text. Since it is a process which fleshes out an already received, but not yet realized, potential-for-being, the ritual might be described as a *recollection* of that which has been, in some sense, 'forgotten.' Thus, Walter Benjamin writes:

> Like ultraviolet rays, memory [*Eingedenken*] shows
> to each man in the book of life a script that invisibly
> and prophetically glosses the text.[87]

But 'fleshing out' also connotes *understanding*. Thus, in the remainder of this essay on the living body of tradition, I would like to focus on the process of understanding. Principles of decisive importance for humanistic education are, I believe, involved. Athens certainly thought so, if we may trust Plato's account of education in *The Republic* and *Laws*.

In *Wahrheit und Methode*, Gadamer writes:

> To understand it [a text] does not mean primarily

referring back to past life, but rather present
participation in what is said. It is not really a
question of a relation between persons . . . but
rather, of a participation in the communication
which the text makes to us.[88]

Now, in the case of religious texts, this participation, this
conversation with the text, is always, I submit, a process of
understanding through embodiment. This explains, in part, why
it happens that, as he states in another work,

The real event of understanding goes continually
beyond what can be brought to the understanding
. . . by methodological effort and critical self-
control. It is true of every conversation that
through it something different has come to be.[89]

This is true above all, I believe, when understanding is transmitted in, and as, a process of embodiment. But, in any case,
understanding a text will never be a question of undergoing,
or experiencing, a discrete mental state, or a momentary
'cognitive' episode, in the disembodied 'life' of a transcendental Cartesian *Cogito*. Rather, it needs to be conceived as
'the entering into an event of transmission in which past
and present are constantly mediated.'[90] So far, so good. But
Gadamer fails to pursue to the end of the implications of his
own logic: implications which lead us, here, to explicate the
truth of understanding in hermeneutical terms as a process
of embodiment. How else can we account for the body of
understanding entrusted to us by our textual, and specifically
liturgical, tradition?
    Nietzsche's ruminations, in *The Will to Power*, contain some
fascinating insights which bear on these points. He observes,
for example, that,

Our most sacred convictions, the unchanging
elements in our supreme values, are judgments of
our muscles.[91]

Gathered into our very muscles, and indeed, into our body
as a whole, we will find, if we are attentive,

The stored-up integrity and shrewdness of

generations which are never conscious of their
principles. . . .[92]

According to Nietzsche,

> When morality . . . has been, as it were, stored up
> through the practice of a whole succession of
> generations, then the total force of this accumulated
> virtue radiates even into that sphere where
> integrity is most seldom found, into the spiritual
> sphere.[93]

Thus, he concludes that,

> One acts perfectly only when one acts
> instinctively.[94]

Or, as he says in another note,

> To the extent that it is willed, to the extent that it
> is conscious, there is no perfection in action of any
> kind.[95]

I would unhesitatingly contest Nietzsche's (perhaps polem-
ical) choice of the concept of instinct to describe the embodiment of spiritual 'perfection.' The concept we obviously need
here is that of spontaneity: 'a spontaneity,' as Merleau–Ponty
puts it in his essay 'On the Phenomenology of Language,'
which 'teaches me what I could not know in any other way
except through it.'[96] 'Instinct' accurately describes the environmental attunement of animals. We obviously do not enjoy
that kind of 'fit.' Our consciousness is a separation (*Riss,
écart*) which terminates that animal attunement. But Nietzsche is entirely justified in insisting that we are capable of
transcending the rational attunement of precept morality.
What is *beyond* that kind of attunement? The spontaneity of
Gelassenheit! So I would also have to contest his asseveration
concerning 'consciousness,' unless what he *means* is in fact
what he *should* mean, viz., that perfection lies *beyond* the
process of deliberation according to principles and precepts
– which is simply another way of reaffirming that the essence
of spiritual behavior is spontaneity. Govinda is therefore
accurate in his observation that, 'We can be spontaneously

and yet fully conscious of the forms and forces of tradition.'[97]
In truth, as he says,

> spontaneity is built on practice . . . it is a product
> of long-repeated actions in the past . . . which
> have become so ingrained in one's nature that they
> need no further decision or effort of will.[98]

We might wish only to add, here, that a tradition will become
so ingrained only if it truthfully *corresponds* to a grain of
destiny already inscribed into the very flesh of our
understanding.

In *The Way of the White Clouds*, the report of his pilgrimage
across Tibet, Govinda is kind enough to describe, for our
benefit, the quotidian life of an old Tibetan who incarnates
for him the very spontaneity in question. I will quote it at
some length, so that we have a chance to feel ourselves into
that life and absorb from the enveloping mood (*Stimmung*)
of the place some of the warmth and joy which it emanates,
and which keeps it always open to the meaningfulness of
the Open:

> In spite of his old age I never saw Katchenla
> unoccupied: whether he would glide about the
> temple on two square pieces of felt, in order to keep
> the floor polished, or whether he would attend to
> the hundreds of butter-lamps, water-bowls, and
> other altar-vessels, which had to be kept clean and
> shining and filled with their various ingredients –
> ever was he busy in the service of the temple or
> in the performance of his spiritual duties: reading
> the sacred texts, reciting prayers for the welfare of
> all living beings, and performing the daily rituals
> for their protection and well-being. On special
> occasions he would be making small clay images of
> great beauty, and I was fascinated to see how every
> phase of the work, from the mixing and kneading
> of the clay, the modeling or pressing into forms,
> to the drying or baking in the charcoal fire and the
> subsequent gilding or painting (or both) of the
> delicate details, every process was accompanied by
> *mantras* and prayers, invoking the blessings of the
> Enlightened Ones and the beneficent forces of the
> universe, present in earth and air, water and fire,

i.e., in all the elements which support our life and serve us in the accomplishment of our work. Thus even a manual occupation was turned into a ritual of profound meaning and an act of devotion and meditation, whose forces would saturate even the material objects created in this way.[99]

Dewey, I think, would have immediately recognized in this exemplary life precisely that embodiment of meaning 'carried to full realization' of which he wrote in *Art As Experience*. So much so, in fact, that I do not hesitate at all to use his own words, to say of Katchenla:

In this participation, the varied wonder and splendor of this world are made actual . . . in the qualities he experiences.[100]

The liturgical texts which lay claim to our embodiment in such a way that we are helped to *focus* on *our bodily felt sense* of their textual meaning are texts which have been written with the very deepest kind of wisdom. For they appreciate that there are dimensions of meaning (*Sinn*) which are such that it is only with my body, i.e., only through the process of actually incarnating those dimensions of sense in a disciplined and eventually skillful way, that I may ever come to understand them. The senses do indeed confuse, ambiguate and disseminate cognitively unified meaning; but they also serve to preserve, and to recollect, ancient meanings otherwise lost: meanings which can be *protected* only in a body not subject to reflection, and *retrieved* only in a precognitive way, 'prior to cognition properly so-called'[101] – retrieved, in their amplitude of sense, only in, and only as, a bodily felt gesture, or a bodily felt posture, or a bodily felt movement. There are deep meanings hermeneutically concealed within the liturgical texts: meanings which I need to *hear with my ears* in order to understand, and meanings which I need to *behold with my eyes*, if I would comprehend their truth. The Cartesian *Cogito* needs a *tongue* to taste the sweetness of truthful speech, as it needs *hands* to hand down the teachings of tradition, and needs *hands* to give alms to the poor and the hungry. To understand these things, it is not sufficient to read. There is much in the meaning of charity that we can really learn only by way of the bodily act itself. The meaningfulness of the religious texts *demands* to be woven, therefore, into the textures and tissues of our body.

Even Edmund Husserl, for all his phenomenological sensitivity, could not break free of the rationalism that nurtured him. Like Descartes, he had difficulty adequately appreciating the fact that the bodily 'expression' of a thought, or the bodily reading of a written text, will always, and of necessity, *supplement* the 'original' cognitive meaning. Thus, Husserl passes on, in effect, the Cartesian view of the painter in Lessing's play, *Emilia Galotti*, who lamented the body's mediation as a loss of meaning: 'On the long path from the eye through the arm to the pencil, how much is lost!' It is not easy for philosophers and theologians to respect and appreciate, as practitioners always have, the wonderfully, and indeed essentially pro-creative role of the human body in the process of understanding. When the transmission of sacred knowledge is mediated by the human body, we need to ask ourselves how much is gained! So much may be gained, in fact, that the Jewish thinkers of the Kabbalah insisted on the invisibility, or unintelligibility, of the primordial text. Ultimately, we may realize that there is only a *continuous* process of embodiment; *no* original text, but only the gestures of devotion that perpetuate the writing of the Book of Life.

How well do we understand this kind of gesture? Understanding is, first and foremost, a free surrender or submission of the body. It is the body as receptive, the body as willing to yield to the authority of the text. But in prayer, we do much more than that: we *offer* our body to the text; we submit to it as an act of devotion. And, as we listen to the words we sing, as we consecrate our ears and our mouth to the enchanting spirit whose sounds we echo; as even the frame of our entire body yields itself up to the rhythmic measures and the rising and falling intonations, we gradually recreate within ourselves an intimate, unshakable, non-objectifiable *understanding* of the body of knowledge: the sacred language is woven, is insinuated, into the very fibers and bones of the body. And then we *know* our tradition in a way that we could never have known it, if we had been *pure* minds or souls, separate from the temple of our body. Understanding the texts, we place our body in a stance which supports them and grounds them firmly on the earth where we stand: in brief, we stand *under* the text; we uphold it, too, holding it up to the measure of the sky. *That* is true understanding. Perhaps our reading, our reading together, here, of some ancient religious texts will help us to open our chests of immortal love and realize there, in the heart of wisdom, the concealed body of knowledge which those texts have long treasured, protecting the body's eternal life within the weavings of darkness wrought by their own print. . .

According to Spinoza, 'The intellectual love of God which arises from the third kind of knowledge is eternal.' (*Ethics*, Book V, prop. 33.) The individual body which embodies the ancient, ancestral body of a religious tradition, and which therefore, of course, also *experiences* this living incarnation of its tradition, does, I believe, become 'eternal' and 'immortal.' What this means, in part, is certainly that, 'The more objects the mind understands . . . the less it suffers from those emotions which are evil, and the less it fears death.' (Book V, prop. 38). But Spinoza's discourse is extremely rich in implicit meanings, and proposition 33 means much more than this. We must, for example, take into account Book II, prop. 14, in which Spinoza seems to suggest that the achievement of such emotional serenity requires that the body participate in a process of 'sublimation':

> The human mind is adapted to the perception of many things, and its aptitude increases in proportion to the number of ways in which its body can be disposed. (Book II, prop. 14)

Whatever our interpretation of this proposition may be, however, Spinoza has explicitly stated his belief that,

> the mind passes to a greater or lesser perfection when it is able to affirm of its body, or some part of it, something which involves a greater or lesser reality than before. (Book III, prop. 48)

Insofar as the mind's passage to a greater perfection depends upon its capacity to make such an 'affirmation,' it is necessary for us to recognize that, as he says,

> There is no modification of the body of which we cannot form some clear and distinct conception. (Book V, prop. 4)

Thus, for instance,

> An emotion which is a passion ceases to be a
> passion as soon as we form a clear and distinct idea
> of it. (Book V, prop. 3)

In the context of contemporary psychotherapy, this certainly makes good sense. But Spinoza is not very helpful in making clear the process by which this ideational transformation is supposed to take place. Now, throughout this book, we have kept our attention focused on the body's felt sense (neither a passion nor an idea) and on the process by which this unclear sense, carried by the body, may be lifted up into a more explicit, more conceptually articulate meaning. We have done this in order to clarify precisely the sort of phenomenon Spinoza is describing. We need to enjoy a good understanding of this matter if we would fathom the way in which the ritual appropriation of the body, as a process of visualization working with archetypal images, can initiate a passage from lesser to greater perfection that takes with it both mind and body. (Spinoza specifies this passage in relation to the mind, but neglects to do the same for the body.)

In this regard, I would like to call attention to a provocative statement to be found in Leibniz's *New Essays on the Human Understanding*. In this statement, Leibniz makes a suggestion which perhaps carries Spinoza's ideational method much further:

> As for Spirits: since I hold that every created
> intelligence has an organic body, whose level of
> perfection corresponds to that of the intelligence or
> mind which occupies the body by virtue of the
> pre-established harmony, I hold that a very useful
> way to get some conception of the perfection of
> Spirits above ourselves is *to think of perfections of
> bodily organs which surpass our own.* To raise
> ourselves above ourselves in that manner, what we
> mostly need are the richest and liveliest
> imaginations. . . . And what I have said in defence
> of my theory of harmony, which exalts the divine
> perfections beyond what anyone had dreamed of,
> will also serve to give us ideas of creatures
> incomparably greater than any of which we have
> had ideas up to now.[102]

It is possible, I think, to translate Leibniz's 'Great Chain of

Being' into a developmental conception of human being. Then it is *not* a question of imagining perfections in the bodies of beings other than, and higher than, ourselves, but is rather a question of imagining such perfections in an embodiment which *we* are capable of becoming. The body of the infant becomes the body of the child; this, in turn, becomes the body of the adult. At each stage, there are new capacities, and new perfections are possible. Is the adult body a fixed state? Is it not possible for this body, too, to continue to develop itself? To be sure, there are fundamental limitations. But can we say *a priori* what they must be? It is certainly Spinoza's conviction, strong like a true vision, that,

> In this life . . . it is our chief endeavor to change
> the body of infancy, so far as its nature permits
> and is conducive thereto, into another body which
> is fitted for many things, and which is related to
> a mind conscious as much as possible of itself, of
> God, and of objects. . . . (Book II, prop. 14)

According to Spinoza,

> He who possesses a body fit for many things
> possesses a mind of which the greater part is
> eternal. (Book V, prop. 39)

And he clarifies this for us in a 'Note' which supplements that proposition:

> He who possesses a body fitted for doing many
> things is least of all agitated by those emotions
> which are evil, that is to say, by emotions which
> are contrary to our nature, and therefore he
> possesses the power of arranging and connecting
> the modifications of the body according to the
> order of the intellect, and consequently of causing
> all the modifications of the body to be related to
> the idea of God. . . .

In this chapter, I have been attempting to show how a process of embodiment, guided by the ritual texts of a religious tradition, can awaken and cultivate what Spinoza calls a 'knowledge of God', or an 'intellectual love of God', that will be far deeper and far more meaningful than we might have thought possible. But this demonstration requires that we be willing to recognize 'the essence of this or that body under the form of eternity.' (Book V, prop. 22). For, as he says, 'Our mind, insofar as it knows itself and the body under the form of eternity, necessarily has a knowledge of God.' (Book V, prop. 30). This requirement is not so easy. Are we ready to acknowledge such a body? Can we visualize it? This living body of the spirit, created by – and yet also for – our understanding of the form of eternity, is, I believe, the only authentic 'body of knowledge.' The 'body of knowledge' that is contained within the religious *texts* themselves is, by contrast, just the imprinted *shadow* of this *living* body, without which the tradition and its ancestral body would surely, and abruptly, perish.

It seems to me that the essence of the body 'under the form of eternity' is the body in its ontological wholeness. If this interpretation makes sense, then I submit that we need to give further thought to retrieving the body of infancy whose undeveloped wisdom we always carry with us in the interiority of our adult embodiment. For, our infancy is a time when, as Neumann puts it,

> the psyche is not yet incorporated in an individual
> body, but is suspended in the field of the unitary
> reality, which contains within it something that is
> in a sense pre-psychic and pre-physical, that is still
> psychic and physical in one.[103]

I want to suggest that the infantile body is suspended in the wholeness of an elemental field of Being, enjoying, by way of the flesh, a primordial attunement to Being. Thus, the infant enjoys a special experience of the 'form of eternity' in his prepersonal, pre-ego-logical existence.

The body of our childhood preserves the claim of a dream inscribed into the heart of our memory: a claim against the existence of our adulthood, whose need for the enchantment of openness we have neither wholly forgotten nor wholly realized. Can something of this infantile experience be retrieved? Can we (still) find within ourselves as adults the infant's body of pre-ontological understanding? Can we locate within our adult bodies a *felt sense* of that original wholeness, that matrix of eternity? And could we then attend to such a sense in such a way that it would favor us with the transformative wisdom that is held in the archetypal images of that primordial condition? Neumann observes that,

> The child's still undifferentiated body image is as large and undelimited as the cosmos. Its own sphere is so fused with the world and hence with everything that we call the outside, that it may well be termed cosmic in scope.[104]

We do not want, of course, to regress back into infancy. But, if we could retrieve that body image and stay in contact with our body's felt sense of the wholeness-of-Being condensed in the image, perhaps we could schematize a body of greater perfection, greater well-being, than the conventional body into which we fall and settle in the normal course of our development.

The human body either changes and grows, or else it dies. So it is, too, with a religious tradition. Religious movements characteristically begin in ecstasy – in dream and vision. In the beginning, they promise freedom and health. But, as they establish themselves in the world, they have a tendency to lose touch with their creative vision. A shift in focus takes place, and they tend to become dogmatic, judgmental, punitive, repressive. The heteronomy of established tradition and its visibility as law *conceal* our initial dream of a healthy spontaneity, from which would flow words and deeds of great beauty, truth and virtue. In this chapter, we have selected certain texts which are remarkable (although there are others we have not been able to cite), not only for their poetic power, but also for their unequivocal appreciation of our needs and capabilities as beings with a bodily nature we cannot dispose of, and which we can ignore only at great cost. These texts are also remarkable by virtue of the lucidity with which they articulate, for our benefit, the processes of feeling and perception, and powerfully motivate us, through a poetry strong both in feeling and in understanding, to get in touch with our bodily experiencing and work on its opening up. After all, what is so striking, and so utterly beyond question, is the fact that the texts we are concerned with here ask us to focus on the way we in-habit and experience our bodily nature, and do so, moreover, with but one goal: the nurturing of our capacity for feeling and perceiving in more open, more spontaneous, more creative and meaningful ways.

If we take the texts in question to heart, that is, if we take them seriously, their poetry is not mystical; nor is it the naive expression of myths and superstition. Rather, we will discover that the poetry speaks truthfully and movingly, addressing itself *directly* to the way we are *experiencing* our bodily being; and we will gradually understand the poetry as an expression, besides, of a visionary *standard* by which we can measure, and test, our own experiential growth. The poetry of these great texts addresses itself precisely to that 'ideality . . . not alien to the flesh' which 'gives it its depth, its dimensions,' and of which, in the passage from *The Visible and the Invisible* which opens this study, Merleau–Ponty so eloquently speaks.

Writing on the meaning of Empedocles' *Purifications*, Charles Kahn says:

> In its state of purity the daimon will have, or will be, an elemental body after all, only not one composed of distinct elements. The hatred which the daimon encounters in the elemental zones will reflect the fact that he, like themselves, is estranged from perfect harmony. On this view, release from strife cannot mean physical separation from the elements but rather the attainment of a new (and original) state of freedom from elemental plurality and opposition.[105]

On Kahn's interpretation, it appears that Empedocles believes that human 'salvation,' conceived as a liberation, or release, from the suffering form of the human body, does *not* involve a 'separation' of 'soul' and 'body,' but requires a *spiritualization* of the physical element – a metamorphosis, that is, which brings into its already implicit harmony that which has been suffering from strife and opposition. May we not interpret the 'resurrection' of the body, and its relationship to 'immortality,' in similar terms? Could the body's immortal 'resurrection' be understood as an ideality that is not alien to the flesh? Here is a striking passage from Tertullian's 'De resurrectione carnis':

> Has God combined [the soul] with, or rather, inserted and intermingled it in, the flesh? Yes; and has so closely compacted them together that it can be held to be uncertain whether the body bears

221

about the soul or the soul the body, whether the
flesh is the servant of the soul or the soul of the
flesh. But it is rather to be believed that the soul is
the driver and has the mastery, as nearer to God.
*Yet this also enhances the glory of the flesh, that it
contains that which is nearest to God and makes itself a
partaker in the soul's mastery.* For what use of nature
is there, what enjoyment of the world, what savour
of the elements, that the soul does not feed upon
by means of the flesh? How, indeed, can it be
otherwise? Is it not through it that the soul is
sustained by all the organs of the senses – by sight
and hearing and taste and smell and touch? . . .
Speech, too, takes place by means of a bodily
organ. . . . [So] that, in fine, the whole life of the
soul is so bound up with the flesh that cessation
of life for the soul is nothing but separation from
the flesh.[106]

Tertullian does not let the flesh experience the soul's immortality in a life after death, but for the duration of the soul's
'life', its commingling with the flesh, he does let the flesh
participate in, and even contribute to, the soul's intimations
of immortality.

Where there exists a living body of tradition, then, as
Santayana says, in *The Life of Reason*, 'we are not left merely
with the satisfaction of abstract success or the consciousness
of ideal immortality.'[107] Wherever mortals dwell in the
context of a tradition that has not forgotten the process of
incarnation, there yet remains, as he cogently argues,

an enlightening example, together with faculties
predisposed by discipline to recover their ancient
virtue. The better a man evokes and realises the
ideal, the more he leads the life that all others, in
proportion to their worth, will seek to live after him,
and the more he helps them to live in that nobler
fashion. His presence in the society of immortals
thus becomes, so to speak, more pervasive. He not
only vanquishes time by his own rationality, living
now in the eternal, but he continually lives again
in all rational beings.
Since the ideal has this perpetual pertinence to
mortal struggles, he who lives in the ideal and

leaves it expressed in society or in art enjoys a
double immortality. The eternal has absorbed him
while he lived, and when he is dead his influence
brings others to the same absorption, making
them, through that ideal identity with the best in
him, reincarnations and perennial seats of all in
him which he could rationally hope to rescue from
destruction. He can say, without any subterfuge
or desire to delude himself, that he shall not wholly
die; for he will have a better notion than the vulgar
of what constitutes his being. By becoming the
spectator and confessor of his own death and of
universal mutation, he will have identified himself
with what is spiritual in all spirits and masterful
in all apprehension; and so conceiving himself, he
may truly feel and know that he is eternal.[108]

With these inspiring words, words very much, I feel, in the
spirit of Spinoza's own thinking, we complete our attempt
to flesh out the living body of tradition whose sublime possibility we have found to be inscribed into the liturgical texts
of our various religions. The task we have undertaken is not,
of course, a task we could ever really complete. But I think
that, in penetrating the sedimented meanings buried in
textual palimpsests, and in adumbrating with our light the
body of understanding which incarnates the spiritual life
sought by all religious traditions, we have contributed something I feel to be missing, something in truth essential, to
Heidegger's ontological interpretation of history, and our
mortal way of being historical. At the same time, moreover,
I believe that we have contributed the gift of the body of
tradition to Heidegger's unfolding of that noble existence
which he calls 'the bearing of thought.'

CHAPTER 3

Moral Education – The Body's Felt Sense of Value

Opening Conversation

(1) And if there is an indubitable good within one's reach, one stretches out one's hand.
Iris Murdoch, *The Nice and the Good*[1]

(2) Moralists need the gestures of virtue, also the gestures of truth.
Nietzsche, *The Will to Power*[2]

(3) The human body is the best picture of the soul.
Ludwig Wittgenstein, *Philosophical Investigations*[3]

(4) Naturalism . . . consists in the claim that morality originates in certain natural movements of the psyche which do not themselves require reference to morality either to describe or to explain them.
Richard Wollheim, 'The Sheep and the Ceremony'[4]

(5) There is an organismic base for an organized valuing process within the individual.
Carl Rogers, *Freedom to Learn*[5]

(6) The body stands for wholeness and unity in general, and its total reaction represents a genuine

224

and creative totality. A sense of the body as a whole
is the natural basis of the sense of personality.

Erich Neumann, *The Origins and History of
Consciousness*[6]

(7) Before the child goes to school, he learns with his
hand, eye, and ear, because they are organs of the
process of doing something from which meaning
results.

John Dewey, *Democracy and Education*[7]

(8) We do not teach them to aspire to be all they can.
We do not give them a training as if we believed
in their noble nature. We scarce educate their bodies.
We do not train the eye and the hand. . . . The
great object of Education should be commensurate
with the object of life. It should be a moral one . . .
touching his [the child's] own nature.

Ralph Waldo Emerson, 'Education'[8]

(9) The great rationality of all education in morality
has always been that one tried to attain to the
certainty of an instinct: so that neither good
intentions nor good means had to enter
consciousness as such. . . . In fact, this
'unconsciousness' belongs to any kind of perfection.

Friedrich Nietzsche, *The Will to Power*[9]

Summarizing Rousseau's philosophy of education as it is
conceived, primarily, in *Emile*, Dewey writes:

Education we receive from three sources – Nature,
men and things. The spontaneous development of
our organs and capacities constitutes the education
of Nature. The use to which we are taught to put
this development constitutes that education given
us by Men. The acquirement of personal
experience from surrounding objects constitutes
that of things. Only when these three kinds of
education are consonant and make for the same
end, does a man tend towards his true goal.[10]

On the basis of this pedagogical theory, Rousseau expounds,
and himself attempts to practise, not only an education *of*
the body, but also, rather more radically, an education *with*

225

the body: moral instruction, for example, *as* perception, sensibility, and activity. To be sure, no method of instruction can
entirely ignore the body. Since we are bodily beings, the
body necessarily mediates all processes of learning. The significance of Rousseau, therefore, consists in the degree to
which he is aware of this mediation, is eager to acknowledge
it, attempts to understand it in theory, and undertakes to
put it into living practice.

Even today, the pedagogical ideas of Rousseau, Emerson
and Thoreau – ideas which Dewey, intelligently refining
them, sought to revive – remain for the most part ignored,
untried, unrealized. From time to time, an educator or philosopher will lend an inspiring, or at least an encouraging,
voice to a wisdom we still need to embody in our educational
practice. In 'Democratic Values and Education,' for example,
R. S. Peters (of the University of London) argues that,

> As a member of the natural world . . . the individual
> must have some understanding of how his body
> works, of procreation, aging, and disease. The
> intimate connection between body and mind is
> being spelled out in more and more detail by
> physiology and brain chemistry. Awareness is
> subtly affected by the circulation of the blood, by
> glandular secretions, and by the metabolic rate of
> the body. So not only is instruction in diet, hygiene,
> and the avoidance of disease essential; the body
> must also be cared for by physical exercise of various
> sorts. It is rather out of fashion . . . to emphasize
> the importance of physical fitness and the general
> dexterity and control of the body developed by
> various exercises, swimming, and games. . . . But
> their basic rationale in terms of care of the body is
> seldom stressed. Little is made, too, of the
> enjoyment many derive from them, which can
> provide a lifelong interest.[11]

Despite this appreciation, however, Peters fails to hear,
underlying the 'merely' metaphorical meaning, the truth that
he himself adumbrates, when he asserts, for example, that
we must teach our children a 'basic body of rules': duties
such as the keeping of promises and telling the truth.[12] Is it
not true that, insofar as it would make sense to support,
teach and maintain a 'body of rules' (in Peters's abstract

sense), there must also be an *implicit body* of rules – a wholesome, living body of experience, from out of which the *sense* of rule-governed behavior would be most effectively, and most meaningfully educed? Thus I want to urge that we ask ourselves, as we attend to Wollheim's advocacy of moral naturalism, how are we reading (hearing) his words? We really need to ask, asking with an obstinacy that may very well seem, to some philosophers, quite perverse: Just what kinds of comportments are to count, from the standpoint of our moral code, as the 'natural movements of the psyche'? Or, in other words: What *is* the 'body of thoughts and feelings' (the words are Wollheim's) appropriate to a moral agent?[13] No adequate 'psychology of moral action'[14] can ultimately avoid paying attention to these questions. Indeed, I will even make bold to affirm that the moral plight we are in today is due, at least in part, to our failure to take the embodiment of moral existence – the fact, for instance, that a certain category of action 'is of no value in the agent's eyes' – with the literalness of truth it demands.[15]

To begin with, of course, we need an understanding of the human body – and therefore an experiencing of the body, whether it be our own body or the body of another – which lets it *be* in its truth. What has made this letting-be so very difficult for us is our centuries-old 'patriarchal' religion of shame, guilt and remorse, which not only justifies, but even requires, the most vehement mortification of the flesh. In our attempt, here, to vindicate our incarnation, we must temporarily refuse, or suspend, the patriarchal body of moral law (the nomological ego-body) and retrieve, by a process of radical reflection, our 'first' body of moral wisdom, a body of biopsychic wholeness, whose principle of being, a deep attunement, a *nomos* which *sings*, was laid down by matriarchal culture, and continues to inform generations of mortals by way of the child's primal relationship to the archetypal Mother. In carrying out this critical reflection, we are greatly indebted to Nietzsche, who is, I believe, the very first philosopher of the Judaeo-Christian epoch to refuse the patriarchal falsehood which shrouds the body and conceals its gifts of wisdom. Dewey, however, is the first philosopher to take this critique into the practical field of education. Repudiating the dualism to which our hatred for the body condemns us, Dewey argues that,

it would be impossible to state adequately the evil

results which have flowed from this dualism of mind and body, much less to exaggerate them. Some of the more striking effects may, however, be enumerated. In part, bodily activity becomes an intruder. Having nothing, so it is thought, to do with mental activity, it becomes a distraction, an evil to be contended with. For the pupil has a body, and brings it to school along with his mind. And the body is, of necessity, a well-spring of energy; it has to do something. But its activities, not being utilized in occupation with things which yield significant results, have to be frowned upon. . . . The chief source of the 'problem of discipline' in schools is that the teacher has often to spend the larger part of the time in suppressing the bodily activities which take the mind away from its material. A premium is put on physical quietude; on silence, on rigid uniformity of posture and movement, upon a machine-like simulation of the attitudes of intelligent interest.[16]

And Dewey rightly points out that,

The neglected body, having no organized fruitful channels of activity, breaks forth, without knowing why or how, into meaningless boisterousness, or settles into equally meaningless fooling.[17]

When the educational system is bent on 'raising' children by 'keeping their instincts and active tendencies repressed,' then what it generates are generations of adults 'educated not into responsibility for the significance and graceful use of bodily powers, but into an enforced duty not to give them free play.'[18] The consequences of this approach are, unfortunately, all too visible.

Now, it might perhaps be countered, at this point, that our system does not in fact neglect the body. Is it not true that our children are taught anatomy, hygiene and biology? Are they not required to take some gymnastics, or to participate in some kind of sport? Is it not true that our schools offer workshops in manual training – woodworking, metalworking, ceramics and other crafts? To our affirmative reply Dewey would want to object:

228

But we are very easily trained to be content with a
minimum of meaning, and to fail to note how
restricted is our perception of the relationships
which confer significance.[19]

And there is, moreover, as Dewey observes, a certain 'grace'
to the intelligence of our bodily activities: a grace we destroy,
or anyway suppress, when we train and discipline the body
as if it were merely a machine.[20] Due to the dualism which
reifies the body, and to the underlying hostility towards it
which separates it from the 'essence' of the spirit, the attention we *do* give the body invariably tends to be caught
between forms of negative reinforcement (ascetic disciplining
and punishment) and forms of drilling, of repetitive,
uniform, mechanistic training:

> the senses and muscles are used not as organic
> participants in having an instructive experience,
> but as external inlets and outlets of mind.[21]

Even the various manual crafts, all of which are intrinsically
creative and meaningful processes, get to be taught in a way
that abuses and mortifies the body, denying it the kind of
intelligence and fulfillment of which it is inherently capable:

> Manual training is reduced to a series of ordered
> assignments calculated to secure the mastery of
> one tool after another and technical ability in the
> various elements of construction.[22]

In the pervasive enframing of our present epoch, even the
skills and crafts of the body, even its finest offerings of handi-
work, are reduced to the technical functioning of calculative
thinking. For, as Dewey says,

> *any* way is 'mechanical' which narrows down the
> bodily activity so that a separation of body from
> mind – that is, from recognition of meaning – is set
> up.[23]

In *Joyful Wisdom*, Nietzsche points out that,

> Society feels with satisfaction that it has a reliable
> *tool* ready at all times in the virtue of this one, in

the ambition of that one, and in the reflection and
passion of a third one – it honours this *tool-like*
nature, this self-constancy, this unchangeableness
in opinions, efforts, and even in faults, with the
highest honours. Such a valuation, which prevails
and has prevailed everywhere simultaneously with
the morality of custom, educates 'character,' and
brings all changing, re-learning, and self-
transforming into disrepute.[24]

Our traditional way of teaching morality is, I think, an inherently mechanizing, technologically willful way: it attempts
to teach a morality of autonomy, but does so by implicitly
heteronomous means, i.e., by imposing precepts and principles not derived from the child's own body of morally
perceptive feeling, and by addressing moral education to the
child's tool-like nature, rather than to a creative reserve of
sensibility which is not reducible to its being as an instrument
of moral culture, and which may suffer very seriously from
the instrumental strategy. When precepts are imposed and
not derived, it is not only that we betray our own principles
by treating the child as a tool, but that, since we are giving
him no understanding of moral evaluation as a process of
articulating a body of implicitly moral feeling, we are actually
encouraging and rewarding a tool-like nature, rigid,
constant, reliable, fixed, docile, and essentially reactive,
rather than thoughtful and responsive. This educational
method is therefore implicitly technological, and tends to
reproduce itself in a character which is easily manipulated,
and which knows by example only those kinds of relationship that involve the manipulation of others. We desperately
need a method of moral education which will avoid the
chains of calculative ratiocination and subvert the technological reduction of human nature and comportment.

Dewey's thinking is responsive to our need. He meets us
precisely where Nietzsche is compelled to leave us; going
beyond a vision and theory of education, he offers precious
suggestions for *applying* our vision to the education of our
children. But I think it must be said, with all due respect,
that even his guidance is not quite sufficient. What more is
needed? In the context of an approach to moral education
which is seriously committed, in just the way that ours, for
example, is, to the spirit of 'naturalism,' what we need is to
be able to specify something like a 'method' for facilitating a

real contact with, and an awareness of, what Carl Rogers calls our 'own organismic valuing process.'[25] In other words, when we are faced with the question of helping a child to realize the truth of morality and make it his own, i.e., realize its truth as fulfilling his very own, and deepest, moral sensibilities, how can we facilitate his access to the 'wisdom of his body'?[26] There are three people who have been, for me, especially helpful in accompanying me beyond the place where Dewey leaves off. These three are: Carl Rogers, Frederick Perls and Eugene Gendlin.[27] For the sake of brevity, though, we will concentrate on the argument to be found in Rogers's book, *Freedom to Learn*. The analyses of Perls and Gendlin, although no less significant, will remain in the background of our thinking.

Now, the infant, as Rogers says,

> prefers those experiences which maintain, enhance, or actualize his organism, and rejects those which do not serve this end.[28]

Thus, the normal, healthy child *begins* life with a 'highly efficient, soundly based valuing process.'[29] But the fact is that the child's natural reliance on this primordial body of wisdom is soon jeopardized, and in order to learn from the circle of important elders what is needed to survive and flourish, the child characteristically begins 'relinquishing the locus of evaluation to others.'[30] Rogers explains it this way:

> To buy love, we relinquish the valuing process. Because the center of our lives now lies in others, we are fearful and insecure, and must cling rigidly to the values we have introjected.[31]

Children need, of course, to learn from others. And they need exemplars. Nevertheless, in the stage of moral development which Kant called 'heteronomy,' children typically begin to lose the advantages of that organismic sense of value with which they started life:

> By taking over the conceptions of others as our own, we lose contact with the potential wisdom of our own functioning and lose confidence in ourselves.[32]

It is certainly true, of course, that this loss of contact, and the kind of 'attunement' it involves, is *replaced* by the heteronomous moral guidance that every child initially needs in order to develop a capacity to make independent judgments and rise to the stature of an autonomous existence. But the child who is not encouraged to *continue* moral development, or who fails for some other reasons to outgrow that initially necessary heteronomous basis, will find himself eventually entangled in what Rogers accurately describes as a 'more rigid, uncertain, inefficient approach to values.'[33] In the adult, heteronomy means conformism, insecurity and its attendant psychological stress, imbalance. It is, in fact, dysfunctional.

When Rogers urges us to give weight to 'the organismic base for an organized valuing process,' and Gendlin encourages us to focus on 'our bodily felt sense' of our situational being 'as a whole,' that is because they firmly believe, as Rogers wants to phrase it, that,

> This valuing process in the human being is effective
> in achieving self-enhancement to the degree that
> the individual is open to the experiencing which is
> going on within himself.[34]

As a clinical psychologist, and a highly experienced psychotherapist, Rogers undertakes to elicit, and moreover to clarify, what he refers to as 'universal human value directions emerging from the experiencing of the human organism.'[35] The motivation is a basic 'faith,' so to speak, that,

> when the human being is inwardly free to choose
> whatever he deeply values, he tends to value those
> objects, experiences and goals which contribute to
> his own survival, growth, and development, and
> to the survival and development of others.[36]

I share this faith, painfully, cognizant, at the same time, of the terrible failures and dangers, the difficulties in providing an environment which is really conducive to this kind of 'inward freedom,' and the problems which make the learning of this focusing and contacting process so arduous, so demanding, and so rarely achieved. But, rather than attempting, here, to prove the unprovable, or to convince people who, whatever they may avow, really do *not* want to be convinced, I propose that we concentrate, in the remaining pages of this division of our study, on how we might actually attempt to ground moral education in a naturalism which *begins* with the truth of our body and its entrustment of goodness, inherent in the psyche's most 'natural' movements.

The naturalism which begins (with Hume, for example) by grounding moral principles in forms of sensibility which 'custom' has tactfully in-formed, needs to be *supplemented* by a naturalism which recognizes the antecedents of our moral intuitions, and our moral sensibility in general, in our bodily felt *sense* of existence, and consequently attempts to teach the principles of morality by educing them from the entrustment of goodness and rightness which is truthfully felt in the experienced body of our being-in-the-world. For me, then, 'naturalism' is not adequately defined by the claim (in Wollheim's formulation) that 'morality originates in certain natural movements of the psyche which do not themselves require reference to morality. . . .' Nor is it reducible to Wittgenstein's proposal. Rather, 'naturalism' must include a recognition that, in Rogers's words, 'There is an organismic base for an organized valuing process within the individual.' But, once we have taken the Rogerian step, we will understand that, in terms of a theory of education, 'naturalism' means a certain way of relating to, and a certain way of working (educationally and therapeutically) with, human *nature*. For, if morality really does originate in natural movements of the psyche, and an organized valuing process is *always already* functioning, even in the body of our infancy, then moral education needs to relate to the individual in a way that acknowledges and respects this bodily endowment. Above all, our moral education will demonstrate such respect by acknowledging that it is not necessary to *impose* morality 'against the grain' – as if it were reasonable to assume that processes of moral evaluation are *external* to the child's bodily nature.

What is called for is a gentle and caring approach that provides a truly nurturing space for the child to make *good contact* with his own evaluative processes, and elicit from the gift of his ownmost body of feeling a comportment that is properly grounded in its primordial universality. Naturalism in moral education therefore requires of its teachers, and of the culture at large, a basic *trust* in the innate potential for goodness carried by the universal body. This trust will only be confirmed, however, insofar as the method of education, and social conditions in general, are genuinely conducive to the harmonious unfolding of this potential. Unfortunately, I know of no society in which such conditions have prevailed long enough to demonstrate the truth and the beauty of a consistent moral naturalism.

The practical approach to moral education with which we shall conclude our present theoretical reflections is, of course, nothing more than a sketch. Without undertaking, here, the enormous task of a rigorous and comprehensive phenomenology of moral experience, we can do little more than allude to the possibility of a moral education grounded in the body of felt experience. What we are doing here is simply clearing a place and marking if off for further work. With this limitation acknowledged, let us proceed to the consideration, very briefly, of five different problems in moral development. The aim, in each case, then, will be to bring out, as clearly as our brevity will permit, the *a priori* possibility for educational or transformative work, focused on the body's always implicit capacity to contact, as a beginning, a deeply felt sense of value.

(1) A very fundamental problem in the realm of moral judgment and comportment is what psychologists refer to as 'the problem of psychological rigidity.' In the dimension of existence defined by morality, such rigidity appears with many familiar faces: intolerance, dogmatism, fanaticism, opposition to necessary change, the suppression of creativity, deafness to rational argument, a refusal to see things as they really are, conformism, and a need to submit to the power of 'authority.' Now, in 'The Child's Relations with Others,' Merleau–Ponty, summarizing the work of several clinical psychologists, draws our attention to the fact that manifestations of psychological rigidity can be significantly correlated with manifestations of rigidity on the level of perception.[37] This stands to reason. If, now, we extend our conceptualization of the perceptual correlation, so that, in keeping with the specific focal concern of this chapter, we contemplate the nature of the correlation between psychological rigidity and the 'standpoint' of postural rigidity, which expresses and concerns the body as a whole, the question which must suggest itself, sooner or later, is surely this: If we take this correlation as our starting point, does it not make sense to search for ways of *diminishing* the rigidity of the psychological ego by working with the rigidity of its ego-logical body, and with the ego-body's self-image? This question, of course,

invites us to attend more closely to the natural movements, the posture and stance, of the rigid, inflexible personality. What kinds of movements, what kinds of posture and stance, seem to be invariant, or anyway, characteristic? And how does the rigid moral standpoint 'schematize' or manifest itself in the disposition and comportment of the body?

These questions eventually point, I think, towards the possibility of using procedures of relaxation and the teaching of free-style, self-expressive dancing as valuable ways of working therapeutically with personality-types suffering from a psychological rigidity which seriously impairs their capacity to participate fully and with maturity in the moral dimension of life. Furthermore, they suggest the possibility – something it is surely worth exploring – of teaching our young children some of the moral postures, attitudes, and positions which constitute the underlying somatic *basis* of a moral 'consciousness,' by working *directly* with their (relatively more compliant) bodies, their images of the body, and their contactful bodily awareness, their bodily felt sense. (Similar work might be undertaken, for example, with regard for the shouldering of responsibility; the capacity to lend a hand; the tense and tight-lipped attitude; turning one's back on difficult problems; a chronic inability to face one's problems; the tension we experience trying to balance the stress in holding back against the virtue in self-restraint; the kind of moral rigidity which becomes, as we should say, 'stiff-necked'; the stingy, hostile, tight-fisted approach; and, to name just one more, the timid and weak-kneed protest.) Teaching morality to children in the form of principles and precepts, we teach them abstractly. We are also teaching them dogmatically, i.e., by the force of our authority, since they may be too young to understand the concepts. Such teaching is both difficult and vulnerable in ways that teaching which would deliberately set out to *mediate* its transmission through the child's body of felt experience should not be. If we are seriously committed, for example, to teaching how to enjoy flexibility, movement, and shifting standpoints as intrinsically meaningful, intrinsically satisfying modes of bodily comportment, while at the same time we clearly and carefully focus the child's attention on his deeply *felt sense* of the bodily being in question, it might be possible not only to develop these *implicitly* moral, and morally essential 'forms of consciousness' to a higher degree, but also to facilitate a deeper, better-grounded, and more autonomous correlative *understanding* of some very basic precepts and principles.

(2) In his introduction to Medard Boss's *Existential Foundations of Medicine and Psychology*, Paul Stern focuses our attention on, in his words:

> the therapist's readiness to open himself widely
> (and without the subterfuge of theoretical
> dogmatism) to whatever manifests itself in the
> interpersonal space cleared by therapy, his
> willingness to welcome the phenomena appearing
> there as real, no matter how outlandish their guise
> – this open-armed, hospitable stance frees the
> analysand in his turn to unbend, to experience
> with previously disowned modes of conduct, to
> gradually make them his own.[38]

'Owning,' i.e., appropriating, previously disowned modes of conduct is a question of embodying them, or embodying them more fully, i.e., with a more deeply felt sense of *being* their embodiment. No mortal can sincerely claim fully to embody the *ideal* of moral character. The bodying forth of the kind of openness that we know to be crucial for moral relationships is, therefore, a task we mortals never finish. There is always a more open space into which we are challenged, as moral agents, to stand out. Accordingly, we are called upon, never to cease giving thought to our capacity for responding to this standing challenge.

When we give it our thought, however, does it not become apparent at once that it would be a terrible 'error' – if that be the word for it – to believe, and act on the belief, that an 'open-armed, hospitable stance,' a stance kindly bent to serve as compassion may require, could ever be a question merely of a 'state of mind,' or an 'interior' mood of the soul? The words speak for themselves; they say what they mean, and mean what they say.

But once again, therefore, our thinking logically moves us, step by step, to the primal question of embodiment. If an open-armed, hospitable stance is really *crucial* for the full exercising of our moral nature; if, in fact, it is the very incarnation, an *exemplary* incarnation, of our capacity for moral relationship, then the teaching of this stance, and its open-armed gesture, must surely be essential. And it must also be *the very best way* to teach our children the understanding feeling – the deeply felt meaning – of some basic moral precepts.

A two-phased pedagogical practice would, I think, be involved, here. Let us try to picture it. In the first phase, the children are *shown* that stand and gesture, and invited to replicate it for themselves in a situation which suffices to make it clear as constitutive of a relationship with others. Then, while they are actually putting themselves into that form of embodiment, the teacher helps them to focus their attention in a sort of open, free and meditative way, on the multitude of sensations, feelings, emotions, fantasies, spontaneous memories and ideational associations which come to pass for them; and the teacher encourages them to articulate freely whatever it is that they are experiencing, noting the importance of their articulation as a way of sharing that experiencing and establishing a friendly and open classroom atmosphere. Finally, the teacher works with that articulatory process to deepen the attentional focusing and expand, or enrich, the dimensionality of bodily felt awareness.

In the second phase, while the children replicate that form of embodiment in a number of different interpersonal groupings, and each time with as much 'meditative' attention as they can give, the teacher begins to *stress* the connection between (i) their friendly, relaxed stance, and their open-armed gesture, and (ii) their bodily felt need for mutually open, mutually welcoming postures and gestures, and for the kind of interpersonal relationship which they discover that bodily positionality to make them feel as a need. Finally, after many brief sessions of practice, the teacher slowly and patiently begins to speak to them of the moral attributes they are already bodying forth, and helps them to feel, by their focusing – feel, that is to say, with their bodies – the progressively well-rooted *physiognomic meaningfulness* of these moral attributes. And finally, to 'complete' the practice, the children are instructed to continue to be mindful of their stance, their postures and gestures, even as they fall into them in the course of their daily living. The teacher points out to them that this constant vigilance, this ongoing mindfulness, provides an opportunity for them to *experience* the value of mutually open, mutually friendly, and mutually considerate relationships, and makes it possible for them, moreover, to sense, in the clearest, strongest, and most direct way, just how they are doing and how they could *enhance* the (virtuous) character of those relationships. With still older children and adults, essentially those same practices could be used very effectively, I think, to deepen the visible and tangible embodiment of a non-threatening openness-to-others, and a kind of yielding, which are necessary preparations for the coming to pass of compassion, not just as an 'inner feeling,' but as a meaningful human relationship.

(3) In *The Will to Power*, Nietzsche argues that,

> Empathy with the souls of others is originally
> nothing moral, but a physiological susceptibility to
> suggestion. . . . One never communicates thoughts:
> one communicates movements, mimic signs,
> which we then trace back to thoughts.[39]

What about the 'thought' of compassion? As absolutely fundamental in any system of morality, this 'thought' invariably appears, codified, in its representative principles and precepts. The question is: How is it to be taught? How cultivated? When Sokrates insisted that virtue cannot really be 'taught,' what he meant was that it cannot be taught solely by precept, nor even mainly by precept, but only, in the fullest sense, by example. I agree. But now, if we ponder what it *is* to teach 'by example,' we will soon realize that that kind of teaching works by virtue of an *exemplary embodiment* – an embodiment of virtue which *shows* it in its most visible *beauty*, *clarifies* it in its articulation of the *truth*, and *directly communicates its goodness* through the tangible power of feeling.

Even so – even, that is, when the teacher's presence manifestly embodies the virtue of compassion, so that it visibly *graces* her stance and her gestures, and she is *visibly moved* by it – compassion is not easily communicated and taught. The fact of the matter is, unfortunately, that the teaching of compassion, even by an exemplary teacher who greatly embodies it, requires much preparatory groundwork. The passage from Nietzsche is helpful in this regard, especially when we put it together with Merleau–Ponty's reflections on the same subject in 'The Child's Relations with Others.'

What, then, is the groundwork preparatory for compassion? Nietzsche speaks of (i) a physiological susceptibility to suggestion, (ii) the communicating of movements (which means *either* communication *by way of* movement *or* the communication of movement itself, i.e., a communication *which moves*, or which perhaps means *both* of these), and finally (iii) a process of *mimesis*. Although Husserl would undoubtedly prefer to speak, rather, of an 'analogical' inter-corporeality constituted by way of an intentionality he calls 'coupling,' and Merleau–Ponty would prefer to speak of this intercorporeality by reference to a prepersonal body-subject, and therefore without ascribing it to the constitutive work of a transcendental ego, it is nevertheless, I think, quite clear that there is a very basic region of agreement where their different contributions significantly intersect.

What we find is that this region of their intersection is precisely the groundwork we need to consider in a process of education aimed at the cultivation of compassion – compassion as the fundament of moral existence. Instead of trying to teach compassion by precept – inevitably a very tenuous procedure – we could (and I believe should) attempt to teach it more modestly by working, first, to heighten the rudimentary, and still undeveloped, bodily felt sense of our primordial intercorporeality. Every ego-subject, being also, and by essential necessity, a body-subject, already inheres in an elemental, pre-existent matrix of flesh which is *inherently* social, and which already sets down each subject's incontest-able and inalienable *kinship* with all other sentient and mortal beings long before there is the reflective life of an individual person. When, as adults, we undertake a process of 'radical reflection,' we come to the realization that there is a level, to begin with, where our existential awareness is anonymous, prepersonal: a deep, extensive, generalized existence, which already implicitly foreshadows, and lays the foundation for, a selfless, socially concerned, responsible, and compas-sionately responsive way of being with others.

So the question is not *whether*, but rather *how*, we might undertake, as an essential part of a process of moral educ-ation, the contacting and developing of our bodily felt sense of being-with-others in a primordial intercorporeality – a bodily being, that is to say, which has the character of being anonymous, prepersonal, inherently communicative, and implicitly integrative and communal. Perhaps the most prom-ising procedure to explore, particularly if we are involved with children, is the communicative situation, the communi-cative process, of playful imitation (*mimesis*). As we did before, in the discussion of our second practical context, let us attempt to *picture* to ourselves, as vividly as we can, a teaching situation in which the phenomenon of imitation ('postural impregnation') might be utilized as a way of height-ening our bodily felt sense of belonging, with others of our kind, to 'one single, elemental, communicative flesh.'

Thus, to sketch our approach very briefly, the teaching of compassion as the very heart of moral education would take place in, and consequently as, a carefully timed sequence of progressively more difficult steps, beginning with games of imitation; progressing to a more focused experiencing of the mimetic 'transfer' as a bodily felt sense of being 'coupled' with the Other, touched and touching, and actually being *moved*, even at a distance, by the bodily presence of an Other; passing through the experience of this corporeal interaction, as a next step, in a way that brings out, or makes more explicit, its inherent, but as yet still *implicit* sense as constitutive of our communicative being-one-with-others; and then, eventually, developing this further, into a well-grounded, bodily felt sense of extensive kinship, basis for the articulation of our natural fulfillment through a life of compassion.

Games involving the enactment of imitation are perfect opportunities to teach our children, in the most concrete way possible, namely, through their body of feeling, the morally fundamental meaning of kinship and community: a meaning which is already implicit, for example, in their physiological susceptibility to suggestion – to being caught up, and visibly moved, by the very presence of this Other. Even the mimetic contagiousness of smiles (a phenomenon which Merleau-Ponty discusses in 'The Child's Relations with Others') could, in fact, be turned into a lesson in moral sensibility, if the teacher knows how to help the children to focus on their involuntary participation in a dimension of their incarnation where existence is already deeply shared, and can then help them to feel – in, as, and with their 'own' bodies – the physiognomic meaning of that kind of experience in its much deeper, implicit dimensionality. Once the teacher has moved them to this experience of their natural 'intertwining,' she may, in a new phase of teaching, begin to help these children to find, within themselves (i.e., within their bodily felt sense of that very intertwining) a natural interdependency and kinship on the basis of which they can realize a powerful motivation – realize their need and longing – for the creating of relationships with others that would have, as their value, a mutually responsive, mutually communicative, and mutually concernful character.

(4) In describing a morally exemplary life, we commonly speak of its 'upright' character. Where does this word come

from? If a morally upright character has no connection whatsoever with the postural axis of the human body, why do we generate, and moreover perpetuate, the possibility of such an obviously perilous confusion? And if, on the contrary, there really is a connection?[40] What then? Then, once again, it would seem possible, and would in fact make good sense, for us to consider how an upright character is naturally grounded in, and naturally emerges from, the natural uprightness of our basic vertical posture – and how, therefore, we might make good and efficient use of our understanding of this connection to teach children an uprightness of character which would be more firmly grounded, more stable, better balanced, and consequently more secure and self-reliant, than that which we are presently capable of teaching.

The ethical notions of uprightness and fallenness, together with their psychological correlates, pride and guilt, are existential understandings *grounded* in the child's experiencing of the step-by-step learning which is involved in the ability to stand up (right) and walk forward (into the future) without losing a basic balance, stumbling and falling. This would seem to suggest that the way adults close to the child themselves perceive these abilities, and how they understand and respond to the child's efforts (and especially, the first mistake), must constitute a factor of decisive importance not only in that child's ability to walk in the upright posture, but also in its understanding acquisition of such basic ethical-psychological notions as uprightness and guilt. In fact, I would like to conjecture, with a boldness not, I think, unjustified, that the adults' way of relating to the frustrations in these early situations will very subtly, but nonetheless significantly, influence the child's entire future development as a moral agent, a moral being.

Since there are, obviously, many *different* ways for adults to relate to the steps of this development in regard for its entirety of meaning, we need to give thought to determining *which* of these many possible ways might be most conducive to the character of moral development we wish to encourage, and how we could facilitate it. I would, myself, want to refrain from all ridiculing, mocking, threatening, punishing for mistakes, pushing and pulling, blaming, condemning, and rewarding in ways that would encourage postures of lordly insolence and aloofness. The earliest 'movements of the psyche' are the most crucial in shaping the child's moral character.

(5) Our word *autonomy* is rooted, as etymology tells us, in two old Greek words: *auto-*, which means 'self-' and *nomos*, which means 'law,' in a first approximation of its significance. Autonomy is a normative specification of freedom as a social, political and ethical ideal. How is this ideal embodied? In the context of moral comportment, autonomy is embodied in actions that are self-initiating, self-controlling, self-deter-mining, self-organizing, self-restraining, self-defining, self-imposed, self-sustaining, self-fulfilling. But the actions char-acterized by such attributes appropriate a specific *body* of natural needs, motives, and capacities. What are the 'natural movements' of a psyche whose actions we should wish to characterize by reference to the ideal of autonomy? Our ques-tion is meant to focus our thinking on the question of motility. In the field constituted by the power of our motility, the essential basis of moral autonomy is *already laid down* wherever there is a mode of comportment that is self-init-iated, self-determinative, self-regulated and self-fulfilling.

To describe the essence of autonomy at this most rudimen-tary level, and in this implicitly normative or nomological way, however, is only to recognize what is appropriate to the disclosure of motility in its deeper truth, its more cultivated beauty, and its inherent potential for goodness. (We should give thought, for instance, to the movements and gestures which extend the reach and range of compassion. When, how, and where do we find ourselves *moved* by compassion? What is it for mortals to be *visibly moved* in this way?) I would like to make explicit the implicitly moral character of human motility. And I would like to bring out the truth that it is inherent in the very nature (*nomos*) of motility to be *always already motivated* to achieve the ideal of moral autonomy by which it would be most deeply moved and fulfilled. (Need I also say that there is a strong tendency, often the stronger, for this motivation to be suppressed and left undeveloped, in favor of a motivation that adjusts motility, and comport-ment in general, to standards of a more heteronomous character?)

Heidegger points out, in his 'Letter on Humanism,' that,

> In Greek, to assign is *nemein*. *Nomos* is not only law,
> but more originally the assignment contained in
> the dispensation of Being [*Seinsgeschick*]. Only the

MORAL EDUCATION

assignment is capable of dispatching man into Being. Only such dispatching is capable of supporting and obligating.⁴¹

This observation introduces the ontological dimension. It locates the origin of our moral autonomy, and the gestures and movements which are geared to it, within a field of action governed by the dispatching of Being. Our obligation to realize autonomy is an assignment which we receive simply by the fact that we are beings released into the openness of Being. Now, according to Heidegger, we mortals fulfill the gift of our nature insofar as we submit ourselves to the 'measurement' of the *Nomos*. Since it is possible to misrepresent and, in particular, to reduce the 'moral nature' whose body is at stake in our attempt to vindicate moral naturalism, it is necessary that we keep in mind the full dimensionality of this 'nature.' I am calling attention here to Heidegger's discussion of the *Nomos* in order to emphasize as strongly as I can that the bodily nature that is addressed by the process of moral education derives its proper measure, its inherent rationality (*ratio*), its true law of development and fulfillment, from a nature whose order is of the deepest depth.

But how does the *ratio* of the *Logos* lay claim to our *bodily* nature? I suggest that it works through the incipient rationality of the primordial *Nomos*, which assigns the moral law to the infant through the body of his motility. The lawfulness with which the human body is inscribed and informed is as deep as the *Logos* itself. *A fortiori*, the field of motility, the field of motivation, which gives rise to the morally upright body, and to which this body belongs inseparably, is as extensive, as deep, as its gift of lawfulness. And we are *capable* of a moral existence only because our bodily nature is *always already informed* by the inscription of the *Logos* as a primordial, universal *Nomos*, laying down the parameters of its rational claim to our nature and gathering us into the harmony of a potential community on the ground of its moral principles.

According to Heidegger, the *Logos* calls us. But the question I want to pursue is: How does it speak and claim us? I submit that the *Logos* is the source of our moral law, and that it speaks to us and lays down its claim to our nature in its manifestation as *Nomos*. (*Nomos* is, after all, but another name for *Logos*.) And I submit, further, that the moral law *first*

243

speaks, first sings to us through our universal body of feeling, our bodily felt sense of value. This elemental, bodily felt sense of value, this *nomos*, this song, is always already laid down for us by virtue of the gift of embodiment; and it is already gathering us into the dream of a universal moral community even before we are old enough to speak – and long before we are strong enough – and weak enough! – to contest its original claim. (The human body exists, therefore, in the *tension* which spans the difference between its individuality and its universality.)

Since the original claim is always contested, even if only through our ontological indifference, it is essential to bear in mind that the 'body' which is susceptible to the kind of moral education we have been attempting to formulate is *not* the *reduced* phenomenon of our science and technology; nor is it, for that matter, the body as conceived by naive thought. The flesh of the body belongs, as Merleau–Ponty says, to the elements of Being. Thus, the lawfulness with which it is inscribed and informed is as deep and as vast as the elemental field, the *Logos* as original *ratio*. In the beginning was the Word: the word that is the laying down of the law for our nature; the word that is entrusted to our nature, that speaks to us from the depth of that nature and through its depth, and that speaks most articulately, most truthfully, in the logical educing and unfolding of our natural potential for being human.

As a manifestation and incarnation of *Logos*, then, our motility is the inscription of the primordial *Nomos*, which establishes the nomological conditions for our fulfillment as self-moved, self-moving agents, capable of initiating a binding self-restraint that is the first laying-down (*legein*) of our creative participation in a field of action where the virtue and goodness of a moral existence may really flourish in the beauty of its truth. By the same token, motility, as the dispensation of *Nomos*, is the inscription of the primordial *Logos*, which always and already *speaks* to us of our 'supersensible destination,' and, in laying down the most basic trajectories of a field of sensible motivations, lays claim *from the very beginning* to the education, the recollective gathering up, of our fullest moral capacities. (As *legein*, *Logos* is both a *laying-down* and a *gathering-collection*: It lays down the primordial *Nomos*, the very *Logos* or *meaning* of our being; and in doing so, it makes possible a gathering recollection of mortals on the basis of moral principles.)

I would maintain that, if we wish to show the moral law a proper respect, we must not fail to recognize the true depth of the *nomos*, which is inscribed into our mortal flesh and which it is the duty of moral education to help our children find and realize within themselves. Our phenomenology of the body must not fall prey to a form of naturalism that reduces the dimensionality of the body. It is to avoid this reductionism that I have attempted to disclose the *nomos* to which Nietzsche, Rogers and Gendlin seem to be pointing, as being, in its truth, the primordial, transpersonal *Nomos*, which is not other than that original *Logos*, source of our moral law. Heidegger understands the way that the *Logos* calls to us, but he does not recognize that *another name* for this *Logos* is *Nomos*. Consequently, he does not examine the *Logos* as *source* of our moral order. Still further from the horizon of his thinking is the *way* that this *Logos*, precisely in its manifestation as *Nomos*, lays claim to our nature, and indeed our respect, by its gifts to the human body. Once we understand this ontological claim on our bodily being, we can recognize, correspondingly, that the *Nomos* we encounter through a phenomenology of embodiment, or through a genetic epistemology, must be understood in its truth as originating in a dimension of Being that we cannot reduce to the naturalism of our objective sciences. Moral education is concerned for the well-being of a body whose feeling and valuing go very deep.

It would seem to follow from this hermeneutical understanding of motility that, insofar as we are concerned about our children's capacity for moral autonomy, we would also be concerned to see to it that moral education of the young begins with the child's first experiencing – and first understanding – of motility. By working with the child in this way, at this most rudimentary level, we might find it possible to raise even the most ordinary child to a very high and high-principled level of motivation; and we might make it possible for such a child to experience autonomy, and understand its nature, in a way that is really not at all possible so long as our educational approach remains stubbornly abstract and focused on a merely intellectual kind of understanding.

Since an intellectual or conceptual kind of understanding always emerges from, and is best kept in contact with, a field of sense constitutive of an implicit preunderstanding, we should be able to recognize the need for a way of teaching and communicating the value of autonomy (in the moral sphere of action) that (1) helps the child to develop the moral capacity whose potential is *intact* in a natural motility; (2) helps the child actually to *experience* this capacity for autonomy in its emergence from a more basic level of motility; and (3) helps the child to understand the value of such autonomy by communicating a way to continue and maintain its original motivating contact with the motility that constitutes its most basic structural and organizing ground.

In conclusion, I would like to emphasize that the teachers to whom we entrust the moral education of our children should know how to help them find their own bodily felt sense of the needs, motives and inherent potential for goodness by which they are always and already moved, always and already motivated – simply by grace of their bodily nature. Teachers, then, must be experienced, and indeed skillful, at creating around their charges an atmosphere of trust and care conducive to the opening up of bodily dimensions of feeling. The moral law (*Nomos*), as the ancient Greeks so clearly perceived, is always already given to us, and is always already singing to us, from the moment of our birth, ingrained, as a bodily felt song, in the very fibers of our body. (In its original Delian meaning, a *nomos* was a song in praise of morally exemplary heroic deeds.) The question is, therefore, whether and how our methods of education can successfully create an environment in which to let it sing into being a joyful body of lucid moral knowledge.

Summary

Beginning with a basic conviction that moral naturalism articulates a fruitful understanding of our moral experience, I have attempted to translate that conviction into a project for existential phenomenology, focused on the experienced embodiment of moral principles. Although the working out of a phenomenology of moral experience is a project whose conception is nearly as old as the phenomenological movement itself, the conception behind this chapter, namely, the conception of a phenomenology focused on the *body* of moral experience, is not at all a familiar one – not even in the reflections on moral experience that are currently claiming the attention of phenomenological circles.

This chapter brings together the theory of moral naturalism and the phenomenology of moral experience by focusing both approaches on the being of the human body as it is experienced. This focus enriches both approaches, I believe, and indeed fleshes them out in essentially necessary ways.

The aim of this chapter, however, goes beyond the attempt to formulate a theoretically adequate framework for understanding our moral experience. Its ultimate aim is more practical, namely, to explore the possibility of deepening our present phenomenological understanding of moral experience by bringing this understanding to bear on the process of moral education, and by concentrating our attention, above all, on the body of moral experience – the body of inborn moral principles – that the young child always brings, as his natural endowment, to the openness of the teaching-and-learning situation. When a phenomenological dialogue takes place in such a situation, the child is helped to focus on his own body of experience, just as it is lived and felt. Since this way of focusing helps the child to realize what he has always already 'known,' and since it accordingly respects the child's most basic gift of autonomy, it is a process that is bound to feel good, bound to educate, and bound to eventuate in a deeper self-understanding. But self-understanding never leaves the child unchanged, and, in this case, where the self-understanding involves the disclosure of moral principles and moral predispositions that the child can contact and feel in a bodily sensible way, the process of phenomenological explicitation initiates an education with especially salutary and enduring consequences. For the child does not only learn, or gradually realize, those fundamental moral principles that claim him simply by virtue of the fact that he is a being embodied in the human form of flesh; he also learns, or realizes, a very basic, very 'natural' procedure for *reflecting* on his experience of the moral claims that various situations will make on him, and for reaching significant conclusions that pass the tests of good bodily feeling, good bodily sense.

I therefore submit that a moral education based on this bodily felt sense is a more autonomous-making foundation, and consequently a much superior foundation, for the moral community we commonly envision, than is the older approach, which is based on teaching abstract precepts and on the insinuation of a capacity for experiencing the claims of an always 'guilty' conscience. It is the joyful teaching, and not the punitive, that opens the child most deeply to the learning space of truth.

CHAPTER 4

The Body Politic

Opening Conversation

(1) In the dance of peace what we have to consider is
     whether a man bears himself naturally and
     gracefully, and after the manner of men who duly
     conform to the law.

                              Plato, *Laws* VII (815)[1]

(2) every form of the reality principle must be embodied
     in a system of societal institutions and relations,
     laws and values which transmit and enforce the
     required 'modification' of the instincts. This 'body'
     of the reality principle is different at the different
     stages of civilization. . . .

                   Herbert Marcuse, *Eros and Civilization*[2]

(3) What mode of investment of the body is necessary
     and adequate for the functioning of a capitalistic
     society like ours? . . . One needs to study what kind
     of body the current society needs. . . . It's as
     though 'revolutionary' discourses were still steeped
     in the ritualistic themes derived from Marxist
     analyses. And while there are some very interesting
     things about the body in Marx's writings, Marxism
     considered as an historical reality has had a terrible
     tendency to occlude the question of the body, in
     favour of consciousness and ideology.

                     Michel Foucault, *Power/Knowledge*[3]

248

(4) Let us ask . . . how things work at the level of on-
going subjugation, at the level of those continuous
and uninterrupted processes which subject our
bodies, govern our gestures, dictate our
behaviours. . . .

Foucault, *Power/Knowledge*[4]

(5) an ideal community of embodied subjects, of an
intercorporeality.

Merleau–Ponty, 'The Concept of Nature'[5]

(6) the intertwining of my life with the other lives, of
my body with the visible things, by the intersection
of my perceptual field with that of the others. . . .

Merleau–Ponty, 'Reflection and Interrogation'[6]

(7) The communication or comprehension of gestures
comes about through the reciprocity of my
intentions and the gestures of others, of my gestures
and intentions discernible in the conduct of other
people. It is as if the other person's intention
inhabited my body and mine his.

Merleau–Ponty, *Phenomenology of Perception*[7]

(8) Now I mean by education that training which is
given by suitable habits to *the first instincts of virtue*
in children; – when pleasure, and friendship, and
pain, and hatred, are rightly implanted in souls *not
yet capable of understanding the nature of them*, and
who find them, *after* they have attained reason, to
be in harmony with her. This harmony of the soul,
taken as a whole, is virtue; but the particular training
in respect of pleasure and pain, which leads you
always to hate what you ought to hate and love
what you ought to love, from the beginning of life
to the end, may be separated off; and, in my view,
will rightly be called education.

Plato, *Laws* II (653)

(9) For men say that the young of all creatures cannot
be quiet in their bodies or in their voices; they are
always wanting to move and cry out; some leaping
and skipping, and overflowing with sportiveness
and delight at something, others uttering all sorts of
cries. But, whereas the animals have no perception
of order or disorder in their movements, that is, of

rhythm or harmony, as they are called, to us, the
Gods, who, as we say, have been appointed to be
our companions in the dance, have given the
pleasurable sense of harmony and rhythm; and so
they stir us into life, and we follow them, joining
hands together in dance and songs; and these they
call *choruses*, which is a term naturally expressive
of cheerfulness. Shall we begin, then, with the
acknowledgement that education is first given
through Apollo and the Muses? What do you say?

Plato, *Laws* II (653–4)

Part I
Political Education in Classical Greece

At *Ion* 536, Plato repeats an ancient myth, probably related
to the myth of the Tree of Creation, and telling, with a music
we cannot forget, of the cosmological dimension within
which the spirit of dance takes place. In *Laws*, however, Plato
discusses the dance, not in the context of myth, but rather
in that of education. According to him, the cultivation of the
body's instinctive feeling for movement and its propensity
for dancing, coupled with the experience of community that
such dancing provides, are essential for the moral and political education of every Athenian citizen. So much so, in
fact, that at *Laws* II: 654, the 'uneducated' man is called
'achoreutos' ('danceless') while the 'educated' is named
'kechoreukos' ('skilled in dance'). Since human beings are
both bodies and souls, their personal health and political
welfare must correspondingly nurture them both in body
and in soul. This nurture, or education, has two branches:

One of gymnastic, which is concerned with the
body, and the other of music, which is designed
for the improvement of the soul. And gymnastic
has also two branches – dancing and wrestling;
and one sort of dancing imitates musical recitation,
and aims at preserving dignity and freedom, the
other aims at producing health, agility, and beauty
in the limbs and parts of the body, giving the
proper flexion and extension to each of them, a

harmonious motion being diffused everywhere,
and forming a suitable accompaniment to the dance.
(*Laws*, VII, 795. Also see *Laws* II, 673)

This kind of education rests on the classical Greek conviction,

that all bodies are benefited by shakings and
movements, when they are moved without
weariness, whether the motion proceeds from
themselves, or is caused by a swing, or at sea, or
on horseback, or by other bodies in whatever way
moving. (*Laws*, VII, 789)

But certain kinds of motion, of 'measure', namely 'the gentle
and benign' (792), are especially beneficial, 'producing in
them [i.e., in children] a sound mind, which takes the place
of their frenzy' (791), and shaping a strong, well-balanced,
and beautiful body (788). The aim of education is *virtue*: a
'gentle and cheerful' soul (792) and an agile, harmonious,
well-balanced embodiment (795), the shining, exemplary
embodiment of moral goodness and civic justice. But such
goodness of character (*ethos*) is exemplified in its glory only
when the process of education is true, not only to the beauty
of mind (soul), but also to the inherent nobility of its bodily
element. (See *Laws* VII, 816.) Thus the aim of political education is to *teach* the political virtues in a *mimesis* of their bodily
comportment: teach them, that is, by a 'method' which, being
'true' to the deepest nature of the body, is able to *bring out*
its intrinsic potential for goodness.

For the Greeks, however, it is in the *dance* that we find a
process of education especially appropriate to the embodying
of civic virtue:

Choric movements are imitations of manners
occurring in various actions, fortunes, dispositions,
– each particular is imitated, and those to whom the
words, or songs, or dances are suited, either by
nature or habit or both, cannot help feeling pleasure
in them and applauding them, and calling them
beautiful. (*Laws* II, 655. Also see 654 and 657)

When learned 'in the earliest years of life,' the kind of movement which imitates the *body* of virtue 'greatly contributes to
create a part of virtue in the soul.' (*Laws* VII, 791.) This

251

mimetic instruction is of course especially helpful in the education of children, since it teaches virtue *not* by abstract precepts difficult for them to understand, but *much more directly*, by maieutic movements immediately felt and intelligible in themselves. Thus, Plato says that dancing continues 'ancestral customs of great antiquity' (793), teaching the virtues of a culture by embodying its rhythm, harmony and balance. (We will recall, here, Merleau–Ponty's discussion, in his *Phenomenology of Perception*, of a 'global bodily knowledge which systematically embraces all its parts.'[8] By helping us to *feel* our way to this holistic *knowledge*, dancing facilitates the embodiment of a wholesome civic virtue.) The dance continues, also, an individual process which begins, in infancy, with nursing, cradling and moving about. Given this noble ideal, it is fitting that the very movements of infancy, and later, the very movements of dance, should attempt to cultivate, above all, the qualities of 'gentleness and benevolence and kindness' (*Laws* VII, 792). For these movements are 'appropriate to noble bodies and generous souls' (816). So Plato has the Athenian say:

> The affection both of the Bacchantes and of the children is an emotion of fear, which springs out of an evil habit of the soul. And when some one applies external agitation to affections of this sort, the motion coming from without gets the better of the terrible and violent internal one, and produces a peace and calm in the soul, and quiets the restless palpitation of the heart. . . . (*Laws* VII, 791)

Dancing continues this early child-rearing approach; and, when successful, it helps the young to experience *directly*, and even 'in the [very] bearing of their bodies' (797), that is, in the *felt sense* of their bodily nature, the consummate value of 'the middle state,' the proper measure, the just and fair proportion – qualities of character essential for well-being, good living, and responsible citizenship (792). The Athenian, in fact, explicitly states the conclusion:

> We ought to live sacrificing, and singing, and dancing, and then a man will be able to propitiate the gods. (*Laws* VII, 803)

As a discipline of embodiment, dance teaches civic ideals

and values in the most direct and unforgettable way, realizing them in the living body of their tradition. The ancient Greeks, it seems, understood the need for a healthy athletic body (athletic in a sense very different from our modern one), and for a wholesome, non-dualistic attitude toward the bodily nature of human being: an attitude of acceptance, and yet free of hedonism, or self-indulgence. In the well-being of the body – in its harmonious gestures, gracefully humbled bearing, well-grounded stance and agile movement, the soul, which is feeling at home, can rest: correspondingly graced with the political virtues of equanimity, balanced judgment, and a sense of just proportion. By directly embodying the classical ideals – those of justice and noble humility, for example – dancing makes political culture into second nature, ensuring a binding devotion that maintains, and celebrates, the harmonious order (*nomos*) of nature and culture.

Part II
Corporeal Schemata

In *The Yellow Emperor's Classic of Internal Medicine*, there is a detailed mapping of the analogy between the functional systems that constitute the individual human body and the functional systems that comprise the body politic.[9] For a superficial reading, the text is merely a metaphorical narrative and offers no more than a systematic analogy. However, for a more hermeneutical reading, the text suggests that the health of the individual and the welfare of the political organization are functionally intertwined and interdependent. In fact, the text suggests very specific *function correlations* between the two systems:

> the heart is like the minister of the monarch who
> excels through insight and understanding; the
> lungs are the symbols of the interpretation and
> conduct of the official jurisdiction and regulation;
> the liver has the functions of a military leader who
> excels in his strategic planning; the gall bladder
> occupies the position of an important and upright
> official who excels through his decisions and
> judgment; the middle of the thorax [the part

253

between the breasts] is like the official of the center who guides the subjects in their joys and pleasures; the stomach acts as the official of the public granaries and grants the five tastes; the lower intestines are like the officials who propagate the Right Way of Living, and they generate evolution and change; the small intestines are like the officials who are trusted with riches, and they create changes of the physical substance; the kidneys are like the officials who do energetic work, and they excel through their ability and cleverness; the burning spaces are like the officials who plan the construction of ditches and sluices, and they create waterways; the groins and the bladder are like the magistrates of a region or a district, they store the overflow and the fluid sections which serve to regulate vaporization. These twelve officials should not fail to assist one another.

When the monarch is intelligent and enlightened, there is peace and contentment among his subjects; they can thus beget offspring, bring up their children, earn a living and lead a long and happy life. And because there are no more dangers and perils, the earth is considered glorious and prosperous.

But when the monarch is not intelligent and enlightened, the twelve officials become dangerous and perilous; the use of Tao [the Right Way] is obstructed and blocked, and Tao no longer circulates warnings against physical excesses. When one attains Tao [the Right Way], even in small and trifling matters, the change will not exhaust and impoverish the people, for they know how to search for themselves.

But the text remains silent, especially for our deeper reading, in one crucial sense: it does not help us to find these correlations and retrieve them within our *experience* of the lived body, the body which we are. Would it be possible for us to actualize within ourselves, within our bodily being, a *felt sense* of these correlations? We need to carry around within us a much clearer understanding of how the maintenance of our bodily well-being and commitment to the harmony of the body politic are really one and the same. Is there some way for us to retrieve, from the elemental dynamics of our being, a powerfully motivating *sense* of our ontological intercorporeality?

The interaction between the laws of a political economy and the body of its investment can be extremely complex, and sometimes quite difficult to discern. But political theory cannot prudently continue to ignore the body of our political life: above all, the political protection, the political control, and the political interpretation of the human body. The body is shaped by its society, shaped in conformity with a specific vision, a specific image of the political. Once it has been shaped in that image, the body carries within its frame an implicit schema of comportments, a 'tacit knowledge,' the character of which is defined through its experience of the body politic.

For the sake of a completeness required by the architectonic of our project, we are therefore giving it our thematic attention. It is, however, a problem that both needs and merits a much lengthier study. This we cannot accomplish. What can be done here, though, will prepare the ground for later work. I would therefore like to *highlight* the human body as a locus for the *investment* of political power and a source of *resistance* to the politics whose will to power is the annihilation of Being. In particular, I would like to call attention to the fact that, relative to the existing political reality, the human body, as a natural or 'wild' being, as flesh, is always already the metaphor, the bearer, of a utopian political destination. Thinkers like Foucault concentrate on the ways in which a political regime externally appropriates the human body, imposing its demands on an essentially passive material; and they will explore strategies of resistance suggested by the body's experience of political institutionalization. But they neglect to acknowledge the body's own intrinsic political wisdom, its own uncommonly good *sense* of good political order, the *sensus communis*. The infant's body is in a 'state of nature': initially, it is relatively untouched by the political norms that will gradually appropriate it by way of the embodiments (the schematizations) it encounters in the early socializing relationships. And yet, this body is *already informed*, in its state of nature, by an operative schema of the ideal body politic: a schema which inhabits the wild body, having already inscribed in its organs and limbs the rudimentary and unconscious image, the incarnate dream, of a political order in which and through which the justice of its deepest nature would enjoy real fulfillment.

Near the end of his life, as we already noted in the Introduction, Merleau–Ponty began to think of the human body in terms of the concept of 'flesh.' Since we have already considered this concept in earlier chapters, I shall reiterate only very briefly the significance of this concept. For Merleau–Ponty, 'flesh' is an *ontological* concept which designates our most primordial, elemental dimension of Being: our bodily inherence in the field of Being as a whole.[10] This designation is further specified, however, in terms of three characteristics that are of particular significance for an ontologically radicalized political theory, viz., (i) openness, (ii) intertwining, and (iii) reversibility. As for the first of these, Merleau–Ponty observes that,

> In reality, there is neither me nor the other as positive, positive subjectivities. There are . . . two opennesses, two stages where something will take place.[11]

This disclosure is one which takes place for the first time when his thinking finally moved into the ontological dimension of embodiment he calls 'flesh': together with the other two, this disclosure is the articulation, and fleshing out, of a radically new body of understanding.

The second, 'intertwining,' designates our 'intercorporeality': the fact that human existence in its most elemental dimensionality is a field of bodily awareness pervasively determined by interactions with other beings that conclusively demonstrate our interdependence and interpenetration. The seemingly universal phenomenon which Husserl calls 'intentional transgression' and which Wallon calls 'postural impregnation' unquestionably attests to the ontological fact of 'intercorporeality' which Merleau–Ponty's concept of 'flesh' is meant to make explicit.[12] As for the third, namely 'reversibility,' Merleau–Ponty wants to call our attention to the sense in which the intertwining of existences, of beings (for example, the seer and the seen, the one who is touching and the one who is touched), sets in motion a dynamic of reciprocity, a mirroring and doubling, such that, for example, the being of the seer is invariably reflected back by the being of that which is seen, and the one who touches is necessarily touched by the being of that which he touches.[13]

Now, I would like to argue that Merleau–Ponty's conceptualization of the 'flesh' can be understood in such a way that it will function as a radically ontological schematization for a new body politic. Let me explain this suggestion in other words. I believe that the flesh can be interpreted as schematizing our most primordial attunement to political order, our most elemental, most rudimentary pre-ontological understanding of the essence (ideality) of political community. In the nature of the flesh, we can experience what Merleau–Ponty calls an 'initial sympathy' and an 'initial community.'[14] In this sense, the flesh may be said to schematize *a priori* a possible body politic. When we consider Merleau–Ponty's account of the three principal characteristics of the flesh, i.e., the ontological dimensionality of our embodiment, we will, I think, be quite struck by the fact that they implicitly authorize a political interpretation: they schematize corporeally our attunement to a political order very different from the ones that have ruled for so long over our history.

The schematic body politic whose sense is carried by the body's pre-ontological understanding (ontological pre-understanding) is, however, only an implicit potential. It needs the modeling of education; it calls for cultivation through social interactions – forms of intercorporeality – which will engage *harmoniously* with this bodily potential and schematize, or demonstrate, the civic ideal of corporeality. In the course of such socialization, it is possible for the ideal body image to connect so intensely and lucidly with the child's bodily predispositions that it gets mirrored and transmitted in a very powerful spontaneous *mimesis*. But it must be emphasized that it is possible to bring forth the ideal corporeality *only insofar as* the intercorporeality constitutive of the process of socialization lucidly demonstrates a body politic that resonates harmoniously with the child's body of pre-ontological understanding. If the body image that is demonstrated for the child *fails* to resonate in this way – if, that is, it fails to demonstrate a 'legible' attunement with the implicit sense of political being always already carried by the child – then the *fulfillment* of the child's inborn potential will not be possible. This fundamental point is, of course, the lesson we need most to learn from the discussion of civic education in Plato.

Radical social theory is very much in need of a grounding truth from the standpoint of which it would be possible to articulate not only a powerful cross-cultural critique of ideology, but also some theoretically well-grounded strategies of resistance to the institutions of domination and repression. In closing this chapter, therefore, I would like to venture the suggestion that the body's implicitly felt sense of harmonious political order, i.e., its pre-ontological understanding of political being, could perhaps provide the most universal, most radical grounding that is possible for political theory, since the infantile body's 'wild being' – its primordial nature – has always already schematized a potential body politic at a stage of life which virtually precedes the political process of socialization. I can think of no better, more radical basis for measuring and contesting any actual political regime. I believe that political theory should accordingly engage this primordial body politic in a hermeneutical process of education. Our collective recollection of this ontological gift could perhaps prepare us in some small way for a new chapter in political history.

In *Epidemics*, a work attributed to Hippokrates, it is said that 'nature [*Physis*] heals disease.'[15] Is there also, then, a message of healing for the body politic, a hint for our political welfare, in that dimension of our embodiment through which we are most fully attuned by *Physis*? Let us not forget that *Physis* is an ancient word for Being. Thus, if the functional analogy is valid, it is possible that the ultimate glory of our commonwealth may lie in our capacity, as individuals, to find within the gift of embodiment a vital sense of our political community through the intercorporeality that has always been implicit in its ontological nature.

Although there are compelling reasons for considering the body politic in a separate chapter, as we have here, I very much regret the classificatory isolation of 'the political' as a separate concern – for example, when our understanding of the potential for spiritual development is detached from the question of our political responsibility or when, conversely, political activity is alienated from any sense of spiritual values. This separateness of 'the political' is, in effect, its negation; it conceals the very possibility of radical political critique and limits political action to superficial reforms. Thus, I should like to emphasize my hope that the brevity and sketchiness of this chapter will not obscure the fact that, throughout this study, I have been reflecting on matters that do have political significance, and have been attempting to articulate an ontological interpretation of human gesture, and motility in general, that makes sense to me in relation to my political commitments and objectives. It would be a source of great satisfaction for me if the sharing of this interpretation in the community of thought could contribute in some way to the enhancement of our political life. For me, therefore, this entire book is a political work, a gesture with political motives and effects. In other studies that were forthcoming at the time of writing, I concentrate on matters of political significance as they arise in the context of an attempt to reach an ontological understanding of our visionary, auditory, and communicative being. I allude to these forthcoming studies because I believe that they will provide some of the specificity and detail that could not be incorporated here.

CHAPTER 5

Taking the Measure in Stride

Opening Conversation

(1) I am in the deepest sense an unfortunate individual, who has from the earliest age been nailed fast to one suffering or another, and on the very edge of insanity, which may have its deeper ground in a disproportion between my soul and my body.

Søren Kierkegaard, *Journals*[1]

(2) if the balance of processes is destroyed, then the underlying unity of the cosmos will cease.

G. S. Kirk, 'Natural Change in Heraclitus'[2]

(3) We do not sustain ourselves in virtue by our own strength, but by the balancing of two opposed vices, just as we remain upright amidst two contrary gales.

Blaise Pascal, *Pensées*[3]

(4) What is upright is the existence that is threatened by weight.

Merleau–Ponty, 'Working Notes'[4]

(5) a man standing upright, firmly planted on that ground as a cosmic axis, stepping firmly.

Desana Indian informant
of the Colombian Amazon[5]

260

(6)   Happy are they that are upright in the way,
      Who walk in the law of the Lord.
                              Book of Psalms 119:1

(7)   The Lord upholds all who fall,
      And raises all who are bowed down.
                              Psalms 145:14

(8)   More honestly and purely speaks the healthy body
      that is perfect and perpendicular: and it speaks of
      the meaning of the earth.
            Friedrich Nietzsche, *Thus Spake Zarathustra*[6]

(9)   my moral carriage is that of a man who limps with
      one foot in life and one in death. . . .
                              Jean Cocteau[7]

(10) This whole human existence . . . is merely the
      consequence of a false step.
                              Kierkegaard, *Journals*[8]

(11) Let our virtues be easy and nimble-footed in
      motion. . . .
                        Nietzsche, *The Joyful Wisdom*[9]

(12) to go through life with a quiet eye and a firm
      step. . . .
                        Nietzsche, *The Joyful Wisdom*[10]

(13) Great peace have they that love thy law;
      And there is no stumbling for them.
                              Psalms 119:165

(14) For thou hast delivered my soul from death. . . .
      And my feet from stumbling.
                              Psalms 116:8

(15) Thy word is a lamp unto my feet,
      And a light unto my path.
                              Psalms 119:105

(16) I thought on my ways, and turned my feet unto
      thy testimonies.
                              Psalms 119:59

(17) And I have refrained my feet from every evil way,
      that I might keep thy word.
                              Psalms 119:101

261

(18) And I will walk at ease,
      for I have sought thy precepts.
                              Psalms 119:45

(19) Thou hast enlarged my steps under me,
      and my feet have not slipped.
                                  Psalms 18:37

(20) He maketh my feet like hind's feet,
      and setteth me upon my high place.
                                  Psalms 18:34

(21) Thousands of Buddhas come forth from the tips of
      his feet.
                              Mumon's verse on Isan[11]

(22) It is the very inner form of earth that continues to
          move within me,
      that has arisen with me,
      that is standing with me,
      that indeed remains stationary with me. . . .
      Navajo 'Song of the Earth,' from *The Blessing Way*[12]

(23) With visible breath I am walking.
      A voice I am sending as I walk.
      In a sacred manner I am walking.
      With visible tracks I am walking.
      In a sacred manner I walk.
      'Song of the Buffalo Cow Woman' (Oglala Sioux)[13]

(24) In beauty I walk.
      With beauty before me I walk.
      With beauty behind me I walk.
      With beauty above me I walk.
      With beauty above and about me I walk.
      It is done in beauty.
      It is finished in beauty.
      Navajo Shaman's Song, *The Night Chant*[14]

Part I

The Measure

(1) Keeping time,
    Keeping the rhythm in their dancing
    As in their living in the living seasons
    The time of the seasons and the constellations
    The time of milking and the time of harvest
    The time of the coupling of man and woman
    And that of beasts. Feet rising and falling.
    Eating and drinking. Dung and death.

    T. S. Eliot, 'East Coker'

(2) in this rhythm I am bound.

    Aeschylos, Prometheos (241)

(3) The destiny of man is a single celestial rhythm.

    Hölderlin[15]

(4) Time does not itself belong to motion but embraces
    it. The intratemporality of a being means its being
    embraced by time (now) as number (counted). The
    factor of the *periechesthai*, being embraced, stresses
    that time does not itself belong among the beings
    which are in time. So far as we measure a being,
    either in motion or at rest, by time, we come back
    from the time that embraces and measures the
    moving thing to that which is to be measured. . . .
    It [is time which] embraces or holds around the
    moving and resting things.

    Heidegger, The Basic Problems of Phenomenology[16]

(5) it is the body which comes to bestride time . . . the
    body's grip upon the soil . . . ways of taking hold
    of time.

    Merleau–Ponty, 'Eye and Mind'[17]

In *The Will to Power*, Nietzsche argues that a growing sense of emptiness in our daily lives, and a powerful nihilism which reflects this in our thinking, may be virtually inevitable, because 'We have measured the value of the world according to categories that refer to a purely fictitious world.'[18] If we recognize the prophetic foresight in Nietzsche's diagnosis, we will want, I think, to devote ourselves to finding the (more) appropriate measure. Following Nietzsche's own hints – hints which he did not permit himself, or perhaps was not by circumstance enabled, to follow out – I would like to suggest the possibility that we could open ourselves to the dictates of this (more) appropriate measure, not by a continuation of metaphysical thinking, but rather by a more thoughtful way of walking the earth.

Now, in '. . . Poetically Man Dwells . . .' Heidegger sees to it that the question of measure and proportion, the very heart of justice as well as of poetry, is given a sounding which will claim our attention:

> The taking of measure is what is poetic in dwelling.
> Poetry is a measuring. But what is it to measure?
> If poetizing is to be understood as measuring, then
> obviously we may not subsume it under just any
> idea of measuring and measure.[19]

And he continues:

> Poetry is presumably a high and special kind of
> measuring. . . . In poetry, there takes place what
> all measuring is in the ground of its being. Hence
> it is necessary to pay heed to the basic art of
> measuring. That consists in man's first of all taking
> the measure which is then applied in every
> measuring act. In poetry the taking of measure
> occurs. To write poetry is measure-taking,
> understood in the strictest sense of the word, by
> which man receives the measure for the breadth
> of his being.

At *Laws* IV, 716, Plato says:

> Things which have no measure are in harmony
> neither with themselves nor with the things which
> have.

According to Heidegger, human beings *receive* this measure by way of their (experienced) mortality: it is our being 'capable of death as death.'[20] So, in *Der Satz vom Grund*, Heidegger says:

> Death is the still unthought measure of the

immeasurable, i.e., of the highest play in which
man is brought on earth, upon which he is staked.[21]

But our *mortality* must be measured against that which is
not mortal. 'Man, as man, has always measured himself with
and against something heavenly.'[22] That is why Hölderlin
writes: 'Man measures himself against the godhead.'[23] And
Heidegger comments:

> The godhead is the 'measure' with which man
> measures out his dwelling, his stay on the earth
> beneath the sky. Only insofar as man takes the
> measure of his dwelling in this way is he able to
> *be* commensurately with his nature. Man's dwelling
> depends on an upward-looking measure-taking of
> the dimension, in which the sky belongs just as
> much as the earth.[24]

In the final sentence of this passage, Heidegger invites us to
experience the earth as a symbol of the godhead. Thus, the
earth becomes our measure. But what does this mean? In
measure-taking, we measure the span of our mortality,
taking the measure from the broad, deep earth and the
immeasurable sky; but we also 'gauge,' as he puts it, 'the
between, which brings the two, heaven and earth, to one
another.'[25] And yet, we cannot measure earth and sky; nor
could they serve us as measure if they were nothing but
projections of our will to power, and appeared in the world
as measures ready-to-hand. (Our hands must overcome their
inveterate tendency to 'abruptly grasp'; we must learn to be
'guided by gestures befitting the measure here to be taken.')[26]
When the poet asks:

> Is there a measure on earth?

he answers, as he must, 'There is none.'[27] So Heidegger then
inquires:

> how can that which by its very nature remains
> unknown ever become a measure? For something
> that man measures himself by must after all impart
> itself, must appear. But if it appears, it is known.
> The god, however, is unknown, and he is the
> measure nonetheless.[28]

265

Following the poet's hints, Heidegger ventures an initial resolution of the enigma:

> The measure consists in the *way* in which the god, who remains unknown, is revealed *as* such by the sky. God's appearance through the sky consists in a disclosing that lets us see what conceals itself, but lets us see it not by seeking to wrest what is concealed out of its concealedness, but only by guarding the concealed in its self-concealment. Thus the unknown god appears as the unknown by way of the sky's manifestedness.[29]

And he concludes, therefore, that,

> This appearance is the measure against which man measures himself.[30]

This appearance, however, is problematic. It requires that what the poet calls 'kindness' govern within our hearts.[31] Thus, when we listen for the ontological measure, the meter, of poetry, we must *also* listen to the measure which is meted out, and felt as a claim, by the beating heart. Only then can we, as mortals, begin to understand how to dwell, standing *on* the earth and standing *under* the sky, and learning from both the true measure of our being.

As our concern, in this study, is for the emerging of a radically new body of understanding, I would like to focus our attention on the body's *experience* of the ontological measure, i.e., on how this measure appropriates our flesh and lays claim to our thought. If we are ever going to overcome the metaphysical tradition, we need to find a way out of the metaphysical representation of the ontological measure. I submit that our way out may be found in a retrieval of that presence-to-Being which is granted us through the body of experience. What I am suggesting in this context, then, is that, through the rhythm in our stride, it may be possible for us to experience the measure of an openness-to-Being that we could not dream of realizing in any other way.

The bodily felt sense of measure – in our heartbeat, for example – is a deep source of wisdom in regard for this true measure. Understanding *begins* in, and begins *as*, a bodily granted feeling. But this does not mean – and it would in fact be a fatal error to presume that it means – a merely ontic, factual feeling. When we locate the ontological in our body of felt experience, it must not be assumed that we are proposing to *reduce* the dimensionality to be spanned by that experience. We are attempting, rather, to *clarify* how that measure of Being, or Being as the immeasurable, can actually claim us *even* in our body of feeling, *even* in our heartbeat. As James Hillman puts it (but perhaps too paradoxically, too provocatively) in his 'Critique of Modern Humanism's Psychology,'

> All areas of feeling shrivel in significance when man
> becomes the measure, when feeling becomes only
> a problem to work on and grow from. Feeling that
> is a merely human function loses its power to
> reflect psyche beyond the human to the unknowns
> of the soul. Therefore it is necessary to
> dehumanize, depersonalize, and demoralize the
> psyche in order to deepen the meaning of its
> human experiences beyond the measure of man.[32]

Surely, however, it is not only the poets who can hear and repeat the sound of the measure, the measure which tells of our mortality; nor are they the only ones who can feel it in the song of their heart. For example, do not those who dance also sometimes open themselves so fully to the song of the earth that they can *hear* this immortal measure when it sounds forth, still heavy with the gravitational weight of the earth? And can they not likewise *feel* its beat, and not merely in their hearts, but also with their feet? Listen to a dance-song, a *hyporchēmē*, attributed to Timotheos of Miletos:

> As for the others the while, they set them up
> trophies to be a most holy place of Zeus, and
> hymned the great healing-god men cry to, beating
> the ground to the tune in high-stept dance.[33]

And this, an ancient folk-song called 'Hymn to Delos':

> The men sing the song of the Lycian ancient, the
> song the prophet Olen brought from the bank of
> the Xanthos, and the maidens that dance to them
> beat with their feet the stable earth.[34]

I submit, then, that the earth, the immeasurably deep and

267

dark, can be our measure of life and death, and that we can receive it through the very steps of our feet. In the measured steps of dance, we, as mortals, together with the gods or dreams we invoke, can celebrate the joining of Earth and Sky. In the measured steps of a dancing stride, we, as mortals, can become more mindful of our earthbound mortality, timed for a certain span. We can learn the true rhythm, the true proportions, of our present embodiment.

In his 'Letter on Humanism,' Heidegger reminds us that *humanus* and *humilitas* are both rooted in *humus*, the Latin word for the nourishing and supportive ground, our fertile earth. Whether we are dancing or simply walking from one place to another, we are claimed by this earth, and therefore we move most appropriately when our motility serves to *commemorate* the ancient endurance of the earth – our Mother Earth, which is Being, Being itself, manifesting as the ground we mortals *need* in order to stand being ourselves; our Mother Earth, into which, as into an abyss, we individually perish when it is our apportioned time to die.[35] 'Everything moves in the midst of death,' said Santayana, 'because indeed it moves.'[36] The resounding rhythms of the dancing or walking step, the step made audible by its contact with the earth, lets us *hear* the passing measure of time – and not just in our feet, but in our body as a whole. The *intactness* of this measure is crucial, and always timely: since it is felt by the *body* as a whole, we are able to undergo an experience of *time* as a whole, and it is this which grants us, in turn, an experience of our own mortality, rounding out the movement of a lifetime. As *we* move, the *earth* sounds; it sounds in *time*. The passage of time passes *through* our body, measuring the span of our life, while *we* pass time, pass through life, taking in the measure of this earth. Time *is* the steadfast earth itself, understanding our gait of mortality. The deep sounding of time is an *energy* given us with the earth's blessing; it is, in fact, that which most deeply *moves* us, that which most powerfully enables *us* to move. And the earth lets us *hear* this – lets us hear its steadfast *support* for our being-in-repose and our being-in-movement. And when we hear this underlying support with a body of understanding, it is possible that we may find ourselves deeply and powerfully moved, moved as never before. Even for others, even for their seeing, we may be visibly moved . . . moved, that is, by a power that is *not* our own, but an energy rising up into the compliant body, a blessing from the earth.

Let us go more deeply into the argument I would like to draw out of this experience. In the stride of our walking, a rhythm is always singing. This rhythm is time's *embrace* of our movement, our walking body. It is also the sensing of an encompassing measure: a measure which reverberates through the body experienced in its wholeness and lays claim to the fleshing out of our being. But the rhythm does not originate in the body; it originates, rather, in the flesh of the world: the body's *relationship* to the elemental ground, our underlying earth. In other words, it is the earth, always present as the grounding for our stride, which implicitly determines the measure that binds us. Since the earth *is* Being in its presencing as a primordial geology, our sensing of a rhythm in our stride is at the same time the receptivity of a guardian awareness (*Wahrnehmung*) to the ontological measure into which we find ourselves always already bound. We move, each one of us, with his own distinctive stride. When we *find* our own true stride, the stride that uniquely fits our bodily being, we can begin to realize in its rhythm the individuating measure of our being.

I would like to suggest that, by interpreting the question of measure in terms of our experiencing of the stride, we can begin to *break out* of the historically dominant framework of metaphysical concepts and representations, as well as the systems of thought (e.g., ethics) that have been determined by them. To the degree that we allow ourselves to experience a *ratio* in our stride, an appropriate measure for our being, which is truly ontological (truly, that is, opening and deepening in relation to the wholeness of Being), and yet not thinkable in the terminology of our traditional metaphysics, we leave behind us the metaphysical rationality which has dominated our experience of the ontological measure. The implicit measure that we continually receive from the earth by virtue of our stride is a measure that originates in the grounding of Being. Now, I realize that, when I say this, it may seem as if I am repeating the metaphysics of rational ground and origin. But this is not the case, for the grounding in question, here, is much more elemental: it is too primordial for metaphysical conceptualization. Its presencing *eludes* the will to power that demands an objective re-presentation of its presence. And it announces itself only for a thoughtful stride attuned to the sounding *logos* of the earth. What makes such a stride 'ontological,' then, is the *openness* of its awareness to the deepest meaning of the ground encountered by motility and the intense *energy* (*physis*) this openness lets burst in.

Submission to the earth is submission to time, the sounding of the earth. The resounding rhythms of the dancing or walking gait can teach us mortals to *trust* the ground, a presencing of Being, so that we can take its measuring, the measuring of our mortality, always in stride.

Part II

In Balance

It will be recalled that, in explaining Herakleitos, Kirk observed that, 'if the balance of processes is destroyed, then the underlying unity of the cosmos fails.' 'And this balance,' he adds, 'depends on *metron* [measure].' Now that we have interpreted the way in which this measure, this presencing of the *Logos*, lays claim to us as mortals through our bodily being-in-the-world, and in particular, through our gait and stride, we need to reflect on the question of balance. Balance is a necessary primordial condition for the emerging body of understanding that our project has been aimed at articulating. A well-balanced mind, clear and steady, requires a well-balanced body, a body relaxed into a restful equilibrium. Our sanity is inseparable from our balance. Likewise, a morally upright life begins with, and is inseparable from, a balanced, upright posture: a body standing up right, firm and steady in its gait, steadfast in its commitment to a life of high principle. Most of us no more achieve such an upright, well-balanced posture than we achieve an upright life. The one may be as difficult as the other; but if their achievement should really be inseparable, ontologically intertwined, then we need to ask ourselves in what way we are still unbalanced, still stumbling, not upright.

A good upright posture is, I believe, a necessary condition for the emerging truth of a deep, full-bodied (i.e., whole-bodied) awareness (*Gewähren*) that the speech, the *logos* of the earth is our most primordial grounding, our most fundamental support, a principal source of our energy. This geological awareness is very powerful. From out of its primordial relatedness-to-Being (*Physis*), it determines the principles of our moral life, regulating our comportment (*Gebärde*) and enabling us to sustain the posture, the bearing and behavior

– finally, the implicit destiny – of a morally upright being. The body's uprightness, attentive to the earth's speech, translates its grounding into a support for our moral rectitude. And, with the body's emerging understanding of itself, the grounding which grants it, and always underlies, its upright stature can accordingly become an *ontological* support for the 'new' morality, the new political community.

In *The Will to Power*, Nietzsche laments the fact that,

> We are losing our center of gravity by virtue of which we have lived; we are lost for a while. . . .[37]

Retrieving that center of gravity, finding our centeredness in that true center of meaning around which our life can pivot in a relaxed, well-balanced way, is crucial not only for our health; it is critical for our emotional well-being, and therefore also for our steadiness of principle as moral agents. Such steadiness, such *Gelassenheit*, is in fact necessary for our ontological well-being, as Heidegger himself very nearly understands. It will be noted that, when he diagnoses the plight in which we of the modern epoch find ourselves, he suggests that he is contemplating our 'standing' in its corporeal, as well as its spiritual sense. The human being, he says,

> is coming to the very brink of precipitous fall; that is, he is coming to the point where he himself will have to be taken as standing-reserve. Meanwhile, man, precisely as the one so threatened, exalts himself to the posture of lord of the earth.[38]

We are easily tempted to exalt ourselves in this posture. But it is a posture of pride and insolence, a posture which makes manifest, and in fact reinforces, our forgetfulness of the earth. In that posture – a posture prized by our patriarchy – we are not, however, well-balanced. Sooner or later, we shall stumble or fall.

If this fall be avoidable, what kind of comportment would avert it? What kind of posture, what kind of bearing, what kind of motility, is well-balanced? Is it not clear that what is appropriate to our humanity is the dignity in a posture of humility – a posture, I mean, that is well-balanced by virtue of its recollection of the earth? (It should be noted that *this* sense of 'humility' is radically different from the traditional sense, which is inextricably caught up in the repressiveness

271

of moral dualism. Taking a hint from etymology, I propose that the humility which would be exemplified by the body of understanding that has been emerging in this study is to be defined, rather, in terms of a recollection of the earth as the primordial ground of our standing.) We are moving closer to being well-balanced when we stand up on the earth with a mindfulness, or an awareness, that acknowledges its elemental grounding of our being, and understand that the earth's endurance is a first measure of our mortality, while its own steadiness is a first measure for our virtue. We are moving closer to being well-balanced when our standing is thoughtfully centered on the *grounding* provided by the earth. We are moving closer to being well-balanced when the *standing* of our being in relation to the presencing of Being is deeply understood through our embodiment and our understanding has attuned the posture of our standing to that field of wholeness on which it rests.

Balance is the 'virtue' of our posture: our ability to stand up and walk to noble purpose without erring or falling. We will always be indebted, beholden, to the earth, the ground on which we stand and walk. But our virtue consists in acknowledging this beholdenness (*Schuldigkeit*) and making our gratitude manifest in the dignity of a posture that *graces* the earth. We are fulfilling the destiny (*Geschick*) in our beholdenness when, instead of continuing to lose our balance, fall or stumble, we become capable of moving with a poise and grace that *embellish* the ground taken for granted at our feet. This attitude toward earth, our most elemental ground, is, I believe, a preparatory step of decisive historical importance for our relatedness-to-Being.

Being presences in our world as 'ground.' Following the tradition, what most philosophers take this to mean is: in Being is our grounding. But we need to understand that it also means: the experience of being grounded is our first experience of Being as it presences in our world. But whether, and how, we are granted an *experience* of this grounding, or whether, instead, what we experience is its wrathful shuddering and quaking, its withdrawal of underlying support or its sudden opening as a gaping abyss, depends, in part, on how we relate to it. Being is an *upholding* ground when we, for our part, uphold our primordial 'contract,' our primordial belongingness (*Zugehörigkeit*) to the earth. According to this 'contract,' we are mortals raised from the earth, mortals destined to walk the earth for a while tarrying a while in its upholding. But our stay in *its* upholding is conditional: it depends on the *character* of our participation in 'the balance of processes.' Are we then willing to acknowledge our standing and falling in the law of this balance? Are we willing to *uphold* that balance, obedient to its measure? Can we uphold our beholdenness to the earth?

Balance concerns our vertical alignment, our standing in relation to a vertical axis. The two poles of this axis are the earth and the sky, the element of our grounding and the element that teaches us spaciousness. But we forget the earth under our feet: the ground which holds us up and at the same time pulls us down, weighting us with the gravity of our own mortality. In death, it is always the earth which claims us. Likewise, we forget the other pole of the axis, the sky above our head: the celestial space which encompasses us with its measure; enraptures with its vastness; awes with its display of immortal presences; instructs in its eternal, or lawful recurrences; and frightens us by its emptiness. Both the earth and the sky can presence either as the plenitude of Being or as a disorienting nothingness. How they presence for us as individuals and groups who are living in the epoch of modernity is very much a question that refers our thinking to an emerging body of understanding.

Recollecting the destiny of our dwelling between these two poles of the vertical axis – recollecting our alignment in this betweenness not only *while* we are walking, but by, or as, the *way* we are walking – makes all the difference. Specifically, it situates our motility in the span of the ontological difference. This is experienced in many ways. Thus, for example, our gait may assume an almost supernatural kind of power. This may seem very strange, but we do need to bear in mind what Heidegger says, in 'The Nature of Language,' about the possibility of actually *feeling* the powerful flow of the earth, rising up into our body, when we speak with words that, as we experience them, flower through the mouth: 'Body and mouth,' he writes, 'are part of earth's flow and growth, in which we mortals flourish, and from which we receive the soundness of our roots.'[39] These are not mere words; they communicate an actual *experience* of centeredness and groundedness, and do so with the accuracy of a phenomenological report. We may be granted a very similar kind of experience to the extent that we walk with the body's

273

guardian awareness of Being, well-centered and well-grounded in the earth's field of energy.

Balance is a question of centering. When we are properly centered, our experience of Being is in equilibrium. Being well-centered, we can encounter other beings in a more relaxed, open, receptive way. Finding our center is in fact a *necessary* step in the development of our ontological capacity to open ourselves to the larger measure of Being and to encounter other beings with equanimity, justice, and a presence that is deeply responsive, since the life which is lived *without* such a center of balance is ontologically too insecure, too vulnerable, to tolerate that measure of openness. Coming 'home' to our true center of being, we can relax our ego-logical defenses and begin to experience things outside the subject/object polarization. When our encounter with other beings takes place in situations where we are *not* well-centered and well-balanced, we will naturally be preoccupied with our own ego-logical security, our own standing. However, when we can encounter beings in a more relaxed condition, it is easier to *release* them from the structural field constituted by our anxiety: we can begin to *let beings be*. Being well-centered within ourselves, we do not need to cling to other beings, afraid to lose their support; nor do we need to seize and hold things, in mortal dread of letting go; nor, finally, do we need to be so defensive. Being well-centered in Being is therefore at the very root of *Gelassenheit*, that 'way of being' in virtue of which, according to Heidegger, we are going to be most favored with a deeper experience of beings and the presencing of Being as such.

Part III

Walking the Path

In his *Introduction to Metaphysics*, Heidegger observes that, 'Every epoch of world history is an epoch of errancy.'[40] 'Error,' he says in another text, 'The Anaximander Fragment,' is 'the space in which history unfolds.'[41] Now it will be noted that, when Heidegger attempts to formulate the 'methodology' of his response to this crisis in history, he is often disposed to speak of steps of thought and the opening up of space. Thus, for example, he reminds us, in *What Is Called Thinking?* that,

Thinking itself is a way. We respond to the way
only by remaining underway. To be underway on
the way in order to clear the way – that is one thing.
The other thing is to take a position somewhere
along the road, and there make conversation about
whether, and how, earlier and later stretches of
the way may be different, and in their difference
might even be incompatible – incompatible, that
is, for those who never walk the way, nor ever set
out on it, but merely take up a position outside it,
there forever to formulate ideas and make talk about
the way.[42]

But that means, as he says, that,

In order to get underway, we do have to set out.
This is meant in a double sense: for one thing, we
have to open ourselves to the emerging prospect
and direction of the way itself; and then, we must
get on the way, that is, must take the steps by which
alone the way becomes a way.[43]

I submit, however, that one of the new steps we need to
take now, a step that could possibly make way for our overcoming of metaphysical history, consists in an interpretation
of thinking which gives it exemplification in a body of ontological understanding. In other words, the next steps we
need to take are steps we actually must take as bodily beings.
   Heidegger wants to break with the metaphysical tradition.
But of course he never reaches the end of the path that his
thinking suggests: the steps he contemplates remain steps of
thinking, in a sense of 'thinking' which still falls under the
sway of the old Cartesian ontology. Thinking in the wake of
Heidegger's preparatory steps, I feel a need to go beyond
the place where he leaves us. That place is mapped for us
when he says, for example, that,

The way of thinking cannot be traced from
somewhere to somewhere like a well-worn rut, nor
does it all exist as such in any place. Only when we
walk it, and in no other fashion, only, that is, by
thoughtful questioning, are we on the move on the
way.[44]

275

In 'Dance and the Soul,' Paul Valéry transports us back in time and space to ancient Greece, where we are privileged to overhear a dialogue of thought set in motion by the graceful presence of a young dancer. Sokrates exclaims:

> A simple walk, the simplest linking of steps . . .
> what we squander carelessly in the vulgar change
> of steps when we walk about our common
> occasions.[45]

To which Eryximachus adds the observation that,

> Our steps are so easy and so familiar to us that they
> never have the honor of being considered in
> themselves and in their character of strange actions
> (unless, becoming infirm or paralyzed, we are
> induced by privation to admire them). . . .

The historical step I am proposing, therefore, is that, as we walk the path that thinking demands, we give thought to our steps. In the forgetfulness that follows our footsteps, a forgetfulness of Being persists. Our historical destiny is accordingly bound to our willingness to *recollect* the body of understanding that walks the path of thought.

The way we walk is a measure of our character, a measure of our groundedness in the truth of Being — a measure, finally, of the depth of our *experience* of Being. For the most part, we walk in the *oblivion* of Being; we walk without awareness. ('Awareness' is etymologically related to the German words *wahren*, *Wahrnis*, *Wahre*, and *Wahrheit*: awareness is the guardian of truth.) To walk *with* awareness is to walk in the truth: to walk, that is, in a *disclosing* of the meaningfulness of Being. In its essence, walking is itself a poetizing saving of the earth. But, by the same token, it is also a saving and upholding of our ownmost being — our being-on-the-path-of-thinking. When we walk in the wholesomeness of thought, we walk in the openness of the ontological difference; and our walking shifts accordingly into a world-spanning stride, a stride of beauty, gathering the whole of time and the whole of space into its melodic rhythm — into that understanding body which unifies the meditation of our steps.

It might be instructive, at this point in our reflections, to consider Heidegger's 'Basic Questions of Metaphysics,' a series of lectures he gave in 1935–6 on the history of the experience of motion. [46] The primary concern of his discussion is, to be sure, the metaphysical understanding of the motion of 'natural bodies' – bodies, that is to say, which are inanimate, or non-sentient. Our concern here, of course, is the distinctively *human* body. Nevertheless, since, for Aristotle, even the motion of things like stones and leaves is essentially teleological, our strategy, which will extend the concept of 'natural body' to include the body which is human in its nature, is less of a distortion than might at first be supposed. And in fact, this unorthodox strategy may actually turn out, as I think, to *open out* our traditional understanding of the nature of the human body, which has suffered for too long – and already, I mean, in Aristotle – from a conceptual enframing which fails to realize its ontological dimensionality. Thus, paradoxically, we may find ourselves headed towards a new understanding of the human body by taking yet another (hermeneutical) reading of the metaphysical tradition: another reading, for example, of Aristotle's account of 'earthly' and 'celestial' bodies. After all, if we allow ourselves to suspend, just for the moment, the weight of our historical knowledge regarding the actual referents which Aristotle himself must have had in mind, we might very well reach a point in our thinking where we would feel strongly inclined to describe the motion of the human body as being, so to speak, 'in the middle,' partaking of that which is characteristically 'earthly,' yet also striving, at the same time, for a form of motility which would be characteristically 'celestial.' We might perhaps want to say that when we are walking the path of thought, our flowing stride, as we actually experience it (e.g., as highly charged), meaningfully participates in the motions which are characteristic of *both* realms. In order to explore this experience, therefore, we shall now proceed to read Heidegger's analysis hermeneutically – and with an eye for its translation into the realm of *human* motility.

Interpreting Aristotle, then, Heidegger says:

> The motion of bodies, however, is *kath' auta*, according to them, themselves. That is to say, how a body moves, i.e., how it relates to place and to which place it relates – all this has its basis in the body itself. . . . The body moves according to its nature. A moving body, which is itself an *archē kinēseōs*, is a natural body. The purely earthly body

> moves downward, the purely fiery body – as every
> blazing flame demonstrates – moves upward. Why?
> Because the earthly body has its place below, the
> fiery, above. Each body has its place *according to its
> kind*, and it strives toward that place. Around the
> earth is water, around this, the air, and around this,
> fire – the four elements. When a body moves
> toward its place, this motion accords with its nature,
> *kata physin*. . . . All motions against nature are *biai*,
> violent.[47]

When we translate this analysis of physical motion into an
interpretation of human motility, we are eventually
confronted by an ontological question. What motility is
appropriate to (the truth of) our nature? If we are, by nature,
mortal embodiments of thought, then our motility should be
in keeping with this kind of nature. *A fortiori*, movements
and gestures which go *against* the ontological grain of our
being must be characterized as 'violent.' (So Heidegger
misses an opportunity, here, when he is discussing the
nature of physical motion, to focus on the motility of the
human body as it needs to be understood in an ontological
context.)

Continuing his historical recollection, Heidegger points out
that, for Aristotle,

> There is an essential difference between the motion
> of celestial bodies and earthly bodies. The domains
> of these motions are different. How a body moves
> depends upon its species and the place to which
> it belongs. The *where* determines the how of its
> Being, for Being means presence [*Anwesenheit*].[48]

Heidegger then observes that Newton, breaking away from
the Aristotelian understanding of physical bodies, wants to
maintain the proposition that 'Every body left to itself moves
uniformly in a straight line.' And Heidegger astutely
comments: 'That means that the distinction between earthly
and celestial bodies has become obsolete.'[49] Of course,
Newton's axiom was not intended to describe human
motility. Still, it gives us something to think about. What
comes to mind, when we read it with an eye open for its
possible significance in the realm of human motility? Does it
perhaps speak to us, for example, about the pressures for

conformity, the standardization, the linearity, the repetitive, mechanical motions, and the military kind of training, which we find so clearly visible in the modern, technologized world? Is there not a strong pressure on us to conform our movements to the operating conditions of the machines we are using? Is there not an increasingly strong pressure on us to restrict our movements to motions which are uniform, predictable, and 'trackable'? And do we not 'fall into step' all too easily? It is not (yet) too late to look into the danger which threatens us: the danger, I mean, in an increasing restriction of our movement to motions that are deeply oppressive . . . and 'contrary to nature.'

Let us continue with our reading of Heidegger:

> Accordingly the distinguishing of certain places also disappears. Each body is itself changed: place no longer is where the body belongs according to its inner nature, but is only a position in relation to other positions.[50]

In the final chapter, we shall return to the question of place – or, more specifically, the question of a place most congenial to the full dimensionality of human being. What here calls for a comment, then, is simply the fact that the process which Heidegger describes involves a change in our *human* environment, and *not* just a change in Nature. We are in danger of losing our distinctively *human* places. This turn of events, which corresponds to the standardization of motility, is pathologized in our life-world as an experience of displacement, exile, homelessness, and anomie.

Heidegger concludes:

> Therefore the concept of nature changes. Nature is no longer the *inner principle* out of which the motion of the body follows; rather, nature is the mode of the variety of the changing relative positions of bodies, the manner in which they are present in space and time.[51]

What does this seem to suggest in regard to the concept of *human* nature, i.e., the representation in terms of which we (strive to) understand *ourselves*? Is our self-understanding really in accordance with our nature? Do we (still) experience our bodily nature as an 'inner principle' of Being out of which the motility of our body flows? Do we discern any factors, any configuration of events, which might possibly *endanger* this fundamental experience?

The history of classical physics will perhaps not seem so benign any longer. When Heidegger tells us, for example, that Galileo proposed to treat 'the motion of every body' as 'uniform and rectilinear,' perhaps we should not find ourselves so easily comforted by the thought that the kind of bodies Galileo intended did not include human bodies in their essential humanness. Likewise, we should perhaps attempt to hear a darker tone in Heidegger's words, when he noted that Galileo prepared science for Newton's more powerful conceptualization of 'what should be uniformly determinative of each body as such, i.e., for bodily being,' namely, as Heidegger puts it:

> All bodies are alike. No motion is special. Every place is like every other, each moment is like any other. . . . All determinations of bodies have one basic blueprint, according to which *the natural process is nothing but the space-time determination of the motion of points of mass.* This fundamental design of nature at the same time *circumscribes its realm as everywhere uniform.*[52]

In this part of our study, we have certainly confronted a number of upsetting questions, solving none. But who would ever dare to claim that walking the path of thought is an easy matter? We have walked in the goodness of thought, and many good questions have overtaken us. If we now take them in our stride, it is possible that we may find some answers beginning to come to us, the unbidden gifts of our body of understanding. During his week on the Concord and Merrimack Rivers, Thoreau must have enjoyed such gifts. And we can learn from the experience he has to share. Thoreau tells us, in his journal, that:

> All the world reposes in beauty to him who preserves equipoise in his life, and moves serenely on his path without violence. . . . The forms of beauty fall naturally around the path of him who is in performance of his proper work; as the curled shavings drop from the plane, and borings cluster around the augur.[53]

CHAPTER 6

The Ground and its Poetizing

Part I
The Earth: Our Elemental Ground

Opening Conversation

(1) We ask the questions 'How does it stand with Being?' [and] 'What is the meaning of Being?' not in order to set up an ontology in the traditional style, much less to criticize the past mistakes of ontology. We are concerned with something totally different: to restore man's historical openness . . . to the domain of Being.

Heidegger, *An Introduction to Metaphysics*[1]

(2) When philosophy conceives the essence of being as Logos, it is already [making it possible for us to lay it down as] the Logos of domination – commanding, mastering, directing reason, to which man and nature are to be subjected. . . . Freud's interpretation of being in terms of Eros recaptures the early stage of Plato's philosophy, which conceived of culture not as the repressive sublimation, but as the free self-development of Eros. As early as Plato, this conception appears as an archaic-mythical residue. Eros is being absorbed into Logos, and Logos is reason which subdues the

281

instincts. *The history of ontology reflects the reality principle which governs the world ever more exclusively. The insights contained in the metaphysical notion of Eros were driven underground.* They survived, in eschatological distortion, in many heretic movements, in the hedonistic philosophy. Their history has still to be written – as has the history of the transformation of Eros in Agape.

> Herbert Marcuse, *Eros and Civilization: A Philosophical Inquiry into Freud*[2]

(3)   I write for a species of man that does not yet exist: for the 'masters of the earth'.

> Nietzsche, *The Will to Power*[3]

(4)   Lord of the earth. . . .

> Nietzsche, *Thus Spake Zarathustra*[4]

(5)   Why has man rooted himself thus firmly in the earth, but that he may rise in the same proportion into the heavens above?

> Thoreau, *Walden*[5]

(6)   the matriarchal spirit does not deny the native maternal soil from which it stems. It does not, like the Apollonian-solar-patriarchal spirit, present itself as 'sheer being', as pure existence in absolute eternity. . . . Apprehending itself as historically generated, as a creature, it does not negate its bond with the Earth Mother.

> Erich Neumann, *The Great Mother: An Analysis of the Archetype*[6]

(7)   Piety . . . may be said to mean man's reverent attachment to the sources of his being and the steadying of his life by that attachment. . . . This consciousness that the human spirit is derived and responsible, that all its functions are heritages and trusts, involves a sentiment of gratitude and duty which we may call piety.

> George Santayana, *Reason in Religion*[7]

(8)   The closer we come to the danger . . . the more questioning we become. For questioning is the piety of thought.

Heidegger, 'The Question Concerning Technology'[8]

(9) Be – and at the same time know the condition
     of not-being, the infinite ground of your deep
     vibrations,
        that you may fully fulfill it this single time.
                           Rilke, *Sonnets to Orpheus*[9]

Following Nietzsche, I would like to be writing for a species
of human being that does not yet exist. But what kind is
that? Differing from Nietzsche, whose vision, so sublime in
many ways, became tragically distorted by the very nihilism
his 'will to power' was meant to overcome, I wish to dedicate
this project to those who will *fulfill* the ancient dream of the
earth, serving it as best they can in accordance with the
'feminine principle' of its elemental nature.

For Nietzsche, nihilism is the danger. Is this danger manifest only in the realm of pure thought? Not at all. Nietzsche
makes himself very clear on this point. Nihilism means the
devastation of the earth. Nihilism means: the wasteland
grows. And yet, as Heidegger helps us to see, Nietzsche
himself – Nietzsche *despite* himself – must bear some responsibility for the confusion in which we are entangled, trying to
understand the meaning of our situation. For the *character* of
the 'will to power,' Nietzsche's response to the danger, is
unmistakably masculine, whereas the character of the needs
of the earth, as our mythology repeatedly tells us, is just as
unmistakably feminine. Heidegger's critique of the will to
power is deep and sound; but it somehow misses Nietzsche's
tragic servitude, his adherence to the values of the old patriarchy. The groundrules of the old patriarchy must be called
into question. Until they are, the will to power can only
hasten the annihilation of the earth. Can we, without transforming this masculine will to power, sincerely hope to avoid
the possibility which Nietzsche loudly prophesies in *Ecce
Homo*, that 'there will be wars the like of which have never
been yet on earth'?[10]

One point where we surely need to press our questioning
is the point where that which we call 'ground' enters our
awareness – our experience and our thinking. In 'The End
of Philosophy and the Task of Thinking,' Heidegger contends
that,

> since the beginning of philosophy and with that
> beginning, the Being of beings has shown itself as
> the ground. The ground is from where beings as

THE BODY'S RECOLLECTION OF BEING

> such are what they are in their becoming,
> persisting, and perishing. . . . As the ground, Being
> brings beings to their actual presencing. The
> ground shows itself as presence. The present of
> presence consists in the fact that it brings what is
> present, each in its own way, to presence.[11]

Already, in this very articulation, Being begins to show itself *as* the ground in a new kind of way: it is not only the *ratio* which, by giving a standard, measures our thinking; it is also the *ratio* which measures our stride and gait.

Now, we must be careful not to *equate* ground and Being, as if they were identical. To equate them would be to *reduce* the Being of beings to that (being) through which, and as which, it shows itself. However, our thinking will not succeed in breaking out of the metaphysical framework, with its traditional interpretation of 'ground,' and hence 'Being,' until we let Being disclose itself to us, *as* ground, *in relation to our embodiment*.

But, as soon as we begin to think the ground in this historically new relation, do we not find ourselves drawn into what Jung calls the 'power of the chthonic'? Earth, after all, *is* the ground in its elemental presence. To be sure, what we call with our word 'ground' is the *deepest* meaning of earth. But it is precisely in this context that, when we speak of earth, we call to mind the ground *as* an elemental presence. Earth, in its deepest truth, is the Being of beings, presencing *in our world* as its elemental ground: the ground which underlies the mystery of 'the worlding of the world.' Jung recognizes this hermeneutical disclosure of the ground, and even perceives the mediation of the body, when, in discussing 'The Role of the Unconscious,' he reflects on the fact that,

> The soil of every country holds some . . . mystery.
> We have an unconscious reflection of this in the
> psyche: just as there is a relationship of mind to
> body, so there is a relationship of body to earth.[12]

This statement should, however, be thought in resonance with another. In 'Mind and Earth,' the second part of his essay on 'Die Erdbedingtheit der Psyche,' he warns that,

> Alienation from the unconscious and from its
> historical conditions spells rootlessness. This is the

danger that lies in wait for the conqueror of foreign
land, and for every individual who . . . loses touch
with the dark, maternal, earthly ground of his
being.[13]

Jung's remarks are all the more striking in the light of their
affinity to the remarks made by Heidegger, in his Messkirch
Memorial Address in honor of the composer Conradin
Kreutzer:

We grow more thoughtful and ask: What is
happening here – with those driven from their
homeland no less than with those who have
remained? Answer: the *rootedness*, the *autochthony*,
of mankind is threatened today at its core! . . . The
loss of autochthony springs from the spirit of the
age into which all of us were born.[14]

But Heidegger does not leave us without an inspirational
elucidation of his vision:

Thus we ask now: even if the old rootedness is
being lost in this age, may not a new ground and
foundation be granted again to man. . . ?[15]

And he replies, near the end of his Address:

Releasement toward things [*Gelassenheit zu den
Dingen*] and openness to the mystery belong
together. They grant us the possibility of dwelling
in the world in a totally different way. They
promise us a new ground and a foundation upon
which we can stand and endure in the world of
technology without being imperiled by it.

Thus, it is his conviction, borne with the strength of his
experience, that,

Releasement toward things and openness to the
mystery give us a vision of a new autochthony
[*Bodenständigkeit*] which someday even might be fit
to recapture the old and now rapidly disappearing
autochthony in a changed form.[16]

These passages are significant, first of all, because they
authorize the interpretation with which we are working, viz.,
that the Question of Being can be understood in relation to
our groundedness on the earth. And is it not significant that
Heidegger closes his meditation on the possibility of a new
autochthony by quoting – for a second time – the words of
Johann Peter Hebel, who said that 'We are plants which . . .
must with our roots rise out of the earth in order to bloom
in the ether and to bear fruit'?[17] Is it not significant that, in
giving to Hebel the very last word, he *plants* us in the earth?
But if, in our relationship to the earth, we are in truth like
plants, the archetypal symbols of the feminine principle,
what becomes of our Nietzschean will to power?

We must take great pains to protect the ontological difference, which keeps the Being of beings apart from the ground,
and *a fortiori*, apart from its most elemental presence as earth.
However, if we do not let ourselves experience the Being of
the ground (Being presencing *as* the ground) and the Being
of the earth (Being presencing *as* the grounding earth), we
do not overcome the fate of metaphysical thinking. On the
contrary! In the extremism of our struggle to escape it, we
simply fall into the opposite extreme – an extreme which is
still, unfortunately, within the old framework. (In his
'Working Notes,' Merleau–Ponty suggests the need for a
'transcendental geology.'[18] This, I believe, is the beginning
of his attempt to overcome the metaphysics of grounding.)
What we need to experience, what we need to understand,
is another way of dwelling, or being, with the Being of the
ground and the Being of the earth. And, if we may trust an
experience of the ground disclosing its presence in, and its
presence as, the elemental earth, then our shift of focus,
our focus, here, on our experiencing of *earth*, is likely to be
especially useful in the process of overcoming metaphysics.

In 'Building Dwelling Thinking,' Heidegger says:

> To be a human being means to be on the earth as
> a mortal. It means to dwell.[19]

What, then, is 'dwelling'? Thinking, as is his wont, by listening for the root and its gathered family of words,
Heidegger says:

> To dwell, to be set at peace, means to remain at
> peace within the free, the preserve, the free sphere

that safeguards each thing in its nature. *The fundamental character of dwelling is this sparing and preserving.*[20]

And he invites us to meditate on this meaning, so that we may be granted an understanding which fulfills its truth in our existence:

> human being consists in dwelling and, indeed, dwelling in the sense of the stay of mortals on the earth.[21]

The 'stay of mortals on the earth,' however, brings us back to the fact of our embodiment, and to the *truth* of that 'medium,' as that in which, and through which, we become accustomed (*gewohnt*) to the earth of our dwelling (*Wohnen*), accustomed to its holding and keeping, and set at ease in the power of that element.

Jung, as we saw, makes the relationship of body to earth explicit. Unfortunately, he does little to articulate the nature, or the character, of this relationship, except insofar as it is refracted through the symbols of the psyche. This is helpful; but it is not sufficient. From the standpoint of the body of understanding, the 'ground' must (eventually) be understood as 'earth.' What, then, is 'earth,' in its upholding of the stay of mortals?

There is further authorization for our interpretation in the twelfth session of the Seminar on Herakleitos (1966-7), where it is Heidegger himself who carries the dialogue forward, from Fink's discourse on ground and underground to the discourse which Nietzsche began on the crucial mediation of the body.[22] Here are the relevant contributions in their dialogue:

> *Fink*: '. . . a human is not only a cleared being; he is also a natural being and as such is implanted in a dark manner in nature. . . . A human being is predominantly a light kindler, he who is delivered over to the nature of light. At the same time, however, he also rests on the nightly ground that we can only speak of as closed. The sleeping and the dead are figures indicated by human belonging in living and dead nature.'
>
> *Fink*: '. . . insofar as a human is a living being, he

also has . . . [the] character of being with which
he reaches into the nightly ground. He has the
double character: on the one hand, he is the one
who places himself in the clearing, and on the other,
he is the one who is tied to the underground of
all clearing.'
Heidegger: 'This would become intelligible first of all
through the phenomenon of the body. . . .'
Fink: '. . . as, for example, in the understanding of
Eros.'
Heidegger: 'Body is not meant ontically here. . . .'
Fink: '. . . and also not in the Husserlian sense. . . .'
Heidegger: '. . . but rather as Nietzsche thought the
body even though it is obscure what he actually
meant by it.'
Fink: 'In the section "Of the Despisers of the Body,"
Zarathustra says, "Body am I entirely, and nothing
else. . . ." Through the body and the senses a
human is nigh to the earth.'
Fink: '[The human is one who] relates himself to
night or to the nightly ground insofar as he
belongs bodily to the earth and to the flowing of
life. . . .'
Heidegger: 'Can one isolate the dark understanding,
which the bodily belonging to the earth determines,
from being placed in the clearing?'
Fink: 'True, the dark understanding can be
addressed from the clearing, but it doesn't let itself
be brought further to language in the manner of the
articulated joining.'

At a later point in the dialogue, Heidegger, in a rare kind
of concession, acknowledges that, in the context of his thinking, 'the body phenomenon is the most difficult problem.'[23]
His final words on the subject, however, are of the utmost
significance:

The bodily [element] in the human is not something
animalistic. The manner of understanding that
accompanies it is something that metaphysics up till
now has not touched on.[24]

This, I submit, is a crucial insight into the historical essence
of metaphysics. Why has metaphysics failed to illuminate the

288

human body? Why has it not undertaken to articulate its own body of understanding? Why has it scarcely even acknowledged the dark element, the earth, which underlies this body of understanding? Why is it that our most fundamental concepts are framed by a metaphysics which cannot touch, nor let itself be touched by, the body of our understanding without doing it the most horrible violence? I want to take Heidegger's sense of the problem and move one step further. The passages we have just considered indicate that Heidegger does acknowledge the body's ontological destiny. They also indicate that the earth, our source of individuation, bears a decisive ontological significance. It seems to me that, until we acknowledge the human body in a way that upholds its dignity as a body of the deepest inherent understanding, and until, therefore, we fulfill the dream of the earth in the very bearing of our thinking, we cannot reasonably expect to escape the fate which is sealed for us within our metaphysics, nor will we be able to walk the path of beauty, beyond the nihilism of its enframing, into that great openness which thinking calls the very truth of Being.

Fink points out that,

> While *hen kai panta* stands for . . . the relationship in the domain of light, the experience of the dark ground of life is the experience of *hen kai pan*. In *hen kai pan* we must think the coincidence of all distinctions. The experience of *hen kai pan* is the relationship of the human, who stands, in individuation, to the nonindividuated but individuating ground.[25]

This ground is not individuated, because it is earth, the elemental; but it is the source of our individuation, since it let us stand becoming ourselves. This is a point of great importance, in that it helps to make explicit the multi-dimensional significance of our project. The attempt to focus phenomenological interpretation on the body of understanding, standing and walking in the support of the earth, is *already* a move beyond metaphysics since (i) traditional metaphysics can conceptualize only an objective body, not the body which we are and live; (ii) traditional metaphysics separates mind and body in a reification of substances that reflects a historical will to power bent on permanence and certainty; (iii) traditional metaphysics excludes or ignores the wisdom in our bodily felt experience; and finally, (iv) traditional metaphysics cannot hold us open to the historical need for an understanding of the ground as an element in our way of being. We must deconstruct the traditional re-presentation of the 'ground' and our relationship to it. The historical transformation of metaphysics necessitates a new experience of grounding – a fresh encounter with the ground. I submit that this is possible if we are willing to give thought (awareness) to the body and dare to open ourselves to an experience of the ground whose gift we can receive only through the medium of our body.

Now, in his *Introduction to Metaphysics*, Heidegger contends that,

> Being human defines itself from out of a relation to
> what is as a whole. The human essence shows
> itself here to be the relation which first opens up
> Being to human beings.[26]

But, as this passage demonstrates, Heidegger's interpretation remains abstract and formal. If we want to understand more fully the process of individuation and the emergence of an ontological Self, then we must consider how the Selfhood of human being is defined by the wholeness it experiences through its openness-to-Being. This means, however, that we must consider the embodiment of human being, for our wholeness and our openness-to-Being cannot be understood apart from the question of our embodiment. As Neumann points out, in *The Origins and History of Consciousness*,

> A sense of the body as a whole is the natural basis
> of the sense of personality.[27]

(It must be emphasized, here, that he is understanding 'personality' in a Jungian sense, so that, for him, 'personality' is a process of individuation which necessarily involves 'the ancestral experience within us,' rooted in chthonic instincts and chthonic intentionalities, and rooted also, therefore, in the maternal energies of the primordial earth.)[28] Now, this 'sense of the body as a whole' is a sense which originates in, and is a gift from, the grounding earth, since, as Fink strongly implies, it is precisely this element, itself non-individuated, which enables us human beings, us mortals, who attempt to stand on it and move on it in a thoughtful way, to draw from our rootedness, our element of steadfast support, that mysteriously uplifting energy by grace of which we can stand being ourselves and stand out, as individuals, into the openness of Being.

Let me state the argument in another form. (i) The human 'personality' is capable of being deepened. (ii) Its capacity for being deepened (i.e., Selfhood) is a function of our experience of the ground – an experience which is itself open to being deepened. (For example, this experience of ground is significantly deepened in relation to the history of metaphysics when 'grounding' is finally understood in terms of our embodiment.) (iii) And, in fact, it is becoming increasingly clear, when we reflect on the history of metaphysics, that the deepening of this experience must eventually be understood as a question of our elemental groundedness as bodily beings. (iv) As bodily beings, we are graced with a sense of the body as a whole. This felt sense can likewise undergo a process of deepening, and as this process unfolds, an even deeper sense of Being in its wholeness may gradually inform our understanding. (v) When we *walk* with a guardian awareness (*Wahr-nehmung*) of our stride, our center of gravity, and our being-grounded, we may realize that we can enjoy a powerfully energizing sense of the body *as a whole made whole* through our rootedness in the depth of the earth. (The 'energizing sense' is an experience of *Physis*, as it surges up through our mortal frame.) (vi) This bodily felt sense of wholeness, hermeneutically disclosive of Being, is *necessary* for the unfolding of the Self as an *ontological* being. (vii) I am therefore proposing that, in a walking moved by awareness, we can take a small 'preparatory step' towards the overcoming of our metaphysical tradition.

Heidegger's study on 'Hölderlin und das Wesen der Dichtung' returns us, as we let this process of individuation engage our thinking, to an appropriate relationship to the Being of the earth:

> Man is the one who is who he is precisely in the attestation [*Bezeugung*] of his own existence. . . .
> But what should man attest? His obedience to the earth. [*Seine Zugehörigkeit zur Erde.*][29]

We are, or can be, fully human only by virtue of our relationship to the earth. For, insofar as our humanity emerges in the depth of our experience of mortality (our *Sein-zum-Tode*), we can move toward ontological fulfillment only by virtue of our acknowledgment of the indebtedness, the beholdenness, in which we always stand with respect to the primordial earth. Mortality is our weight, the gravity of our earthliness. The earth holds us and keeps us through a flesh of mortality. But it holds us most benevolently, and keeps us most protectively, when we demonstrate our 'obedience' with a body of understanding, a body which responds to the earth's presence by giving itself away in what Merleau–Ponty would call an *ekstase* of 'consecratory gestures.'[30]

Because of their destined closeness to the four elements of Nature, and perhaps especially the earth, the North American Indians understood the hold of the earth on the flesh of all who are mortals. Here is Black Elk, who walked as a holy man among the Sioux, speaking about their ancient sun dance:

> the flesh represents ignorance, and, thus, as we
> dance and break the thong loose, it is as if we were
> being freed from the bonds of the flesh. It is much
> the same as when you break a young colt; at first
> a halter is necessary, but later, when he has become
> broken, the rope is no longer necessary. We too
> are young colts when we start the dance, but soon
> we become broken and submit to the Great Spirit.[31]

Accompanying one of their other sacred dances, though, is a song of the most moving beauty. And it is with the powerful sound of that song of the earth that I would like to close our meditation on the ontological grounding of the human essence in a ground whose elemental presence is the earth on which we walk:

> My relatives, Grandmother and Mother Earth, we
> are of earth and belong to you. O Mother Earth,
> from whom we receive our food, you care for our
> growth as do our own mothers. Every step we
> take upon you should be done in a sacred manner;
> each step should be as a prayer. O Mother, may
> your people walk the red path of life, facing the
> strong winds! May we walk firmly upon you! May
> our steps not falter![32]

But what am I urging here? I would like to make it clear

that I am not suggesting a sentimental return to primitivism. Rather, what I am suggesting is that we can *learn* from the Indian experience, appropriating it *in our own way and in accordance with the exigencies of our present historical situation.* As we lose our foothold, our sense of the ground, as we falter, as we feel ourselves unable to respond to the most extreme danger, it is only sensible that we test the stretch of our capacities and give heed to the wisdom of other times and other cultures. Out of such encounters, it is possible that the capacity for a historically original response might still be granted us.

Part II

The Poetizing Dance

Opening Conversation

(1) the dancer has his ear in his toes.
Nietzsche, 'The Other Dancing Song,'
Thus Spake Zarathustra[33]

(2) The feet listen. . . .
William Carlos Williams, *Paterson*[34]

(3) With sounds, our love dances on many-hued rainbows.
Nietzsche, *Thus Spake Zarathustra*[35]

(4) Dance the dance of David before the ark of the covenant, for I believe that such a dance holds the mystery of walking in the sight of God.
Gregory of Nazianz, *Theological Orations*[36]

Our objectives in this section are two: first of all, to demonstrate that when dance is thoughtful, it is a fundamental form of poetizing (*Dichtung*); and second, to bring the dance to disclosure as the 'origin' or the 'essence' (the *archē*) of movement in general. We are thereby deepening, and at the same time clarifying, the sense in which the spirit of dance is a poetizing of our existence: a bearing of thought in which we are granted an experience of Being.
Hölderlin speaks:

Full of merit, yet poetically, man dwells on this
earth.[37]

According to Heidegger, poetizing

does not fly above and surmount the earth in order
to escape it and hover over it. Poetizing is what
first brings man onto the earth, making him belong
to it; and thus it brings him into dwelling.[38]

As he says in 'Hölderlin und das Wesen der Dichtung,'

In poetizing . . . man is gathered on the ground of
his existence [*gesammelt auf den Grund seines
Daseins*].[39]

Speaking out of experience I myself have undergone, I
want to say: when mortals dance in a spirit of joyful piety,
the Being of all beings itself is presencing, and not only as
ground, but as Earth, the elemental. And this wholesome,
grounding presence can be felt and perceived. Dancing, in
fact, makes us more susceptible to such an experience of
Being, free of metaphysical encumbrances. Experienced
directly, I mean, without any need for questions and reasons;
and experienced in its immeasurable depth, hospitality, and
abundance as a strong, enduring ground for all dwelling; as
a fertile, yielding ground for planting and agriculture; as the
long-patient, resourceful earth; as a place for the dead; as
the ground that silently bears our upright walk through the
rejoicings and sufferings of life.
    In the Hölderlin poem, 'Heimkunft/An die Verwandten,'
which Heidegger discusses in one of his lectures on this poet,
we read:

Often we must be silent; we lack holy names.[40]

But what we cannot invoke by *words* that name, we can
perhaps evoke through our *dance,* just as the sonorous strings
of the lyre, which Homer calls 'dancing,' can gladden the
beings of the Sky and make them welcome on Earth.
Remember that 'David danced before the Lord with all his
might.' (Samuel II, 6:14) Without 'leaping and dancing' (6:16),
how could he have communicated with his God? And
remember, too, the words of the *Psalm* (149:3): 'Let them

praise His name with dancing; let them make music to Him with drum and harp.' (Also see 150:4.) We can *dance* our feelings of gladness in the presence of the gods; and we can celebrate in lively *movement* the incalculable value of mortal existence. Dancing is another way of naming Being: it is akin to the poet's way, and in no respect inferior.

Plutarch is supposed to have said that 'the dance [orchēsin] is a silent poetry [poisin], and poetry a speaking dance.'[41] The question this introduces is whether Heidegger's interpretation of poetizing could be translated into a deeper – that is to say, an ontological – understanding of the experience of dance. To answer this, let us consider the formulation Heidegger offers in 'Hölderlin und das Wesen der Dichtung':

> Poetizing is the founding naming of Being and of
> the essence of all things – no arbitrary or willful
> saying, however, but that, rather, whereby there
> first comes into the open all that which we then
> in everyday speech take up and talk about.
> Poetizing accordingly never takes language for
> granted as an already present-at-hand material;
> rather, poetizing itself first grants language its
> possibility. . . . Thus, in reversal, the essence of
> speech must be understood starting from the
> essence of poetizing.[42]

If the essence of dance, however, be poetizing, then it should be feasible to take what we have just heard Heidegger say and transfer it, with appropriate changes, to the poetizing spirit of dance – and indeed, the ontological depth, of such movement. Let us see if this be so. Making the necessary displacements and substitutions, the text, in one of its disseminations, will now read as follows:

> As poetizing, dance is the founding measure [beat,
> or rhythm] of Being and of the essence of all things
> – no arbitrary or willful movement, however, but
> that, rather, whereby there first comes into the
> open all that which in everyday movement and
> actions we find ourselves concerned with.
> Poetizing dance accordingly never takes movement
> or motion for granted as an already completed
> basis; rather, dancing itself first grants motion and
> movement their very possibility. . . . Thus, in

reversal of common belief, the essence of motility
must be understood starting from the essence
which holds sway in poetizing dance.

Now, I maintain not only that this transposition makes sense,
but that it illuminates the essential nature of dance, and
clarifies the relation between dance and movement in
general. Consequently, there is a double confirmation: first
of all, Heidegger's thinking about poetizing in language
receives indirect support in its extension to another medium;
but secondly, our present interpretation of dance as a form
of poetizing is likewise supported, since the substitutions we
made in Heidegger's text seem to preserve its truth.

However, if this still seems questionable, perhaps we
should ponder the discovery of an anthropologist, Gerardo
Reichel-Dolmatoff, who lived with the Kogi Indians of
Colombia. In learning how the Kogi train their young boys
for the priesthood, he found that, as the Indians themselves
put it,

the child 'first' learns to dance and only later learns
to walk.[43]

What could this apparent paradox mean? Since the children
in question are obviously 'walking' long before the dance-
training begins, we may presume, first of all, that 'dancing'
is not to be understood in the customary sense as something
which is incompatible with (or which excludes) walking, and
secondly, that what is of concern to the elders is ultimately
a different kind, or different spirit, of walking. Why does the
child need, 'first,' to learn the sacred dance? What is it about
the qualities of movement in dance that makes dance more
primordial? Why, or how, does dancing first make it possible
for the child to 'walk' – walk, that is, in a sacred manner?
What is the essence of dance?

The Kogi attitude is instructive. It compels us to consider
ontological questions. It compels us to consider dance in a
surprising sense: as a certain quality, or character of motility,
or as movement inhabited by a certain modality and dimension of awareness. Ontically considered, 'walking' is always
first. Ontologically considered, however it is 'dance' that is
first: first, in the sense that, without that bodily felt quality
of inwrought thoughtfulness, 'walking' in the proper way
would not be possible. We might say that, for the Kogi,

dance is first because it is a sacred movement-of-the-origin (*archē*), an ek-static movement which opens us to the wholeness and expansiveness of Being, and a movement which intensifies our grounding and our contact with the powers of the earth.

But I think we also need to take note of the fact that dance is intrinsically joyful: it is the spontaneous, irrepressible joy in sheer movement as such. Dance is at the very origin (*archē*) of motility, because the ecstasy of dance, an intrinsic recollecting and rejoicing-in-Being that embraces the body as a coherent whole, is a necessary condition for the very possibility of movement.

In *Joyful Wisdom*, Nietzsche's attempt to begin a new science (a 'fröliche Wissenschaft') is amply justified by his description of the nature of motility:

> A continuum stands before us from which we
> isolate a pair of fragments, just in the same way as
> we perceive a movement as isolated points, and
> therefore do not properly see, but infer it. . . .[44]

Merleau–Ponty's phenomenology of movement altogether confirms this account, spelling out what Nietzsche leaves implicit. According to Merleau–Ponty (as we have already seen in Chapter 1), the healthy human being normally enjoys 'a global bodily knowledge which systematically embraces all its parts.'[45] This global, feeling self-comprehension, this 'erotic' proprioception, constitutes the 'pre-objective unity,' the basic integrity, as it were, of my bodily being-in-the-world. Now, in moments of motility, this 'synergic totality,' as he also describes it,[46] is more fully operative; it is also more clearly visible and tangible:

> my body itself I move directly; I do not find it at
> one point of objective space and transfer it to
> another.[47]

Thus, when we focus on our experiencing of movement, we find, or realize, that,

> Each instant of the movement embraces its whole
> span.[48]

Instead of 'a collection of movements strung laboriously

together,' the motility characteristic of healthy human beings will have a certain 'melodic character.'[49] The more focused we are, i.e., the more self-aware we are in regard for our bodily felt sense of the movement or gesture, the more we will experience this 'erotic' embrace, this good-feeling melodic character. (The reader is reminded of the passage quoted earlier, in the 'Opening Conversation' of Chapter 4, Part I, in which Heidegger discusses movement and the embrace of time.) Now, the embrace of the felt melody is heightened and enhanced, to the degree that our movement approaches the kind of movement, or the 'quality' of movement, that we are characterizing, here, as 'dancing.' By the same token, of course, an unfortunate person like Schneider (the patient whose bodily being-in-the-world was fundamentally altered, as Merleau–Ponty shows, by the damage his brain suffered in the War) experiences not only a disintegration of meaningful units of movement, but a paralyzing inertia, an absence of motivation:

> the gesture itself loses the melodic character which it presents in ordinary life, and becomes manifestly a collection of partial movements strung laboriously together.[50]

Because of this 'melody' embracing our movement, there is a very real *sense* in which it is true that every movement is 'magically already at its completion' from the very instant it begins. One way of describing this fact is to speak of a kind of corporeal 'projection':

> The normal function which makes abstract movement possible is one of 'projection,' whereby the subject of movement keeps in front of him an area of free space in which what does not naturally exist may take on a semblance of existence.[51]

But Merleau–Ponty also describes this process as a 'laying down of the first coordinates, the anchoring of the active body' in its vectorially organized space:[52] a description which, though certainly true of our normally 'pedestrian' and 'prosaic' movements, is even more deeply true of – and incalculably more deeply true to – the essential nature of the poetizing movements of a dancing body.

But, now, there is still another dimension to take into

account. The melodic embrace, which is our felt sense of the movement as a whole, forms a sort of 'intentional arc'.[53] And, according to Merleau–Ponty,

> It is this intentional arc which brings about the unity of the senses, of intelligence, of sensibility and motility.[54]

As it begins to become clear, however, that motility is a 'basic intentionality,'[55] the melody, or dance, of the 'intentional arc' begins to disclose itself as arising from an absolutely *primordial* dimension of our bodily being-in-the-world: as, in fact, the *archē tēs kinēseōs* (the 'origin,' or 'principle,' of movement) of the body of ontological understanding; the *archē tēs kinēseōs* which is raised into consciousness, and indeed taken up for reflection, in the second session of the Heidegger/Fink Seminar on Herakleitos, and which, furthermore, by a trajectory of reasoning seemingly unrelated to that which brings Merleau–Ponty to join together, in one single discourse, the concept of the 'arc' and the concept of the 'embrace,' eventually motivates the two thinkers struggling with Herakleitos to move on from a discussion of that *archē* to a discussion of *periechon*, a word which, in their recognition of it, means 'embrace.'[56] (Is this nothing but a sheer coincidence?)

What I would like to suggest, then, is that this embracing melodic arc of motility reaches down into the primordial origin (*archē*) of movement, and that, when our movement is filled with the gift of thought, it can have the felt quality of a poetizing dance: a dance, I mean, in the sense of a primordial, ontological attunement, a deep chthonic intentionality – the very energy of Being (*Physis*) giving rise to various ontic motions, rhythms such as our walking. The earthen ground of Being is such that only my *whole* body, and moreover my body *felt in its wholeness*, can 'espouse' its primordial geometry, its transcendental geology. Understood in relationship to the earth, its ground of support, 'dance' is the joyful feeling of an ontological movement, a movement which, by virtue of its guardian awareness, attunes us to the primordial Being of the ground and gathers us into the embracing arc (*archē*) of its ecstatic energy. As such, dance is indeed the poetizing which makes all our movements possible. Because we are forgetful, however, we are rapidly losing our groundedness. Metaphysics simply reflects a nihilism that is already affecting the body of our experience. It is for this reason that I contend that our traditional ontology desperately needs renewal through a thinking born of the rejoicing dance, the rejoicing stride.

Part III

The Ecstatic Leap of Faith

Opening Conversation

(1) I know not what the spirit of a philosopher would be like better than to be a good dancer. For the dance is his ideal . . . in the end, his sole piety, his 'divine service'. . . .

Nietzsche, *Joyful Wisdom*[57]

(2) Precious firmness . . . O the feel of the ground, My step had found on you its blessed stay! But under the living foot that feels its way, Knowing with dread its natal pact is near, This firm earth has touched my foothold. Not far, among these steps, dreams my precipice. . . .

Paul Valéry, 'La Jeune Parque'[58]

(3) the very brink of a precipitous fall. . . .
Heidegger, 'The Question Concerning Technology'[59]

(4) God amuses himself at the leaps and springs and contortions of these millions of men to get hold of the truth without suffering.

Kierkegaard, *Journals*[60]

(5) How much truth [can] a spirit *endure*, how much truth does it *dare*? More and more that became for me the real measure of value.

Nietzsche, *Ecce Homo*[61]

(6) every elevation of man brings with it the overcoming of narrower interpretations . . . every strengthening and increase of power opens up new perspectives and means believing in new horizons. . . .

Nietzsche, *The Will to Power*[62]

(7)   Every movement of infinity comes about by
      passion, and no reflection can bring a movement
      about.
                    Kierkegaard, *Fear and Trembling*[63]

(8)   he who is accustomed to it [Nietzsche's new
      'science'] may live nowhere else save in this light,
      transparent, powerful, and electric air. . . . In this
      clear, strict element he has his power whole: here
      he can fly!
                    Nietzsche, *The Joyful Wisdom*[64]

(9)   Now I am light, now I fly, now I see myself
      beneath myself, now a god dances through me.
                    Nietzsche, *Thus Spake Zarathustra*[65]

(10) He [i.e., 'the knight of faith'] constantly makes the
      movements of infinity, but he does this with such
      correctness and assurance that he constantly gets
      the finite out of it, and there is not a second when
      one has a notion of anything else. It is supposed
      to be the most difficult task for a dancer to leap
      into a definite posture in such a way that there is
      not a second when he is grasping after the
      posture, but by the leap itself he stands fixed in
      that posture. Perhaps no dancer can do it – that
      is what this knight does. . . . The knights of infinity
      [i.e., the knights of infinite resignation] are
      dancers and possess elevation. They make the
      movements upward, and fall down again; and this
      too is no mean pastime, nor ungraceful to behold.
      But whenever they fall down they are not able at
      once to assume the posture, they vacillate an
      instant, and this vacillation shows that after all
      they are strangers in the world. This is more or less
      strikingly evident in proportion to the art they
      possess, but even the most artistic knights [of
      infinity] cannot altogether conceal this vacillation.
      One need not look at them when they are up in
      the air, but only the instant they touch or have
      touched the ground – then one recognizes them.
      But to be able to fall down in such a way that the
      same second it looks as if one were standing and
      walking, to transform the leap of life into a walk,
      absolutely to express the sublime in the pedestrian

301

– that only the knight of faith can do – and this
is the one and only prodigy.

Kierkegaard, *Fear and Trembling*[66]

(11) we are attempting to learn thinking. The way is
long. We dare take only a few steps. If all goes
well, they will take us to the foothills of thought.
But they will take us to places which we must
explore to reach the point where only the leap will
help further. The leap alone takes us into the
neighborhood where thinking resides. We
therefore shall take a few practice leaps right at the
start, though we won't notice it at once, nor need
to. . . . In contrast to a steady progress, where we
move unawares from one thing to the next and
everything remains alike, the leap takes us abruptly
to where everything is different, so different that
it strikes us as strange. Abrupt means the sudden
sheer descent or rise that marks the chasm's edge.
Though we may not founder in such a leap, what
the leap takes us to will confound us.

Heidegger, *What Is Called Thinking?*[67]

(12) Leap and vision require long, slow
preparation. . . .

Heidegger, *What Is Called Thinking?*[68]

(13) To grasp here means consciously to experience
what has been named in its essence and so to
recognize in what moment of the hidden history
of the West we 'stand'; to recognize whether we
do stand in it, or are falling, or already lie prostrate
in it, or whether we neither surmise the one nor
are touched by the other two. . . . To think
'nihilism' thus does not mean to produce 'mere
thoughts' about it in one's head. . . . Rather, to
think 'nihilism' means to stand in that wherein
every act and every reality of this era in Western
history receives its time and space, its ground and
background . . . in a word, its 'truth'.

Heidegger, *Nihilism*[69]

Our concern in this chapter is the modern experience of
'ground.' What is the character of our relationship, in this
modern epoch, to the presencing of Being *as* our 'ground,'

302

our 'grounding'? The metaphysically determined relationship to the ground and its grounding is a relationship which reflects, and at the same time encourages, the nihilism, or loss of Being, that has long remained implicit in the *technological* standpoint of our Western civilization. It is becoming increasingly apparent that this *standpoint*, characterized by our 'need' to master the ground on which we stand and place its presence firmly under our command as an always available standing reserve (*Bestand*), locates us, not on *firm* ground, but on the edge of an *abyss*. The ground which, since ancient times, immemorial times, has been giving us a ground on which we could in fact *depend*, is finally beginning to manifest, rather, as a frightening void. And we are in the gravest danger of falling into the horror of its nihilism. (Nihilism, as the negation of Being, and eternalism, as the reification, or securing, of Being, are but two aspects of the same phenomenon, as the Madhyamika logic of Buddhism tried to show, many centuries ago.)

I would like to demonstrate that the overcoming of nihilism calls for an historically new relationship to the grounding of the ground, and that the truth of this new relationship is symbolized by, and may be realized through, the deeply joyful *release* of a poetizing movement. Because we know, and are only comfortable with, the *commanding standpoint*, an immobility which of course is required by our attempt to get a permanent fix on the horizon and bring everything within it to an absolute standstill, we need to learn how to make the graceful leap of hermeneutical understanding: a mode of comportment by virtue of which we may be granted an historically new experience of that which grounds our existence. This, I think, is the unthought hint to be read into Nietzsche's surmise that,

> one could imagine a delight and a power of self-determining, and a *freedom* of will, whereby a spirit could bid farewell to every belief, to every wish for certainty, accustomed as it would be to support itself on slender cords and possibilities, and to dance even on the verge of abysses.[70]

If we could learn from the *release* of the dance – from its leaps of ecstasy – how to be with the ground in a non-dogmatic, less willful and more compliant posture, perhaps we might then begin to enjoy a grounding which does not withhold from us its yield of treasures and leave us with nothing to stand on, nothing at all on which to depend.

In order to 'place' the thoughtful dance and its leap of faith in their proper dimensionality, I propose that we refer our reflections to passages from Heidegger's discourse on Nietzsche. The passages on which we will focus first take up a fundamental existential question: the question, namely, of decision and its ground. Heidegger maintains that,

> The essential thinkers are those whose sole thought tends in the direction of a single and highest decision, either preparing for this decision or accomplishing it definitively. . . . The almost fantastic misuse of the word 'decision' cannot ignore that word's content, by virtue of which it is related to the most inward discrimination and the most extreme distinction. This, however, is the distinction between beings as a whole, including gods and men, world and earth, and Being [itself], whose dominance alone grants or denies to each being that it be that being which it is able to be.
>
> The highest decision which can come to pass, and which in each case becomes the ground of all history, is that between the primacy of beings and the dominance of Being. Thus, whenever and however beings as a whole are expressly thought, thinking stands in the dangerous scope of this decision. This decision is never made and carried out [solely] by man.[71]

The thinker, he says, is the one who 'stands within the decision of what there is at all and what beings are.'[72] Daring to stand out into the openness of this truth, an opening in our history which the decision itself has certainly not made, but in which the thinker stands only by virtue of that decision, the courageous one confronts challenges which are 'unanticipated and can never be anticipated.'[73] And the movements of thought which are most responsive to these challenges will, of course, be correspondingly unpredictable – and perhaps even astonishing. In fact, the farther away a thinker goes from the field where the historical force of metaphysics would hold him captive, the more his movements, his way of bearing the gift of thought, will take on a form, a character, that could not have been anticipated:

304

Nietzsche's thought of the will to power thinks
beings as a whole in such a way that the
metaphysical ground of history of the present and
future age becomes visible and at the same time
decisive. . . . Care moves every thinker who thinks
in the direction of the decision. . . .[74]

Do we really want to know 'what is at stake in the path of
thought of a thinker'?[75] Do we dare to find out for ourselves?
Would we risk even 'madness' to follow a path of thought
where it goes? Heidegger gives us his warning:

To tread Nietzsche's path of thought to the will to
power means to encounter this historical
decision.[76]

Are we prepared, then, to entrust ourselves to the 'care'
which 'moves every thinker'? What is it, in fact, to be
involved in this kind of decision? And how are we moved,
when we are moved by care in virtue of our thinking? Finally,
we might want to ask, perhaps only asking ourselves: How
do we *move* in the spirit of that care?

But let us return, for the time being, to the question of
decision. The 'matter for thought,' here, as Heidegger says,
is 'the highest decision which can come to pass, and which
in each case becomes the ground of all history,' namely: the
decision 'between the primacy of beings and the dominance
of Being.' Or, in other words, words, however, which are
still Heidegger's: the decision by virtue of which 'beings as
a whole are expressly thought.' What I would like to suggest,
now, is that, when this decision (this de-cision, this *écart*) is
visualized by reference to the body of understanding, it is
symbolized as . . . a leap: the highest possible *de-cision* in
relation to the historical ground of our understanding.

The leap is the coming-to-pass (*Ereignis*) of this earth-
shaking historical de-cision: it is the way this ontological de-
cision appropriates and individuates (*ereignet*) our being as a
body of understanding. The leap is the coming-to-pass of
the existentially individuating and differentiating decision to
span with our guardian awareness the space, the ground, of
the ontological difference. And it is the ecstatic *acknowledgment* of this fundamental ground of difference; it is the body's
ecstasy in this acknowledgment. In the melodic arc (*archē*) of

the leap is the possibility of an original (*ursprünglich*) experience of the ground, the origin of (*Ursprung*) its rejoicing.

Although every single movement, every single step we take, requires – is – an act of faith, a 'passion' of trust which entrusts our balance, our sanity, our very existence, to the *support* of the grounding earth, the leap is unquestionably our most *supreme* act of faith. And yet it is also, at the very same time, the *infinite passion* of our trust in, and our obedience to, the earth. For, while it is certainly true that the leap is a decisive leave-taking, a momentary defiance of gravity, it is also true that the earth is given an opportunity to assert the finality of its claim, and that the leap is a preparation for the body's return, and the passion of the homecoming: the leap is that decisive event in our historical lives which makes it possible for us to experience our faith in the moment of its greatest risk. Furthermore, the leap is that appropriation of our body which makes it possible for us to experience our obedience to the earth with the *whole* of our being, i.e., with our being *in its wholeness*, and to experience this obedience precisely *as* an infinite submission, an infinite passion.

In its commemoration of the ground, of Being in (and as) the primordial (*ursprünglich*) grounding of our mortal being and dwelling, our thinking *needs* to give its 'propositions' (*Sätze*) a *non-metaphysical* grounding: a grounding and origin (*Ursprung*) which traditional metaphysics could not be counted on to represent. The appropriate grounding, therefore, is in the primordial leap (*ursprünglicher Satz*), which springs with high ecstasy, thanks to its release from the hold of metaphysics, off the original ground of its most radical questioning. 'Why are there beings?' Heidegger asks, in his *Introduction to Metaphysics*. And he says, by way of answer, that this question

> has its ground in a leap through which we thrust
> away all the previous security . . . of our life. The
> question is asked only in this leap; it *is* the leap;
> without it there is no asking.[77]

Furthermore, because of its character as a movement which is both primordial and ecstatic,

> the leap in this questioning *opens up* its own *source*
> – with this leap the question arrives at its own
> *ground*. We call such a leap, which *opens up* its own

source, the original source, or origin [*Ur-sprung*], the finding of one's own ground.[78]

Of course, the passages we have just been considering could be interpreted just as appropriately as passages concerned with the formulation, or the articulation, of a certain kind of principle. But why take Heidegger's words to be metaphors – and 'mere' metaphors, at that? The German word, *Satz*, lends itself to both translations, both interpretations. The German word for 'origin,' for that which is 'primordial,' does, however, give its stress to the leap; if we listen, we can actually *hear* this 'leap' suddenly leaping out from the very sounding of the word. And what happens when we listen for the resonance of the word for 'ground' with our feet as well as our ears? Perhaps it may become easier for us, after a while, to understand the nature of the ground from a standpoint which is *outside* the rational framework of metaphysics!

There certainly can be no question about Heidegger's way of hearing these words. Even if he is not dancing and leaping with the whole of his body, his *hearing* certainly participates in this spirit of play. In the play of *words*, Heidegger's thinking leaps and dances. And this is not a mere contingency. Not at all! Rather, this is the way thinking is finally *moved*, when it is moved by a care for its ground – moved by a caring which takes it ecstatically *outside* the restrictions imposed by the rigid framework of our metaphysics, which *binds* thinking to linear chains of ratiocination.

In *Der Satz vom Grund*, Heidegger is concerned simultaneously – the simultaneity is essential – with *both* dimensions of the *Satz*. In both the leap and the proposition, the thinker is related to the ground. The leap, of course, is a mode of comportment, a way of moving, or being moved, in relation to the ground. But the same may be said about the proposition. The attempt to formulate the principle of the ground, the attempt to bring it to articulation, is, neither more nor less than the leap, a mode of comportment, a way of moving, or being moved, in relation to the ground. What are we moved to say, as we go into the 'innermost depths' of our experiencing of the ground? What are we moved to say and do?

Der Satz vom Grund is a meditation on the possibility of different relationships to the ground (and, by implication, the earth, its element). It is an exploration which moves into the realm of possibility, where Heidegger can begin to 'undergo' an experience in regard for Being – Being, that is, *as ground* – which would no longer be completely determined, completely restricted, by the traditional authority of meta-physical representation. Metaphysics cannot re-present the presence of the ground; when it fails, it pronounces the ground 'elusive'. In the modern epoch, this means nihilism: the more willfully we posit it in a drive for permanence (*Bestand, Gestell*), the more deeply Being withdraws, and the more we lose our foothold, our needed grounding. Heidegger's meditation therefore makes room, as it must, for the necessary *play* of thought. But what this approach to the question of the ground begins to suggest, sooner or later, is that, given the conceptual elusiveness ('playfulness') of the 'ground,' a playful spirit, a playful relationship to the ground, may be absolutely *decisive* in opening up our thinking to a dimensionality of the ground which has been, until now, historically closed to us. If the spirit of play be decisive in this way, or in this sense, then our understanding of the ground, and of Being in its historical determination *as* the ground, would naturally expand most vigorously – 'growing by leaps and bounds,' as we say – to the extent that our thinking becomes capable of taking leaps and dancing with ideas. We must ask ourselves how well-prepared we are to let go of the metaphysical encumbrances in our history which weigh us down and restrict our freedom of movement.

In his study on Nietzsche, Arthur Danto notes the fact that Nietzsche's writing

> is difficult for the casual reader to follow. He wants to know *where Nietzsche stands*, and to this a simple answer cannot be given.[79]

And he goes on to explain that,

> There is a crucial tension throughout Nietzsche, between a free-wheeling critic, always prepared to *shift ground* in attacking metaphysics, and a metaphysical philosopher seeking to provide a basis for his repudiation of any such enterprise as he is practicing.[80]

If we put to one side the question of whether Danto's inter-pretation is reasonable, we are free to focus on the character of Nietzsche's bodily comportment. It is, of course the move-ment of a graceful dancer. But why should we be surprised? And why does Danto, whose eyes are acute enough to *see* the dance, fail explicitly to interpret its significance?[81] Nietzsche himself says, in *Thus Spake Zarathustra*:

> And once I wanted to dance as I have never danced before; over all the heavens I wanted to dance. . . . Only in the dance do I know how to tell the parable of the highest things.[82]

Nietzsche is entirely right about the decisive importance of the spirit of dance. Heidegger understands this as the spirit of play, and indeed himself exemplifies this spirit in his astonishing leaps of thought. But he misses the opportunity to make this spirit *explicit* as a bearing of thought: misses the opportunity, I mean, to illuminate it in the beauty of its fulfillment as a *body* of ontological understanding, a body standing on the earth, its incalculably deep ground of Being, and moving about, with high purpose, in a way that is, and will always remain, utterly inconceivable from a metaphysical standpoint. Heidegger *knows* that it is only in the spirit of play, in the graceful movements of its leaps and turns and steps, that thinking will overcome the power of metaphysics. It is unfortunate, though, that he does not *say* this, for the clearest *saying* of this is itself very liberating.

In thinking, the historical thinker must be capable of the highest historical de-cision. The highest de-cision is the de-cision which *articulates* the ontological difference between Being and beings – articulates it in a way that makes it stand out – while at the very same time it *spans* the space first opened up by that de-cision. But this kind of de-cision, requiring of us that we break away from the gravity and rigidity of our metaphysical history, could only come to pass as (and in) a leap of faith, a leap of infinite passion. The gravity of metaphysics will *never* understand the graceful dancing of thought; nor will it ever unbend enough to approve a thinking which moves, or is moved, in leaps of ecstatic self-abandon.

In *Der Satz vom Grund*, Heidegger takes up the question of grounding, which he perceives – accurately, I believe – to be at the very heart of our historical entanglement with metaphysics:

> Insofar as Being is, it itself has no ground. Yet this
> is not so because it is self-grounded, but rather
> because every form of its grounding, even and
> precisely that [which comes to pass] through itself,
> remains inappropriate to Being as ground.[83]

We ask, then: is there any posture of thinking, any bearing, any gesture at all which would be *appropriate* to Being as ground? Or perhaps we should ask: Is there any way of comporting ourselves which would be appropriate precisely because it can understand and acknowledge that *every* form of grounding remains in some sense *inappropriate*? The answer I wish to suggest is that the poetizing *dance* of thought – its true *Gelassenheit* – is the most appropriate way for us mortals to comport ourselves in relation to this 'elusive' ground. Let us test this suggestion. Let us stop everything for a moment and, in that space, let us ask ourselves: When the highest de-cision comes to pass, and we are moved by the beauty and the good feeling in its truth, how shall we comport ourselves? All around the world, the answer, every-where the same, appears. Mortals *leap* and *dance* in obedience to the earth, the elemental presence of ground; mortals leap and dance with a *rhythm* of power, a rhythm which gets its measure from the immeasurable ground which stands under their feet. Being skillful, the gestures of dance are celebratory. They commemorate and give thanks. They surrender the ego's will to power, giving it back, as the acceptance of our mortality, to the all-powerful earth, ground of our body of understanding.[84]

In the poetizing dance, a mortal's thinking of Being is always well-grounded. In the poetizing movements of dance – in the leap, for example – the Being of the ground, the presencing of Being *as* the *ground* of our being, finally becomes unconcealed in a new historical experience. Being can presence in a new way for a thinking which does *not* ask 'Why?', but simply *moves freely and with rejoicing* in the open space of the ontological difference. In the poetizing dance, the metaphorical leap, thinking can finally *experience* the ground in (and despite) its conceptual elusiveness. For, this is a thinking which has learned, in the vision of the leap, how to play:

The 'because' submerges in the play. The play is

310

without 'why.' It plays because it plays. It remains only play, the highest and deepest.[85]

To be sure, the metaphysician will continue to argue that,

'Why' is the word for the question into the ground. 'Because' contains the answer which indicates the ground. The 'why' seeks the ground; the 'because' brings it forth.[86]

But as the history of metaphysics carries us ever closer to the brink of the abyss of nihilism, it begins to become more and more evident that only a leap, a leap of thought right *into* that abyss – or perhaps a dance of surrender on the very edge – might yet serve to save us. So Heidegger contests the metaphysician's assumption that *nothing* is *without* ground, in the sense of a reason ('because. . .') that sufficiently answers, or totally settles, the question 'Why?'[87] According to Heidegger,

The question remains whether and how we, hearing the movements of this playing, play along with and join in the playing.[88]

Playing, then, himself with the tonal qualities of different vocal stresses, Heidegger hears the 'Principle of Ground,' which traditionally *sounds* like '*Nothing* is *without* ground,' in a new and different way:

Nothing *is* without *ground*. Being and ground: the same. Being as grounding has no ground, but as the abyss plays that game which . . . plays to us Being and ground.[89]

As he notes, letting the sounds of the words dance in his ears:

the stress [now] lets us hear a *harmony* between the 'is' and 'ground'. . . .[90]

So it would seem that we *can*, in this manner, directly and authentically *experience* –

The belonging-together of Being and ground.[91]

311

For indeed,

> Being is ground-like [grundartig], ground-related
> [grundhaft].[92]

But how can we experience that harmony outside the realm where thinking is a question of hearing? How can we open ourselves to hear it in a play which does not destroy us in a fall through the abyss? These questions are meant to remind us that we could also hear that fundamental harmony through the dancing and leaping of our feet. But what about the proximity of the abyss?

In 'What Are Poets For?' Heidegger points out that,

> The word for abyss – Abgrund – originally means
> the soil and ground towards which, because it is
> undermost, a thing tends downward.

And then he writes:

> But in what follows, we shall think of the Ab- as the
> complete absence of the ground. The age for which
> the ground fails to come, hangs in the abyss.[93]

Now of course, we cannot entirely elude the history which awaits our epoch as a whole. Neither as individuals nor as communities. But if we are not to despair altogether, to lie down and die, or, for that matter, to throw ourselves aimlessly into an abyss of certain death, then we need to ask ourselves how we might comport ourselves so that the ground does not deny us the possibility of its saving presence. Thus we need to reflect on our experience: at what point does the ground become an abyss? And as we reflect on this question, we may begin to realize the significance of Heidegger's emphasis on the spirit of play. If play in the sense of Gelassenheit (letting be) is the ontologically most appropriate comportment towards the ground, we might surmise that the opposite of play (das Gestell) could possibly be decisive with regard to whether we are granted an experience of the ground in its presence as ground, or whether we are destined to experience the ground in its absence, again and again, as an abyss. In the melodic arc (archē) of the leap, in its rejoicing, I believe that we can prepare ourselves for a new experience of the primordial ground.

The ground in its immeasurableness *is* elusive. Consequently, the most harmonious relationship to the ground – that relationship which would grant us the deepest, most uplifting experience of its resonance – would be a relationship characterized by play: a ludic mode of comportment, a play of discursive allusions. The ecstatic leap of infinite passion precisely responds to the historical need for a less willful, more playful relatedness to the Being of the ground. The nihilism into which our metaphysics has finally fallen can perhaps be understood, in this light, as a natural consequence of the rigid, grasping, very unplayful character of our concepts. The concepts with which our metaphysics has attempted to grasp the nature of the ground do *not* let the ground presence as it is, i.e., in its necessary elusiveness; rather, they willfully insist on representing it entirely on its own rational terms. Metaphysics finds itself facing the horror of an abyss, rather than the kindness of a ground, because it has vehemently refused to *be with* the ground in a way that is truly harmonious, refused to bend its thinking in obedience to the earth. The ground is, however, a mirror-play: it simply reflects back to us the character of our own understanding. To what extent is our metaphysical need for a secure rational foundation a compensation for, and a symptom of, our loss of a proper bodily grounding – and our loss, too, of a bodily felt sense of ratio?

The leap symbolizes joy: our joy in the earth's presence. It symbolizes, therefore, our commemoration and thanksgiving. But it also manifests a way of relating to the ground which releases it from our control, our mastery, our will to power. The leap *corresponds* to the unreifiable truth of the ground.

And precisely here we may perhaps begin to realize the significance of the movements of dance in the history of all religions. So long as they kept those movements, just that long have they joyfully *cared* for the earth of their mortal grounding. Is it not a striking fact, a matter worth our pondering, that the most diverse religions – and by no means only the primitive – have experienced the ecstatic movements of dance at the very heart of their faith? Erwin Straus will help, I think, to explain this:

> the tension between subject and object, between I and world, is dissolved in the immediate experience of dancing. . . . [But] we [should] never

> for a moment forget that the experience itself is
> not conceptual, that the dance does not overcome
> the subject-object dichotomy conceptually, but that
> it actualizes a union of the separated in a far more
> elementary manner – by em-bodying its
> meaning.[94]

According to Straus, dancing effects a 'transformation in one's immediate experience of his own body,' and it does this by *shifting* the center of felt energy from the region of the head (center of energy for the masculine intellect, the *ego cogito*) to the region of the trunk (center of energy for the more feminine modes of awareness). This downward, earthward shift is, of course, of the utmost importance for the religious experience, since, as he states, the 'gnostic attitude is reduced and the pathic moment in experience comes to the fore.'[95] By dissolving the ego-logical structure of subject-and-object, the leap of faith *opens* us to the space of the ontological difference; and it envisions a different history of Being. In leaping from the ground (i.e., in our *Satz vom Grund*), a new historical experience is made possible.

But metaphysics needs to get in touch with the 'pathic' mode of thinking. Without that contact, it is essentially powerless to overcome a historical destiny in which we both suffer and make suffer. Our metaphysics desperately needs to recollect the ancient maternal power of the earth if it is to see us through the historical danger of total nihilism. (From an archetypal standpoint, nihilism is related to the historical predominance of a masculine and patriarchal interpretation of the will to power. Thus, the first stage of its 'overcoming' necessitates a balancing shift to a more feminine, matriarchal principle.) Or, to put this another way: Our metaphysics needs a well-grounded thinking, a thinking which rejoices in Being, and in rejoicing, gives thanks. We need a thinking which finally can leap and dance . . . leap and dance as never before. It is useful to bear in mind that, as Hermann Hesse says in his essay on 'Zarathustra's Return': 'As a child grows in a woman's womb, so destiny grows in each person's body. . . .'[96]

But now I want to bring out for reflection that which I consider to be the very highest purpose, the inborn destiny, which grows in each person's gift of motility. If we return to the epigrams at the very beginning of this section and read over again the concluding sentence of the lengthy passage we abstracted from *Fear and Trembling*, we find Kierkegaard proclaiming that,

> to transform the leap of life into a walk, absolutely to express the sublime in the pedestrian – that only the knight of faith can do – and this is the one and only prodigy.

But Kierkegaard, whose characterization of the leap of faith has not been, and could not be, I wager, surpassed, has very little more to say about the *walk* of the knight of faith. We may of course *presume* that this walk is also a movement of infinite passion. But the question is: what does that really mean?

Let us move somewhat closer to an answer by considering, first of all, that this walk, as a movement of infinite passion, must be a gait whose every step is graced by its *infinite receptivity* to the gifts of the earth over which it passes. What, then, is a receptive step? And what are the gifts of the earth? Our steps are receptive when they are made with guardian awareness. And their gracefulness consists in the quality of their recollection of Being. Now, what are the earth's gifts? Is it not true that one of its gifts is the teaching of equality, and of the compassion which understands that end? (From dust to dust: the earth eventually claims the body of every mortal. The earth's claim continually speaks to us of our humility.) What this tells us is that, in obedience to the earth, its elemental ground, the movement of infinite *passion* gradually becomes a movement of the most inexhaustible *compassion*.

The true gait of power is not a gait moved by the egological or egocentric will, Nietzsche's 'manly' will to power; it is, rather, a gait moved by that which is *beyond* the will, beyond both the 'activity' and the 'passivity' of the egocentric person. The truly powerful gait is moved, as Heidegger says, by the gracefulness of 'Care':

> Care moves every thinker who thinks in the direction of the decision.

Kierkegaard says that the infinite passion in the leap must become one's walk of life. By the same token, it needs to be said that the dimensionality of the thinker's caring extends, of course, beyond the realm of human existence. On that

315

point we must be absolutely clear. Nevertheless, the thinker's efforts to extend his caring *beyond* that realm must not distract him from that which needs to be cared for, and that which needs to be done, *within* the human realm. Thus, when the thinker moves *within* this realm, the caring which moves him – the caring by which he is visibly moved – is called 'compassion,' our openness to all beings.

Moved by compassion, the gait of power takes one wherever there is need. Moved by compassion, we go wherever our abilities and gifts are needed. Moved by compassion, we are moved by a de-cision not entirely of our own making: a de-cision which originates in the space of the ontological difference itself, which appropriates us in the heart of our body of understanding, and which speaks to us most directly through the resonance of the earth, that presencing of the ground whose compassion for our historical dwelling is most audible when we are obedient to its rhythmic measure.

Perhaps, then, if the leap (*Satz*) of our gait could learn to spring from a faith in the earth's own ways and from a joyful fidelity to the earth's prior claims, the Being of our original groundedness (i.e., *der ursprünglichen Grund*) would no longer open up before our steps as an abyss (*Abgrund*) of nihilism. The historical significance of Heidegger's *Der Satz vom Grund* – that which, in this work, has until now remained unthought – is the ecstatic leap of faith and fidelity. From out of our experience of its primordial (*ursprüngliche*) truth, it is possible that a new body of ontological understanding might someday emerge, and that a turn in our historical destiny, the earth's song and geology, will favor our steps with its resonance.

CHAPTER 7

The Gathering
Round-Dance

Opening Conversation

(1) In infinite time, every possible combination would
at some time or another be realized an infinite
number of times. And . . . a circular movement of
absolutely identical series is thus demonstrated:
the world as a circular movement that has already
repeated itself infinitely often and plays its game
in infinitum.

Nietzsche, *The Will to Power*[1]

(2) Circular motion and motion in a straight line are
the simple movements, *haplai.* Of these two,
circular motion is first, i.e., is the higher, and thus,
of the highest order. . . . In circular motion, the
body has its place in the motion itself; for this
reason such motion is perpetual and truly in
being. In rectilinear motion the place lies only in
one direction, away from another place, so that
motion comes to an end over there. . . . The purest
motion, in the sense of change of place, is circular
motion; it contains, as it were, its place in itself. A
body that so moves itself, moves itself completely.
This is true of all celestial bodies. Compared to this,
earthly motion is always in a straight line, or
mixed, or violent, but always incomplete.

Heidegger, 'Basic Questions of Metaphysics'[2]

(3) in modern thought, circular motion is understood only in such a way that a perpetual attracting force from the center is necessary for its formation and preservation. With Aristotle, however, this 'force', *dynamis*, the capacity for its motion, lies in the nature of the body itself. The kind of motion of the body and its relation to its place depend upon the nature of the body. The velocity of natural motion increases the nearer the body comes to its place; that is, increase and decrease of velocity, and cessation of motion, depend upon the nature of the body.

Heidegger, 'Basic Questions of Metaphysics'[3]

(4) with the creation of the universe the dance too came into being, which signifies the union of the elements. The *round dance* of the stars, the constellation of planets in relation to the fixed stars, the beautiful order and harmony in all its movements, is a *mirror* of the original dance at the time of creation. The dance is the richest gift of the muses. . . . Because of its divine origin, it has a place in the mysteries and is beloved by the gods and carried out by human beings in their honor.

Lucian, *On the Dance*[4]

(5) In playing their part in the cosmic dance, all creatures are bound together in an intricate web of life. By his nature, man too participates in all cosmic events and is inwardly and outwardly interwoven with them. Increasingly, he becomes aware of the mutual dependency whereby influences pass between the universe and man's body. . . . On the way to himself he has recognized that the . . . universe, which he once peopled with countless divinities, is . . . moving within man himself.

Maria-Gabriele Wosien, *Sacred Dance:
Encounter with the Gods*[5]

(6) Celestrial motion being circular, man, by imitating it, partakes of the cosmic dance-round and begins to experience reality as order round a center. . . . This experience of the center becomes basic to

318

worship and eventually results in man's orientation toward an objective reality.

Wosien, *Sacred Dance*[6]

(7)   The earliest rituals are therefore rituals of ego-concentration, circle-mandala forms of ritual, whose probable earliest form, common to all early mankind, is the round-dance, in which the human group sets itself apart from the world and gathers into a community. In the mandala of the psyche, the Self forms the center, whereas the ego is the center of the mandala of consciousness. In both cases, the circle is a defence and fortress of the psychic content.

Erich Neumann, *The Child: Structure and Dynamics of the Nascent Personality*[7]

(8)   Originally, all ritual was a dance, in which the whole of the corporeal psyche was literally 'set in motion'.

Erich Neumann, *The Great Mother: An Analysis of the Archetype*[8]

(9)   There is thus a shifting of the center of the personality into the warmer region of heart and feeling, while the inclusion of intuition suggests a groping, irrational apprehension of wholeness.

Carl G. Jung, 'Concerning Mandala Symbolism,' *The Archetypes and the Unconscious*[9]

(10)   the body's gesture toward the world introduces it into an order of relations of which pure physiology and biology do not have the slightest idea. Despite the diversity of its parts, which makes it fragile and vulnerable, *the body is capable of gathering itself into a gesture which for a time dominates their dispersion.* . . .

Merleau–Ponty, 'Indirect Language and the Voices of Silence'[10]

(11)   In poetizing . . . human beings become gathered on the ground of their ek-sistence.

Heidegger, 'Hölderlin und das Wesen der Dichtung'[11]

(12)   without goal, unless the joy of the circle is itself a

319

goal; without will, unless a ring feels good will
toward itself. . . .

Nietzsche, *The Will to Power*[12]

(13) To each and all it is given to dance. . . . He who
joineth not in the dance knoweth not the way.

St John, 'Hymn of Jesus,' *Apocryphal Acts*[13]

(14) And just as he who dances with his body, rushing
through the rotating movements of the limbs,
acquires a right to share in the round dance, in the
same way, he who dances the spiritual dance,
always moving in the ecstasy of faith, acquires a
right to dance in the ring of all creation.

St Ambrose[14]

(15) It is something very wonderful
to be initiated into the Mysteries
with rhythm and dance.

Lucian, *On the Dance*[15]

(16) Before man expresses his experience of life through
materials, he does so with his own body. Early
man dances on every occasion: for joy, grief, love,
fear; at sunrise, death, birth. The movement of
the dance provides him with a deepening of his
experience. In his dancing, the imitation of sound
and movement observed around him, and
especially the involuntary expression of motion
through sound and gestures, precedes any
consciously articulated sound and dance
formation. Before the dance develops into a
deliberate religious rite, it is a rhythmic release of
energy, an ecstatic art. . . . As an act of sacrifice,
as man giving himself to his god, the dance is
total surrender.

Wosien, *Sacred Dance*[16]

(17) The Medicine Wheel Circle is the Universe. It is
change, life, death, birth and learning. This Great
Circle is the lodge of our bodies, our minds, and
our hearts. It is the cycle of all things that exist.
The circle is our Way of Touching, and of
experiencing Harmony with every other thing
around us. And for those who seek Understanding,
the Circle is their Mirror.

Hyemeyohsts Storm, *Seven Arrows*[17]

(18) The Medicine Wheel is the living Flame of the
Lodges, and the Great Shield of Truth written in
the sign of the Water. It is the Heart and the Mind.
It is the Song of the Earth. It is the Star-Fire and
the Painted Drum seen only in the eyes of children.
It is the Red Pipe of the Buffalo Gift smoked in
the Sacred Mountains, and it is the Four Arrows of
the People's Lodge. It is our Sun Dance.
Hyemeyohsts Storm, *Seven Arrows*[18]

(19) every culture which has lost myth has lost, by the
same token, its natural healthy creativity. Only a
horizon ringed about by myths can unify a
culture.
Nietzsche, *The Birth of Tragedy from the Spirit of
Music*[19]

(20) Although the beginnings of the psychological-
matriarchal age are lost in the haze of prehistory,
its end at the dawn of our historical era unfolds
magnificently before our eyes. Then it is replaced
by the patriarchal world, and the archetype of the
Great Father or of the Masculine, with its different
symbolism, its different values, and its different
tendencies, becomes dominant.
Erich Neumann, *The Great Mother: An Analysis
of the Archetype*[20]

(21) He [Jesus] gathered all of us together and said:
Before I am delivered up to them,
let us sing a hymn to the Father,
and so go forth to that which lieth before us.
He bade us therefore make as it were a ring,
holding one another's hands,
and himself standing in the midst, he said:
Answer Amen to me.
He began then to sing a hymn and to say:
Glory be to thee, Father,
And we, going about in a ring, answered him:
Amen!
St John, 'Hymn of Jesus,' *Apocryphal Acts*[21]

(22) Just as the chorus always moves in a circle around
the leader, and sings best when it turns towards
him, so we must also surround him, and when we
regard him we can behold our end and our place,

> our voice is in harmonious accord with him and we
> dance around him in a dance inspired by truth.
> In this dance we can find the source of life, the
> source of intelligence, the principle of existence,
> the cause of goodness and the origin of the soul.
>
> Plotinus, *Enneads*[22]

(23) To consecrate every sort of dance or melody. First
we should ordain festivals – calculating for the year
what they ought to be, and at what time, and in
honor of what gods, progeny of gods, and heroes
they ought to be celebrated; and, in the next place,
what hymns ought to be sung at the several
sacrifices, and with what dances the particular
festival is to be honored. This has to be arranged
at first by certain persons, and, when arranged,
the whole assembly of the citizens are to offer
sacrifices and libations to the Fates and all the
other gods, and to consecrate the several odes to
gods and heroes: and if any one offers any other
hymns or dances to any one of the gods, the priests
and priestesses, acting in concert with the
guardians of the law, shall, with the sanction of
religion and the law, exclude him, and he who is
excluded, if he do not submit, shall be liable all his
life long to have a suit of impiety brought against
him by any one who likes.

Plato, *Laws* VII, 799

Part I

A Place of Clearing

In the sixth strophe of *Brot und Wein*, Hölderlin asks:

Why does the holy dance not [any longer] rejoice?[23]

The poet's question moves me. It moves me to think.
Although it undoubtedly falls short of an answer to the poet's
question, this kind of movement – thinking – can itself be a
joyous response. So we will, as before, attempt to let
ourselves be moved wherever the matter for thought takes
us. If this movement should awaken an experience of joy,

then our thinking will indeed have brought us closer to the spirit of dance. In any event, by giving thought to the poet's question and letting ourselves be moved by it, we are already holding open the future of mortal existence for the ecstatic space of the sacred dance.

Now, there are, so far as I know, only – or at least – two major essays in which Heidegger explicitly discusses the dance. About one of them, 'Hölderlins Erde und Himmel,' it could, I suppose, be argued that Heidegger is concerned with dance only because the poet is. But we still need to account for Heidegger's initial attraction to the Hölderlin work and for his willingness to give the dance so much space in his thinking. In the other essay, however, which is devoted to understanding the essential nature of the thing – it is, in fact, called 'The Thing' – Heidegger's discussion of dance cannot in any respect be explained away. Much as they might wish to ignore the dance in Heidegger's thinking, philosophers must sooner or later give it the gift and tribute of their own thought.

Let us consider, first, the Hölderlin essay. In Hölderlin's poem 'Griechenland', we come across the following passage:

> But like the round-dance
> at the wedding,
> to the nimble and compliant too can come
> a great beginning.[24]

Who are the participants in the marriage? And what is the significance of the round-dance (*der Reigen*)? Heidegger wants to emphasize that the participants gathered for the wedding are four:

> The marriage is the wholeness of intimacy [*Innigkeit*]
> gathering Earth and Sky, men and gods. It is the
> festival and celebration of the unending
> relationship.[25]

'The bride is the Earth,' he says, 'to whom comes the song of the Heavens.' And 'the round-dance [*der Reigen*] is the drunken coming-together [*Zueinander*] of the gods themselves in the heavenly fire of joy.'[26] (In *Zarathustra*, a book Heidegger knew well, Nietzsche speaks of 'the nuptial ring of rings, the ring of [eternal] recurrence.')[27] Thus, the round-dance is a gathering of the Fourfold (*das Geviert*): the two cosmological elements, the Earth and Sky themselves, together with their representative embodiments, mortals of the earth and gods from the sky. Since the gathering is joyous, it takes the form of, and is called, a dance. Since the gathering is also, however, a commemoration, a hermeneutical returning to 'the beginning,' and celebrates what is, in fact, an *unending* relationship, a relationship *without* beginning and end, the dance takes the form of a circle, a ring, a round-dance.[28] But this interpretation is just a beginning: the time-place where our own thinking happened to enter the circle. Heidegger himself says:

> We have not been given the power to scoop up the riches which, in the word 'round-dance,' are spoken with simple reticence. [*Wir vermögen der Reichtum des einfacher Scheu gesagten Wortes 'Reigen' nicht aufzuschöpfen.*] For it names the treasure itself, namely, that ['great destiny'] which still might come.[29]

In the round-dance, the ring of gathering, the ring which brings together gods and mortals, Earth and Sky, something of the greatest importance takes place. Within the ring of the Fourfold, gods and mortals are appropriately *turned*, both in relation to one another and in relation to the 'elements' of Being, which enable them to become what they are:

> 'Gering' is the intensified word for *ring*, which means the light and nimble [*das Leichte*], the pliant and compliant [*Geschmeidige*], the submissive and yielding [*Fügsame*]. . . .[30]

The round-dance, therefore, is a symbol, a prototype, of 'the coming of the great beginning':

> This [beginning] comes . . . in the form [*Weise*] of the round-dance.[31]

Why is this so? If we read it to snatch up from the philosopher a clarifying interpretation we do not get from the poet, we are bound, I would say, to be frustrated: the 'Erde and Himmel' essay ultimately leaves us very much in the dark. Some of our questions may be answered, however, when we turn to 'The Thing' and 'Building Dwelling

Thinking.' The first of these two works, the essay on 'The Thing,' is the only other study to take up the event of the round-dance; but, since both works are concerned with the dwelling of mortals in the gathering of the Fourfold, we can make use of them to spell out some of the implications of the 'Erde und Himmel' essay.

We might note that there is a discussion of 'beauty,' in 'Hölderlins Erde und Himmel,' which we could use as our interpretive beginning. Heidegger does say there that, in the round-dance, mortals 'let beauty dwell on Earth.'[32] And he even defines beauty in a way that implicitly *names* this dance:

> Beauty is the pure appearing of the unconcealment of the whole unending relationship around the center.[33]

The round-dance, then, is a possibility of dwelling; it is a commitment, on the part of those who are gathered, to the building of a world of beauty, a world for the dwelling, not only of mortals, but also of the gods who reflect them. The round-dance is a ring of gathering for the preservation of the Fourfold: not only gods and mortals, but also the Earth and the Sky. The dance takes place in a clearing on the earth; and its protection is the canopy of the sky. In the round-dance, we are gathered around a center. Being is welcomed in that center. The round-dance is a hermeneutic circle gathering the Fourfold in a recollection which turns toward the central meaning of Being. We are gathered into a hermeneutical understanding of Being:

> Mortals dwell in the way they preserve the Fourfold [Earth and Sky, mortals and divinity] in its essential being, its presencing.[34]

'Accordingly,' he says, 'the preserving that dwells is Fourfold':

(1) 'Mortals dwell in that they save the earth.' ('To save really means to set something free into its own presencing.')
(2) 'Mortals dwell in that they receive the sky as sky.'
(3) 'Mortals dwell in that they await the divinities as divinities.' ('They do not make their gods for themselves and do not worship idols.')

(4) 'Mortals dwell in that they initiate their own nature –
     their being capable of death as death – into the use
     and practice of this capacity, so that there may be a
     good death.'[35]

The round-dance is a coming-together of the Four in a re-
affirmation, a renewal, of the cosmic order. In the very
rhythm of the dance, the moving power of *Dikē*, another
word for *to metron*, is called into presence, and is bodily felt.
The dance is a re-enactment of the cosmic *justice* which
gathers the Four into the beauty, the truth, and the goodness,
of a universal order. The round-dance gathers us into the
recollection, therefore, of that which, in Plato's *Gorgias*
(507–8), Sokrates tells Kallikles:

> Wise men say that the heavens and the earth, gods
> and men are bound together by fellowship and
> friendship, and orderliness and temperance and
> justice, and that for this reason they call this
> universe order, or *cosmos*, and not a world of
> disorder or misrule.[36]

Since the round-dance plays an essential role in the life-
world of the Oglala Sioux, I would like to record, here, their
own interpretation of the event which used to gather them
into a sacred ring for the chant and the dance. Lame Deer
never read Sokrates; but, as this description of the Pipe
Ceremony shows, he would have understood him at once:

> With us the circle stands for the togetherness of
> people who sit with one another around the
> campfire, relatives and friends united in peace while
> the pipe passes from hand to hand. The camp in
> which every tipi had its place was also a ring. The
> tipi was a ring in which people sat in a circle, and
> all families in the village were in turn circles within
> a larger circle, part of the larger hoop which was
> the seven campfires of the Sioux, representing one
> nation. The nation was only a part of the universe,
> in itself circular and made of the earth, which is
> round, of the sun, which is round, of the stars,
> which are round. The moon, the horizon, the
> rainbow – circles within circles within circles, with
> no beginning and no end. To us this is beautiful

and fitting, symbol and reality at the same time, expressing the harmony of life and nature.[37]

Returning, now, to Heidegger's paper on 'The Thing,' we find that the circle of the Fourfold sets in motion a kind of mirroring. The round-dance is an interplay of reflections:

> Each of the four mirrors in its own way the presence of the others.[38]

(See Lucian, *supra*, the fourth text in the 'Opening Conversation.') Furthermore, the circle is an In-gathering of beings (*legein, Sammeln*) in relation to their original center: in the reflectiveness of the mirror-play, the participants are turned 'inward,' toward the center of Being from which, once again, they come, and around which they move in a dance of self-abandon. Thus, the round-dance (*Reigen*) is an event of appropriation (*Ereignis*): an event in which each participant, whether god or mortal, realizes its own most central existential truth:

> The appropriate mirroring sets each of the four free into its own, but it binds these free ones into the simplicity of their essential being towards one another.[39]

The mirroring which takes place in the round-dance is an interplay of reflections which *opens* the participants to the meaningfulness of their ontological In-gathering:

> The mirroring [*Der Spiegel*] that binds into freedom is the play [*das Spiel*] that betroths [or entrusts] each of the four to each through the enfolding clasp of their mutual appropriation [*Ereignis*].[40]

The round-dance is not just a gathering of human beings; it is a gathering of mortals: a gathering of *mortals in their interplay with immortals*; a gathering of the two, dancing in the light of human reflection. And it is more: it is also a gathering which includes the participation of *every worldly thing*. Nothing, no thing, is excluded from the circle of Being. Nothing, therefore, is denied recognition in the round-dance of ontological remembrance. Echoing Leibniz, but only after an appeal to our lived perception, Merleau–Ponty argues, in

his *Phenomenology of Perception,* for the truth that 'every object
is the mirror of all others.'[41] But Heidegger's thought moves
more freely. In 'The Thing,' he actually describes this Leibni-
zian mirroring, this vast intertwining, as a cosmological gathering in the form of the joyful round-dance:

> The fouring presences as the worlding of the world.
> The mirror-play of world is the round-dance of
> appropriating. [*Das Spiegel-Spiel von Welt ist der
> Reigen des Ereigens.*] Therefore, the round-dance
> does not encompass the four like a hoop. The
> round-dance is the ring that joins while it plays as
> mirroring. [*Der Reigen ist der Ring, der ringt, indem
> er als das Spiegeln spielt.*] Appropriating, it lightens
> the four into the radiance of their simple oneness.
> Radiantly, the ring joins the four, everywhere
> open to the riddle of their presence. The gathered
> presence [*Wesen*] of the mirror-play of the world,
> joining in this way, is the ringing [*das Gering*]. In
> the ringing of the mirror-playing ring, the four
> nestle into their unifying presence, in which each
> one retains its own nature. So nestling [*gering*],
> they join together, worlding the world.[42]

The worlding of the world does not necessarily take place,
however, in the *rejoicing* of the sacred dance. It may, for
example, take place in a war of nuclear energy, a fire of total
annihilation. That, presumably, is the point of Hölderlin's
question – the one, I mean, which moved us to open this
phase of our thinking to the event of the round-dance. With
a courage akin to the poet's, Nietzsche faces into the danger
which threatens to close our epoch; and in *The Birth of
Tragedy*, he clearly names it:

> a culture without any fixed and consecrated place
> of origin, condemned to exhaust all possibilities.[43]

As we let these words reverberate, we can begin to hear,
perhaps, in something Heidegger says, a matter for thought
which he himself has left for the circle which remains
unthought. In Hölderlin's 'Erde und Himmel,' Heidegger
notes that,

> The round-dance in Greek is *choros*, the festive

singing, the dance which celebrates the god: *chorois timan Dionyson, Bacchae* (220). [44]

Here, for example, is a *choros* described by Sappho:

Thus once upon a time the Cretan woman danced rhythmically with delicate feet around a lovely altar, treading upon the soft, smooth flowers of the meadow. (Fragment 114)[45]

The vintage dance depicted on Achilles' shield, a dance rejoicing the place of the harvest, is also a *choros*:

Young maidens and youths, gay of spirit, were carrying the fruit, sweet as honey, in woven baskets. And in their midst, a boy played charmingly upon a clear-toned lyre, and sang sweetly in accompaniment, with delicate voice; and the dancers followed along with him, leaping [*posi skairontes*] with song and shouts of joy. [46]

So is the dance which Hephaistos places near the rim of the shield, and which Homer describes thus:

Youths and marriageable maidens were dancing [*orcheomai*] . . . with their hands on one another's wrists, the girls in fine linen with lovely garlands on their heads, and the men in closely woven tunics showing the faint gleam of oil, and with daggers of gold hanging from their silver belts. Here they ran lightly round, circling as smoothly on their accomplished feet, just as the wheel of the potter when he sifts and works it with his hands to see if it will spin; and there they ran in lines [*threxaskon*] to meet each other. A large crowd stood round enjoying the delightful dance [*choron*], with a minstrel among them singing divinely to the lyre, while a couple of acrobats, keeping time with his music, threw cart-wheels in and out among the people. [47]

In the dance-song we heard earlier in this chapter, the one by Timotheos of Miletos, we may now hear another accent: not so much, this time, an accent on the beating of the ground, but rather more an accent on the dance (*Reigen*) as an event (*Ereignis*) *taking place*, and in truth, *taking its own* (*eigenen*) *place*:

> As for the others the while, they set up trophies to
> be a most holy place [*hagnotaton temenos*] of Zeus,
> and hymned the great healing-god men cry to,
> beating the ground to the tune of high-stept dance
> [*hupsikrotois choreiais*].⁴⁸

I want to say, using Heidegger's own words, that it is in the com-pliance of the round-dance, first and foremost, that 'all holy places are gathered.'⁴⁹ Heidegger comes very close to this understanding of the round-dance; but he does not avail himself of the evidence – historical, etymological, and phenomenological – which would make it possible for us to experience, simultaneously, both the *dance* and the *place* in the truth (*alētheia*) of their coming to pass (their being, and taking place, as *Ereignis*).

What set my own thinking in motion was a passage in Heidegger's *Introduction to Metaphysics*, in which he ponders the Greek experience of place:

> For clarification of the meaning of *paremphainō*, let
> us consider what has been said. . . . That wherein
> something becomes refers to what we call 'space.'
> The Greeks had no word for 'space.' This is no
> accident; for they experienced the spatial on the
> basis, not of extension, but of place (*topos*); they
> experienced it as *chōra*, which signifies neither place
> nor space, but that which is occupied by what
> stands there. The place belongs to the thing itself.
> Each of all the various things has its place. That
> which is in process of becoming is placed in this
> local 'space' and emerges from it. But in order that
> this should be possible, 'space' must be free from
> all the modes of appearance that it might derive
> from anywhere. For if it were similar to any of the
> modes of appearance that enter into it, it would,
> in receiving forms of antithetical or totally different
> essence, manifest its own appearance and so
> produce a poor realization of the [original] model.
> That wherein the things in process of becoming
> are placed must precisely not present an aspect and

appearance of its own. (The reference to the passage in *Timaeus* [50e] is intended not only to clarify the link between the *paremphainon* and the *on*, between also-appearing and being as permanence, but at the same time to suggest that the transformation of the barely apprehended essence of place (*topos*) and of *chōra* into a 'space' defined by extension was initiated by the Platonic philosophy, i.e., the interpretation of being as *idea*. Might *chōra* not mean: that which abstracts itself from every particular, that which withdraws [into its depth, the unbounded], and in such a way precisely admits and 'makes place' for something else?)[50]

This last query is a natural one, since the Greek words for *place* (*chōra*, *chōros*, *chōrē*), are related etymologically to their words *chōreō* and *chōrēsomai*, which mean: 'make room for,' 'give way to,' 'fall back,' 'withdraw,' and 'retire.' But my question is, rather, this: does not the etymological kinship which binds together the Greek words for place (*chōra*, *chōros*) and round-dance (*choros* and *choreia*) suggest that, for the earliest Greeks, and in a time immemorial, it was the *ring* of the gathering Fourfold, the Fourfold gathered in the recollection of a round-dance, which first cleared and defined a 'real' place? (We should also bear in mind here, that the Greek word for 'separate,' 'differentiate,' 'divide' is *chorizō*. And that which they call *chōrismos* is a separated and differentiated place, a place of essential difference.)[51]

But this question takes me to a place in my thinking from which I find myself formulating another question, namely: is it possible that, by giving the gift and tribute of our thought to the sacred round-dance, i.e., by letting our thinking *participate* in the joy of the Fourfold which its spirit gracefully gathers, we might actually be *opening* ourselves to the disclosure of a radically new way for us, as the mortals we are, to experience the yielding of our 'places' and dwell in the ecstasy of an open and gracious space?

A space is something that has been made room for, something that is cleared and free, namely, within a boundary, Greek *peras*. A boundary is not that at which something stops but, as the Greeks recognized, the boundary is that from which

> something *begins its presencing*. . . . Space is in
> essence . . . that which is let into its bounds.[52]

I submit that the round-dance is the delimiting and clearing
of a location, a place within whose boundaries mortals bound
to the earth let Being appear *as* a gathering of the Fourfold.
The earliest Greeks must have *experienced* the ontological significance of the round-dance in the hermeneutical process of
making, or clearing, a place; but they did not need to – or
anyway did not – thematically understand, nor did they ever
contemplate as a question, the essential *truth* (the ecstasy of
alētheia) in the original relationship. We, however, do not
(any longer) *experience* this relationship; but, unlike the anci-
ents, we have been granted the possibility of *making* the
connection in a movement of our thought, returning, in a
dance of thought, to that place of origin where the truth
(*alētheia*) of Being is received in recollection by the body of
understanding. But is it then certain that the ancient *experience* of this 'original place,' circumscribed by the rejoicing of
the dance, cannot be reclaimed? Is it certain that not even a
leap of thought could retrieve for us, in a form appropriate
to our modernity, that essential truth, which appeared for a
time, and with such beauty, in the culture of ancient Greece?
When Heidegger speaks, in his 'Erde und Himmel' paper,
of the 'treasure' hidden at the center of the round-dance, he
lets his words resonate with the hint of a 'great destiny,' and
'the coming of the great beginning.' Could it be that the
'treasure' which belongs for safekeeping within the ring of
the round-dance is an event of Being which *re-establishes* the
space of the ontological difference? Could it be, I mean, that
our thinking might eventually find, precisely in the taking
place of this round-dance, the fateful treasure of an understanding which retrieves the archaic symbolism of the dance,
not in order to *repeat* an answer whose time is past, but
rather, in order to open itself up to a *transcendence* of the
metaphysical representation of space? Could it be, then, that
the treasure which comes to thinking 'in the form of the
round-dance' is not other than the beginning of a radically
new *experience* of 'place'? In hermeneutics, the treasure is
always enclosed in a circle. Perhaps we need to go back to
the kind of place which is compliantly cleared when the
round-dance of old takes place, in order to move, when
favored, beyond the enframed place of metaphysics into a

resting-place (*Aufenthalt*) that would feel more appropriate for the openness which is our being.

This resting-place, as a 'region,' is a major topic for thought in Heidegger's work on 'Logik: Heraklits Lehre vom Logos.' There is, he argues, a 'fundamental connection' (*Wesenszusammenhang*) between *Logos* and *chōra* 'in the sense of "region" [*Gegend*].'[53] 'Region' he defines as:

> the open realm and the vastness [*Weite*], in which something takes its resting-place [*Aufenthalt*], [and] from which it arises [*herkommt*], takes leave [*entkommt*], and rejoins [*entgegnet*].[54]

In wrestling with Fragment 108, Heidegger is compelled to rethink the severing (*kechōrismenon*) and the making of the difference (*chōrizein*); and he takes up for reflection, accordingly, the problematic those ancient words propose. *Chōrizein* is the establishing of a place (*chōra*):

> The *chōra* is the self-opening, yielding [*entgegenkommende*] expanse.[55]

It is:

> the surrounding, the all-giving environment [*umgebende Umgegend*], which clears a space for a resting-place and continues to sustain it [*einräumt und gewahrt*].[56]

Heidegger, however, is not fully satisfied with this level of interpretation. Digging still deeper in the 'geology' of Being, he traces these words for 'place' to the more elemental *chaō*, source of *our* word for *chaos*, and meaning: 'to gape, to split open, to become receptive to, and to open.'[57] The place, therefore, as the gathering of a region whose depth is an utterly open expanse, cannot be experienced in its truth as some kind of *object* (*Gegen-stand*): it is not a region whose boundaries can be absolutely determined, willfully measured with finality, and willfully brought to a conceptualizable standstill. Beyond the local place looms the neighbouring region; beyond the familiar region, an utterly open expanse: an openness which is order or is chaos, depending on how willfully attached we may be to our prevailing conceptual scheme. Perhaps the experience of space undergone in the round-dance would *liberate* us from a process of conceptual enframing which makes it difficult for us to experience that *open* expanse as an *order* of harmony. Perhaps a thoughtful experience of the hermeneutical round-dance would open *us* to the possibility of experiencing that openness of Being as a field of dancing energy – as, in a word, *Phusis*. (I think it is worth noting that, in *The Prelude*, Book VIII, line 627, in the 1805–6 version, Wordsworth speaks of the 'pulse of Being.')

Let us keep in mind, here, that Being, experienced as *Logos*, *Legein*, is the In-gathering region of all regions, the encompassing region of Being, which articulates all regions and gathers them into the openness of its embrace.[58] It is 'the original preserving gathering,' a primordial geology that sets in motion the arising, staying, and perishing of all human divisions on the earth. It is that which gathers and, in its very gathering, lets the *truth* of beings come to appearance within its ring of deep entrustment. But the sacred round-dance is *also* a gathering; it too is a *legein*: a collective human enactment, in the sense of a *homologein* which corresponds to, and is appropriate to, the more primordial gathering of the geological *Logos*. If that which we call the 'Logos' is the 'original word' (*Vorwort*) of human speech,[59] then the gathering for the round-dance, as an event which gathers the Fourfold, could perhaps be described as a recollection of the primal taking-place of space: an event taking place in, and taking place as, an *appropriation* of the mortal body in a movement for the sake of the coming-to-presence of truth in its communal ring of protection. The gathering of the round-dance is a recollection and repetition of the primordial geological gathering of Being as such. It is, therefore, an ontological *homologein*: an event (*Ereignis*) through which the human body comes into its own (*eigen*) and finds its place as a body of ontological understanding.

The place is inseparable from the round-dance which takes place there where the place in its disclosedness-of-Being comes-to-be. Preserved in their truth by an etymology which still gathers them into its timely embrace, the words for *round-dance* and *place* keep us appropriately open, as we heed the reminder that it is, in fact, *owing* to the hermeneutical *round-dance* – an event of the highest awareness, gathering the Fourfold into a graceful ring – that a place, as such, is first brought into being. For the round-dance is a gathering which rings off a place, clears a place, a round place of heartfelt enclosure, and places that which it surrounds in the protection (truth) of the taking-to-heart. The human beings whose hearts have gathered them for a round-dance are *mortals* gathering in a sacred ring, inviting the 'gods' to join with them, there in the place at the center of their heart, for a celebration of cosmic order, and a time when earth and sky may come together.

When Heidegger speaks of 'a movement whereby there first comes into the open. . . .'[60] I suggest that we think of the movement which gathers mortals into the sacred round-dance of life. Here we indeed find a movement of thought *appropriate* to the primordial articulation (*legein*) of the *Logos*. For the round-dance clears a place of truth, a place for the disclosure of the ontological difference (*kechōrismenon*) as a decisive appropriation (*Ereignis*) of our bounded world-space:

> The place opens, each time, a region, in that it
> gathers things by their belonging-together with it.
> In the place there plays the gathering in the sense
> of the protective enclosing [*frei-gebenden Bergens*]
> which frees things in their region.[61]

In *Die Kunst und der Raum*, Heidegger honors the work of sculpture, calling it an 'embodiment of the truth of Being.'[62] Can we, however, without depriving our culture's greatest sculpture of its glorious work in the epochal disclosure of Being, somehow find a place in our heart to acknowledge the altogether *special* fittingness of these words with regard to the ecstatic event of dance?

Now the round-dance, as a dance gathering the Fourfold, belongs to what Lawler describes as

> the great group of magic encircling dances in which
> an 'object' is set apart from things of everyday life
> by the living wall of the dancers' bodies, and is
> thereby symbolically consecrated, protected, and
> worshipped.[63]

The 'magic circle', or *mandala*, has of course often appeared, and since time immemorial, wherever the deepest processes of healing have been known to take place. Inscriptions of the circular *mandala* are, as Jung points out,

> instruments of meditation, concentration, and self-

immersion, for the purpose of realizing inner
experience. . . . At the same time, they serve to
produce an inner order. . . . They express the idea
of a safe refuge, of inner reconciliation and
wholeness.[64]

Wosien points out that,

Truth, being beyond sound and rhythm, is the
invisible divine center around which all creation
dances.[65]

But this tells us that, when the healing of the psyche is to
take place in relation to the taking place of truth, it must be
understood that what makes all of this possible is the primordial *ekstasis*, the energy-dance of Being. The energy of this
ekstasis takes over the motility of the ego-logical body-subject
and dissolves all its barriers to the sheer flow of the energy-
fields of Being. The healing transformation is possible only
when the round-dance *turns* the ego's body into a 'synergic
body,'[66] a passionate guardian of the unending vitality of
truth, encircling the hidden treasure of Being, which is the
ecstasy of Being itself, at the very center of its heartfelt dance.

Before we proceed to the last two parts of this chapter, I
would like to summarize, in the form of a table, the interpretation of motility that we have developed thus far. The table
brings together the analyses worked out in Chapter 1 (which
is concerned, first, with the genesis and unfolding of motility
and second, with the hermeneutical character of gesture),
Chapter 5 (which is concerned with the measure and balance
of our stride), and Chapter 6 (which concerns the ground
and our poetizing), as well as Part I of this chapter (which
concerns the place of the round-dance as a topology, geology,
and archaeology of Being). Table 7.1 correlates three stages
in a developing self-understanding with an interpretation of
five modes of articulation (*logos*) in the presencing of Being
(see column 2). Finally, in the third column, the five modes of
articulation are characterized more concretely in experiential
terms, so that the formal, ontological language of the second
column can be understood in reference to the emerging body
of understanding as actually experienced.

TABLE 7.1

Stages of human self-understanding in relation to the Question of Being	A history of the articulations of Being as reconstructed by the ontological self-understanding that inhabits our motility	How we may experience Being in relation to our motility when we have followed a course of ontological recollection and understanding
(1) Prepersonal, pre-egological, pre-ontological understanding of human motility in relation to Being.	(1) *Topo-logy*: Being as the original opening of space.	(1) Being is the original ecstasy of openness, a primordial dance of energy.
	(2) *Geo-logy*: Being as gathering clearing of a field and laying out of a ground.	(2) Being is a center of gathering and a laying-down, clearing a field and preparing a ground for *Dasein*.
(2) Personal, ego-logical, ontical understanding of motility in relation to Being: the preceding stage remains implicit, forgotten, suppressed, concealed. Human motility is (mis)understood in a forgetfulness of Being.	(3) *Patho-logy*: Being as worlding.	(3) Being is in concealment as it makes way for ego-logical centers of motility, which emerge into the clearing from out of the original dance of Being. With the arising of these energy-centers, characteristic patterns begin to take shape and solidify. The centers tend to be moved and motivated by positive and negative emotions, habitual patterns of attraction, aversion, and indifference that determine the character and course of all our motility and activity.
Existential leap: commitment to the path of thinking.	Being as the field of de-cision, as ontological difference.	Being is the call for a reversal of our direction. We reach a turning point as we move on the path.

TABLE 7.1 – continued

(3) Process of authentic appropriation: what takes place when an individual Self is committed to developing a transpersonal, non-ego-logical, deeply ontological understanding of motility, and actually embodying it in his motility. This process calls for a recollection of Being and a retrieval of the implicit understanding given in stage (1).	(4) *Archaeo-logy*: The grounding and gathering of Being, as the articulation (*legein*) of a primordial claim on our body's felt sense of motility.	(4) Being is the energy which surges into the body and passes through it as our motility becomes the hermeneutical medium for an ontological recollection.
	(5) *Homo-logy*: The topology and geology of Being as they give themselves to unconcealment through the *homologein* of human motility.	(5) Through the hermeneutical grace and elegance of our motility, Being as the primordial dance of energy becomes manifest as the origin of our own motility.

Part II

Space

But we still do not know, we who know so much, what 'space as space' really *is*. We do not know, as Heidegger phrases it, 'the ownmost character' ('das Eigentümliche') of space.[67] Thus he initiates, in *Die Kunst und der Raum*, a fundamental critical questioning of our experience of space:

> But can the physical-technical projection of space,
> whatever its further determination may be, hold
> its own as the only true space? When compared
> with it are all spaces otherwise structured . . . only
> subjectively determined primitive forms and
> transformations. . . ?[68]

338

The deepest significance of this questioning is perhaps stated most forcefully, however, in 'The Turning,' where Heidegger contends that,

> modern man must first and above all find his way back into the full breadth of the space proper to his essence. That essential space of man's essential being receives the dimension that unites it to something beyond itself – solely from out of the conjoining relation that is the way in which the safekeeping of Being itself is given to belong to the essence of man as the one who is needed and used by Being. Unless man first establishes himself beforehand in the space proper to his essence and there takes up his dwelling, he will not be capable of anything essential within the destining now holding sway.[69]

The modern experience of space has been pervasively shaped by the will to power. Both the space we customarily live in and the Newtonian space which corresponds to our scientific, technological projection have been organized around the linearity of goal-directed, object-oriented activity: actions motivated by institutionalized acquisitiveness and possess-iveness, alienated modes of productivity, strategies of mastery and domination, and an aggressively calculative rationality. I would like to suggest that, from out of the hermeneutical spirit of the round-dance, a motility-body of ontological understanding eventually might emerge, and that this spirit could gather us most poetically into a new history of dwelling. By grace of our participation in the round-dance of Being, we are gathered into the freedom of a planetary dwelling-space *unknown* to objective science. And this takes place because we have let ourselves be gathered into a synergic field, gathered as centers of ecstatic awareness, centers themselves gathered in a round – to protect the orig-inal gift ('Es gibt'), the most central event (*Ereignis*): the gath-ering and centering of energy as the spatializing of Being as such.

A good place to continue our ruminations might be found, I think, in a passage from Merleau–Ponty's *Phenomenology of Perception*, where he describes the character of geometrical space:

> The notion of geometrical space, indifferent to its
> contents, that of a pure movement which does not
> by itself affect the properties of the object, provided
> phenomena with a setting of inert existence in
> which each event could be related to physical
> conditions responsible for the changes occurring,
> and therefore contributed to this freezing of being
> which appeared to be the task of physics.[70]

We are now realizing that the space of Euclidean geometry,
the space which has been so hospitable to Newtonian
physics, the present-day theory of physiology, and our entire
modern technology of building and producing, is after all
only *one* modulation of space among *many other* equally
coherent, equally possible formations. And we are beginning
to understand how the homogeneous world-space of
Newtonian physics necessitates a freezing of being, a solid-
ifying of boundaries, a condensing of energies. This world-
space favors an ontology of objectification, permanence,
constant positions, egocentricity. Despite our essential open-
ness-of-being (*Dasein*), this world space (de)posits us in thing-
like positions and locations. In order to challenge this representation of our spatiality, Heidegger writes, in 'Building
Dwelling Thinking,' that,

> we always go through spaces in such a way that we
> already experience them by staying constantly
> with near and remote locations and things. When I
> go toward the door of the lecture hall, I am already
> there, and I could not go to it at all if I were not
> such that I am there. I am never here only, as this
> encapsulated body; rather, I am there, that is, I
> already pervade the room, and only thus can I go
> through it.[71]

Merleau–Ponty's unfolding of our most deeply enfolded
experience of spatiality, and especially that unfolding of our
experience of *motility* through which he guides us in his
Phenomenology of Perception, fully accords with Heidegger's
description, and furthermore fleshes it out. As
Merleau–Ponty says in 'Eye and Mind,'

> We must take literally what vision teaches us:
> namely that through it we come into contact with

the sun and the stars, that we are everywhere all at once.[72]

When we get deeply in touch with our bodily felt sense of *motility*, when we can feel the *depth* of its melodic arc (*archē*), we will find ourselves suddenly *released* into a space of tremendous energy, a space of much greater openness, greater richness, and greater emotional hospitality, than our customary experience, to whose claustrophobia we tend to become habituated, would ever give us reason to believe possible.

There is a *binding* of energy, a confining and closing off which tends to take place with the emergence of the willful ego and its establishment, in adulthood, at the very center of our everyday experience of being-a-bodily-being-in-space, and which is not only parallel to, but actually in some complicated ways interdependent with, the *representational* confining and closing off which tends to take place where physical theory of space intersects with our lived experience of an *ego-logically constituted* space. Marvin Casper's discussion of 'Space Therapy and the Maitri Project' will perhaps be useful for our focus. (The Maitri Project, unfortunately no longer in operation, attempted to help severely neurotic patients by taking them, over a span of many days, and sometimes weeks, through a specially designed sequence of 'rooms,' each one shaped and colored to provide a very specific experience of space and make room for the most urgent transformations in space awareness. Supporting this therapy is the theory that neurosis and health are ways of being-bodily-in-space, and that carefully structured spaces can therefore intervene with salutary effect in the spatialization of certain forms of neurosis.) Casper, a clinical psychologist, points out that,

> the basis of neurosis is the tendency to solidify
> energy into a barrier that separates space into two
> [solid, opposing, and even conflicted] entities, 'I'
> and 'Other', the space in here and the space out
> there. This process is technically termed 'dualistic
> fixation'. First there is the initial creation of the
> barrier, the sensing of other, and then the inference
> of inner, or I. This is the birth of the ego. We
> identify with what is here and struggle to relate to
> what is out there.[73]

341

The emergence of the ego-subject and the taking shape of an ego-logical space of embodiment are not only simultaneous; they are, as we discover, two processes which are deeply interdependent and essentially inseparable. But the story Casper has to tell is not yet over. He continues:

> After the initial creation of I and Other, I *feels* the territory outside itself, determining if it is threatening, attractive, or uninteresting. *Feeling* the environment is followed by: impulsive action-passion, aggression, or ignoring – pulling in what is seductive, pushing away what is threatening or repelling, ignoring what is uninteresting or irritating. But feeling and impulsive action are crude ways of defending and enhancing ego. The next level, [or phase of] response is conceptual discrimination, fitting phenomena into categories, which makes the world much more manageable and intelligible.

So much for the basic psychogenesis. Now we reach the point where phenomenological description cannot be clearly separated from clinical diagnosis. According to Casper,

> The degree of neurosis and suffering that a person experiences is related to the amount of 'inner' space and clarity which are available to him. If a person feels that his 'inner' resources for coping with and appreciating life are very limited, then the world outside seems highly alien, seductive, and threatening. He feels compelled to struggle to remove threats and draw in what is valuable.

But, as he accurately observes,

> the struggle is self-defeating. It intensifies the solidity of the barrier and results in feelings of inner poverty and restricted space.

By the same token,

> to a highly neurotic person, the outer world is extremely claustrophobic and confusing.

Psychic pathology is always played out, always mirrored, in the agonies of space. But space is social as well as personal and, indeed, social space precedes all personally individuated spaces. For this reason, though, it becomes possible to alleviate psychic distress, distress in our 'inner space', by changing the qualitative character of our socially organized 'external space.'

Casper's diagnosis calls for thought. What if we are all, as adults, in the ego-logical stage of maturity, somewhat 'pathologized' by neurotic structures of anxiety and defense? What if the protective structuring necessary for the formation of the adult ego-subject retains, as a tendency, the impulse to solidify, objectify, partition, and fixate *beyond* the stage – or degree – where such defenses are actually needed for survival or growth? Even Freud, who could not conceive, or could not relinquish, an ego-centric psychology, had to acknowledge that the ego, being *born* in a condition of anxiety, serves to *perpetuate* the anxiety of its origins in defensive and aggressive behaviors. For our purposes, then, pathology (neurosis) might be defined as 'getting stuck' in a space which is frozen into a dualistically polarized, and hence deeply *conflicted*, structure that is inimical to change, growth and, in general, a meaningful creative existence.

What Casper's diagnosis suggests is that, insofar as we human beings cannot altogether transcend the suffering of neurosis, the suffering peculiar to the corporeal nature of the stabilized ego-subject, our lived space will be shaped and warped, narrowed and tightened, in relation to that neurosis. And, since the most fundamental neurosis, the pathology through which we must all pass, is intimately bound up with the maintenance of an ego-centric framework of representing and experiencing, the pathological character towards which our being-in-space inherently tends must be understood as implicating an ego-centric and ego-logical body-subject – an ego-determined way of being embodied in space, spatialized in existence.

If it is the case that a certain pathologizing tendency *does* characteristically structure our everyday experiencing of this space of embodiment, we might begin to consider the possibility that there is some deeply significant connection between (i) our tendency to structure the space we bodily live in – our 'psychological space,' you might say – through various projections, centerings and encirclements of a neurotic nature, and (ii) our participation in the emergence of the objective space of classical physics. The objective, uniform, causally determined technical space of Newtonian physics, together with its Euclidean geometry of straight lines, rigid planes and solid masses, must really be understood as emerging and developing on the basis of our *everyday* experiencing of space: it arises as a *transformation* of this anterior experiencing, this synergic spatialization which we *are*. What this implies, however, is that, in our relation to Euclidean-Newtonian physical space, there will be, in addition to its fruits, its benefits, at least a *tendency* for that space also to express, to reflect, and even to exacerbate the ego-logical, ego-centric process of 'dualistic fixation': the process of polarizing space and reifying what is polarized into opposites inflexibly opposed not only to one another, but also to salutary changes. Such fixation is *already inherent* in the everyday experience of being-in-space, and of space as such.

Although science and its technology are certainly *not* essentially pathological in their origin and their intent, and certainly *no more* essentially, or inevitably, pathological than the ego itself, it is nevertheless true that the objective space of classical physics cannot escape its origin in the ego-logically constituted social space of normal, i.e., ego-centric, adult experience. So that, insofar as the ego-logical body-subject tends to stabilize, in adulthood, in a structuring of lived social space which gets stuck in manifestations of the ego's round of anxieties, defensiveness and projections, the kind of objectification which is essential to the space of classical science *will* tend to perpetuate, and *may* even intensify, certain latent characteristics of our everyday experience which are rooted in the neurotic dispositionality of ego-centric embodiment. In other words, the pathological tendency always already inherent in the ego-logically constituted space of everyday mundane existence – the tendency towards objective fixation, restriction, and polarization – readily 'couples' with a parallel tendency inherent in the physical space of classical science, so that, in the end, they reflect and mutually reinforce one another.

Consider, once again, a uniform, homogeneous space (space as represented in Euclidean geometry and Newtonian physics): a static space of solid, theoretically impermeable masses, rigid planes, fixed boundaries, straight and inflexible lines, and minimal qualitative differentiation. Is it not evident that the totalizing grid of this space matches up in a certain natural way with the 'rigid personality' of the ego-logical, ego-centric character? Is it not characteristic of the ego-logical structuring to endeavor, as much as possible, to get things straight, to put things in their proper place, to pin down, to make secure, and place under a standardizing control? And are we not prone, all of us, to habitualities which standardize, routinize and stereotype what the generosity of space gives us, from out of its unfathomable richness, to encounter? In part, it is the objectivating capacity behind these tendencies (by no means entirely undesirable) which *makes possible* the constitution of an objective physical space. But, once we are living in a space shaped and influenced by our involvement in the spatial dimension constituted through normal science, certain latent propensities in the adult's ego-centric spatiality, some of which are not altogether wholesome, are encouraged to manifest their power.

Here we might ponder, for example, the ways in which the uniformity of physical space introduces into our life-world certain pressures to conform and standardize; and how the spatialization into which technology inserts us intensifies the problem we confront, as individuals, in getting in touch with our felt sense (a global, physiognomic, holistic sense) of bodily-being-in-the-world. The local polarization of subject and object into which the everyday (mundane) space-experience of the adult ego tends to fall has given birth to a science and a technology of space – a building and dwelling – which not only reflect this polarization in another existential dimension, but also even strengthen its hold. We even begin to experience our own bodies as mere 'furniture,' mere objects *in* space; we lose touch with our *experience* of embodiment as a dynamic 'synergic' process, a perpetual *ek-stasis*, situated in being in a way that could not be more *unlike* that of the physical thing. (The 'thing,' too, of course, which for Heidegger is a center for the gathering of the Fourfold, also gets distorted and, as it were, 'injured' through the reification and ontological indifference of its surrounding space.)

According to my interpretation, Heidegger is arguing that human beings tend to live, for the most part, in a space whose potential openness, implicit richness, and beauty, too, they cannot easily feel – a space which, in that sense and to that degree, has taken shape as a reflection and expression, a mirroring, of a fundamental ontological tendency to project our ego-centered social pathology, and to suppress, or anyway leave undeveloped, that other, equally inherent – but much weaker – tendency, which is our capacity to *continue* opening and expanding and deepening our experience of Being as a whole, once the ego has presided over our survival into the social world of the adult existence.

The homogeneity of Newtonian space certainly does authorize a conception of the ideal observer which puts us everywhere at once, and in this sense breaks down our defensive egocentricity. But the fact of the matter is that the very same properties of space also conspire to deny us any *affective contact* with things. Out of our indifference to the ontological difference, the space of Being as such, we have spatialized the world of our dwelling in a space that is indifferent to our deepest needs and concerns. Our entanglement with the objective space of classical physics has in fact *encouraged* us to deny, to forget, or to devalue our pre-ontological, bodily felt sense of the intrinsic richness, meaningfulness, and openness of our space for living. Who can dispute the fact that the sway of this conception has made it considerably more difficult for us to experience the receptivity of our space to the healthy emotional needs, feelings and concerns that would most fulfill us as human beings? We have expanded our civilization into the envelope of outer space; yet we cannot make room, here on earth, for people very different from ourselves. We control a far reach of space; yet we still have no resting place, no near abode, for the weary and desperate soul. We 'contact' the most distant stars, but do so in a space without any room for deeply meaningful feeling, since the spatial uniformity which makes such contact possible derives from a theoretical framework that *requires* the relinquishing of qualitative, bodily felt experience.

The round-dance is healing not only because its *ekstasis* breaks down the defensive rigidity of our culturally acquired ego-body, but because, in so doing, it awakens our ontologically most primordial body – 'my synergic body,' as Merleau–Ponty would say. In the *ekstasis* of the round-dance, therefore, we are opened to a space whose dimensionality can be experienced in relation to the 'energy' of Being (*Physis*) as a whole.

In *The Will to Power as Art*, the first volume of his work on Nietzsche, Heidegger attempts to articulate his sense of the ontological dimension into which what he calls 'rapture' (*Rausch*) opens us:

Rapture is feeling, an embodying attunement, an

346

embodied being that is contained in attunement,
attunement woven into embodiment. But
attunement lays *Dasein* open as an enhancing, and
conducts it into the plenitude of its capacities, which
mutually arouse one another and foster
enhancement.[74]

Rapture, then, is 'a mode of the embodying, attuned stance
towards beings as whole. . . .'[75] It is unfortunate that, in his
dialogue with Nietzsche, Heidegger did not think to interpret
that 'rapture,' a bringing-forth of Being, in relation to the
gathering circle of the communal round-dance.

Dance is the original geo-graphy of our placement on earth,
the original geo-metry of ontological space. In the synergic
rapture of the round-dance, the gift of a *sacred* place is gathered into the hermeneutic circle of human awareness, gathered out of the sheer openness of space. And it will be,
therefore, by way of the round-dance, the round-dance of
archaic thought, that we shall finally retrieve the lost gift of
sacred space; for, as Heidegger says,

> Profane spaces are always the *privation* of sacred
> spaces often lying far back.[76]

The round-dance is an enactment of our pre-ontological
understanding: our most radical knowledge of sacred space
and the geology of Being. It is our decisive initiation into the
wholesome space of the ontological difference. It is our
release from ego-centricity, and our experiencing of a
synergic, trans-personal center of meaning. It is the ecstasy
of our synergic body, our openness to the primordial space of
Being as a whole, endlessly gathering beings into its original
clearing and dispersing its unreckonable gifts in a mirror-
play of dancing, spinning, circling energies. The round-dance
is the taking-place of our pre-ontological awareness of Being;
it is our way of acknowledging that we are transitory dances
of energy, briefly gathered for a moment of disclosure. The
round-dance is the hermeneutical enactment of our In-gathering, our recollection in the history of Being.

Merleau–Ponty argues, in his *Phenomenology of Perception*,
that,

> As far as bodily space is concerned, it is clear that
> there is a [prepersonal, bodily carried] knowledge

347

of place which is reducible to a sort of co-existence [i.e., attunement] with that place, and which is not simply nothing, even though it cannot be conveyed in the form of a description or even pointed out without a word being spoken.[77]

There is a prepersonal, 'unconscious' understanding of place, and it is this understanding, borne by the 'phenomenal body', which is claimed by, and accordingly recognizes, the sacredness and enchantment of its ontological origin. The 'origin' of our places is to be found or retrieved in the round-dance of Being, in an ekstatic dance of primordial energies gathering themselves into a ring of hermeneutical disclosure. This gathering is at the same time the event (*Ereignis*) of clearing that gives us mortals an abiding place in the world for our time of dwelling.

What Heidegger does not acknowledge, though, is the fact that this history of sacred and profane spaces is correlated with another history: a history of the human body as species and individual. For there is an implicit understanding of the sacredness of space that is carried by the ancient ancestral body which always still lives within us, even when we are deprived of any genuine understanding, and which is always most in evidence in the *child*'s primordial experience of space. It is easier for the child to experience a space as a place of enchantment, because he naturally inhabits it with a kind of openness that makes him exceptionally attuned to the full dimensionality of his places, more unselfconsciously responsive to the transformations of mood taking place in his surroundings, and more receptive than most adults to the very fact, the ontological gift, of presencing as such.

In 'The End of Philosophy and the Task of Thinking,' Heidegger allows himself to dream. His thinking dances, moved to speak out, but with a message of restrained hope:

> we may suggest that the day will come when we will not shun the question whether the opening [*Lichtung*], the free open, may not be that within which alone pure space and ecstatic time, and everything present and absent within them, have the place which gathers and protects everything.[78]

I doubt that we have answered the poet's question – the one with which we opened our thinking, in this study, to the spirit of dance. And I am sure that, although we have not shunned the question which concerns the opening, we have not yet responded adequately to its entrustment of wisdom – a wisdom, really, that is ultimately *beyond* the categorial duality of hope and despair. But perhaps, if our bearing can become, in time, more thoughtful, our gestures more obedient to the compassion which calls them forth, and our walking more open to feeling the support of the earth and taking its measure in our stride, we may be blessed, eventually, with answers that only our 'phenomenal' body, moved by its ancient and irrepressible dream to make every single movement a celebration of Being, could ever give us to understand.

Part III
Resting

In *De partibus animalium*, Aristotle notes that 'man alone of all animals stands erect.' To this, however, he immediately adds his recognition of our corresponding vulnerability, that ontological limitation by which our noble stature is ultimately measured:

> But to man it is no easy task to remain for any
> length of time on his feet, his body demanding
> rest in a sitting position.[79]

Perhaps, if we have found some measure of inspiration in the round-dance of our thought, and have let the dance gather us into the measured breathing of the *Logos*, and have let it release us into a more expansively felt, more ecstatic space of openness-to-Being, we will want to share what we have learned, sitting together on the ground of our present understanding, sitting together and sitting apart, sitting with the process of learning, sitting well-grounded in the aliveness of our deepening repose.

Notes

Preface

1 Sigmund Freud, *Civilization and Its Discontents*, trans. Joan Riviere (New York: W. W. Norton, 1962), p. 105.
2 Martin Heidegger, 'Zur Seinsfrage,' in *Wegmarken*, 'Gesamtausgabe', Bd. 9 (Frankfurt am Main: Vittorio Klostermann, 1976), p. 215.
3 Heidegger, 'Metaphysics as History of Being,' in *The End of Philosophy*, trans. and ed Joan Stambaugh (New York: Harper & Row, 1973), pp. 14–15.
4 Heidegger, 'The Age of the World Picture,' in *The Question Concerning Technology and Other Essays*, trans. and ed William Lovitt (New York: Harper & Row, 1977), p. 136.
5 Heidegger, *An Introduction to Metaphysics*, trans. Ralph Manheim (New York: Doubleday, 1961), p. 32.
6 Carl C. Jung, *Psychological Reflections: A New Anthology of His Writings, 1905–1961*, trans. and ed Jolande Jacobi and R. F. C. Hall (New York: Pantheon Books, 1945), p. 277.
7 Heidegger, *Being and Time*, trans. John Macquarrie and Edward Robinson (New York: Harper & Row, 1962), Part II, ch. 3, sect. 64, p. 357.
8 *Ibid.*, p. 276.
9 *Ibid.*, p. 233.
10 Heidegger, 'Hölderlin und das Wesen der Dichtung,' in *Erläuterungen zu Hölderlins Dichtung* (Frankfurt am Main: Vittorio Klostermann, 1971), p. 36.
11 Heidegger, *Being and Time*, p. 167.
12 Heidegger, *ibid.*, p. 184.
13 Heidegger, 'Introduction,' *The Basic Problems of Phenomenology*, trans. Albert Hofstadter (Bloomington: Indiana University Press, 1982), p. 20.
14 John Dewey, *Democracy and Education* (New York: Macmillan, The Free Press edn, 1966), p. 123.
15 Heidegger, *What Is Called Thinking?*, trans. J. Glenn Gray and Fred Wieck (New York: Harper & Row, 1968), p. 78.
16 Heidegger, *An Introduction to Metaphysics*, p. 142.

17 Albert Hofstadter, 'Translator's Introduction' to Martin Heidegger, *The Basic Problems of Phenomenology*, p. xxiv.
18 *Ibid.*
19 Heidegger, *What Is Called Thinking?* p. 89.
20 Hofstadter, 'Translator's Introduction,' *op. cit.*, p. xxiii.
21 Heidegger, *Being and Time*, p. 61.
22 *Ibid.*
23 *Ibid.*, p. 60.
24 *Ibid.*, p. 58.
25 *Ibid.*, p. 56.
26 *Ibid.*, p. 179.
27 *Ibid.*, p. 59.
28 *Ibid.*, pp. 61–2.
29 Heidegger, *The Basic Problems of Phenomenology*, Sec. 22, p. 328.
30 *Ibid.*
31 Medard Boss, 'Martin Heideggers Zollikon Seminars,' *Erinnerung an Martin Heidegger* (Pfullingen: Gunther Neske, 1977), pp. 31–45. Translated by Brian Kenny and reprinted in *The Review of Existential Psychology and Psychiatry*, vol. XVI, nos 1–3 (1978–9), p. 7.
32 Heidegger, *What Is Called Thinking?* p. 14.
33 Heidegger, 'The Age of the World Picture,' Appendix 10, in *The Question Concerning Technology and Other Essays*, p. 153.
34 Heidegger, 'Recollection in Metaphysics,' in *The End of Philosophy*, p. 82. Italics added.
35 Heidegger, *Nihilism*, 'Nietzsche,' vol. 4, trans. David Farrell Krell (New York: Harper & Row, 1982), pp. 139–40.
36 *Ibid.*, p. 140.
37 *Ibid.*, p. 141.
38 Heidegger, 'Introduction,' *The Basic Problems of Phenomenology*, Section 5, p. 19.
39 Heidegger, 'The Age of the World Picture,' in *The Question Concerning Technology and Other Essays*, p. 154.
40 See Joan Stambaugh's 'Introduction' in Martin Heidegger, *The End of Philosophy*, p. xi.
41 Heidegger, 'The Question Concerning Technology,' in *The Question Concerning Technology and Other Essays*, p. 3.
42 Friedrich Nietzsche, *The Will to Power*, ed Walter Kaufmann, trans. Walter Kaufmann and R. J. Hollingdale (New York: Random House, 1968), Book II, Note 455, p. 249.
43 *Ibid.*, Book II, Note 418, pp. 224–5.
44 Harry Stack Sullivan, *The Interpersonal Theory of Psychiatry* (New York: W. W. Norton, 1953), p. 193.
45 Heidegger, 'The Question Concerning Technology,' *The Question Concerning Technology and Other Essays*, p. 3.
46 *Ibid.*, p. 6.
47 Heidegger, 'Nihilism and the History of Being,' *Nihilism*, 'Nietzsche', vol. 4, p. 233.

48 Heidegger, *The Will to Power as Art*, 'Nietzsche,' vol. 1, trans. David Farrell Krell (New York: Harper & Row, 1979), p. 112.

Introduction

1 Richard Ellman, *Yeats: The Man and the Masks* (New York: W. W. Norton, 1978), p. 289.
2 Richard Rorty, *Philosophy and the Mirror of Nature* (Princeton: Princeton University Press, 1979), p. 239.
3 Gershom Scholem, *On the Kabbalah and its Symbolism* (New York: Schocken, 1969), p. 116.
4 See Philip Wheelwright, *The Pre-Socratics* (New York: Odyssey Press, 1966), p. 70.
5 See Erich Fromm, *Marx's Concept of Man*, with a translation from Marx's *Economic and Philosophical Manuscripts* by T. B. Bottomore (New York: Frederick Ungar, 1961), p. 134.
6 *Ibid.*
7 *Ibid.*
8 *Ibid.*, p. 135.
9 *Ibid.*
10 Heidegger, *Being and Time*, p. 277.
11 Maurice Merleau–Ponty, 'The Intertwining – The Chiasm,' *The Visible and the Invisible*, ed Claude Lefort, trans. Alphonso Lingis (Evanston: Northwestern University Press, 1969), p. 155.
12 Nietzsche, *The Will to Power*, Book II, Note 419, pp. 225–6. Also see Book II, Note 195, p. 115 and Note 437, p. 240, and Book III, Note 674, p. 355.
13 *Ibid.*, Book III, Note 489, p. 270. Also see Note 492, p. 271.
14 *Ibid.*, Book II, Note 255, p. 148.
15 *Ibid.*, Book II, Note 314, p. 173.
16 See, e.g., *ibid.*, Book III, Note 665, p. 350 and Note 674, p. 355.
17 See *ibid.*, Book III, Note 532, p. 289.
18 See *ibid.*, Book III, Notes 489–92, pp. 270–1; Note 518, p. 281; and Note 549, pp. 294–5.
19 *Ibid.*, Book I, Note 115, p. 70.
20 *Ibid.*, Book I, Note 118, p. 72.
21 *Ibid.*, Book I, Note 117, p. 72. Also see Book II, Notes 226–7, p. 131.
22 Nietzsche, *Joyful Wisdom*, trans. Thomas Common (New York: Frederick Ungar, 1960), Book V, Note 322, p. 351.
23 Nietzsche, *The Will to Power*, Book IV, Note 105, p. 540. Also see Note 419.
24 See *The Dialogues of Plato*, vol. I, trans. Benjamin Jowett (New York: Random House, 1937), pp. 6–7. Also see *Phaedrus* 270, p. 273: 'Hippocrates the Asclepiad says that the nature even of the body can be understood only as a whole.'
25 Nietzsche, *The Will to Power*, Book III, Note 674, p. 355.

26 *Ibid.*, Book III, Note 659, p. 347.
27 *Ibid.*, Book IV, Note 1045, p. 537.
28 *Ibid.*, Book III, Note 676, pp. 357–8.
29 *Ibid.*
30 *Ibid.*, Book IV, Note 1046, p. 538.
31 *Ibid.*, Book IV, Note 1051, p. 540.
32 *Ibid.* Also see Book I, Note 196, pp. 115–16, where Nietzsche attacks the Judaeo-Christian tradition: 'instead of the deification of man, his undeification,' and a course of history which discloses our 'deepest self-contempt.'
33 *Ibid.*, Book III, Note 820, p. 434.
34 Nietzsche, *Joyful Wisdom*, Book III, Note 110, p. 156.
35 Heidegger, *Being and Time*, Part I, ch. III, sect. 23. p. 143.
36 *Ibid.*, ch. III, p. 138.
37 *Ibid.*, Part II, ch. IV, p. 419.
38 Heidegger, 'What Are Poets For?' in *Poetry, Language, Thought*, trans. Albert Hofstadter (New York: Harper & Row, 1975), p. 138.
39 Heidegger, 'Building Dwelling Thinking,' in *Poetry, Language, Thought*, p. 157.
40 Heidegger, 'Letter on Humanism,' *Basic Writings*, ed David Farrell Krell (New York: Harper & Row, 1977), p. 204. Also see pp. 202–3.
41 Heidegger, *What Is Called Thinking?* p. 58.
42 *Ibid.*, p. 68.
43 Heidegger, *Nihilism*, 'Nietzsche', vol. 4, pp. 139–41.
44 *Ibid.*
45 *Ibid.*, p. 10.
46 Heidegger, 'What Are Poets For?' *Poetry, Language, Thought*, p. 134.
47 *Ibid.*, p. 135.
48 Eugen Fink and Martin Heidegger, *Heraclitus Seminar, 1966/1967*, trans. Charles H. Seibert (University, Alabama: University of Alabama Press, 1979), p. 144.
49 *Ibid.*, p. 145.
50 See Erich Neumann, *The Child: Structure and Dynamics of the Nascent Personality*, trans. Ralph Manheim (New York: Harper & Row, 1976), pp. 124–8 for a discussion of body, darkness, ground and earth. Also see p. 145 for a discussion of vegetative symbolism (e.g., rooting) in relation to the child's first phase of life.
51 Fink and Heidegger, *Heraclitus Seminar*, p. 146.
52 *Ibid.*
53 Heidegger, *The Will to Power as Art*, 'Nietzsche', vol. 1, p. 209.
54 *Ibid.*, p. 99.
55 *Ibid.*
56 *Ibid.*, pp. 99–100.
57 *Ibid.*, pp. 98–9.
58 *Ibid.*
59 Heidegger, *Nihilism*, 'Nietzsche', vol. 4, p. 218.
60 Heidegger, *The Will to Power as Art*, 'Nietzsche', vol. 1, p. 100.
61 *Ibid.*, p. 105.

62 Heidegger, *Being and Time*, p. 179.
63 Heidegger, *The Will to Power as Art*, 'Nietzsche', vol. 1, pp. 98–100.
64 Medard Boss, *Existential Foundations of Medicine and Psychology*, trans. Stephen Conway and Ann Cleaves (New York: Jason Aronson, 1979), p. 110.
65 Nietzsche, *The Will to Power*, Book III, Note 676, pp. 357–8.
66 George Santayana, *Platonism and the Spiritual Life* (New York: Harper & Row, 1957), p. 260.
67 Heidegger, *Nihilism*, 'Nietzsche', vol. 4, p. 140.
68 Nietzsche, *The Will to Power*, Book II, Note 461, p. 253.
69 Scholem, *On the Kabbalah and its Symbolism*, p. 116.
70 See Heidegger, *Heraklit*, Bd. 55, 'Gesamtausgabe,' II Abteilung, *Vorlesungen 1923–1924*, ed Manfred Frings (Frankfurt am Main: Vittorio Klostermann, 1979), p. 130.
71 Nietzsche, *The Will to Power*, Book IV, Note 1021, p. 528. Also see Erich Neumann, *The Child: Structure and Dynamics of the Nascent Personality*, pp. 125–9, for a discussion of the traditional Western attitude toward the flesh of the body, especially the *lower* body, and for Neumann's analysis of the concomitant stage of its polarization into 'upper' and 'lower,' 'above' and 'below,' 'clean' and 'unclean,' especially in relation to the *positive* valorization of the head-pole, the *negative* valorization of the anal-pole, and in relation to the earth and the sky, and the transition from the matriarchal to the patriarchal archetypes. Also see Neumann's *The Origins and History of Consciousness*, trans. R. F. C. Hull (Princeton: Princeton University Press, Bollingen Series XLII, 1970), p. 310. Neumann attempts to demonstrate – with success, in my opinion – that aversion for the body and mortification of the flesh are directly related to the rule of the patriarchy (the rule of the masculine ego) and the suppression of the feminine principle. (The body, especially the body of infant and child, is always primarily in the care of the matriarchy.)
72 Nietzsche, *The Will to Power*, Book IV, Note 1021, p. 528.
73 *Ibid.*, Book II, Note 461, p. 253.
74 *Ibid.* Also see Book II, Notes 407–8, p. 220.
75 Max Scheler, 'Das Ressentiment im Aufbau der Moralen,' *Vom Umsturz der Werte: Abhandlungen und Aufsätze*, ed Maria Scheler (Bern: A. Francke Verlag, 4th edn, 1955), pp. 87–8.
76 Carl G. Jung, 'The Spiritual Problems of Modern Man,' *Civilization in Transition*, 'Collected Works,' vol. 10, trans. R. F. C. Hull (Princeton: Princeton University Press, Bollingen Series XX, 1964), para. 195, p. 94.
77 *Ibid.*
78 *Ibid.*
79 *Ibid.*
80 *Ibid.*
81 See, for example, Erich Neumann's work on *The Child: Structure and Dynamics of the Nascent Personality*, esp. pp. 125–9.
82 Nietzsche, *The Will to Power*, Book III, Note 674, p. 355.

83 *Ibid.*, Book IV, Note 1046, p. 538.
84 Samuel B. Mallin, *Merleau–Ponty's Philosophy* (New Haven: Yale University Press, 1979), p. 31.
85 Maurice Merleau–Ponty, *Phenomenology of Perception*, trans. Colin Smith (London: Routledge & Kegan Paul, 1962), p. 351. Italics added.
86 *Ibid.*, p. 350.
87 *Ibid.* Italics added.
88 Merleau–Ponty, 'The Intertwining – The Chiasm,' *The Visible and the Invisible*, p. 155.
89 Merleau–Ponty, *Phenomenology of Perception*, p. 215.
90 Merleau–Ponty, 'The Intertwining – The Chiasm,' *The Visible and the Invisible*, pp. 139, 146.
91 *Ibid.*, p. 146.
92 *Ibid.*, p. 147.
93 *Ibid.*, p. 123.
94 *Ibid.*, p. 147.
95 *Ibid.*, p. 153–4.
96 *Ibid.*, p. 148. Also see his 'Working Notes' (January 1959), p. 168, where he refers to the 'spiritual' aspect of the body.
97 Merleau–Ponty, 'The Intertwining – The Chiasm,' *The Visible and the Invisible*, p. 136.
98 Walter Pater, *Marius the Epicurean* (London: Macmillan, 1907), vol. I, p. 146.
99 Merleau–Ponty, 'The Intertwining – The Chiasm,' *The Visible and the Invisible*, p. 248.
100 *Ibid.*, p. 147. Anaximenes says: 'As our souls, being air, hold us together, so breath and air embrace the entire universe.' See Philip Wheelwright, *The Pre-Socratics* (New York: Odyssey Press, 1966), p. 60.
101 Merleau–Ponty, 'The Intertwining – The Chiasm,' *The Visible and the Invisible*, p. 139.
102 The two main texts of importance for a theory of the body politic are 'The Intertwining – The Chiasm' and 'The Child's Relations with Others,' trans. William Cobb, in *The Primacy of Perception*, ed James M. Edie (Evanston: Northwestern University Press, 1964).
103 Heidegger, 'The Word of Nietzsche: God is dead,' *The Question Concerning Technology and Other Essays*, p. 112.
104 Heidegger, *An Introduction to Metaphysics*, p. 32.
105 *Ibid.*, p. 31.
106 *Ibid.*, p. 37. See John Dewey, *Democracy in Education* (New York: Macmillan, The Free Press edn, 1966), for a discussion of our tendency to turn education into forms of training and drill.
107 Heidegger, *An Introduction to Metaphysics*, p. 37.
108 Heidegger, 'Metaphysics as History of Being,' *The End of Philosophy*, pp. 14–15.
109 Heidegger, 'The Age of the World Picture,' *The Question Concerning Technology and Other Essays*, p. 142.
110 Heidegger, 'Letter on Humanism,' *Basic Writings*, p. 230.

111 Fink and Heidegger, *The Heraclitus Seminar*, Eleventh Session, p. 126.
112 Heidegger, 'Letter on Humanism,' *Basic Writings*, p. 230.
113 Heidegger, *An Introduction to Metaphysics*, p. 130.
114 See Heidegger, *Being and Time*, p. 191 and 'The Word of Nietzsche,' *The Question Concerning Technology and Other Essays*, p. 56.
115 Søren Kierkegaard, *Repetition*, trans. Walter Lowrie (Princeton: Princeton University Press, 1946), p. 12.
116 Nietzsche, *The Will to Power*, Book III, Note 812, p. 430.
117 Heidegger, 'Nietzsche's Overturning of Platonism,' *The Will to Power as Art*, 'Nietzsche', vol. 1, p. 203.
118 Heidegger, *Being and Time*, Part II, ch. V, sect. 74, p. 437.
119 See Heidegger, *An Introduction to Metaphysics*, pp. 135–42, 147–8.
120 Barrington Moore, Jr, *Reflections on the Causes of Human Misery and upon Certain Proposals to Eliminate Them* (Boston: Beacon Press, 1969), pp. 1–2.
121 See Herbert Marcuse's 'Preface,' in *Eros and Civilization: A Philosophical Inquiry into Freud* (Boston: Beacon Press, 1962), where he connects psychological thinking with political awareness.
122 Fink and Heidegger, *Heraclitus Seminar*, p. 160.
123 Nietzsche, *Human, All Too Human*, trans. H. Zimmer and Paul Cohn, in *The Complete Works of Friedrich Nietzsche*, vol. 6, ed Oscar Levy (New York: Macmillan, 1909–11; reissued by Russell & Russell, 1964), Note 153.
124 Heidegger, *Being and Time*, p. 422.
125 Heidegger, *Nihilism*, 'Nietzsche', vol. 4, p. 229.
126 Heidegger, *What Is Called Thinking?* p. 180.
127 Heidegger, 'The End of Philosophy and the Task of Thinking,' *Basic Writings*, p. 387.
128 Heidegger, 'Overcoming Metaphysics,' *The End of Philosophy*, p. 110.
129 *Ibid*.
130 See Andrew T. Scull, *Decarceration: Community Treatment and the Deviant: A Radical View* (Englewood Cliffs, New Jersey: Prentice–Hall, 1977), pp. 15–40.
131 Heidegger, 'Overcoming Metaphysics,' *The End of Philosophy*, p. 110.
132 Heidegger, *What Is Called Thinking?* p. 84.
133 Heidegger, 'Recollection in Metaphysics,' *The End of Philosophy*, p. 91.
134 Heidegger, 'Language,' *Poetry, Language, Thought*, p. 205. Also see his *Erläuterungen zu Hölderlins Dichtung* (Frankfurt am Main: Vittorio Klostermann, 1971), p. 26.
135 Heidegger, 'Overcoming Metaphysics,' *The End of Philosophy*, p. 102.
136 Heidegger, 'Recollection in Metaphysics,' *The End of Philosophy*, p. 83. Also see p. 79.

Chapter 1 The Bearing of Thought

1 Heidegger, *On The Way to Language* (New York: Harper & Row, 1965), p. 75.
2 Henry David Thoreau, 'Economy,' in *Walden*, Joseph Wood Krutch (ed.) (New York: Bantam Classics, 1962), p. 112.
3 Heidegger, 'Recollection in Metaphysics,' in *The End of Philosophy*, p. 82.
4 *Ibid.*, p. 78.
5 Heidegger, *What Is Called Thinking?* p. 89. Italics added.
6 Herbert V. Guenther, 'Indian Buddhist Thought in Tibetan Perspective,' *Tibetan Buddhism in Western Perspective* (Berkeley: Dharma Publishing, 1977), pp. 115–38.
7 Medard Boss, *Existential Foundations of Medicine and Psychology*, p. 131.
8 Heidegger, 'Logos (Heraclitus, Fragment B50),' *Early Greek Thinking*, trans. and ed David Farrell Krell and Frank A. Capuzzi (New York: Harper & Row, 1975), pp. 59–78. The reader is urged to consult the original German edition of the essay, published in *Vorträge und Aufsätze* (Pfullingen: Günther Neske, 3rd edn 1959).
9 Katsuki Sekida, *Two Zen Classics: Mumonkan and Hekiganroku* (New York: John Weatherhill, 1977), p. 263.
10 John Dewey, *Democracy and Education*, p. 162.
11 Merleau–Ponty, *Phenomenology of Perception*, p. 144.
12 Heidegger, *What Is Called Thinking?* p. 16. Also see André Leroi-Gourhan, *Le geste et la parole* (Paris: Albin-Michel, 1965) and Jean Brun, *La main et l'esprit* (Paris: Presses Universitaires de la France, 1963).
13 Heidegger, *What Is Called Thinking?* p. 16.
14 *Ibid.*, p. 23.
15 *Ibid.*
16 Katsuki Sekida, *Two Zen Classics*, p. 329.
17 Heidegger, 'Logos (Heraclitus, Fragment B50),' p. 68.
18 Heidegger, *What Is Called Thinking?* p. 14.
19 *Ibid.*, p. 187.
20 *Ibid.*, p. 195.
21 Heidegger, 'The Age of the World Picture,' in *The Question Concerning Technology and Other Essays*, p. 142.
22 See David Farrell Krell's 'Analysis,' in his translation of Heidegger, *The Will to Power as Art*, 'Nietzsche', vol. 1, p. 237.
23 Heidegger, 'The Turning,' in *The Question Concerning Technology and Other Essays*, p. 37.
24 *Ibid.*
25 Henri Bergson, *The Two Sources of Morality and Religion*, trans. R. Ashley André and Cloudesley Brereton (New York: Greenwood, 1935), p. 246.
26 Boss, *Existential Foundations of Medicine and Psychology*, p. 42.
27 See Heidegger and Fink, *Heraclitus Seminar 1966/1967*, pp. 120–33. Also see p. 141, where Heidegger refers to 'the reaching of hands' and meditates on the significance of the utterance, 'I give you my hand'.
28 Boss, *Existential Foundations of Medicine and Psychology*, pp. 102–3. Also

see Merleau–Ponty, 'The Intertwining – The Chiasm,' in *The Visible and the Invisible*, pp. 133–4.

29 Heidegger, 'Building Dwelling Thinking,' in *Poetry, Language, Thought*, p. 157.

30 Nietzsche, *The Will to Power*, Book II, Note 388, p. 209.

31 Bhagwan Shree Rajneesh, *Only One Sky: On The Tantric Way of Tilopa's Song of Mahamudra* (New York: E. P. Dutton, 1976), p. 236.

32 Daisetz Suzuki, *Essays in Zen Buddhism*, First Series (New York: Grove Press, 1961), p. 234.

33 Heidegger, 'The Turning,' *The Question Concerning Technology and Other Essays*, p. 40.

34 Merleau–Ponty, *Phenomenology of Perception*, p. 194.

35 *Ibid.*, p. 314.

36 *Ibid.*, p. 317.

37 *Ibid.*, p. 98.

38 *Ibid.*, p. 140.

39 *Ibid.*, p. 105.

40 *Ibid.*, p. 136.

41 *Ibid.*, p. 365.

42 *Ibid.*

43 *Ibid.*, pp. 353, 336.

44 *Ibid.*, p. 329.

45 *Ibid.*, p. 254. Italics added.

46 *Ibid.*

47 *Ibid.*, p. 347. Italics added.

48 *Ibid.*, p. 288.

49 *Ibid.*, p. 100.

50 *Ibid.*, p. 326.

51 *Ibid.*, p. 242.

52 *Ibid.*, p. 251.

53 *Ibid.*, p. 254. Italics added.

54 Hyemeyohsts Storm, *Seven Arrows*, (New York: Ballantine Books, 1973), p. 21.

55 Ronald Blythe, *Akenfield: Portrait of an English Village*, (New York: Dell Publishing, 1969), p. 166.

56 Rainer Maria Rilke, *Letters 1910–1926*, trans. Jane Bannard Greene and M. D. Herter Norton (New York: W. W. Norton, 1969), p. 334. From a letter to Alfred Schaer, February 1924 (at Muzot).

57 Blythe, *Akenfield*, p. 131.

58 *Ibid.*, p. 136.

59 Adrienne Rich, *Of Woman Born* (New York: W. W. Norton, 1976; Bantam edn, 1977), p. 6. This report is interesting because it articulates an experience which is multi-dimensional. In one sense, or on one level, it is, or could be, an experience of the traditional oppression that women in our society are continually compelled to endure. But on another level, perhaps a deeper one, it could be, and for the author apparently it is, an experience of liberation by virtue of her personal consent (a

bodily felt consent) to transpersonal identification with the woman's ancestral body.

60 Rilke, *Sonnets to Orpheus*, trans. M. D. Herter Norton (New York: W. W. Norton, 1962), Part I, Sonnet XVI, pp. 46–7.
61 Rilke, *Duino Elegies*, trans. J. B. Leishman and Stephen Spender (New York: W. W. Norton, 1939), Elegy II, p. 16, p. 6.
62 W. S. Merwin, *The Miner's Pale Children* (New York: Atheneum, 1976), p. 124.
63 Freud, *Beyond the Pleasure Principle*, trans. James Strachey (New York: W. W. Norton, 1961), p. 46.
64 *Ibid.*, p. 68.
65 *Ibid.*, p. 57.
66 Heidegger, 'The Question Concerning Technology,' *The Question Concerning Technology and Other Essays*, p. 19.
67 Heidegger, *Introduction to Metaphysics*, p. 146.
68 Merleau–Ponty, *Phenomenology of Perception*, p. 353.
69 Nietzsche, *The Will to Power*, Book IV, Sect. 1044, p. 537.
70 See J. H. van den Berg, *The Changing Nature of Man* (New York: Dell Publishing, 1975), pp. 211–12.
71 Heidegger, *What Is Called Thinking?* p. 11.
72 Heidegger, 'Recollection in Metaphysics,' *The End of Philosophy*, p. 77.
73 Shibayama Zenkei, *Zen Comments on the Mumonkan* (New York: New American Library, Mentor edn, 1974), p. 291. Also see p. 204.
74 Heidegger, 'The Question Concerning Technology,' *The Question Concerning Technology and Other Essays*, p. 8.
75 Heidegger, 'Logos,' *Early Greek Thinking*, p. 121.
76 *Ibid.*, p. 120.
77 *Ibid.*, p. 121.
78 Herbert V. Guenther, 'The Natural Freedom of Mind,' *Crystal Mirror*, vol. 4 (Berkeley: Dharma Publishing, 1975), p. 113. Since a *mandala* is a 'perfect' *Gestalt*, it is worth noting that, in his 'Working Notes,' Merleau–Ponty writes: 'My body is a *Gestalt*, and it is co-present in every *Gestalt*.' See *The Visible and the Invisible*, p. 205. Also note this (p. 207): 'since the *Gestalt* arises from polymorphism, this situates us entirely outside the philosophy of the subject and the object.'
79 Herbert V. Guenther, *Buddhist Philosophy in Theory and Practice* (Boulder: Shambhala Publishing, 1971), p. 198.

Chapter 2   The Living Body of Tradition

1 Lame Deer and Richard Erdoes, *Lame Deer: Seeker of Visions* (New York: Simon and Schuster, 1972), p. 157.
2 Merleau–Ponty, 'The Philosopher and Sociology,' *Signs*, trans. Richard McCleary (Evanston: Northwestern University Press, 1964), p. 110.
3 Merleau–Ponty, 'The Indirect Language,' in *The Prose of the World*, trans. John O'Neill, ed Claude Lefort (Evanston: Northwestern University Press, 1973), p. 83.

4 Merleau–Ponty, *Phenomenology of Perception*, p. 254.
5 *Ibid.*, p. 81n.
6 Nietzsche, *The Will to Power*, Book III, section 676, p. 358.
7 Erich Neumann, *The Origins and History of Consciousness*, trans. R. F. C. Hull (Princeton: Princeton University Press, Bollingen Series XLII, 1970), p. 303.
8 Merleau–Ponty, 'The Indirect Language,' *The Prose of the World*, p. 83.
9 *Ibid.*, p. 94.
10 Jung, 'Two Kinds of Thinking,' *Symbols of Transformation: An Analysis of the Prelude to a Case of Schizophrenia*, 'Collected Works', vol. 5, trans. R. F. C. Hull (New York: Pantheon Books, Bollingen Series XX, 1956), p. 28.
11 Merleau–Ponty, *Phenomenology of Perception*, p. 351.
12 Merleau–Ponty, 'The Indirect Language,' *The Prose of the World*, p. 83.
13 Jung, 'Two Kinds of Thinking,' *Symbols of Transformation*, p. 29.
14 Neumann, *The Origins and History of Consciousness*, p. 284.
15 *Ibid.*, p. 287.
16 Jung, 'Instinct and the Unconscious,' in *The Structure and Dynamics of the Psyche*, in 'Collected Works', vol. 8, p. 133.
17 Freud, 'Formulations Regarding the Two Principles in Mental Functioning,' in *Collected Papers*, trans. and ed Joan Rivière (London: Hogarth Press, 1953), vol. 4, p. 14. Cited in Jung, *Symbols of Transformation* (New York: Pantheon Books, Bollingen Series V, 1965), p. 28.
18 Neumann, *The Origins and the History of Consciousness*, p. 288.
19 *Ibid.*, p. 289. The phrase 'our ancestral body' will be found on p. 290.
20 George Santayana, *Platonism and the Spiritual Life* (New York: Harper & Row, 1957), p. 260.
21 Merleau–Ponty, *The Visible and the Invisible*, p. 152.
22 Michel de Montaigne, 'Apology for Raymond Sebond,' *The Complete Essays*, trans. Donald M. Frame (Stanford: Stanford University Press, 1965), Book II, p. 327.
23 See *The Hundred Thousand Songs of Milarepa*, trans. and ed. Garma C. C. Chang (Boulder: Shambhala, 1977), vol. 1, p. 29.
24 Nicholas Cusanus, 'De Sapientia,' in *Unity and Reform: Selected Writings of Nicholas of Cusa*, ed John Patrick Dolan (Notre Dame, Indiana: University of Notre Dame Press, 1962), p. 109.
25 Merleau–Ponty, *Phenomenology of Perception*, p. 146.
26 Neumann, *The Origins and History of Consciousness*, p. 291.
27 Thoreau, *Walden*, in *The Portable Thoreau*, ed with an Introduction by Carl Bode (New York: Viking Press, 1964), pp. 467–8.
28 Neumann, *The Origins and History of Consciousness*, p. 292.
29 Søren Kierkegaard, *The Last Years: Journals 1853–1855*, ed and trans. Ronald G. Smith (London: Collins, 1965). Quoted by John Updike, 'The Fork,' in *Kierkegaard: A Collection of Critical Essays*, ed Josiah Thompson (New York: Doubleday, 1972), p. 172.
30 Neumann, *The Origins and History of Consciousness*, p. 292.
31 *Ibid.*, p. 310.

32 Rainer Maria Rilke, *Letters 1910–1926*, pp. 238–9. From a letter to Phia Rilke, 17 December 1920 (Schloss Berg am Irchel, Zurich).

33 See *The Jewish Daily Prayer Book: Ha-Siddur ha-Shalem*, trans. and annot. Philip Birnbaum (New York: Hebrew Publishing Co., 1949) pp. 331–4. Also see the morning service for *Yom Kippur*, in *Service for the Day of Atonement*, trans. Simon Glazer (New York: Hebrew Publishing Co., 1935), p. 130.

34 See *Talmud Berakhoth* 11a; 60b, *Daily Hebrew Prayer Book*. Also see *Psalm* 135 and the *Yom Kippur* morning service, in *Service for the Day of Atonement*, p. 92. According to Gershom Scholem, the doctrine of the ten *Sefirot* connects moral attributes, and even political character, to different realms of the human body. In so doing, it provides very specific guidance concerning the cultivation of the capacities and skills centered in these various regions. See Scholem, *Major Trends of Jewish Mysticism* (New York: Schocken, 1961), pp. 141–55.

35 Neumann, *The Origins and History of Consciousness*, p. 287.

36 *Talmud Pesahim* 118a, *The Daily Hebrew Prayer Book*, p. 331. In regard for 'hands spread out in prayer as the eagles in the sky,' see also the discussion of *Mahamudra*, a gesture 'stretching across the whole of time,' in Herbert V. Guenther, *The Life and Teaching of Naropa* (New York, London, Oxford: Oxford University Press, 1963), p. 223.

37 Heidegger, *Metaphysics Anfangsgründe der Logik im Ausgang vom Leibniz*, ed Klaus Held, vol. 26, 'Gesamtausgabe' (Frankfurt am Main: Vittorio Klostermann, 1978), p. 247. *The Old Testament* abounds in references to parts and organs of the body (e.g., lips, tongue, ears, face, head, heart, bones, feet, hands), postures and attitudes of the body (e.g., sitting, standing, uprightness, reclining), and activities which require embodiment (e.g., the singing of praises, walking, crying, beholding). I am suggesting, then, that we may interpret these references as ways of 'calling' and 'binding' the human body.

38 See Rilke's letter of August 1915 to Princess Marie von Thurn und Taxis-Hohenlohe, in *Letters of Rainer Maria Rilke, 1910–1926*, pp. 139–40.

39 Merleau–Ponty, *Phenomenology of Perception*, p. 55.

40 Cusanus, 'De Visione Dei,' in *Unity and Reform*, p. 180.

41 Cusanus, 'De Sapientia,' *ibid.*, p. 110.

42 Wallace Stevens, 'Things of August,' in *The Palm at the End of the Mind*, ed Holly Stevens (New York: Knopf, 1971), p. 357.

43 Walter Benjamin, 'One-Way Street,' in *Reflections*, ed with an introduction by Peter Demetz, and trans. Edmund Jephcott (New York: Harcourt, Brace & Jovanovich, 1978), p. 66.

44 Jean-Paul Sartre, *What Is Literature?* trans. Bernard Frechtman (New York: Harper & Row, 1965), p. 45.

45 See Benjamin, 'The Art Work in the Age of Technical Reproducibility,' *Illuminations* (New York: Schocken Books, 1969).

46 Friedrich Hölderlin, 'Brot und Wein,' VI, *Sämtliche Werke*, ed Paul Stapf (Berlin and Darmstadt: Tempel-Verlag, 1960), p. 279. The original German reads as follows: 'Warum zeichnet, wie sonst, die Stirne des

Mannes ein Gott nicht/Druckt den Stempel, wie sonst, nicht dem Getroffenen auf?'

47 Nietzsche, *Dawn of Day*, trans. J. M. Kennedy, in 'The Complete Works of Friedrich Nietzsche', vol. 9, ed Oscar Levy (New York: Gordon Press, 1974), p. 127.

48 Merleau–Ponty, *Phenomenology of Perception*, p. 150.

49 *Service for the Day of Atonement*, p. 194. Also see *Psalm* 145:21.

50 Michel Foucault, 'Nietzsche, Genealogy, History,' in *Language, Counter-Memory, Practice*, ed, with an Introduction, by Donald F. Bouchard (Ithaca: Cornell University Press, 1977), p. 148.

51 Merleau–Ponty, 'The Intertwining – The Chiasm,' in *The Visible and the Invisible*, p. 139.

52 Merleau–Ponty, *Phenomenology of Perception*, p. 166.

53 Jacques Derrida, 'Freud and the Scene of Writing,' in *Writing and Difference*, trans. Alan Bass (Chicago: University of Chicago Press, 1978), p. 199. Also see the use of scriptural metaphors for the body in Michel Foucault, *The Birth of the Clinic: An Archaeology of Medical Perception*, trans. A. M. Sheridan Smith (New York: Random House, 1975).

54 Derrida, *ibid.*, p. 199.

55 Julia Kristeva, 'Quelques problèmes de sémiotique littéraire à propos d'un texte de Mallarmé: "Un coup de dés",' in A. J. Greimas (ed.) *Essais de sémiotique poétique* (Paris: Larousse, 1972), p. 216.

56 Jorge Luis Borges, 'The God's Script,' *Labyrinths* (New York: New Directions, 1964), p. 170. Also see Richard Jacobson, 'Absence, Authority, and the Text,' in *Glyph: Johns Hopkins Textual Studies* (Baltimore: Johns Hopkins University Press, 1978), vol. 3, pp. 137–47.

57 Scholem, *Major Trends in Jewish Mysticism*, p. 283.

58 *Service for the New Year*, trans. Simon Glazer (New York: Hebrew Publishing Co., 1935), pp. 323–4. Also see Scholem, *Kabbalah* (New York: New American Library, Meridian Books, 1978), p. 165.

59 Scholem, *Kabbalah*, p. 128.

60 John Welwood, 'Meditation and the Unconscious: A New Perspective,' *Journal of Transpersonal Psychology*, vol. 9, no. 1 (1977), p. 14.

61 Jung, 'The Structure of the Psyche,' *The Structure and Dynamics of the Psyche*, 'Collected Works', vol. 8, p. 157.

62 *Ibid.*, para. 342, p. 158.

63 Jung, 'The Relations Between the Ego and the Unconscious,' in *Two Essays on Analytical Psychology*, 'Collected Works', vol. 7, p. 174.

64 Neumann, 'Introduction,' *The Origins and History of Consciousness*, p. xvi.

65 Jung, 'Concerning Mandala Symbolism,' *The Archetypes and the Collective Unconscious*, 'Collected Works', vol. 9, Part I, p. 384. Also see 'The Concept of the Collective Unconscious' and 'Archetypes of the Collective Unconscious,' in *The Archetypes and the Collective Unconscious*, 'Collected Works', vol. 9, Part I. Note, finally, Heidegger's comments about the superiority of the historical *archē*, in *An Introduction to Metaphysics*, p. 130.

66 Neumann, *The Origins and History of Consciousness*, p. 295.

67 *Ibid.*, p. 288.
68 See Neumann's discussion (*ibid.*, p. 290) of archetypal 'images of wholeness'.
69 Merleau–Ponty, 'The Child's Relations with Others,' trans. William Cobb, in *The Primacy of Perception*, ed James M. Edie (Evanston: Northwestern University Press, 1964), p. 118.
70 Merleau–Ponty, *Phenomenology of Perception*, p. 254.
71 See Geshé Wangyal, *The Door of Liberation: Essential Teachings of the Tibetan Buddhist Tradition* (New York: Maurice Girodias Associates, Inc., 1973), p. 162. Also see pp. 194–235.
72 Merleau–Ponty, *Phenomenology of Perception*, p. 164.
73 For a discussion of 'coupling,' 'associative sense transfer,' and the active and passive 'syntheses of sense,' see Edmund Husserl, 'Fifth Meditation,' *Cartesian Meditations*, trans. Dorion Cairns (The Hague: Martinus Nijhoff, 1960), especially pp. 108–36 (sections 50–8).
74 Foucault, 'Nietzsche, Genealogy, History,' *Language, Counter-Memory, Practice*, p. 148.
75 *Service for the Day of Atonement*, p. 194.
76 See the *Jewish Daily Prayer Book*, p. 761, *Genesis* 17:10–14, and *Deuteronomy* 10:16.
77 See Derrida, *Of Grammatology*, trans. Gayatri Spivak (Baltimore: Johns Hopkins University Press, 1976).
78 See *The Book of Creation: Sepher Yetzirah*, ed and trans. Iving Friedman (New York: Samuel Weisner, 1977), pp. 1–3.
79 Freud, *Project for a Scientific Psychology, Standard Edition of the Complete Psychological Works of Sigmund Freud* (London: Hogarth Press), vol. I, p. 47.
80 Derrida, *La dissémination* (Paris: Larousse, 1973), p. 113.
81 William Blake, *Milton* (Boulder: Shambhala Publishing, 1978), Book I, p. 91.
82 Gerardo Reichel-Dolmatoff, 'Training for the Priesthood among the Kogi,' in Johannes Wilbert (ed.), *Enculturation in Latin America: An Anthology* (Los Angeles: UCLA Latin America Center Publications, University of California, 1977), p. 279. Also see Marcel Mauss, *Essai sur les techniques du corps* (Paris: Les Editions de Minuit, 1968–9), 3 vols, ed Victor Karady.
83 Reichel-Dolmatoff, *ibid.*, pp. 279–80.
84 *Ibid.*
85 John Dewey, *Art as Experience* (New York: G. P. Putnam's Sons, 1958), p. 22.
86 *Ibid.*, p. 39.
87 Benjamin, 'One-Way Street,' *Reflections*, p. 79.
88 Hans-Georg Gadamer, *Wahrheit und Methode: Grundzüge einer philosophischen Hermeneutik* (Tübingen: J. C. B. Mohr, 1960), p. 369. Also see Benjamin, 'Ueber den Begriff der Geschichte,' in *Gesammelte Schriften* (Frankfurt: Suhrkamp, 1974), Bd. I, p. 704.
89 Gadamer, *Philosophical Hermeneutics*, trans. David E. Linge (Berkeley: University of California Press, 1976), p. 58.

90 Gadamer, *Wahrheit und Methode*, pp. 274–5. Also see p. 261.
91 Nietzsche, *The Will to Power*, Book II, Note 314, p. 173.
92 *Ibid.*, Book II, Note 439, p. 242.
93 *Ibid.*, Book II, Note 440, p. 242.
94 *Ibid.*
95 *Ibid.*, Book II, Note 434, p. 238.
96 Merleau–Ponty, 'On the Phenomenology of Language,' *Signs*, trans. Richard C. McCleary (Evanston: Northwestern University Press, 1964), p. 93.
97 Lama Anagarika Govinda, *Creative Meditation and Multi-Dimensional Consciousness* (Wheaton, Illinois: Theosophical Publishing House, 1976), p. 269.
98 *Ibid.*, p. 268.
99 Govinda, *The Way of the White Clouds* (Berkeley, Shambhala Publishing Co., 1970), p. 18.
100 Dewey, *Art As Experience*, p. 22.
101 Merleau–Ponty, 'On the Phenomenology of Language,' *Sings*, p. 63.
102 Gottfried Wilhelm Freiherr von Leibniz, *New Essays on the Human Understanding*, translated and edited by Peter Remnant and Jonathan Bennett (New York: Cambridge University Press, 1981), Book III, ch. 6, p. 307. Italics added. For an example which satisfies Leibniz's proposal, see H. H. The Second Dalai Lama, Gyal-wang ge-dun gya-tso, *The Steps of Visualization for the Three Essential Moments: A Stairway for Ascending to the Tusita Buddha-fields* (Dharamsala, India: Library of Tibetan Works and Archives, 1975), p. 16.
103 Neumann, *The Child: Structure and Dynamics of the Nascent Personality*, p. 12.
104 *Ibid.*
105 Charles H. Kahn, 'Religious and Natural Philosophy in Empedocles' Doctrine of the Soul,' in Alexander Mourelatros (ed.), *The Pre-Socratics: A Collection of Critical Essays* (New York: Doubleday Books, 1974), p. 455.
106 Tertullian, 'De resurrectione carnis,' cited in Arthur O. Lovejoy (ed.), ' "Nature" as Norm in Tertullian,' *Essays in the History of Ideas* (New York: G. P. Putnam's Sons, Capricorn Books, 1960), p. 327. Italics added.
107 George Santayana, *Reason in Religion*, vol. III, of *The Life of Reason* (New York: Collier Books, 1962), p. 185.
108 *Ibid.*, p. 186.

Chapter 3 Moral Education – The Body's Felt Sense of Value

1 Iris Murdoch, *The Nice and the Good* (New York: Penguin, 1978), p. 130.
2 Nietzsche, *The Will to Power*, Book II, Note 304, p. 171.
3 Wittgenstein, *Philosophical Investigations*, trans. G. E. M. Anscombe

(New York: Macmillan, 1953), p. 178.

4 Richard Wollheim, 'The Sheep and the Ceremony,' *The 1979 Leslie Stephen Lecture* (Cambridge: Cambridge University Press, 1979), p. 16.

5 Carl Rogers, *Freedom to Learn* (Columbus: Charles E. Merrill and Co., 1969), p. 251. Also see Jung's 'Archetypes of the Collective Unconscious,' *The Archetypes and the Collective Unconscious*, 'Collected Works', vol. 9, Part I, pp. 19–20. Jung argues that, 'The unconscious is the psyche that reaches down from the daylight of mentally and morally lucid consciousness into the nervous system that for ages has been known as the "sympathetic". This does not govern perception and muscular activity like the cerebrospinal system, and thus control the environment; but . . . it maintains the balance of life and, through the mysterious paths of sympathetic excitation, not only gives us knowledge of the innermost life of other beings, but also has an inner effect on them.' If we recognize that 'the unconscious' is our *bodily nature*, then Jung is saying that our bodily nature is that dimension of our psyche which 'reaches down from the daylight of mentally and morally lucid consciousness into the nervous system . . . [that] maintains the balance of life and . . . gives us knowledge of the innermost life of other beings. . . .' But if the body functions in this way, it makes a fundamental contribution to our moral life.

6 Neumann, *The Origins and History of Consciousness*, p. 288.

7 Dewey, *Democracy and Education*, p. 142.

8 Ralph Waldo Emerson, 'Education,' *The Portable Emerson*, ed Mark Van Doren (New York: Viking Press, 1946), pp. 254–5.

9 Nietzsche, *The Will to Power*, Book II, Note 430, p. 234.

10 Dewey, *Democracy and Education*, p. 113.

11 R. S. Peters, 'Democratic Values and Education,' *Teachers College Record*, vol. 80, no. 3 (February 1979), p. 476.

12 *Ibid.*, p. 475. Also see p. 469.

13 Wollheim, 'The Sheep and the Ceremony,' *The 1979 Leslie Stephen Lecture*, p. 5.

14 *Ibid.*

15 *Ibid.*

16 Dewey, *Democracy and Education*, p. 141. Also see Neumann, *The Child: Structure and Dynamics of the Nascent Personality*, pp. 90–135. Neumann correlates the pre-ego-logical and ego-logical stages in the child's moral development with the matriarchal and patriarchal stages in the history of culture; and he correlates these with stages in a process of incarnation.

17 Dewey, *Democracy and Education*, p. 141.

18 *Ibid.*, p. 144.

19 *Ibid.*, p. 153.

20 *Ibid.*, p. 142.

21 *Ibid.*, p. 198.

22 *Ibid.*, p. 142.

23 *Ibid.*

24 Nietzsche, *Joyful Wisdom*, Book IV, Note 296, p. 231.

25 Rogers, *Freedom to Learn*, p. 244.
26 *Ibid.*
27 See Frederick Perls, Ralph Hefferline, and Paul Goodman, *Gestalt Therapy: Excitement and Growth in the Human Personality* (New York: Dell Publishing Co., 1951), Eugene T. Gendlin, *Focusing* (New York: Bantam Publishing Co., 1981), and Carl Rogers, *On Becoming A Person* (Boston: Houghton Mifflin, 1961).
28 Rogers, *Freedom to Learn*, p. 243.
29 *Ibid.*
30 *Ibid.*, p. 246.
31 *Ibid.*, p. 256.
32 *Ibid.*, p. 247.
33 *Ibid.*, p. 243.
34 *Ibid.*, p. 251.
35 *Ibid.*, p. 255.
36 *Ibid.*, p. 254.
37 Merleau–Ponty, 'The Child's Relations with Others,' trans. William Cobb, in *The Primacy of Perception*, ed James M. Edie (Evanston, Northwestern University Press, 1964), pp. 96–155.
38 Paul J. Stern, 'Introduction,' to Medard Boss, *Existential Foundations of Medicine and Psychology*, p. xxi.
39 Nietzsche, *The Will to Power*, Book III, Note 809, p. 428.
40 See Erwin Straus, 'Born to See, Bound to Behold: Reflections on the Function of the Upright Posture in the Esthetic Attitude,' in *The Philosophy of the Body: Reflections of Cartesian Dualism*, ed Stuart Spicker (New York: Quadrangle, 1970), pp. 334–61.
41 Heidegger, 'Letter on Humanism,' in *Basic Writings*, pp. 238–9.

Chapter 4 The Body Politic

1 Plato, *Laws* VII, 815, in Jowett, vol. I, p. 291. All references to Plato are taken from the two-volume Jowett translation, *The Dialogues of Plato* (New York: Random House, 1937).
2 Marcuse, *Eros and Civilization: A Philosophical Inquiry into Freud* (Boston: Beacon Press, 1962), p. 34.
3 Michel Foucault, 'Body/Power,' in *Power/Knowledge: Selected Interviews and Other Writings, 1972–1977*, ed Colin Gordon, trans. Leo Marshall, John Mepham and Kate Soper (New York: Pantheon, 1980), pp. 58–9.
4 Foucault, 'Two Lectures,' *ibid.*, p. 97.
5 Merleau–Ponty, 'The Concept of Nature,' Part I, in *Themes from the Lectures at the Collège de France, 1952–1960*, trans. John O'Neill (Evanston: Northwestern University Press, 1970), p. 82.
6 Merleau–Ponty, 'Reflection and Interrogation,' *The Visible and the Invisible*, p. 49.
7 Merleau–Ponty, *Phenomenology of Perception*, p. 85.
8 *Ibid.*, p. 314.

263

9 See *Huang Ti Nei Ching Su Wen: The Yellow Emperor's Classic of Internal Medicine*, trans. Ilza Veith (Berkeley: University of California Press, 1966), pp. 133–4.
10 See Merleau–Ponty, 'The Intertwining – The Chiasm,' *The Visible and the Invisible*, p. 155. Also see pp. 130–54.
11 Merleau–Ponty, 'Working Notes,' *The Visible and the Invisible*, p. 263.
12 See Merleau–Ponty, 'The Child's Relations with Others,' *The Primacy of Perception*, pp. 118–19.
13 See Merleau–Ponty, 'Working Notes,' *The Visible and the Invisible*, pp. 264, 354.
14 See Merleau–Ponty, 'The Child's Relations with Others,' *The Primacy of Perception*, pp. 119–20.
15 See William F. Peterson, *Hippocratic Wisdom: For Him Who Wishes to Pursue Properly the Science of Medicine* (Springfield, Illinois: Charles C. Thomas, 1946), p. 137.

Chapter 5   Taking the Measure in Stride

1 See John Updike, 'The Fork,' in Josiah Thompson (ed.), *Kierkegaard: A Collection of Critical Essays* (New York: Doubleday, 1972), p. 167.
2 G. S. Kirk, 'Natural Change in Heraclitus,' in Alexander P. D. Mourelatos (ed.), *The Pre-Socratics: A Collection of Critical Essays* (New York: Doubleday, 1974), p. 193.
3 Blaise Pascal, *Pensées*, trans. W. F. Trotter (New York: E. P. Dutton, 1958), Note 359, p. 99. Referring to Kierkegaard, Stephen Crites observes that, 'one shuns situations in which he would have to walk out in the open, supported by his own powers alone, for then he could not conceal his shaky condition.' See Crites, 'Pseudonymous Authorship as Art and as Act,' in Josiah Thompson (ed.), *Kierkegaard: A Collection of Critical Essays*, p. 192.
4 Merleau–Ponty, 'Working Notes,' *The Visible and the Invisible*, p. 272. Also see Erwin W. Straus, 'The Upright Posture,' *Phenomenological Psychology*, translated by Erling Eng (New York: Basic Books, 1966), p. 148: 'Human gait is, in fact, a continuously arrested falling.'
5 Gerardo Reichel-Dolmatoff, *Amazonian Cosmos: The Sexual and Religious Symbolism of the Tukano Indians* (Chicago: University of Chicago Press, 1971), p. 94.
6 Nietzsche, *Thus Spake Zarathustra*, trans. Walter Kaufman (New York: Viking Press, 1956), p. 33. Also see pp. 76–7.
7 See André Fraigneau, *Cocteau* (New York: Grove Press, Evergreen Books, 1961), p. 100.
8 See John Updike, 'The Fork,' in Josiah Thompson (ed.), *Kierkegaard: A Collection of Critical Essays*, p. 177.
9 Nietzsche, *The Joyful Wisdom* (New York: Frederick Ungar, 1960), Book I, p. 14.

10 *Ibid.*, Book IV, p. 236.
11 See Katsuki Sekida, *Two Zen Classics: Mumonkan and Hekiganroku*, a translation with commentaries (New York: John Weatherhill, 1977), p. 116.
12 See Leland Wyman and Berard Haile, *Blessing Way* (Tucson, Arizona: University of Arizona Press, 1970), p. 136.
13 See John G. Neihardt, *Black Elk Speaks: Being the Life Story of a Holy Man of the Oglala Sioux* (New York: Simon and Schuster, Pocket Books, 1972), pp. 3–4.
14 See Washington Matthews, *The Night Chant, A Navajo Ceremony.* Memoirs of the American Museum of Natural History, Whole Series, vol. VI, Anthropology, vol. V. Publications of the Hyde Southwestern Expedition, 1902 (New York: American Museum of Natural History, 1902), pp. 73, 140–42, 296–304.
15 See documentation on Hölderlin's conversation (circa 1804), with Isaak von Sinclair on the theme of madness. I have not been able to retrace my steps back to the documentary source.
16 Heidegger, *The Basic Problems of Phenomenology*, trans. Albert Hofstadter (Bloomington: Indiana University Press, 1982), p. 252.
17 Merleau–Ponty, 'Eye and Mind,' *The Primacy of Perception*, p. 185.
18 Nietzsche, *The Will to Power*, Note 12B, p. 13.
19 Heidegger, '. . . Poetically Man Dwells . . .' *Poetry, Language, Thought*, p. 221. 'Measure' is the subject of discussion on pp. 220–7.
20 *Ibid.*, p. 222.
21 Heidegger, *Der Satz vom Grund* (Pfullingen: Günther Neske, 1957), pp. 186–7.
22 *Ibid.*, p. 221.
23 *Ibid.*
24 *Ibid.*
25 *Ibid.*
26 *Ibid.*, p. 223.
27 *Ibid.*, p. 220.
28 *Ibid.*, p. 222.
29 *Ibid.*, p. 223.
30 *Ibid.*
31 *Ibid.*, pp. 227–9.
32 James Hillman, *Re-Visioning Psychology* (New York: Harper & Row, 1975), p. 190.
33 J. M. Edmonds (trans. and ed.), *Lyra Graeca*, vol. III (Cambridge: Harvard University Press, Loeb Classical Library, 1927), pp. 322–3.
34 *Ibid.*, pp. 488–9.
35 See Tarthang Tulku, *Time, Space, and Knowledge* (Berkeley: Dharma Publishing, 1980), p. 198.
36 George Santayana, *Reason in Religion*, vol. III of *The Life of Reason* (New York: Collier Books, 1962), p. 178.
37 Nietzsche, *The Will to Power*, Note 30, p. 20.
38 Heidegger, 'The Question Concerning Technology,' in *The Question*

Concerning Technology and Other Essays, ed William Lovitt (New York: Harper & Row, 1977), p. 27. It is worth looking, besides, at *What Is Called Thinking?* (New York: Harper & Row, 1968), p. 77, where Heidegger's discussion involves him in references to 'staying on the way,' 'falling down,' 'walking,' and 'standing upright.'

39 Heidegger, 'The Nature of Language,' in *On The Way to Language*, trans. and ed Joan Stambaugh and Peter Hertz (New York: Harper & Row, 1971), p. 98.

40 Heidegger, *An Introduction to Metaphysics*, pp. 11–12.

41 Heidegger, 'The Anaximander Fragment,' *Early Greek Thinking*, p. 26.

42 Heidegger, *What Is Called Thinking?* p. 168.

43 *Ibid.*, p. 169.

44 *Ibid.*

45 Paul Valéry, 'Dance and the Soul,' trans. Dorothy Bussy, in Anthony Bower and James Laughlin (eds), *Selected Writings of Paul Valéry* (New York: New Directions, 1964), pp. 188–9.

46 See Heidegger, 'Basic Questions of Metaphysics,' in *What Is A Thing?* trans. and ed W. B. Barton, Jr and Vera Deutsch, with a commentary by Eugene Gendlin (Chicago: Henry Regnery Co., 1967). Pages 66–108 of this translation have been included in David Farrell Krells' anthology, *Martin Heidegger: Basic Writings* (New York: Harper & Row, 1977). For the sake of convenience, our page citations will refer to the Krell anthology.

47 Heidegger, *Basic Writings*, p. 260.

48 *Ibid.*, p. 261.

49 *Ibid.*, p. 262.

50 *Ibid.*, p. 263.

51 *Ibid.*, p. 264.

52 *Ibid.*, pp. 266–7.

53 Henry David Thoreau, 'A Week on the Concord and Merrimak Rivers,' in *The Portable Thoreau*, ed Carl Bode (New York: Viking, 1964), pp. 194–5.

Chapter 6   The Ground and its Poetizing

1 Heidegger, *An Introduction to Metaphysics*, p. 34.

2 Marcuse, *Eros and Civilization: A Philosophical Inquiry into Freud*, p. 114. Italics added.

3 Nietzsche, *The Will to Power*, Book III, Note 958, p. 503.

4 Nietzsche, *Thus Spake Zarathustra*, Note 320, p. 89.

5 Thoreau, 'Economy,' in *Walden*, ed Joseph W. Krutch (New York: Bantam, 1962), p. 67.

6 Neumann, *The Great Mother: An Analysis of the Archetype* (Princeton: Princeton University Press, Bollingen Series XLVII, 1972), p. 55.

7 George Santayana, *Reason in Religion*, p. 125.

8 Heidegger, 'The Question Concerning Technology,' *The Question Concerning Technology and Other Essays*, p. 35.

9 Rilke, *Sonnets to Orpheus*, Part III, No. 13, p. 95.
10 Nietzsche, *Ecce Homo*, trans. Walter Kaufmann and R. J. Hollingdale (New York: Random House, 1967), Note 1153. Cited in Tracy Strong, 'Nietzsche and Politics,' in Robert Solomon (ed.), *Nietzsche: A Collection of Critical Essays*, p. 288.
11 Heidegger, 'The End of Philosophy and the Task of Thinking,' in *On Time and Being*, trans. and ed Joan Stambaugh (New York: Harper & Row, 1972), p. 56.
12 Jung, 'The Role of the Unconscious,' *Civilization in Transition*, in 'Collected Works', vol. 10, trans. R. F. C. Hull and ed Herbert Read, Michael Fordham and Gerhard Adler (Princeton: Princeton University Press, Bollingen Series XX, 1970), p. 13.
13 Jung, 'Mind and Earth,' in *Civilization in Transition*, 'Collected Works', vol. 10, p. 49.
14 Heidegger, 'Memorial Address,' *Discourse on Thinking*, trans. John M. Anderson and E. Hans Freund (New York: Harper & Row, 1966), pp. 48–9.
15 *Ibid.*, p. 53.
16 *Ibid.*, p. 55.
17 *Ibid.*, p. 57.
18 Merleau–Ponty, *The Visible and the Invisible*, p. 258.
19 Heidegger, 'Building Dwelling Thinking,' in *Poetry, Language, Thought*, p. 147.
20 *Ibid.*, p. 149.
21 *Ibid.*
22 Eugen Fink and Martin Heidegger, *Heraclitus Seminar 1966–1967*, trans. Charles H. Seibert (University, Alabama: University of Alabama Press, 1979), p. 144–6.
23 *Ibid.*, p. 146.
24 *Ibid.*
25 *Ibid.*, p. 147.
26 Heidegger, *An Introduction to Metaphysics*, p. 142.
27 Neumann, *The Origins and History of Consciousness*, p. 288.
28 *Ibid.*, p. 289.
29 Heidegger, 'Hölderlin und das Wesen der Dichtung,' in *Erläuterungen zu Hölderlins Dichtung*, p. 36.
30 Merleau–Ponty, *Phenomenology of Perception*, p. 146.
31 Black Elk, *The Sacred Pipe: The Seven Rites of the Oglala Sioux* (New York: Penguin Books, 1971), p. 85.
32 *Ibid.*, pp. 13–20.
33 Nietzsche, *Thus Spake Zarathustra*, p. 224.
34 William Carlos Williams, *Paterson* (New York: New Directions, 1963), p. 129.
35 Nietzsche, *Thus Spake Zarathustra*, p. 217.
36 Gregory of Nazianz, *Theological Orations*, cited by Maria-Gabriele Wosien, in *Sacred Dance: Encounter with the Gods* (New York: Avon Books, 1974), p. 29.
37 Friedrich Hölderlin, *Sämtliche Werke*, ed Paul Stapf (Berlin and

Darmstadt: Der Tempel-Verlag, 1960), p. 416. Also see Heidegger, 'Poetically Man Dwells,' in *Poetry, Language, Thought*, pp. 213–29.
38 Heidegger, 'Poetically Man Dwells,' *ibid.*, p. 218. I have changed Hofstadter's translation of *Dichtung* as 'poetry' to the richer word, 'poetizing'.
39 Heidegger, 'Hölderlin und das Wesen der Dichtung,' in *Erläuterungen zu Hölderlins Dichtung*, p. 45.
40 Heidegger, 'Heimkunft/An die Verwandten,' in *Erläuterungen zu Hölderlins Dichtung*, p. 26.
41 See J. M. Edmonds, *Lyra Graeca*, vol. III (Cambridge: Harvard University Press, Loeb Classical Library, 1927), pp. 330–2.
42 Heidegger, 'Hölderlin und das Wesen der Dichtung,' *Erläuterungen zu Hölderlins Dichtung*, p. 43.
43 Gerardo Reichel-Dolmatoff, 'Training for the Priesthood Among the Kogi of Colombia,' in Johannes Wilbert (ed.), *Enculturation in Latin America: An Anthology* (Los Angeles: UCLA Latin America Center Publications, University of California, 1977), p. 279. The words of the Navaho Night Chant, words which accompany one of the Navaho people's most important dances, implicitly disclose this same understanding of dance as the 'origin' of all motility. See Washington Matthews, *The Night Chant, A Navaho Ceremony*. Memoirs of the American Museum of Natural History, Whole Series, vol. VI, *Anthropology*, vol. 5. Publications of the Hyde Southwestern Expedition, 1902.
44 Friedrich Nietzsche, *Joyful Wisdom*, Note 112.
45 Merleau–Ponty, *Phenomenology of Perception*, p. 314.
46 *Ibid.*, p. 317.
47 *Ibid.*, p. 94.
48 *Ibid.*, p. 140.
49 *Ibid.*, p. 105.
50 *Ibid.*, p. 104.
51 *Ibid.*, p. 111.
52 *Ibid.*, p. 100.
53 *Ibid.*, p. 136.
54 *Ibid.*
55 *Ibid.*, p. 137.
56 Eugen Fink and Martin Heidegger, *Heraclitus Seminar 1966–1967*, pp. 24 (Seminar Two) and 29 (Seminar Three).
57 Nietzsche, *Joyful Wisdom*, Book V, Note 381, p. 351.
58 Paul Valéry, 'La Jeune Parque,' in *Paul Valéry: Selected Writings*, ed Anthony Bower and James Laughlin (New York: New Directions, 1964), pp. 22–3. I have been guided by Dorothy Bussy's translation; but the one I offer here is my own.
59 Heidegger, 'The Question Concerning Technology,' in William Lovitt (ed.), *The Question Concerning Technology and Other Essays*, p. 27.
60 Kierkegaard, *Journals*. Cited by John Updike, in 'The Fork,' in Josiah Thompson (ed.), *Kierkegaard: A Collection of Critical Essays*, p. 170.

61 Nietzsche, Preface, *Ecce Homo*, p. 34.
62 Nietzsche, *The Will to Power*, Book III, Note 616, p. 330.
63 Kierkegaard, *Fear and Trembling*, trans. Walter Lowrie (New York: Doubleday, 1954), p. 53n.
64 Nietzsche, *Joyful Wisdom*, Book IV, Note 293, p. 228.
65 Nietzsche, *Thus Spake Zarathustra*, Part I, p. 41. Also see Part III, p. 192, 'On the Spirit of Gravity.'
66 Kierkegaard, *Fear and Trembling*, pp. 51–2. Also see pp. 48–50.
67 Heidegger, *What Is Called Thinking?* p. 12.
68 *Ibid.*, p. 233.
69 Heidegger, *Nihilism*, 'Nietzsche', vol. 4, p. 10.
70 Nietzsche, *Joyful Wisdom*, Book V, Note 347, p. 287.
71 Heidegger, 'Nietzsche as Metaphysician,' a translation by Joan Stambaugh of part of Heidegger's work on *Nietzsche*, vol. I, published in Robert Solomon (ed.), *Nietzsche: A Collection of Critical Essays* (New York: Doubleday, 1973), pp. 109–10.
72 *Ibid.*, p. 110.
73 *Ibid.*, p. 112.
74 *Ibid.*
75 *Ibid.*, p. 113.
76 *Ibid.*, p. 112.
77 Heidegger, *An Introduction to Metaphysics*, p. 5.
78 *Ibid.* Italics added.
79 Arthur Danto, *Nietzsche As Philosopher* (New York: Macmillan, 1965), p. 79. Italics added.
80 *Ibid.*, p. 80.
81 See Carlos Castaneda, *A Separate Reality* (New York: Scribner's and Sons, 1971), pp. 20–1. Sacateca's 'dancing' is his way of learning, knowing, understanding and teaching. Don Juan teaches Castaneda how to walk, how to leap and how to fly.
82 Nietzsche, *Thus Spake Zarathustra*, p. 112.
83 Heidegger, *Der Satz vom Grund*, 3rd edn (Pfullingen: Günther Neske, 1965), p. 185. Also see pp. 95 and 108.
84 *Ibid.*, pp. 186–7: 'Death is the still unthought measure of the immeasurable, i.e., of the highest play in which man is brought on earth, and upon which he is staked.'
85 *Ibid.*, p. 188.
86 *Ibid.*, p. 70.
87 *Ibid.*, p. 48.
88 *Ibid.*, p. 188.
89 *Ibid.*
90 *Ibid.*, p. 86. Italics added.
91 *Ibid.*, p. 180.
92 *Ibid.*, p. 90.
93 Heidegger, 'What Are Poets For?' in *Poetry, Language, Thought*, p. 92.
94 Erwin W. Straus, 'Lived Movement,' *Phenomenological Psychology* (New York: Basic Books, 1966), pp. 25–6.

95 *Ibid.*, p. 26.
96 Hermann Hesse, 'Zarathustra's Return: A Word to German Youth, 1919,' in Robert C. Solomon, *Nietzsche: A Collection of Critical Essays*, p. 376.

Chapter 7   The Gathering Round-Dance

1 Nietzsche, *The Will to Power*, Note 1066, p. 549.
2 Heidegger, 'Basic Questions of Metaphysics,' in *Martin Heidegger: Basic Writings*, ed David Farrell Krell (New York: Harper & Row, 1977), p. 261. This was a lecture, and was originally published in *Die Frage nach dem Ding* (Tübingen: Max Niemeyer Verlag, 1962). The text has been translated by W. B. Barton, Jr and Vera Deutsch, and appears with an analysis by Eugene Gendlin under the title *What Is a Thing?* (Chicago: Henry Regnery Co., 1967).
3 Heidegger, *Basic Writings*, pp. 261–2.
4 Lucian, *On the Dance*, quoted in Maria-Gabriele Wosien, *Sacred Dance: Encounter with the Gods* (New York: Avon Books, 1974), p. 8. Italics added.
5 See Maria-Gabriele Wosien, *Sacred Dance*, p. 126.
6 *Ibid.*, p. 20.
7 Neumann, *The Child: Structure and Dynamics of the Nascent Personality*, p. 148.
8 Neumann, *The Great Mother: An Analysis of the Archetype*, pp. 298–9. Also see Neumann's work on *The Origins and History of Consciousness*, p. 291: 'Centroversion is . . . the functioning of the body as a whole and . . . the unity of its origins.' The round-dance takes place in accordance with the matriarchal principle and the feminine archetype.
9 Carl C. Jung, 'Concerning Mandala Symbolism,' in *The Archetypes and the Unconscious*, 'Collected Works' (Princeton: Princeton University Press, Bollingen Series XX, 2nd edn, 1968), vol. 9, Part I, p. 379.
10 Merleau–Ponty, 'Indirect Language and the Voices of Silence,' in *Signs*, ed Richard McCleary (Evanston: Northwestern University Press, 1964), p. 68. Italics added.
11 Heidegger, 'Hölderlin und das Wesen der Dichtung,' *Erläuterungen zu Hölderlins Dichtung*, p. 45.
12 Nietzsche, *The Will to Power*, Book IV, Note 1067, p. 550.
13 See Wosien, *Sacred Dance*, pp. 7 and 28.
14 *Ibid.*, p. 26.
15 Lucian, *On the Dance*, quoted in Lillian Lawler, *Dance in Ancient Greece* (Seattle: University of Washington Press, 1967), p. 24.
16 Wosien, *Sacred Dance*, p. 8.
17 Hyemeyohsts Storm, *Seven Arrows* (New York: Ballantine, 1973), p. 14.
18 *Ibid.*, p. 1. Also see Wosien, *Sacred Dance*, p. 20.
19 Nietzsche, *The Birth of Tragedy* (New York: Doubleday, 1956), Sect. 23, p. 136.
20 Neumann, *The Great Mother: An Analysis of the Archetype*, p. 92.
21 See Wosien, *Sacred Dance*, p. 28.

22 Plotinus, *Enneads*. Quoted and discussed by Wosien, *Sacred Dance*, p. 20.
23 The German reads: 'Warum freuet sich denn nicht der geweihete Tanz?'
24 Heidegger, 'Hölderlins Erde und Himmel,' in *Erläuterung zu Hölderlins Dichtung*, p. 155. The other work in which Heidegger discusses the round dance is 'The Thing,' *Poetry, Language, Thought*, pp. 180f.
25 Heidegger, 'Hölderlins Erde und Himmel,' *Erläuterung zu Hölderlins Dichtung*, p. 173.
26 *Ibid.*, p. 174.
27 Nietzsche, *Thus Spake Zarathustra*, p. 229.
28 See Max Pulver, 'Jesus' Round Dance and Crucifixion According to the Acts of St John,' in *The Mysteries: Papers for the Eranos Yearbooks*, translated by Ralph Manheim (Princeton: Princeton University Press, Bollingen Series XXX, vol. 2, 1955), pp. 169–93. Also see Neumann's *The Great Mother: An Analysis of the Archetype* (Princeton: Princeton University Press, Bollingen Series XLVII, paperback edn, 1972), and, in particular, his work on *The Origins and History of Consciousness*, p. 291.
29 Heidegger, 'Erde und Himmel,' *Erläuterungen zu Hölderlins Dichtung*, pp. 173–4.
30 *Ibid.*
31 *Ibid.*
32 *Ibid.*, p. 179.
33 *Ibid.*
34 Heidegger, 'Building Dwelling Thinking,' in *Poetry, Language, Thought*, p. 150.
35 *Ibid.*, pp. 154–7.
36 Plato, *Gorgias*, 507–8, *The Dialogues of Plato*, vol. I, trans. and ed Benjamin Jowett, p. 569.
37 Lame Deer and Richard Erdoes, *Lame Deer: Seeker of Visions* (New York: Simon and Schuster, Touchstone Books, 1972), p. 112.
38 Heidegger, 'The Thing,' *Poetry, Language, Thought*, p. 179.
39 *Ibid.*
40 *Ibid.*, p. 180.
41 Merleau–Ponty, *Phenomenology of Perception*, p. 68.
42 Heidegger, 'The Thing,' *Poetry, Language, Thought*, p. 180.
43 Nietzsche, *The Birth of Tragedy*, Sect. 23, p. 137.
44 Heidegger, 'Erde und Himmel,' *Erläuterungen zu Hölderlins Dichtung*, p. 174.
45 See John Maxwell Edmonds, *Lyra Graeca* (New York: G. P. Putnam's Sons, Loeb Classical Library, 1927), p. 107.
46 Homer, *The Iliad*, Book XVIII, lines 567–72. For a good translation, see the one by E. V. Rieu (Toronto: Penguin Books, 1950), p. 352.
47 Homer, *ibid.*, Book XVIII, lines 593–606. Also see the Rieu translation, pp. 352–3.
48 Edmonds, *Lyra Graeca*, vol. III, pp. 322–3.
49 See Heidegger, 'The Thing,' *Poetry, Language, Thought*, pp. 171 and 181. Also see 'Building Dwelling Thinking,' *Poetry, Language, Thought*, pp. 153–7.
50 Heidegger, *An Introduction to Metaphysics*, pp. 54–5.

51 See Heidegger, *What Is Called Thinking?*, p. 227, to connect this analysis to the question of the *ontological difference*.
52 Heidegger, 'Building Dwelling Thinking,' *Poetry, Language, Thought*, p. 154.
53 Heidegger, 'Logik: Heraklits Lehre vom Logos,' *Heraklit*, 'Gesamtausgabe', vol. 55, ed Manfred Frings (Frankfurt am Main: Vittorio Klostermann, 1979), p. 337.
54 *Ibid.*, p. 335.
55 *Ibid.*, p. 337. Also see p. 333.
56 *Ibid.*, p. 335.
57 *Ibid.*, p. 336.
58 *Ibid.*, p. 338.
59 *Ibid.*, p. 383.
60 Heidegger, *Die Kunst und der Raum* (St Gallen: Erker-Verlag, 1969), p. 10.
61 *Ibid.*
62 *Ibid.*, p. 8.
63 Lawler, *The Dance of the Ancient Greek Theatre*, (Iowa City: University of Iowa Press, 1964), p. 11.
64 Jung, 'Concerning Mandala Symbolism,' *The Archetypes and the Unconscious*, 'Collected Works', vol. 9, Part I, pp. 383–4. Also see pp. 389–90.
65 Wosien, *Sacred Dance*, p. 8.
66 See Merleau–Ponty, 'The Intertwining – The Chiasm,' *The Visible and the Invisible*, p. 141. Being 'synergic,' the dancing body preserves the *whole of Being*.
67 Heidegger, *Die Kunst und der Raum*, p. 7.
68 *Ibid.*, pp. 6–7.
69 Heidegger, 'The Turning,' *The Question Concerning Technology and Other Essays*, p. 39. This question constitutes the task of Tarthang Tulku, *Time, Space, and Knowledge* (Berkeley: Dharma Publishing, 1978). I strongly recommend this book.
70 Merleau–Ponty, *Phenomenology of Perception*, p. 54.
71 Heidegger, 'Building Dwelling Thinking', *Poetry, Language, Thought*, p. 157.
72 Merleau–Ponty, 'Eye and Mind,' *The Primacy of Perception*, p. 187.
73 Marvin Casper, 'Space Therapy and the Maitri Project,' *The Journal of Transpersonal Psychology*, vol. 6, no. 1 (1974), pp. 57–8. Also see Heidegger's discussion of 'confinement within the Open' in 'What Are Poets For?' (*Poetry, Language, Thought*, p. 107).
74 Heidegger, *The Will to Power as Art*, 'Nietzsche', vol. 1, p. 105.
75 *Ibid.*
76 Heidegger, *Die Kunst und der Raum*, p. 9. Italics added.
77 Merleau–Ponty, *Phenomenology of Perception*, p. 101.
78 Heidegger, 'The End of Philosophy and the Task of Thinking,' in *Basic Writings*, p. 385.
79 Aristotle, *De partibus animalium*, in *The Works of Aristotle*, trans. and ed J. A. Smith and W. D. Ross (Oxford: Clarendon Press, 1958), Book IV, ch. 10, 689b19–21.

Bibliography

Aristotle, *De partibus animalium*, 'The Works of Aristotle,' vol. 5, Oxford, Clarendon, 1958.

Benjamin, W., *Illuminations*, New York, Schocken Books, 1969.

Benjamin, W., *Gesammelte Schriften*, Frankfurt am Main, Suhrkamp, 1974.

Benjamin, W., *Reflections*, New York, Harcourt, Brace & Jovanovich, 1978.

Bergson, H., *The Two Sources of Morality and Religion*, New York, Greenwood, 1935.

Birnbaum, P. (ed.), *The Jewish Daily Prayer Book*, New York, Hebrew Publishing Co., 1949.

Black Elk, *The Sacred Pipe: The Seven Rites of the Oglala Sioux*, New York, Penguin, 1971.

Blake, W., *Milton*, Boulder, Shambhala, 1978.

Blythe, R., *Akenfield: Portrait of an English Village*, New York, Dell Publishing, 1969.

Borges, J., *Labyrinths*, New York, New Directions, 1964.

Boss, M., *Erinnerung an Martin Heidegger*, Pfullingen, Gunther Neske, 1977.

Boss, M., *Existential Foundations of Medicine and Psychology*, New York, Jason Aronson, 1979.

Brun, J., *La main et l'esprit*, Paris, Presses Universitaires de la France, 1963.

Casper, M., 'Space Therapy and the Maitri Project,' *Journal of Transpersonal Psychology*, vol. 6, no. 1, 1974, pp. 57–67.

Castaneda, C., *A Separate Reality*, New York, Scribner's, 1971.

Chang, G. (ed.), *The Hundred Thousand Songs of Milarepa*, Boulder, Shambhala, 1977.

Danto, A., *Nietzsche as Philosopher*, New York, Macmillan, 1965.

Derrida, J., *La dissémination*, Paris, Larousse, 1973.

Derrida, J., *Of Grammatology*, Baltimore, Johns Hopkins University Press, 1976.

Derrida, J., *Writing and Difference*, University of Chicago Press, 1978.

Dewey, J., *Art as Experience*, New York, G. P. Putnam's Sons, 1958.

Dewey, J., *Democracy and Education*, New York, Macmillan, The Free Press edn, 1966.

Dolan, J. (ed.), *Unity and Reform: Selected Writings of Nicholas of Cusa*, University of Notre Dame Press, 1962.

Edmonds, J. (ed.), *Lyra Graeca*, vol. 3, Cambridge, Harvard University Press, 1927.

Ellman, R., *Yeats: The Man and the Masks*, New York, W. W. Norton, 1978.

Emerson, R., *The Portable Emerson*, New York, Viking Press, 1946.

Erdoes, R., *Lame Deer: Seeker of Visions*, New York, Simon & Schuster, 1972.

Fink, E. and Heidegger, M., *Heraclitus Seminar 1966/1967*, University of Alabama Press, 1979.

Foucault, M., *The Birth of the Clinic: An Archaeology of Medical Perception*, New York, Random House, 1973.

Foucault, M., *Language, Counter-Memory, Practice*, Ithaca, Cornell University Press, 1977.

Foucault, M., *Power/Knowledge: Selected Interviews and Other Writings 1972–1977*, New York, Pantheon, 1980.

Fraigneau, A., *Cocteau*, New York, Grove Press, 1961.

Freud, S., *Collected Papers*, vol. 4, London, Hogarth Press, 1953.

Freud, S., *Project for a Scientific Psychology*, 'Standard Edition of the Complete Psychological Works of Sigmund Freud,' London, Hogarth Press, 1954.

Freud, S., *Beyond the Pleasure Principle*, New York, W. W. Norton, 1961.

Freud, S., *Civilization and Its Discontents*, New York, W. W. Norton, 1962.

Friedman, I. (ed.), *The Book of Creation: Sepher Yetzirah*, New York, Samuel Weiser, 1977.

Fromm, E., *Marx's Concept of Man*, New York, Frederick Ungar, 1961.

Gadamer, H., *Wahrheit und Methode: Grundzüge einer philosophischen Hermeneutik*, Tübingen, Mohr, 1960.

Gadamer, H., *Philosophical Hermeneutics*, Berkeley, University of California Press, 1977.

Gendlin, E., 'Experiential Phenomenology,' in M. Natanson (ed.), *Phenomenology and the Social Sciences*, Evanston, Northwestern University Press, 1973, pp. 281–319.

Gendlin, E., 'Experiential Psychotherapy,' in R. Corsini (ed.), *Current Psychotherapies*, Itasca, Peacock Publishers, 1973, pp. 317–52.

Gendlin, E., '*Befindlichkeit*: Heidegger and the Philosophy of Psychology,' *Review of Existential Psychology and Psychiatry* vol. 16, nos. 1–3, 1978–9, pp. 48–60.

Gendlin, E., *Focusing*, New York, Bantam, 1981.

Glazer, S. (trans.), *Service for the Day of Atonement*, New York, Hebrew Publishing Co., 1935.

Govinda, A., *The Way of the White Clouds*, Berkeley, Shambhala, 1970.

Govinda, A., *Creative Meditation and Multi-Dimensional Consciousness*, Wheaton, Theosophical Publishing House, 1976.

Greimas, A. (ed.), *Essais de sémiotique poétique*, Paris, Larousse, 1972.

Guenther, H., *The Life and Teaching of Naropa*, Oxford University Press, 1963.

Guenther, H., *Buddhist Philosophy in Theory and Practice*, Boulder, Shambhala Publishing, 1971.

Guenther, H., 'The Natural Freedom of Mind', *Crystal Mirror*, vol. 4, Berkeley, Dharma Publishing, 1975.

Guenther, H., *Tibetan Buddhism in Western Perspective*, Berkeley, Dharma Publishing, 1977.

378

BIBLIOGRAPHY

Gyal-wang ge-dun gya-tso, *The Steps of Visualization for the Three Essential Moments: A Stairway for Ascending to the Tusita Buddha Fields*, Dharamsala Library of Tibetan Works and Archives, 1975.

Heidegger, M., *Sein und Zeit*, Tubingen, Max Niemeyer, 1927.

Heidegger, M., *Existence and Being*, Chicago, Henry Regnery, 1949.

Heidegger, M., *Platons Lehre von der Wahrheit, Mit einem Brief über den 'Humanismus'*, Bern, A. Francke, 1954.

Heidegger, M., *Was ist das – die Philosophie?* Pfullingen, Günther Neske, 1956.

Heidegger, M., *Zur Seinsfrage*, Frankfurt am Main, Vittorio Klostermann, 1956.

Heidegger, M., *Der Satz vom Grund*, Pfullingen, Günther Neske, 1957.

Heidegger, M., *Identität und Differenz*, Pfullingen, Günther Neske, 1957.

Heidegger, M., *Einführung in die Metaphysik*, Tübingen, Max Niemeyer, 1958.

Heidegger, M., *Vorträge und Aufsätze*, Pfullingen, Günther Neske, 1959.

Heidegger, M., *The Question of Being*, London, Vision Press, 1959.

Heidegger, M., *Die Gegenwart der Griechen im neueren Denken*, Tübingen, Mohr, 1960.

Heidegger, M., *Gelassenheit*, Pfullingen, Günther Neske, 1960.

Heidegger, M., *An Introduction to Metaphysics*, New York, Doubleday, 1961.

Heidegger, M., *Nietzsche*, 2 vols, Pfullingen, Günther Neske, 1961.

Heidegger, M., *Vom Wesen der Wahrheit*, Frankfurt am Main, Vittorio Klostermann, 1961.

Heidegger, M., *Was Heisst Denken?* Tübingen, Max Niemeyer, 1961.

Heidegger, M., *Die Frage nach dem Ding: Zu Kants Lehre von der transzendentalen Grundsätzen*, Tübingen, Max Niemeyer, 1962.

Heidegger, M., *Die Technik und die Kehre*, Pfullingen, Günther Neske, 1962.

Heidegger, M., *Being and Time*, New York, Harper & Row, 1962.

Heidegger, M., *Holzwege*, Frankfurt am Main, Vittorio Klostermann, 1963.

Heidegger, M., *Was ist Metaphysik?* Frankfurt am Main, Vittorio Klostermann, 1965.

Heidegger, M., *Vom Wesen des Gründes*, Frankfurt am Main, Vittorio Klostermann, 1965.

Heidegger, M., *Aus der Erfahrung des Denkens*, Pfullingen, Günther Neske, 1965.

Heidegger, M., *Unterwegs zur Sprache*, Pfullingen, Günther Neske, 1965.

Heidegger, M., *Discourse on Thinking*, New York, Harper & Row, 1966.

Heidegger, M., *What is a Thing?* Chicago, Henry Regnery, 1967.

Heidegger, M., *What is Called Thinking?* New York, Harper & Row, 1968.

Heidegger, M., *Zur Sache des Denkens*, Tübingen, Max Niemeyer, 1969.

Heidegger, M., *Die Kunst und der Raum*, St Gallen, Erker-Verlag, 1969.

Heidegger, M., *The Essence of Reasons*, Evanston, Northwestern University Press, 1969.

Heidegger, M., *Identity and Difference*, New York, Harper & Row, 1969.

Heidegger, M., *Phänomenologie und Theologie*, Frankfurt am Main, Vittorio Klostermann, 1970.

BIBLIOGRAPHY

Heidegger, M., and Fink, E., *Heraklit*, Frankfurt am Main, Vittorio Klostermann, 1970.

Heidegger, M., *Erläuterungen zu Hölderlins Dichtung*, Frankfurt am Main, Vittorio Klostermann, 1971.

Heidegger, M., *On the Way to Language*, New York, Harper & Row, 1971.

Heidegger, M., *Frühe Schriften*, Frankfurt am Main, Vittorio Klostermann, 1972.

Heidegger, M., *On Time and Being*, New York, Harper & Row, 1972.

Heidegger, M., *The End of Philosophy*, New York, Harper & Row, 1973.

Heidegger, M., 'The Principle of Ground,' trans. K. Hoeller, *Man and World*, vol. 7, 1974, pp. 207–22.

Heidegger, M., *Die Grundprobleme der Phänomenologie*, 'Gesamtausgabe,' vol. 24, Frankfurt am Main, Vittorio Klostermann, 1975.

Heidegger, M., *Poetry, Language, Thought*, New York, Harper & Row, 1975.

Heidegger, M., *Early Greek Thinking*, New York, Harper & Row, 1975.

Heidegger, M., *Logik: Die Frage nach der Wahrheit*, 'Gesamtausgabe,' vol. 21, Frankfurt am Main, Vittorio Klostermann, 1976.

Heidegger, M., *Wegmarken*, Frankfurt am Main, Vittorio Klostermann, 1976.

Heidegger, M., *Basic Writings*, New York, Harper & Row, 1977.

Heidegger, M., *The Question Concerning Technology and Other Essays*, New York, Harper & Row, 1977.

Heidegger, M., *Metaphysische Anfangsgründe der Logik im Ausgang vom Leibniz*, 'Gesamtausgabe,' vol. 26, Frankfurt am Main, Vittorio Klostermann, 1978.

Heidegger, M., *Heraklit*, 'Gesamtausgabe,' vol. 55, Frankfurt am Main, Vittorio Klostermann, 1979.

Heidegger, M. and Fink, E., *Heraclitus Seminar 1966/1967*, University of Alabama Press, 1979.

Heidegger, M., *The Will to Power as Art*, 'Nietzsche,' vol. 1, New York, Harper & Row, 1979.

Heidegger, M., *Nihilism*, 'Nietzsche,' vol. 4, New York, Harper & Row, 1982.

Heidegger, M., *The Basic Problems of Phenomenology*, Bloomington, Indiana University Press, 1982.

Hillman, J., *Re-Visioning Psychology*, New York, Harper & Row, 1975.

Hölderlin, F., *Sämtliche Werke*, Berlin and Darmstadt, Tempel-Verlag, 1960.

Homer, *The Iliad*, Toronto, Penguin, 1950.

Husserl, E., *Cartesian Meditations*, The Hague, Martinus Nijhoff, 1960.

Husserl, E., *Ideas*, New York, Collier Books, 1964.

Husserl, E., *The Crisis of European Sciences and Transcendental Phenomenology*, Evanston, Northwestern University Press, 1970.

Jacobson, R., 'Absence, Authority, and the Text,' *Glyph: Johns Hopkins Textual Studies*, Baltimore, Johns Hopkins University Press, vol. 3, 1978, pp. 137–47.

Jung, C., *Psychological Reflections: A New Anthology of His Writings, 1905–1961*, New York, Pantheon Books, 1945.

Jung, C., *Symbols of Transformation: An Analysis of the Prelude to a Case of*

Schizophrenia, 'Collected Works,' vol. 5, New York, Pantheon Books, 1956.

Jung, C., *Civilization in Transition*, 'Collected Works,' vol. 10, Princeton University Press, 1964.

Jung, C., *Two Essays in Analytical Psychology*, 'Collected Works,' vol. 7, Princeton University Press, 1966.

Jung, C., *The Structure and Dynamics of the Psyche*, 'Collected Works,' vol. 8, Princeton University Press, 1968.

Jung. C., *The Archetypes and the Collective Unconscious*, 'Collected Works,' vol. 9, Part 1, Princeton University Press, 1968.

Kierkegaard, S., *Concluding Unscientific Postscript*, Princeton University Press, 1941.

Kierkegaard, S., *Repetition*, Princeton University Press, 1946.

Kierkegaard, S., *Fear and Trembling*, New York, Doubleday, 1954.

Kierkegaard, S., *The Last Years: Journals 1853–1855*, London, Collins, 1965.

Lame Deer and Erdoes, R., *Lame Deer: Seeker of Visions*, New York, Simon and Schuster, 1972.

Lawler, L., 'Terpsichore: The Story of Dance in Ancient Greece,' *Dance Perspectives* 13, 1962.

Lawler, L., *The Dance of Ancient Greek Theatre*, Iowa City, University of Iowa Press, 1964.

Lawler, L., *Dance in Ancient Greece*, Seattle, University of Washington Press, 1967.

Leibniz, G., *New Essays on the Human Understanding*, New York, Cambridge University Press, 1981.

Leroi-Gourhan, A., *Le geste et la parole*, Paris, Albin-Michel, 1965.

Mallin, S., *Merleau–Ponty's Philosophy*, New Haven, Yale University Press, 1979.

Marcuse, H., *Eros and Civilization: A Philosophical Inquiry into Freud*, Boston, Beacon Press, 1962.

Matthews, W. (ed.), *The Night Chant: A Navaho Ceremony*, New York, American Museum of Natural History, 1902.

May, R., *The Courage to Create*, New York, Bantam, 1976.

Merleau–Ponty, M., *La structure du comportement*, Paris, Presses Universitaires de France, 1942.

Merleau–Ponty, M., *Phénoménologie de la perception*, Paris, Gallimard, 1945.

Merleau–Ponty, M., *Les sciences de l'homme et la phénoménologie*, Paris, Centre de Documentation Universitaire, 1953.

Merleau–Ponty, M., *Signes*, Paris, Gallimard, 1960.

Merleau–Ponty, M., *Phenomenology of Perception*, London, Routledge & Kegan Paul, 1962.

Merleau–Ponty, M., *The Structure of Behavior*, Boston, Beacon Press, 1963.

Merleau–Ponty, M., *Sens et non-sens*, Paris, Editions Nagel, 1963.

Merleau–Ponty, M., *Le visible et l'invisible*, Paris, Gallimard, 1964.

Merleau–Ponty, M., *Signs*, Evanston, Northwestern University Press, 1964.

Merleau–Ponty, M., *L'Oeil et l'esprit*, Paris, Gallimard, 1964.

Merleau–Ponty, M., *The Primacy of Perception*, Evanston, Northwestern University Press, 1964.

Merleau–Ponty, M., *Résumés de cours, Collège de France 1952–1960*, Paris, Gallimard, 1968.

Merleau–Ponty, M., *The Visible and the Invisible*, Evanston, Northwestern University Press, 1969.

Merleau–Ponty, M., *Themes from the Lectures at the Collège de France 1952–1960*, Evanston, Northwestern University Press, 1970.

Merleau–Ponty, M., *The Prose of the World*, Evanston, Northwestern University Press, 1973.

Merwin, W., *The Miner's Pale Children*, New York, Atheneum, 1976.

Montaigne, M., *The Complete Essays*, Stanford University Press, 1965.

Moore, B., *Reflections on the Causes of Human Misery and upon Certain Proposals to Eliminate Them*, Boston, Beacon Press, 1969.

Mourelatos, A. (ed.), *The Pre-Socratics: A Collection of Critical Essays*, New York, Doubleday, 1974.

Murdoch, I., *The Nice and the Good*, New York, Penguin, 1978.

Neihardt, J., *Black Elk Speaks: Being the Life Story of a Holy Man of the Oglala Sioux*, New York, Simon & Schuster, 1972.

Neumann, E., *Art and the Creative Unconscious*, Princeton University Press, 1959.

Neumann, E., *The Origins and History of Consciousness*, Princeton University Press, 1970.

Neumann, E., *The Great Mother: An Analysis of the Archetype*, Princeton University Press, 1972.

Neumann, E., *The Child: Structure and Dynamics of the Nascent Personality*, New York, Harper & Row, 1976.

Nietzsche, F., *The Birth of Tragedy*, New York, Doubleday, 1956.

Nietzsche, F., *Thus Spake Zarathustra*, New York, Viking Press, 1956.

Nietzsche, F., *Joyful Wisdom*, New York, Frederick Ungar, 1960.

Nietzsche, F., *Human, All Too Human*, 'The Complete Works of Friedrich Nietzsche,' vol. 7, New York, Russell & Russell, 1964.

Nietzsche, F., *Ecce Homo*, New York, Random House, 1967.

Nietzsche, F., *The Will to Power*, New York, Random House, 1968.

Nietzsche, F., *Dawn of Day*, 'The Complete Works of Friedrich Nietzsche,' vol. 9, New York, Gordon Press, 1974.

Pascal, B., *Pensées*, New York, E. P. Dutton, 1958.

Pater, W., *Marius the Epicurean*, London, Macmillan, 1907.

Perls, F., Hefferline, R., and Goodman, P., *Gestalt Therapy: Excitement and Growth in the Human Personality*, New York, Dell, 1951.

Peterson, W., *Hippocratic Medicine: For Him Who Wishes to Pursue Properly the Science of Medicine*, Springfield, Charles Thomas, 1946.

Plato, *Dialogues*, New York, Random House, 1937.

Pulver, M., 'Jesus' Round Dance and the Crucifixion According to the Acts of St. John,' *The Mysteries: Papers for the Eranos Yearbooks*, vol. 2, Princeton University Press, 1955.

Rajneesh, B., *Only One Sky: On the Tantric Way of Tilopa's Song of Mahamudra*, New York, E. P. Dutton, 1976.

Reichel-Dolmatoff, G., *Amazonian Cosmos: The Sexual and Religious Symbolism of the Tukano Indians*, University of Chicago Press, 1971.

Reichel-Dolmatoff, G., 'Training for the Priesthood among the Kogi,' in J. Wilbert (ed.), *Enculturation in Latin America: An Anthology*, Los Angeles, UCLA Latin America Center Publications, 1977.

Rich, A., *Of Woman Born*, New York, W. W. Norton, 1976.

Rilke, M., *Duino Elegies*, New York, W. W. Norton, 1939.

Rilke, M., *Sonnets to Orpheus*, New York, W. W. Norton, 1962.

Rilke, M., *Letters 1910–1926*, New York, W. W. Norton, 1969.

Rogers, C., *On Becoming a Person*, Boston, Houghton Mifflin, 1961.

Rogers, C., *Freedom to Learn*, Columbus, Charles Merrill, 1969.

Rorty, R., *Philosophy and the Mirror of Nature*, Princeton University Press, 1979.

Rosner, F., *Meditation in the Bible and the Talmud*, New York, Yeshiva University Press, 1977.

Sallis, J. (ed.), *Heidegger and the Path of Thinking*, Pittsburgh, Duquesne University Press, 1970.

Sallis, J., *Phenomenology and the Return to Beginnings*, New York, Humanities Press, 1973.

Santayana, G., *Platonism and the Spiritual Life*, New York, Harper & Row Torchbooks, 1957.

Santayana, G., *Reason in Religion*, 'The Life of Reason,' vol. 3, New York, Collier Books, 1962.

Sartre, J.-P., *What is Literature?* New York, Harper & Row, 1965.

Scheler, M., *Vom Umsturz der Werte: Abhandlungen und Aufsätze*, Bern, A. Francke Verlag, 1955.

Scholem, G., *Major Trends of Jewish Mysticism*, New York, Schocken, 1961.

Scholem, G., *On the Kabbalah and its Symbolism*, New York, Schocken, 1969.

Scholem, G., *Kabbalah*, New York, New American Library, Meridian Books, 1978.

Scull, A., *Decarceration: Community Treatment and the Deviant: A Radical View*, Englewood Cliffs, Prentice-Hall, 1977.

Sekida, K., *Two Zen Classics: Mumonkan and Hekiganroku*, New York, John Weatherhill, 1977.

Solomon, R. (ed.), *Nietzsche: A Collection of Critical Essays*, New York, Doubleday, 1973.

Spinoza, B., *Ethics*, New York, Hafner, 1949.

Stevens, W., *The Palm at the End of the Mind*, New York, Alfred Knopf, 1971.

Storm, H., *Seven Arrows*, New York, Ballantine Books, 1973.

Straus, E., *Phenomenological Psychology*, New York, Basic Books, 1966.

Sullivan, H., *The Interpersonal Theory of Psychiatry*, New York, W. W. Norton, 1953.

Suzuki, D., *Essays in Zen Buddhism*, New York, Grove Press, 1961.

Tarthang, T., *Time, Space and Knowledge*, Berkeley, Dharma Publishing, 1980.

Tertullian, 'De resurrectione carnis,' in A. Lovejoy (ed.), *Essays in the History of Ideas*, New York, G. P. Putnam's Sons, 1960.

Thompson, J. (ed.), *Kierkegaard: A Collection of Critical Essays*, New York, Doubleday, 1972.

BIBLIOGRAPHY

Thoreau, H., *Walden*, New York, Bantam Classics, 1962.

Thoreau, D., *The Portable Thoreau*, New York, Viking, 1964.

Valéry, P., *Selected Writings*, ed A. Bower and J. Laughlin, New York, New Directions, 1964.

van den Berg, J., *The Changing Nature of Man*, New York, Dell, 1975.

Wangyal, G., *The Door of Liberation: Essential Teachings of the Tibetan Buddhist Tradition*, New York, Maurice Girodias Associates, 1973.

Welwood, J., 'Meditation and the Unconscious: A New Perspective,' *Journal of Transpersonal Psychology*, vol. 9, no. 1, 1977, pp. 1–24.

Welwood, J., 'Reflections on Psychotherapy, Focusing, and Meditation,' *Journal of Transpersonal Psychology*, vol. 12, no. 2, 1980, pp. 18–35.

Wheelwright, P., *The Pre-Socratics*, New York, Odyssey Press, 1966.

Williams, W., *Paterson*, New York, New Directions, 1963.

Wittgenstein, L., *Philosophical Investigations*, New York, Macmillan, 1953.

Wollheim, R., 'The Sheep and the Ceremony,' *The 1979 Leslie Stephen Lecture*, Cambridge University Press, 1979.

Wosien, M., *Sacred Dance: Encounter with the Gods*, New York, Avon, 1974.

Wyman, L., and Haile, B., *Blessing Way*, Tucson, University of Arizona Press, 1970.

Zenkei, S., *Zen Comments on the Mumonkan*, New York, New American Library, 1974.

Index

INDEX

Collective unconscious, 18, 100, 171–2, 196
Compassion, 96–8, 150–1, 153, 315–16
Corporeal schema, 67, 101, 150, 159, 163, 182–4, 189–90, 195–201, 209, 217–23, 235, 253–9; of the child, 218–20; in relation to Leibniz, 217; in relation to Spinoza, 216–19, 223
Cusanus, Nicholas, 175, 182

Dance: and the *archē*, 297; in classical Greek education, 250–3; and place, 330–5; as poetizing and grounding, 293–316; as round-dance, 317–36; and truth, 335–6
Depression, and nihilism, 70
Derrida, Jacques, 191, 205
Descartes, René, 50, 121, 215; *see also* Cartesianism
Deuteronomy, 190, 203
Dewey, John, 8, 121, 208, 214, 225–31
Dwelling, 286–7
Dzogs-chen, 109

Earth, 281–316, 323–5
Education, 224–7, 250–3
Ego, 18, 100–1, 111, 114–15, 133, 139, 143–4, 164–6; and ego body, 96–7, 234, 239, 341–4; and masculinity, 176
Ekstasis, ecstasy, 26, 159, 173–4, 292, 297, 336, 345–6; and care-structure, 97; and dance, 297; as ekstatic inherence, 78; in the leap, 305–6; and topology, 145
Eliot, T. S., 30, 263
Embrace, 297–9; and Eros, 141, 145; as gathering into a circle, 164; and *legein*, 140–4; and *periechon*, *periechesthai*, 263, 297–9; and time, 269
Emerson, Ralph Waldo, 225–6
Empedocles, 30, 221
Epidemics, 258

Ereignis, 305, 327–8, 330, 334, 339
Erikson, Erik, 19
Erinnerung, 53, 77; *see also* Recollection
Eros, 141, 147–50; 153; and Logos, 147–8, 281–2; and nihilism, 1–3, 5; or *Thanatos*, 1–3
Euclidean geometry, 162, 340, 344
Exile of the body, 55, 73, 123, 206, 279
Existential decision, 103–4, 174, 337; and the leap, 300–16

Falling, 44, 110, 115, 260–2, 270–4, 302
Feeling, 16, 48–9, 54, 61, 103–5, 108, 128; and the attunement of mood, 50–4; the body of, 54; and gathering, 148–9
Felt sense, 16, 43, 48–9, 53, 55, 61–2, 69, 89, 103–4; 109–10, 116, 147, 156–7, 214, 224, 234–5, 240, 266, 291, 299; *see also* Attunement
Feminine principle, 58–9, 163, 175, 282–3, 286, 314, 321
Fink, Eugen, 46–7, 83, 135, 287, 289
Flesh, 58, 64–8, 79, 98, 108, 142, 170, 177, 183, 190–223, 239–40, 244, 247, 255–7, 266, 269, 291–9; the sublimation of, 37
Foucault, Michel, 43, 191, 201–2, 248–9, 255
Foundationalism, 106; and grounding, 106–8
Fourfold, 323–8, 331; and *mandala*, 166
Freedom: and truth, 24
Freud, Sigmund, 1, 2, 19, 147, 153, 191, 195, 203–4, 343; and psychoanalysis, 17
Friedman, Irving, 202

Gadamer, Hans Georg, 210–11
Galileo, 280
Gathering *see Legein, Logos*
Gelassenheit, 165, 129–30, 134, 212, 310; and balance, 271–4, 285
Gendlin, Eugene, 19, 53, 231, 245

INDEX